How to Accept German Reparations

PENNSYLVANIA STUDIES IN HUMAN RIGHTS

Bert B. Lockwood, Jr., Series Editor

A complete list of books in the series
is available from the publisher.

HOW TO ACCEPT
GERMAN REPARATIONS

SUSAN SLYOMOVICS

PENN

UNIVERSITY OF PENNSYLVANIA PRESS

PHILADELPHIA

Published by
University of Pennsylvania Press
Philadelphia, Pennsylvania 19104-4112
www.upenn.edu/pennpress

Printed in the United States of America on acid-free paper
10 9 8 7 6 5 4 3 2 1

Library of Congress Cataloging-in-Publication Data
ISBN 978-0-8122-4606-3

For my son

What is here?
Gold? yellow, glittering, precious gold? No, gods,
I am no idle votarist: roots, you clear heavens!
Thus much of this will make black white, foul fair,
Wrong right, base noble, old young, coward valiant.
Ha, you gods! why this? what this, you gods? Why, this
Will lug your priests and servants from your sides,
Pluck stout men's pillows from below their heads:
This yellow slave
Will knit and break religions, bless the accursed,
Make the hoar leprosy adored, place thieves
And give them title, knee and approbation
With senators on the bench: this is it
That makes the wappen'd widow wed again;
She, whom the spital-house and ulcerous sores
Would cast the gorge at, this embalms and spices
To the April day again. Come, damned earth,
Thou common whore of mankind, that put'st odds
Among the route of nations, I will make thee
Do thy right nature.

> —William Shakespeare, *Timon of Athens*,
> Act IV, Scene 3, ll. 1689–1708

CONTENTS

Prologue: Reparations and My Family

My father, Josef Slyomovics, has been forced to flee his country twice: first in 1938 when Hitler annexed the Sudetenland and again in 1948 when the Soviet Union occupied Czechoslovakia. In the summer of 1998, while on vacation in the town where he grew up, Karlovy Vary (in Czech; Karlsbad in German), he announced to his astonished family that he intended to stay in the Czech Republic and was not returning to Canada. Vera Hollander Slyomovics, his wife and my mother, refused to remain with him despite their fifty-year absence from a homeland she now dismissively categorizes as "the third world." She was going home to Canada.

My father's Czech citizenship was restored to him two years later, on September 25, 2000, and, subsequently, so was his passport. Immediately, he presented me with a bound copy of his request, a thick dossier consisting of random documents retrieved from the Czech government archives held safely while their subject was exiled elsewhere for half a century. A series of official certificates chronicles my father's army career: a French-Czech document, dated May 4, 1940, proves his enlistment at the Czechoslovakian exile army recruiting headquarters in Paris; the Czech Brigade injury list, item number 90, attests that Lance Corporal Josef Slyomovics, army number A-4879, tank brigade, was wounded in Dunkirk on November 5, 1944; and an army form procured back in his hometown of Karlovy Vary, dated July 31, 1945, marks his demobilization and return to Czechoslovakia. Ominously, the final Czech document is a police report, dated March 24, 1948, refusing an application for a passport because "his travel abroad would endanger the security of the state." He had been imprisoned briefly the month before as a "capitalist" during the 1948 Communist takeover of Czechoslovakia and found not guilty by a sympathetic judge, while more than fifty of his fur factory workers came to the courtroom to declare that he was a great boss. The judge advised him to disappear since new arrests on faked charges were imminent.[1] He and his pregnant wife trekked three weeks across the Semmering Mountains in the spring of 1948 to a Displaced Persons (DP) Camp in Salzburg, Austria, where my brother Peter was born on June 12 as they waited for a visa to any country willing to admit them.

My father would never file for indemnities from the post-Communist Czech Republic government to regain his factory and house confiscated by the Czech Communists in 1948,[2] just as he refused in 1945 similar reparations stemming from the post-World War II redrawing of national boundaries between Czechoslovakia and the Soviet Union. Following the June 1945 Treaty, Czechoslovakia was forced to cede its easternmost province, Subcarpathian Ruthenia, my father's birth province, to the Soviet Union. Although a Czech-Soviet committee headquartered in Prague was "charged with making the final accounting of mutual claims for compensation to be paid by each state to its respective transferred co-nationals,"[3] in 1945 my father chose not to file a claim. Neither did he apply for his soldier's pension for six years of army service during World War II in the Czechoslovakian Brigade. He served his country Czechoslovakia, he said, with no thought of recompense. Between 1998 and 2004, my father resided in Prague, fulfilling residency requirements, but somehow we never found time to finish the process of completing paperwork to confer his Czech nationality on me, his daughter. He knew that I would never live in the Czech Republic, yet he wanted to bestow on me his gift of a future European citizenship and, thus, the right to work anywhere in Europe.

My father was warmly welcomed officially, bureaucratically, and personally as a returning Czechoslovakian Jew, a war hero, a member of the non-Communist Czech Left, and a rare native of Karlovy Vary, a city devoid of its Jewish minority, who were largely exterminated in Theresienstadt/ Terezín Camp, and now populated with Moravians and Bohemians from elsewhere. My father's welcomed return contrasts with the fates of the two-and-a-half million Sudeten Germans of Czechoslovakia who were expelled in 1945 by the postwar Edvard Beneš government on charges of mass collaboration with the Nazis; this expulsion, which many call Europe's first postwar ethnic cleansing, continues to roil relations between the governments of Germany and the Czech Republic, while individuals and groups of former inhabitants, usually residing in Germany, actively campaign for restitution.[4]

My mother, who together with my grandmother survived the Auschwitz Concentration Camp, long refused to file for reparations, calling it "blood money." She was not alone in her views. Many Jews from Israel's community of Holocaust survivors, estimated at a third of the immediate postwar population, refused negotiations with West Germany. Joseph Sprinzak, then the Speaker of Israel's Knesset, maintained "the honor of the Jewish people precluded any acceptance of restitution from Germany even if it were voluntary and spontaneously offered."[5] Israel should not accept "blood money," concurred a writer in 1951 in the *Jewish Herald* of New York, reflecting the revulsion of the diasporic community.[6] My mother was encouraged in her refusal by my father who described to me specific events that shaped their decision. Testifying in hearings would intensify already severe traumatic symptoms, they believed. Moreover, in 1948, they had fled their Czechoslovakian homeland and established a new life in Canada. In the following years, they paid less attention to deadline dates for reparation claims and gave priority to concerns about their safety and financial security.

Nonetheless, at age seventy-three in 1999, my mother undertook her first claim to reopened initiatives. Responding to an official notice by German authorities conducting a worldwide search for those eligible for a German pension, especially World War II forced laborers, she requested workers' benefits from the German government as a slave laborer in the munitions factory owned and operated by Junkers in Markkleeberg, Leipzig, where there was a satellite camp of Buchenwald.[7] The universe of Germany's wartime slave labor was vast. By 1944, the number of largely foreign forced laborers in Germany peaked at 7.6 million men and women; German workers were unavailable, as most had been conscripted into the armed forces. So great was the shortage that

> the SS gave up their intention to make Germany "judenrein," clean of Jews. Concentration camp inmates were hauled back from the East where they had been transported, with the declared intention of working them to death. But also working them for lucrative ends: the SS rented them to German industry just as the Army rented prisoners of war for daily fees, guaranteeing replacement in case of failure.[8]

My mother's request for a pension as a slave laborer was turned down on the grounds that neither in Auschwitz from June 6 to October 2, 1944, nor in Markkleeberg from October 2, 1944, to April 13, 1945, did she deposit payments, presumably on a monthly basis, to any existing German pension fund. The letter writer, citing German regulations, distinguishes in bold print between forced labor and forced labor in a concentration camp:

> After careful consideration of all the information you supplied, we must unfortunately come to the conclusion, that you are not eligible for a pension from Germany as you were in a concentration camp. **Despite the physical hardship you endured, incarceration does not qualify for the German pension, as contributions to the German pension fund would not have been made. According to the pension law, this does exclude persons who were in concentration camps from pension entitlements.**

While it is unimaginable to me that even forced laborers outside the concentration camp system contributed to any German pension fund, I find myself wondering sympathetically about the letter writer, who stated forthrightly that this assessment did not "reflect in any way how we feel about your case; we can only state the facts as outlined by the law." I picture a German bureaucrat my age; he is blond, balding, and born after the Second World War as he sweats over my mother's dossier in which starvation, beatings, and twelve-hour, six-day assembly-line work weeks building the fearsome JU-87 Stuka dive-bomber engines could not be made to conform to regulations.

Similarly, until new protocols were introduced in 2000, months in the Jewish ghetto of Mátészalka preceding my family's deportation to Auschwitz had no bearing on indemnification, despite a 1972 report by the organization that negotiates for world Jewry—namely, the Conference on Jewish Material Claims Against Germany (henceforth, the Claims Conference) —contesting such spurious distinctions:

> Claimants for damage to health who suffered in concentration camps for a year or longer were granted a legal presumption that the disabilities complained of were causally linked to the Nazi persecution, even if they came to light years later. But the German authorities refused to extend that presumption to inmates of ghettos and labor camps, even though the hardships suffered in them were as severe as those in concentration camps.[9]

On March 15, 1939, the Czechoslovakian province of Subcarpathian Ruthenia was annexed unilaterally by the Axis Hungarian government. The fate of Czechoslovakian Jews from my family's village and adjacent border villages strung along the foothills of the Carpathian Mountains was henceforth linked to the fate of Hungarian Jewry. Four days later, on my mother's eighteenth birthday, March 19, 1944, German troops occupied Hungary. My mother's village of Bishtine (or Bishtina in Yiddish, Bustino in Czech, and Bustyaháza in Hungarian) was emptied of its Jewish population in the spring of 1944, when they were deported to the Mátészalka Ghetto in northeastern Hungary across the shifting lines of the Czech-Hungarian border. At that time, approximately one-third of Hungary's population of 763,000 Jews, swelled by various annexations, originated from the former Czechoslovakian region of Subcarpathian Ruthenia.

Scholars at Yad Vashem, Israel's immense Holocaust archive and museum in Jerusalem, provide this overview of conditions in the Mátészalka Ghetto, where my mother, her parents, and her maternal grandmother were together for the last time:

> When the Germans entered Hungary in 1944, Mateszalka [*sic*] and some areas in its vicinity were declared a military zone. The Russian army was then in the Carpathian Mountains, close to this town. One of the biggest concentration camps [ghetto] in Hungary was built in Mateszalka. Jews from the towns of the Marmoros district, among them Raho, Nagybocsko, Korosmezo, Okormezo, Bustyahaza [my mother's hometown], and Tecso [*sic*], were sent to it. There were about 17,000 people in this camp [ghetto]. The attitude of the policemen to the arrested Jews was most brutal. Tortures, hunger, density, and diseases were their lot. At the beginning the arrested were kept outside. After a short time, they were crowded into a few little houses, some dilapidated. The community dished out meager food rations every day, plus soap and bread. The arrested stood on lines to get the food. At last they were brought to the railroad station, and were put into closed railroad cars, about eighty people to a car, and the railroad took to them to Auschwitz.[10]

One of my mother's stories about life in the Mátészalka Ghetto of 1944 distills the apocalyptic despair of the ghetto's inhabitants:

5

The conditions were appalling. It was one short street, and they emptied the people from the street and they jammed us in a room of this
kind, even in the attic, it was unbelievable. That's why we were full of
lice. The hygiene conditions were terrible; it was impossible to keep it
clean. The Hungarian police were more cruel than the Germans, they
had little fights, there was a lot of cruelty in the Hungarian, and my
Hungarian was perfect, I finished seven grades, I needed one more
grade to get the degree, so I spoke fluent Hungarian, and they kept
saying you should convert. Will that help me? It might. I tried not to
have anything to do with them. . . . In Mátészalka there were cattle
trains going to Auschwitz and back, Auschwitz and back. So nothing
happened, and to tell you, which was a very remarkable thing that
I never forgot, ten rabbis got together to pray, a *bet din* (religious
court) and they called our Lord to an account of Himself (*ins rif
mir dikh zu din torah*), how He could let the children perish, not to
do anything. They called Him to account for, and I was totally fasci-
nated by it. And I stood there waiting for the sky to open, it didn't
open and then there was a deadly silence after. And I walked over
and in my Yiddish, I asked what was going to happen, and they said
now we're going to pray. That was the end of it. And unfortunately we
were the last ones to leave, my dad, my mom and I, my grandmother.
The rest of the family left before us.[11]

Although my mother's original request in 1999 for a German pension was
initially refused, it was finally settled in 2000 in a later round of German
reparations protocols. The German government sent a one-time, lump-sum
payment of US $5,000 in acknowledgment of her "detention" in Auschwitz.
My mother never submitted any supplementary application, yet, unexpect-
edly on August 2, 2002, she received in the mail a single payment of $1,000
(as Slave Labor Class I) arising from the settlement with Swiss banks over
dormant accounts and heirless assets of Holocaust victims.[12] Finally, in
2002, with assistance of the New York City office of the Conference on Jewish
Material Claims Against Germany under provisions of the "Article 2
Fund,"[13] my mother applied for and continues to receive since age seventy-
six, the sum of €270 each month, roughly the equivalent of $370, as a life-
time pension. In response to another initiative, with a May 14, 2004
deadline, my mother filed a claim for heirs wishing to pursue an application
under the Program for Former Slave and Forced Laborers. She did so in her

own name and as the heir of her father, Samuel Sandor Hollander, my grandfather after whom my son is named. And on August 2, 2004, the office of the Claims Conference handling former slave and forced laborers reported to my mother that, as "the *second and final* installment of the one-time payment" for herself and her mother, she would receive the maximum amount of $5,000 from the Foundation "Remembrance, Responsibility and the Future" (in German, *Stiftung Erinnerung, Verantwortung, und Zukunft*).[14] The purpose of the Foundation fund was to cover all further claims by forced laborers from the Nazi era, hitherto excluded from reparations, to assure "legal peace"[15] for those German industries that had profited from their servitude. Among the 3,527 contributing corporate groups and their subsidiaries is Junkers Luftverkehr of Dessau, my mother and my grandmother's employer, so to speak.[16]

The fact that I was fortunate to have my parents alive and well when I wrote this chapter in 2010—no evil eye, my father had turned ninety-seven and my mother eighty-three—did not mean that my father was available for interviews. He refuses to be officially audiotaped unless the topic is his expertise, sardonic Yiddish jokes. Our family spent two summers in Karlovy Vary before he admitted that he could not lead us to his boyhood house. Not since his first return in 1945 could he approach the apartment where he last saw his parents before they fled to Prague in 1938 to be transported in 1941 to the Theresienstadt/Terezín Camp, a site of death he will never visit or speak about. My father is the one member of my close family who escaped the Nazi concentration camp system and soldiered in the Czechoslovakian Brigade. In 1938, with the help of the underground Czech exile government network, my father had been spirited away to safety in Antwerp. Two years later, in May 1940, he barely escaped the advancing German army blitzkrieg into Belgium by fleeing to Paris, where he and his brother joined up with the exiled Czechoslovakian forces. In memory of his murdered parents, he dispatched my mother and me in his stead to tour the Theresienstadt/Terezín ghetto and camp, where we two traced with our fingers on page 802 of the camp's second oversized memorial volume the names of my paternal grandparents.[17] My father becomes unsettled and anxious when questioned, so I cobble together decades of surreptitious questions and laconic, indirect replies. Elsewhere, my family's past sufferings repose bureaucratically inside a plethora of Nazi archives about concentration camp inmates. Documenting their reparations became my way to make their respective pasts unfold.

Slowly and carefully, I have pieced together a rudimentary chronology from family members. I located my father's home in Karlovy Vary with the help of a former Czech policeman whom my father hired to chauffeur us around town. There is a family photograph taken in 1998 of my mother, my son, and me smiling at the camera as we clutch each other in front of my father's former apartment house, Zeeland Haus, in the lower town. Then it was a shabby building undergoing renovations. Wealthy Russians were investing in second vacation homes in this beautiful spa town, architecturally untouched by war or occupation and long a favorite of former Soviet President Leonid Brezhnev and his coterie. Just moments before the photograph, an elderly Czech lady had spat and cursed us as Russian usurpers. In impeccable Czech, my mother pointed out that this had been home before 1948, and rather she, the elderly Moravian lady brought to this Sudeten region after the expulsion of us natives, was in fact the interloper. Successive waves of antagonistic populations have inhabited the same architectural structures, lending Karlovy Vary an air of melancholy beauty. The town's baroque facades resembled a multilayered wedding cake, as if to represent its complicated ethnic history: the economically depressed Czechs, few native to the town, resented the newer, wealthy Muscovite residents, while descendants of the former Jewish population came to take the waters, mixing with former Sudeten Germans of Czechoslovakia, now prosperous citizens of Germany on seasonal pilgrimages to the villages from which they had been expelled in 1945. My one attempt to conduct fieldwork in the nearby spa town of Jachimov—the current Czech name of the former German St. Joachimstaal—crashed to a halt, after my mother and I interviewed the son of the former Nazi *Gauleiter*, the governor of the region. When he recounted that he too planned to resettle from Germany to the Sudeten Czech village of his youth—"*because the years from 1939–45 were the happiest, most carefree time of my life*"—we departed trembling from our encounter with a joyful Nazi past.

During that same summer of 1998, I photographed my father elegantly attired in his three-piece white summer suit and boater, seated in the baroque splendor of the ballroom in Marienbad, a spa town in the Karlovy Vary district. He was eighty-five years old, six feet tall, a handsome, blue-eyed, blond man who walked with the ramrod posture of a former soldier, surrounded by East European tourists dressed in cheap tracksuits and sneakers. I was unable to photograph a subsequent moment, when he broke down weeping in the pump room of the spa, barely whispering, "I used to dance here with my sisters Margit and Helen." We whisked him away and put him to bed in his luxurious hotel room to obliterate the memory that they too were killed. My father rarely talks about his father, Hayim David Slyomovics, killed in the Theresienstadt/Terezín Camp. On rare occasions, he speaks about his mother, Bluma Holder Slyomovics, murdered in Auschwitz when the Czech "family" camp was obliterated, but never without tears. She was sent to the Auschwitz crematoria to make room for the Hungarian Jewish transports on the very same day that brought my mother and grandmother from the Mátészalka Ghetto to Auschwitz, a fact I learned from my father's sister Ida, who witnessed her mother's death and the arrival of the Hungarian Jews throughout April 1944.

My mother and grandmother were among ten thousand Jews selected from Auschwitz for slave labor to construct Germany military barracks at the Plaszow Camp outside Krakow, Poland. Plaszow, made famous by Steven Spielberg as the site of his movie *Schindler's List*, was worse than Auschwitz, my mother said. Inmates were overseen by a brutal woman commandant named Ilse. My mother recalled that a soccer goal post was erected and only the fittest, defined as those who could jump and touch the top, survived. The rest Ilse shot on the spot, wielding her gun from its holster like a cowboy.[18] On June 6, 1944, my mother and grandmother were transported back to Auschwitz from Plaszow, which had no crematoria, and were among two hundred Jewish women of some five thousand Plaszow Camp inmates spared for another slave labor assignment.[19] This date is famously D-Day. My father was waiting in a ship along the French coast for the signal to disembark with the Czechoslovakian Brigade tank corps, while his mother in the Czech family camp transported from Theresienstadt/Terezín to Auschwitz was liquidated to make room for the arrival of my mother, whom he had not yet met. Meditating on the deaths of Hungarian Jews transported to Auschwitz on D-Day, historian Randolph L. Braham writes,

> The magnitude of the crime committed by the Nazis and their Hungarian accomplices is dramatically illustrated by the following comparative statistical data. Three transports arrived in Auschwitz-Birkenau with close to 12,000 Jews from Northern Transylvania on 6 June 1944. Better known as D-Day, this was one of the most magnificent days in the annals of military history, when the greatest multinational armada ever assembled under one command stormed the beaches of Normandy. By the end of that day, the number of invading Allied

troops killed was about half that of the Hungarian Jews. While the Allies' killed-in-action figures declined dramatically after the toehold had been gained on Normandy later that day, the Hungarian Jews continued to be murdered at almost the same high rate day after day until 9 July, continuing the awesome daily massacre rate that began on 16 May. In the end, the wartime losses of Hungarian Jewry significantly exceeded those incurred by the military forces of the United States in all theaters of war, just as they also significantly exceeded the combined military and civilian war deaths of the British, a nation that bore much of the German military onslaught. These comparisons are cited not to minimize the sacrifices or diminish the heroism of the Western Allies but simply to underscore the magnitude of the Holocaust in Hungary.[20]

On December 11, 1997, my mother recounted her experience to an interviewer sent from the Survivors of the Shoah Visual History Foundation, an oral history project established by filmmaker Steven Spielberg in 1994 after filming *Schindler's List*:

> It was D-Day, June 6, when we arrived at Auschwitz, and the Normandy invasion started. That day, they were very busy. The [crematoria] didn't smoke as much, there was still some burning. We started to be counted, we went into groups, and those over eighteen and those under forty went left, and those working went on the other side and they were, at the time we were still not believing we were going into the, we believed it a few hours later, that we were going to the crematorium. The crematoriums were so built that in one place came the water and the other place came the gas, there was very little difference to see. After a while you could see that it was this and this, and we were going like sheep to the slaughter, and nobody complained. (Vera Slyomovics, interview by Steven Spielberg Survivors of the Shoah Visual History Foundation, Netanya, Israel, December 11, 1997)

My mother's father was separated from his wife and daughter during the selection process in Auschwitz and transported to Austria's Mauthausen-Melk Camp in April 1944. My mother learned about his death in 1945, the summer of her liberation from the Markkleeberg Camp, an event told to the

Spielberg Holocaust project interviewer. To the interviewer's question—at what stage did you hear about your father?—my mother gave this partial account:

> This was very traumatic. I was on my way from Budapest to Prague. In a train. And they were discussing, and I heard from somebody that dad went there near the end, which was near Vienna, and they said, two people were telling me, this guy was there, Hollander, because he spoke six languages, and he did the interpretation. Later on, I was sitting on the train and another man came by, and he said what were you talking about, and we said Hollander, and he said, "He was a wonderful man," and I said, "Was?" and he said, "On December the 8th," I know the date, I keep it, it's going to be this time nineteen days in Kislev, I never forget this anniversary because I figured it out. I'm sorry, twenty-one days in Kislev? Nineteen days I do the candles. He said, "He was wonderful, but one day he got diarrhea, and when he came back to get his job back, they wouldn't give it to him, so he had to go and do construction, and he died on 8 of December." My first instinct, the train was going, I was lifting the window, I really wanted to die. I said if he didn't make it I wouldn't want to live. I didn't do it and I'm glad I survived it. That's where I found out, on the train between Budapest and Prague that my dad didn't make it. (Vera Slyomovics, interview by Steven Spielberg Survivors of the Shoah Visual History Foundation, Netanya, Israel, December 11, 1997)

In contrast to documents that possess no feelings but elicit strong emotions, my mother was unhappy with her interview experience conducted under the auspices of Spielberg's Holocaust survivor project. She reported that the interviewer rigidly followed a template of questions to plow through and did not seem to see her as an individual, neither looking at her nor responding to her questions and curiosity. As I watch the videotape of this interview, my mother resembles a butterfly nailed to a board, fluttering and evading as much as possible. She apologizes repeatedly to the interviewer for her twitching and inability to sit still.

Nevertheless, I acknowledge an immense debt to the interviewer from the Spielberg documentation project: finally, in 1997, I possessed a chronology of my mother's precise movements through the Nazi extermination system. In fact, all direct quotations in this chapter are transcribed from the

Spielberg interview videotape. In the dogged pursuit of oral history and victim testimony, the interviewer resisted, as I cannot, my mother's charm: attractive husky European accent; warm, brown eyes; and exotic high cheekbones. Moreover, my mother's compelling storytelling skills, a delightful exercise in free association, derailed all my attempts at rational exposition. My parents ceaselessly circle around the black hole of the past, recast horrific experiences humorously and heroically, and enmesh me in their prewar paradise.

On rare occasions, it slipped out that my mother's beloved father was so weakened by diarrhea and forced labor in Mauthausen-Melk's infamous stone quarries that at the age of forty-two he perished, thus escaping the inevitable selection to the crematoria. To know the date and circumstances of a loved one's death is said to give solace to mourners who commemorate anniversaries calendrically, annually. To know the precise date of any Jew's death in the Nazi extermination camps was rare. Four months after her liberation on the train that carried my mother from Budapest (where she successfully made up lost academic years to pass her Hungarian advanced high school *matura* examinations) to Prague (where she had been admitted to Charles University Medical School), can one speak of death freely chosen by my grandfather, the camp linguist and interpreter whom I will never know? My mother called reparations "paying the blood of my dad with money." Her reasons for filing fifty years later were that she felt justified in requesting compensation neither as victim nor as survivor but as a worker. During her 1997 interview, my mother provided additional reasons for her making claims for reparations as a slave laborer:

> To tell you how idealistic I was I never accepted German money, I never took the *Wiedergutmachung* because I felt they are paying the blood of my dad with money. So I was young enough I didn't want to accept, and I was interrupted in my studies so I could have had more. Now I met the president of Germany and now I'm ready to accept. I have a thyroid problem, glaucoma in my eyes and I have very bad osteoporosis. (Vera Slyomovics, interview by Steven Spielberg Survivors of the Shoah Visual History Foundation, Netanya, Israel, December 11, 1997)

Although age, illness, and recurrent financial uncertainty were factors in making claims, central to my mother's acceptance of reparation finally in 1999 was a chance encounter with the then president of Germany, Richard von Weizsäcker, whom she adores. She was deeply moved by his 1985 speech commemorating the fortieth anniversary of Germany's defeat by the Allied forces: "The 8th of May was a Day of Liberation. It freed us all from the inhuman system of national-socialist rule by force. . . . We had the chance for a new beginning."[21] While visiting the German consulate near her home in Vancouver, my mother was introduced to him by a clerk. Von Weizsäcker kissed her on the cheeks, then bowed to kiss the Auschwitz tattoo. When he held my mother's arm in a warm embrace and implored, "Promise me you will apply," she replied, *Ich verspreche Ihnen* (I promise *you*).

Fifty years after Auschwitz on a family visit to Australia, my mother encountered again her tattooer, a Slovakian Jewish *Kapo* who exclaimed on seeing her arm in a sleeveless dress, "My God, that's my handwriting!" Her evening was ruined, she said, especially when she discovered that he had changed his name to that of a famous Zionist leader to avoid persecution as a *Kapo*, the appellation for Jews in the camps who policed their people for the Nazis.[22] No, my mother had replied to the Spielberg interviewer, responding to a question I never dared ask, the application of the tattoo was not physically painful; it was humiliating. The number tattooed on my grandmother's arm, A-19459, is one number before my mother's A-19460, just as my grandmother preceded her own daughter on two separate occasions as they passed under the examining gaze of Josef Mengele, Auschwitz's doctor and anthropologist, the notorious "Angel of Death." He directed the two of them, my grandmother aged thirty-nine and her eighteen-year-old daughter, not to the gas chambers on the left but to the right, to life, for showers and delousing. Although my mother and grandmother survived together in various camps, they diverged on the issue of reparations. Unlike my mother, my grandmother Gizella Elefant Hollander accepted German reparations money as soon as it was offered in the 1950s and died in Netanya, Israel, in 1999 at ninety-six, living for more than fifty years on her monthly stipend of approximately $600.

It could be said that the Holocaust hovers over my life in the form of my grandmother's document in support of reparations. As her only granddaughter and in my role as the family archivist, I hold fast to her gift of a single translucent and fragile onionskin page. "I had just begun to understand what a document really is," writes Raul Hilberg, preeminent historian of the Holocaust. "It is first of all an artifact, immediately recognizable as a relic. It is the original paper that once upon a time was handled by a bureaucrat and signed or initialed by him. More than that, the words on that paper constituted an action: the performance of a function. If the paper was an order, it signified the entire action of its originator."[23] My grandmother's document is dated April 27, 1945. By the time the American Army liberated my mother and grandmother in Markkleeberg on April 13, 1945, a date they celebrated annually, my grandmother weighed eighty pounds. My mother tells the story:

> We were three Jewish women who decided to return to Markkleeberg [Camp, escaping from the Death March] reasoning no one would think of looking for us there. We found ten more Jewish women hiding there. And it was there that the American Army came to rescue us. The soldiers cried. Their first act was to cut the electrical wires, their second was to shoot up the camp and destroy the perimeters, and their third was to supply medical care and food. When they reached Markkleeberg they were expecting five hundred Jewish women according to their information. We were only thirteen women and two SS men hiding in the back. By then the Americans knew what they would encounter in the camps. I'll never forget the sound of the army bullhorn, like the *shofar* that sounds each year, and an American voice shouting in Yiddish: *Hob nisht kayn moyre, mir zaynen eyrer menshen* (Have no fear, we are your people). We were [in Markkleeberg] until April 13. Everybody asked me, I was born April 13, 1945, and on April 13 an American division freed us. They shot through all of the, [to the interviewer] you're not American are you? I've got a big love for Americans; I always feel that they've given me my life. My husband claims that this Texan [who liberated me] has grown through the years. At first he was 6 feet tall and now he's 7. He came and it was April 13 and I remember Mom was very sick, she was bad. I tried to get her better. They brought me a piece of pork, the worst thing they could give her, they had to pump her stomach and take her to the hospital, she was very sick. Friday night the rabbi, the chaplain came, he and the Texan cried and they can't believe that, I still wasn't fat, but I wasn't emaciated . . . they asked me what I wanted and I said bread, my whole bed covered with bread. So they covered my bed with 15 breads, I couldn't part with them, and they were good. . . .
>
> [After the Americans came in] we were very anxious to eat. We looked like animals. The Germans divided us, Momma couldn't come,

those who were younger we went. My first feeling was, they served us coffee and cake. I didn't know how to drink the coffee. I didn't know how to drink. I dropped the cup, I spilled everything, I hadn't seen a cup in all these years and I spilled everything, back to civilization, I couldn't handle it. I wasn't angry. I always surprised myself that I wasn't angry, I should have been much angrier. I kept saying if my father survived, every time my father, people would come from Vienna, all over, and I would say, "You remember Mr. Hollander?" There wasn't a person that I wouldn't ask for dad if he was alive. I never thought he wouldn't make it, I thought he had a better chance. This was my first feeling. Food, depending which came first, food or dad. I was very hungry. (Vera Slyomovics, interview by Steven Spielberg Survivors of the Shoah Visual History Foundation, Netanya, Israel, December 11, 1997)

Two weeks after liberation while awaiting repatriation at Markkleeberg Camp—and it is this act that astonishes me—my grandmother marched over to the civilian German engineer, the overseer of slave laborer battalions, and demanded a document proving that she, Gizella Hollander, had indeed been in Markkleeberg. Her single page from the Junkers aviation company, Markkleeberg factory, sports the official Junkers logo, a stylized man in white with arms outstretched as if flying within the black triangle that surrounds him. It is numbered 394181 and titled *Arbeitsbescheinigung*, a "work certification" (Figure 1). The German text, validated by an illegible signature, is followed by a later addition, an English translation at the bottom of the page for the purposes of my grandmother's reparation claim:

By the SS-Konzentrationslager Buchenwald Gizella Hollander born 24.6.1905, from the SS-Konzentrationslager Auschwitz has been assigned to our factory the 2nd of October 1944 to work there. She was dismissed on the 18th of April 1945, date of the occupation by the American troups [sic]. This certification is drawn up for the return to her country.

Consider that it is April 1945, the war not over, bombs falling, Germany in chaos, and my grandmother wills a self-created work certificate from the German engineer placed under arrest in the cell of the camp he formerly oversaw. The bureaucratic language confected by my grandmother and the

JUNKERS FLUGZEUG- UND MOTORENWERKE AKTIENGESELLSCHAFT

MOTORENBAU ZWEIGWERK MARKKLEEBERG

WERKLEITUNG

MARKKLEEBERG I 27.April 1945
FERNRUF: SAMMEL-NR. LEIPZIG xxxx 39 41 81
Eth/Do.

Arbeitsbescheinigung
- - - - - - - -

Durch das SS-Konzentrationslager Buchenwald wurde am 2.10.1944
aus dem SS-Konzentrationslager Auschwitz

Gizella H o l l ä n d e r, geb. 24.6.1905,

unserem Werk zur Arbeitsleistung zugewiesen. Sie ist von uns mit
dem Tage der Besatzung durch die amerikanischen Truppen entlassen
worden.

Diese Bescheinigung wird ausgestellt zum Zwecke des Rücktransporte
in ihre Heimat.

JUNKERS FLUGZEUG UND MOTORENWERKE AG
MOTORENBAU ZWEIGWERK MARKKLEEBERG

Certification
By the SS-Konzentrationslager Buchenwald Gizella HOLLÄNDER,
born the 24.6.1905, from the SS-Konzentrationslager Auschwitz
has been assigned to our factory the 2nd of October 1944 to work
there. She was dismissed on the 18th of April 1945, date of the
occupation by the american troups.
This certification is drawn up for the return to her country.

Figure 1. Gizella Hollander, Markkleeberg *Arbeitsbescheinigung* (work certification). Author's collection.

engineer defies the fact of her liberation, defining the end of forced labor in terms of a job "dismissal." My mother tells me she knew nothing about this document, only that my grandmother carried important papers in her underwear for the duration of the war, her return to Prague, through the Communist takeover of Czechoslovakia, and in transit in Havana for a year before rejoining her daughter in Montreal. At the same time in April 1945, while both were still in Markkleeberg, my mother, on behalf of the same civilian German engineer, testified in a makeshift American army court that he had assigned my grandmother a privileged job, one where she could sit as she measured Junkers plane parts. With a single bowl of soup as nourishment per twelve-hour shift, other camp laborers collapsed from malnutrition, but also from exhaustion because they were forced to stand as they worked.

Before the war my grandmother had been a successful, well-traveled businesswoman, accustomed to far-flung financial ventures and complex written transactions between Czechoslovakia and nearby Hungary, Romania, and Austria. Did my grandmother envision a world remade sane by paperwork, did she dare to contemplate the possibility of remuneration and reparation, or did she imagine that, without written proof from the perpetrators, no one would believe where she had been and what had been done to her?

CHAPTER 1

Financial Pain

No one is beyond the pale of human existence, provided
he pays for his guilt.

—Karl Jaspers

My particular family history illuminates justifications for and against
reparations through discussions of indemnification, the anthropology of
"blood money," guilt, and responsibility embedded in the ways these approaches both do and do not shed light on my mother's refusal to accept reparations for Auschwitz, in contrast to my maternal grandmother's implacable
pursuit of reparations from Germany, Hungary, and the Ukraine for over four
decades until her death in Israel in 1999 (Figure 2). My research project inves-
tigates aspects of histories and legal instruments of international human
rights law relevant to remedies and specifically to a historical moment during
which my family and their larger surrounding Jewish community after World
War II were forced to confront the perils and possibilities of redress.

Why do people pursue reparations? The effect of financial indemnities
as the primary form of reparation to survivors of torture and disappearance and the pursuit, or refusal, of reparation are part of a growing literature in human rights legal studies, with Holocaust survivors an obvious,
much-studied group. When human rights violations are presented primarily through material terms for indemnification, acknowledging an indemnity claim becomes one way for victims to be recognized. Remedy and
redress are processes that not only afford a vindication to the injured but also
assume, or perhaps create, the existence of legal instruments with practical
outcomes that determine what is to be done and how to rectify wrongs.

Figure 2. My mother and grandmother in Prague, 1946, one year after their liberation. Author's collection.

When a government commits wrongs against a group, money emerges as the potent remedy to restore justice. In all its varied meanings and typologies, the term "reparations" is currently the preeminent remedy,[1] owing much to the unprecedented legal history of the Nuremberg Trials prosecuting the Nazi leadership and to German redress programs for victims of Nazi persecution in the aftermath of World War II. The most recent example to draw on these German precedents is the United Nations guideline on remedy and reparation, dated April 2005 and worth quoting fully:

> Restitution refers to actions that seek to restore the victim to the original situation before the gross violations of international human rights law or serious violations of international humanitarian law occurred. Restitution includes restoration of liberty, enjoyment of human rights, identity, family life and citizenship, return to one's place of residence, restoration of employment and return of property. Compensation refers to economic payment for any assessable damage resulting from violations of human rights and humanitarian law. This includes physical and mental harm, and the related material and moral damages. Rehabilitation includes legal, medical, psychological, and social services and care. Satisfaction includes almost every other form of reparation including measures that halt continuing violations, verification of facts and full and public disclosure of the truth in rights protective ways, the search for the missing, identification of bodies, and assistance in recovery, identification and reburial in culturally appropriate ways. Satisfaction also includes official declarations or judicial decisions that restore the dignity, reputation, and legal rights of the victim and persons connected with the victim, public apology and acceptance of responsibility, judicial sanctions against responsible parties, commemorations and tributes to the victims. Guarantees of non-repetition include measures that contribute to prevention, ensure effective control over the military and security forces, ensure proceedings occur with due process, fairness and impartiality, strengthen the independent judiciary, protect human rights defenders, prompt the observance of codes of conduct and ethical norms, including international standards, by public servants, promote mechanisms for preventing and monitoring social conflicts and their resolution; review and reform laws contributing to or allowing the gross violation of international human rights laws.[2]

In sum, the reach of reparations as a remedy encompasses restitution, compensation or indemnity, rehabilitation, satisfaction, and guarantees of non-repetition.

An early post-World War II German remedy, a legal measure imposed in 1947 during the Allied Occupation of Germany, was the restitution (*Rücker-stattung*) of Jewish properties that the Nazis stole, confiscated, or, according to their racial terminology, "Aryanized."[3] But how to deal with heirless personal and communal property once owned by eradicated Jewish communities? The eventual fate of material goods and assets belonging to a destroyed European Jewry presented complex problems. Because a defeated Germany was the cause of the disappearance and death of Jewish owners, the impetus to formulate laws and administrative practices arose from a fear that any disposition of assets might revert, as was customary, to the benefit of the state, namely, Germany, in this case the acknowledged perpetrator. Assets estimated at $14 billion would otherwise go to enrich Germany. In addition, historian Ronald Zweig summarizes the dilemma of postwar Jewry facing the daunting tasks, both moral and organizational, of how to press claims: "How could Jews negotiate with Germans so soon after the crematoria and the gas chambers of Hitler's Third Reich? What recompense was possible for the murder of six million people and the destruction of communities hundreds of years old? How was it possible to estimate the value of individual and communal Jewish material assets, which the Germans had plundered between 1933 and 1945?"[4] The postwar Federal Republic of Germany (West Germany), nonetheless, took responsibility for meeting *material* claims by Jews in a widely publicized speech by Chancellor Conrad Adenauer addressed to the German parliament on September 27, 1951:

> Unspeakable crimes have been committed in the name of the German people calling for moral and material indemnity, both with regard to the individual harm done to Jews and to the Jewish property for which no legitimate individual claimants still exist. . . . The Federal government is prepared, jointly with representatives of Jewry and the State of Israel, which has admitted so many stateless Jewish fugitives, to bring about a solution of the material indemnity problem, thus easing the way to the spiritual settlement of infinite suffering.[5]

A year later, September 10, 1952, the Federal Republic of Germany signed Protocol No. 1 "to enact laws that would compensate Jewish victims of Nazi persecution directly" and Protocol No. 2 that would "provide funds for the relief, rehabilitation and resettlement of Jewish victims of Nazi persecution," laws both confirmed and partially extended on the unification of East and West Germany in 1990.[6] Policies enacted were based on sincere government apologies and the principles of restitution, indemnification, and reparations: restitution as the restoration of actual individual assets, indemnification as compensatory payments, and reparations in the form of collective payments made by one state to another, in this case to the Jewish people and eventually to the State of Israel after its establishment in 1948.

German reparations are called *Wiedergutmachung*—literally, "making good again." Germany has created the largest sustained redress program, amounting to more than $60 billion in payments, a landmark process that set into motion a global legal transformation in how abuses by a state may be evaluated. In contrast to this German model, the absence of governmental atonement and apology is assumed to signal that a more common legal category is operating, one in which parties agree to a settlement: one side pays without acknowledging or apologizing for violating any laws, and the other side, the aggrieved party, receives a cash award; no liability is implied or assumed.[7] Therefore, ways to gauge the worth of reparations in the case of Germany were based on a government that admitted to harm committed in the name of Germany and that sought to atone for past injustices, in part by paying victims money.

Money and Suffering

Money is looked upon as an impersonal, colorless social abstraction, according to Georg Simmel in his foundational 1878 treatise on *The Philosophy of Money*:

> Money is the purest reification of means, a concrete instrument which is absolutely identical with its abstract concept; it is a pure instrument. The tremendous importance for understanding the basic motives of life lies in the fact that money embodies and sublimates the practical relation of man to the objects of his will, his power and his impotence; one might say, paradoxically, that man is an indirect human being. I am here concerned with the relation of money to the totality of human life only insofar as it illuminates our immediate

problem, which is to comprehend the nature of money through the external and internal relationships that find their expression, their means or their effects in money.[8]

Exemplifying Simmel's notions about money's abstract, neutral, and rational qualities is the use of cash payments between individuals and collectivities to atone for murder, torture, and disappearance. Although Simmel described the frequency of compensatory money payments before the twentieth century, since World War II, a plethora of mechanisms has emerged most prominently to promote the concept that a life damaged or lost as a consequence of violence can be paid for. This chapter draws on aspects noted in Simmel's survey of the complex properties of money payback, especially the ways in which he was forcefully struck by the "*intensity* with which the relationship between human value and money value dominates legal conceptions."[9] Buttressed by numerous cross-cultural examples from the anthropological literature, Simmel concluded in relation to an omnipresent "intensity" that offenders who pay money to resolve murder cases constitute a clear and public admission of guilt to the surrounding society.

Some conclusions based on Simmel's key insights are, first, that an admission of guilt accompanied by cash underpins the historical basis for any legal system of fines and, second, that such a system evolves effectively into mechanisms with which to buy social peace and avoid endless retribution and feuding.[10] Systems of fines and payments—grouped by sociologist Viviana Zelizer under the rubric of "the monetization of guilt"—in turn produce varied and unintended consequences. An objective monetary value may be attached to human beings, just as Simmel taught, but also dynamically and reciprocally, money involved in such an exchange becomes endowed with social significance. What are new meanings attached to special purpose money payments?[11] Especially following the work of scholars Daniel Levy and Natan Sznaider and expanding on Simmel's insights, how are we to understand the politically charged realm of financial reparations disbursed not by individuals but instead emanating from the state? What is different when the state bestows funds on recipients who are its current or former citizens? Levy and Sznaider provide some answers:

> At the level of states and ethnic collectivities, money is exchanged for forgiveness. Legal and politically consequential forgiveness are distinct from feelings of forgiveness. And at the level of individuals, the

act is one of closure. Money symbolizes the irrevocable admission that a crime has been committed. As Marcel Mauss had already stated in 1925 in his analysis of *The Gift*, symbolic exchanges are relations between people as much or more than they are relations between objects. In the case of restitution, the acceptance of the money symbolizes the acceptance of the giver. And that is an acceptance that would never be possible on the basis of personal relations.[12]

Drawing on aspects of financial reparations raised by Simmel, Zelizer, Mauss, and Levy and Sznaider, I investigate several related themes throughout this book. (1) How are current reparations related to "blood money"? (2) Can Simmel's "intensity" be understood in relation to the ways in which money is "sacralized," that is, made sacred, both by an association with the damaged, tortured or missing body of the citizen and by means of the state's financial reparation procedures? (3) While the acceptance of money may signal the acceptance of guilt by the giver, does it truly signal any kind of acceptance by a recipient designated the injured party, as Levy and Sznaider suggest? Finally, and what lies at the heart of my inquiry, (4) why are restitution and reparation *necessary but never enough*, at least not always and not uniformly everywhere? What, if anything, does my intimate knowledge of Holocaust survivors' sufferings grant me? Beyond the subjective language of daughterly empathy, what should I do as an anthropologist caught up in the contemporary concerns of social scientists who are shifting away from the abstractions of money toward the impact of moral sentiments?

"Blood Money"

Reparations (the plural form routinely used) now mean primarily one thing—money.[13] It is not easy to come to grips with the messy realities of those who receive reparations—a group variously called victims, survivors, persecutees, claimants, deponents, litigants, heirs, my extended family, my mother and grandmother. Is the principal problem a central incompatible relationship that posits a link, a direct exchange between money and suffering? Rational choice economic theories that once privileged *homo economicus*, a self-interested money-maximizing "economic human," offer little clarity because the intensity of victim emotions plays a salient role. While many victims choose not to speak, and even those who do speak do not speak with one voice, they do pronounce a strikingly consistent reaction to money. Irrespective of an individual's decision to claim or reject reparation funds, most describe participation in monetary remedies as the calculating, materialist, instrumental monetization of their sufferings. Money received through reparations is, therefore, "morally earmarked," following sociologist Viviana Zelizer's descriptor for the social life of money: "In everyday existence, people understand that money is not really *fungible*, that despite the anonymity of dollar bills, not all dollars are equal or interchangeable."[14] In many historic and legal cases, financial reparations have been morally earmarked as "dirty" sullied money and labeled in diverse cross-cultural settings "blood money."

Anthropological theories have long posited a progressive evolutionary model from "blood money" to reparations according to which feuding communities without compensation mechanisms evolve into advanced societies with blood money payments that exclude the retaliatory *lex talionis*, an eye for an eye. The centuries long use of a form of quantifiable scale, either money or goods, to substitute for a life as blood debts also points to the monetization of interpersonal relations in early societies long before our capitalist, state-backed deployment of moneys. A final stage of sociocultural sophistication occurs when, for example, a suprajuridical body is established, such as the tribal assembly or a court to adjudicate damages and specify blood money in cases of death, rape, and violent disputes.[15] Thus, for victims to refuse financial compensation precisely because it is "blood money" is to remain mired in the primitive stages of perpetual feuding, revenge, bitterness, and savagery.[16]

Nonetheless, many refuse. Some fifty years after Germany's postwar indemnities, recipient responses pronounce the same epithet. "Blood money" has reappeared in widely disparate cases based on financial reparations, whether the atrocity indemnified is ethnic cleansing, genocide, or a state's ideological war against its own citizens. My mother refused the postwar German *Wiedergutmachung* compensation program because, she informed me, it was "blood money": nothing could compensate for her father's murder in Austria's Mauthausen Camp. Refusing money had once been her cleansing process:

> I didn't betray my father's memory by taking money from the killers. Since I started receiving monthly reparation checks in 2004 [for slave labor], they have become a constant reminder of my father's

murder. They prevent healing and building a new life in a new country. Before I was clean, I took nothing. (Vera Slyomovics, interview by author, Vancouver, Canada, June 1, 2007)

Many concentration camp survivors who refused compensation reputedly reasoned, "If I don't get the money, the Germans will feel more guilty."[17] So, too, the Mothers of the Plaza de Mayo, the organization of families of those disappeared during Argentina's "Dirty War," divided rancorously in 1986. The president of one splinter group, Hebe de Bonafini, rejected exhumations of cadavers ("we will not be contented by a bag of bones") and government indemnification ("blood money").[18] Similar reactions were voiced in Algeria as a result of disappearances occasioned by the country's brutal internal war of the 1990s. The head of the Algerian Mothers of Disappeared Children, Nacéra Dutour, disdainfully rejected the extensive 2005 Algerian financial reparations protocols by refusing to file for reparations for her son, Amine Amrouche, forcibly disappeared in 1997. Subsequently, Dutour told me that Algerian reparations were "tribal," as if the Algerian regime could force a retrogade return to some imagined prelapsarian tribal collectivity that subsumes each victim's experience on behalf of the public good (interview with Nacéra Dutour, Paris, November 22, 2003). Like my mother, Dutour exemplifies the rights-bearing citizen motivated by her own conscience and unwilling to take into account the persuasiveness of moral imperatives emanating from sources of authority such as the state.[19]

Cash awards to the living on behalf of the dead are so deeply enmeshed with the repugnant notion of blood money that all those associated with claims processes, even outsiders such as lawyers and administrators, are morally implicated as if by contagion. Kenneth Feinberg, the American lawyer charged by the George Bush administration as the "Special Master" to dispense the September 11 Victim Compensation Fund of 2001, decided to forego lawyer's fees for his work "to avoid additional criticism . . . that some families would accuse [him] of earning 'blood money' on the backs of the injured."[20] Lawyers, in particular, are singled out as blood-sucking moneygrubbers. Burt Neuborne, one of the foremost litigators representing plaintiffs against German companies that employed forced labor as well as insurance companies that failed to pay off claims, was quick to defend the role of lawyers:

Most lawyers behaved responsibly. Thus far, the only grant of fees has been a total of approximately $50 million payable to fifty-one lawyers by the German Foundation at the recommendation of Nicholas Katzenbach and Kenneth Feinberg. In the interests of full disclosure, the arbitrators awarded me approximately $4.3 million for my efforts on behalf of the German Foundation. In connection with the Swiss case, Mel Weiss, Mike Hausfield and I have waived fees in connection with obtaining the settlement in the Swiss case, leading to a total fee structure in that case for achieving the settlement of approximately $6 million, of which $1.6 million is being donated to Columbia Law School. If that is profiteering, we could use more of it.[21]

Comparing families of the World Trade Center dead to agents in a business deal, or worse, suggesting that victims are rationally strategizing games—see Feinberg's inadvertent metaphors below—is loathsome and challenges the recipient's belief that these were special sacred funds, at once and the same time "marked" and "earmarked" money. The slightest allusion to monetary metaphors, Feinberg concluded, endangered the U.S. government's desired outcome of a single mass settlement versus the feared thousands of individual suits:

I committed a couple of genuine faux pas during early town meetings. On one occasion when trying to stress the uniqueness of the 9/11 fund, I remarked, "This program is not business as usual." Eyes got wide in the audience, and some families exchanged glances. Then a stricken husband got to his feet and angrily retorted, "This is not a *business* you're talking about, Mr. Feinberg. You're talking about my *wife*." Another time, I was urging a group of Staten Islanders to participate in the fund rather than mount lawsuits, a path I was convinced would lead nowhere. To emphasize my conviction, I told the families, "This is the only game in town." As soon as the words escaped my lips, I caught a glimpse of my lieutenant, Camille Biros, wincing in the front row of the audience. With a sinking feeling I realized what I had said. The room practically erupted in anger. One outraged wife spoke for the group. "To you, this may be a game," she spat, "But not to us." Heads nodded around the room. What could I do? I apologized profusely and inwardly vowed to never, ever use that kind of language again. I never did.[22]

When my mother reread this chapter, she zeroed in on Feinberg's unfortunate use of the phrase about U.S. government reparations as the "only game in town." She commented that beatings did not hurt her as much as the harmful power of words that echoed Feinberg's approach. Words wounded her most, even unintentional ones. She responded with a story that my family had heard many times, but her reflections on Feinberg's phrases framed new contexts and comparisons to this often repeated, familiar morality tale of resistance:

> We went out to the [Markkleeberg camp Junkers] factory, and we were passing a garbage dump, marching to work in camp. When I jumped out of line to get the potato in the garbage, the *Oberschafüh-rer* [Alois Knittel] hit me on the head with his wooden baton. My skull opened, and the blood flowed into my mouth. I looked at him and said, "It tastes like tea." He laughed and said I always turned things to the good. He liked me. I was the only one invited to his house to clean, and he gave me butter and potatoes. (Vera Slyomovics, interview by author, Vancouver, Canada, August 11, 2010)[23]

Just as I struggle to write about my mother's long-term disdain for Auschwitz reparations, so too did Feinberg have difficulties in fathoming that, among the potential claimants to the 9/11 Fund, seven tabulated cases of outright refusal remained, despite the 97 percent rate of agreement among those eligible to submit a claim: "Mrs. Jones stared at me blankly. In a flat, robotic tone she responded, 'Go away, Mr. Feinberg. Thank you for coming but no amount of money can replace him. Leave the application on the kitchen table. I'll look at it later.' I never heard from her and the application was never filed. Why would a family forego the opportunity to receive millions?"[24]

Blood money notwithstanding, once legal and administrative mechanisms of reparations are launched, perpetrators and victims must face each other, inevitably. In the immediate postwar period in West Germany, Germans and Jews were forced to confront each other's memories of past ethnic persecution and genocide—if for no other reason than to deal with the combination of legal and financial remedies emerging from restitution and reparations processes. As the *Wiedergutmachung* program launched German reparations to Jewish victims of National Socialism, all parties involved experienced negative associations.[25] Jewish emotions and actions attached to Germany's financial compensation—protocols that evolved into the most the extensive and expansive to date—produced anxiety and resentment. The actual work of carrying out programs of German reparations to Jews has been researched by Christian Pross, the medical director of the German Center for the Treatment of Torture Victims in Berlin. His research in the 1980s, based on reviewing early files, retrieves traumatic moments for Jewish claimants when dealing with early postwar German bureaucracies. Despite the radically changed context of the new West German state forging revitalized connections with its current and former Jewish citizens, many assigned to carry out the German program were imbued with what Pross characterizes below as oppositional attitudes to reparation payments to Jews, reflected in the "spirit" of the first decade of German reparations payments:

> [T]op representatives of the state, such as the finance minister, spread the subliminal message throughout the population that the reparations program was nothing but a playground for clever lawyers and pension cheats. Ordinary Germans believed that perecutees lied, demanding harm for reparations they never suffered. In this atmosphere, German bureaucrats felt empowered to scour each reparations application like police detectives for errors and inconsistencies, and the applicants felt they were being forced to prove their innocence. In casting the German state in the role of plaintiff and the persecutees in that of defendants or supplicants begging favors, the former Nazis in the government, administration, and judicial system ensured that reparations would not become an accusation directed against them. . . . The law, with its wealth of clauses, grounds for exclusion, deadlines, and harassing demands, was structured to allow the state, while acting the part of the kind philanthropist, to cut and slash its benefits to the point of unrecognizability, ultimately leaving a complicated system of settlements, minimum pensions, and hardship funds. After what were years of running the gauntlet between legal clauses, rules, doctors, and bureaucrats, many persecutees were so intimidated that they were willing to accept even the most minimal settlements.[26]

Pervasive psychological, historical, economic, and financial barriers to implementing reparation protocols in postwar Germany were also delin-

eated by Pross. He cites numerous occasions of veiled anti-Semitism from
German administrators when interacting with survivors—most notoriously
in the figure of Ernst Féaux de la Croix, castigated by Pross as a former Nazi
official retooled into a top German bureaucrat post in charge of reparations
when other better trained, even sympathetic, civil servants and jurists were
available.[27] Indeed, I have often read in the early postwar literature, and still
hear even from scholars, the acceptable expression of distaste for Holocaust
survivor reparations couched in the form of an accusation. Numerous court
cases seeking additional reparations have been described as a "movement"—
whether a vibrant human rights outpouring or an unethical financial
shakedown—but nonetheless a movement that is greater than its specific
legal and financial processes against a variety of contemporary European
institutions, among them Swiss insurance companies, Austrian banks, and
German industries. Survivors, it is insinuated, routinely exaggerate, even
lie, to increase indemnity awards. Many scholars, such as Michael J. Bazyler,
discuss troubling questions about the morality of Holocaust restitution lawsuits that began in the 1990s, lawsuits that helped bring about German slave
labor payments in 2000 and thus ensured for the first time my mother's
monthly pension from the German government:

> First, does the demand for financial restitution demean the memory
> of the Holocaust? Second, once the funds are collected, how are they
> to be fairly distributed? This raises the provocative issue of who should
> be deemed a "Holocaust survivor." Third, should some of these resti-
> tution funds be allocated for Holocaust education and remembrance,
> or do they belong solely to survivors? Fourth, while payments to in-
> dividual survivors from these settlements were in the thousands
> of dollars, the class-action attorneys earned fees in the millions.
> Are these attorneys entitled to such fees, even though the fees repre-
> sent less than 2 percent of the total amounts collected through the
> litigation? Fifth, many of the lawsuits were defended by Jewish law-
> yers. Although European corporations accused of wrongful conduct
> both during and after WW II are free to hire Jewish lawyers to de-
> fend their interests, should lawyers who are Jewish have taken on the
> defense of such suits?[28]

Surely, the base materiality of items despoiled—the lists of goods, furnishings, bank accounts, art works, businesses, and insurance policies—conjures

stereotypes about Jewish financial cunning and greed. History affords too many examples linking Jews, usury, and the accumulation of money, even as exemplified by economist John Maynard Keynes who attributed the configuration of deferred gratification, usury, and savings to Jewish notions of immortality: "Perhaps it is not an accident that the race which did most to bring the promise of immortality into the heart and essence of our religion has also done most for the principle of compound interest and particularly loves this most purposive of human institutions."[29]

The Promise of Money and Reparative Values

Filing for reparations calls for a willingness to tell your story. Nonetheless, there are striking differences between a witness in a courtroom setting, whose account accuses a torturer or murderer face to face, and filling in the blanks of forms. Until the year 2000, my mother laid claim to her dream, recounted throughout my adolescence, in which she confronts the Auschwitz doctor Josef Mengele in a court of law and stands before him alive, healthy, productive, and the mother of two children. On hearing of Mengele's death by drowning on a Brazilian beach in 1979, she insisted that the dream of seeing him in a law court was satisfied, because drowning most resembles the fate of his victims choking to death, the doomed struggling to breathe inside the gas chambers. My mother's refusal to seek reparations collided with the launching of newer German reparations for the next millennium. She ignored the 1997 German government Social Security program for ghetto pensions. In response to the fact that few Jews were even qualified for this pension, since paid employment while interned in some 1,000 Nazi ghettos annexed to the Third Reich was unusual, the "German Government Ghetto Work Payment Program" in 2007 funded additional categories of reparations. A one-time payment of €2,000 (around $3,000) was disbursed if claimants could prove their ghetto work was voluntary or "unforced labor."[30] My mother applied to the later 2007 program based on her volunteer work in the Mátészalka Ghetto clinic. When I inquired what volunteer work she did, she laughed and said she perfected the art of delicate hand delousing techniques. Removing each louse was a gentle way of grooming and touching patients for whom rarely were any medicines available.

Determining the value of an individual human life engages armies of actors and participants: lawyers, human rights activists, doctors, economists,

politicians, insurance agents, historians, and social scientists in multiple
processes of conceiving, creating, categorizing, implementing and distrib-
uting reparative outcomes. The terms of reparations—for whom, what purpose, and which monetary calculations recognize the crimes of torture,
disappearance, and imprisonment—but also the institutional bestower of
money compelled potential claimants to distinguish actively among a variety of possible reparations processes. Reparative values, therefore, are also
attached to the *source* of money. That there is a morality to funding sources
and that these standards of morality are set by the recipient seem to hold
true even for litigants in American personal injury cases far removed from
the domain of human rights atrocities. Legal scholar Tom Baker has analyzed the experiences of claims against American insurance companies versus
claims against actual individuals encountered face to face in the courtroom.
He concludes that claimants interpret blood money from individuals as a
good thing because of its resemblance to the biblical "eye for an eye . . . a life
for a life." Especially cases involving physical injury call forth the law of
retribution in which the perpetrators pay directly because they are unable to
hide behind impersonal institutions, companies, or states: "Real money
from real people—money paid directly by defendants out of their own
pocket. As the term reflects, blood money hurts defendants in a way that
money paid on behalf of a defendant by a liability insurance company cannot. For that reason, blood money is an entirely different currency than
what lawyers refer to as 'insurance money'."[31] Baker asks us to imagine impersonal sources of money as "cold, hard, and flat," while money directly
and painfully issuing from the perpetrator is "hot, soft and highly textured."
He concludes for personal-injury cases that "the key assumption is that
people who have harmed others have to feel some financial pain" and, therefore, forms of financial pain may act as a deterrent against future harm.[32]
My grandmother never stopped searching for new reparations programs
that would inflict financial pain on the perpetrators, but, more so, she was
compelled to do so to push back against her own pain. Once a West German
state stood in for its acknowledged antecedent Nazi perpetrators, my grandmother seemed to exemplify another stage in reparation demands, at least
according to Georg Simmel:

> Only here can we talk about *punishment* in the full sense of the word.
> The purpose now is to affect the subject himself, and any penalty as
> practical action is a means towards this end. Money fines thus take

on a totally different meaning for the former monetary compensation for wounding and killing. They are not supposed to compensate for the damage done, but to inflict pain upon the culprit.[33]

My grandmother believed that foremost among the wartime crimes for which Germans must pay was the creation of Jewish monsters in the Nazi image from among her own family and neighbors. Festering psychological and physical wounds that fueled her path toward unrelenting financial punishment of the Germans were highlighted for me in her story of Ada M. Once, a close neighbor and friend, Ada M. in Auschwitz was anointed a petty tyrant, the *Lagerälteste*, or head of a Jewish women's slave labor section, a post ranked higher than the *Sonderkommando*, the "special unit" of Jewish inmates charged with disposing crematoria corpses. Camp inmates who could be forced to identify with the aggressor behavior of sadistic SS men and women were chosen as *Lagerälteste*. One day when Ada M. smashed my grandmother to the ground for some minor offense, my mother rushed to defend her mother by pushing back. Ada M. possessed near total authority over five thousand Jewish women housed in ten barracks in the Auschwitz II-Birkenau camp complex. She took it on herself to make an example of my mother, a narrative my mother first recounted to me in June 2007 when we celebrated my parents' sixtieth wedding anniversary:

Ada M. began beating me over the head with her wooden baton, then made me kneel holding bricks over my head, beating me when I dropped them, throwing cold water on me when I collapsed. I still hear my mother's screaming, *los meyn eynzikes kind*, leave my only daughter alone. My mother always said to me, "If you ever find Ada M., just strangle her." Ada M. would also punish my mother regularly by making her kneel for hours and beating her. Two years after the war in 1947, I went to visit my mother's friend in the country, a woman who was Ada M's cousin. I was young, a medical student at Charles University in Prague, happy and recently engaged to your father who sent me off in a chauffeured car. The cousin told me she had someone hidden in the attic. Down the stairs walked Ada M. The cousin told me that Ada M. had been forced by the Nazis to watch her parents and eight siblings shot before her eyes. To harden her, she was forced to dig their graves and bury them. Then she was given her own office and well treated. In the camps, she was tall, with long dark hair while we were emaciated, heads shaven, and here she came down the stairs bent over, her hair falling out. Ada M. said to me, "Forgive me." I put my head on the table and cried and cried. I had to leave. I returned home and my mother asked me why I was so sad. I was afraid to tell her that I had seen Ada M. and all I could do was cry. My mother was speechless when I told her about meeting Ada M. Finally she asked, "What did you do?" I said, "I cried." And then she wailed, 'How will you ever succeed in life?" (Vera Slyomovics, interview by author, Vancouver, Canada, June 3, 2007)[34]

Neither my mother nor grandmother was capable of reconciling Ada M.'s moral and behavioral conduct in the camps, so deeply at odds with either their pre-Holocaust friendship and neighborly proximity or their post-Holocaust return to normal civilized behavior. In a question-and-answer session with high school students in 1982 on her Holocaust experiences, and twenty-five years prior to my interviews, I was present in the audience when my mother again evoked Ada M.:

She too was totally dehumanized. She was responsible; she was quite open about it. She had no mercy on us. She was the original builder of Auschwitz, she had to dig the graves for her three sisters, four brothers and her parents, and she had absolutely no sympathy for us. And any time she found out there was a mother-daughter combination, she became especially cruel. A year after I saw her when I visited her cousin, Ada M. was arrested. She got two years in prison. She was denounced by someone, tried by a Czechoslovakian court, and couldn't get back her Czech citizenship; she was from Slovakia. We heard that after prison she left for South America.[35]

Psychiatrist Anna Ornstein defines my mother's reactions as a form of "survivor's guilt." Ornstein draws on her experiences as a Hungarian Jew who survived Auschwitz with her mother, although her brother and father did not.[36] Counterintuitively, she claims that survivor's guilt is never the circumstance in which the survivor finds herself alive when a family was obliterated, the normative definition in much of the popular and psychological literature. Instead, she posits paralyzing states of survivor guilt due to the inability to see any continuity between the atrocious acts survivors may have committed or merely witnessed in the camps and what they now face in conducting a life that must be lived in a normal fashion.[37] Thus, my mother and grandmother's responses accord somewhat with Ornstein's radical recasting of psychic manifestations surrounding survivor guilt: my mother wept, turning anguish inward, while my grandmother characteristically lashed outward, entertaining fantasies of revenge and its practical enactment through financial restitution.

Hungarian Reparations and the Story of My Great-Aunt

Instead of courtroom remedies, by the year 2000, my mother had become the claimant who pleads to a third party by recounting facts, dates, and details repeatedly to a variety of listeners with a claim that must conform the past into the framework of the haunting question: how much is a life worth? While witnesses and court cases produced specific typologies of storytelling that resulted in one kind of legal closure, I find myself returning to a question introduced in this chapter: why it is that demands for reparation never end? As long as my grandmother was alive, her demand for reparations endured. While vacationing at my parent's home in 2005, I came upon a pile of unopened letters postmarked Budapest, Hungary, addressed to my grandmother's residence in Netanya, Israel, and forwarded after her death in August 1999 to my mother in Vancouver, Canada. Up until five months before her death, my grandmother had engaged in a lengthy correspondence in Hungarian (a language my mother must translate for me), in which she mailed out forms responding to Hungarian reparation protocols in Hebrew (which I translate for my mother). My mother's initial reaction to these long ignored documents was astonishment. Why, she wondered as she perused the pile of letters revealing a long-standing correspondence unknown to her, had my grandmother applied for reparations from the Hungarian government on behalf of my grandmother's murdered brother-in-law, Avraham Hendler? Why not on behalf of Malka Elefant Hendler, my grandmother's sister and Hendler's wife who shared his fate? Or why not demand reparations, for example, for the family's eight-story apartment building in Munkács, currently the city of Mukačevo in western Ukraine, where Jews once constituted almost half the population? The property, jointly owned by my maternal grandparents, was confiscated in 1944 during the Axis Hungarian occupation of Czechoslovakia's dismembered easternmost province of Subcarpathian Ruthenia. It seems that my grandmother, more knowledgeable than we, was aware of every legal loophole, including one in which Jews despoiled of property during the brief wartime era of Hungarian rule over Subcarpathian Ruthenia are not included under any post-Communist Hungarian laws to compensate dispossessed property owners.[38] But she could potentially file a different claim based on family connections. Subcarpathian Ruthenia, which reverted briefly to Czechoslovakia after Hungary's surrender, was annexed to the Soviet Ukraine in 1945. As my mother ruminated about wartime events that triggered my grandmother's quest for Hungarian reparations, I was instructed for the first time in 2005 about the fates of my grandmother and her three sisters.

Of the four daughters of my maternal great-grandparents David Elefant and Pearl Shreter, only two sisters, my grandmother and her youngest sister Hani, returned from a variety of Nazi slave labor and extermination camps. I have always known that my mother and grandmother survived together and that my great-aunt Hani's two children, six-year-old Oscar and nine-year-old Ruth, were immediately taken away from her and killed in Auschwitz the week before my mother and grandmother arrived. No visit would end at Hani's house, ninety-four when she died in 2009, without her trembling arthritic fingers handing me prewar black-and-white photos of her murdered boy and girl. A third sister, Helen (Haya) Elefant Hollander, who was married to my maternal grandfather's older brother (two brothers married two sisters), was gassed immediately with her two young sons on arrival to Auschwitz in April 1944; the two older sons perished a year later during the spring 1945 death march out of Auschwitz.

I had never known what happened to my grandmother's fourth and eldest sister, Malka Elefant Hendler. Direct questions brought tears and evasions during an adolescent phase when I was immersed in genealogy and family kinship charts. Her fate unfolded first through the leftover paperwork from my grandmother's failed quest for Hungarian reparations and was subsequently interpreted as a tale of murderous wartime Nazi bureaucracy. Beginning June 27, 1941, the Hungarian Axis regime controlling my family's region of Subcarpathian Ruthenia (again, formerly Czechoslovakia) required all Jews to demonstrate Hungarian citizenship by proving uninterrupted residence since 1851, a paperwork demand only possible if wealthy ancestors had been listed on nineteenth-century Austro-Hungarian taxpayer rolls.[39] A description of the process appears in the Holocaust memorial volume that is dedicated to Carpathian Jews, whose communal fates were linked to the geopolitical spaces of a newly reconstituted pre-World War I

Marmorosh region formed by the unilateral annexation by Hungary of the Czechoslovakian province north of the Tisza River:

> This was a very harsh and cruel decree. Some of the Jews of Marmaros—in general, the wealthier and better established financially—ran around from government office to government office, in order to obtain official documentation proving their citizenship and taxpayer status. In the Budapest offices of the "Bureau for the Protection of the Rights of the Jews of Hungary" (the "Magyar Izraelitak Partfogo Irodaja," which served all of the social groupings of Hungarian Jewry, Orthodox as well as "Neolog") there were every daylong lines of Jews waiting to get the necessary documents. Included in the crowd were a substantial number of Jews from Marmaros. Many of the applicants camped at the entrance to these offices during the night, in order to insure their turn when the office opened in the morning. And indeed, most of those who put in the efforts were lucky enough to receive the desired citizenship papers.[40]

Those without papers faced deportation east, meaning certain death as "foreign Jews." My maternal grandfather, Sandor Hollander, after whom my son is named, paid a Budapest lawyer $5,000 to obtain the necessary documents, as did many well-connected members of my maternal lineage fearing to travel some six hundred kilometers in wartime conditions to the distant capital. Fifty Czechoslovakian crowns could buy one American dollar, my mother recalled, and her parents had amassed over $100,000 in the hope of fleeing to Switzerland. According to our cousin Eugene Hollander, in 1830, an ancestor (perhaps my great-great-grandfather?) named Leopold Hollander settled in Berehovo in the Carpathians and was said to have come from America:

> His origins and why he came from America I have never been able to ascertain fully. But the town archives record that in order to build a distillery, he had to pay some sixty thousand gold crowns to the treasury of the regional government. A handsome sum in our day, an astronomical sum then. It was noted in the records that the value of a milch cow was six gold crowns. He was apparently noted for his wealth.[41]

Not so the experience of Avraham Hendler forced to travel by train from Subcarpathian Ruthenia to Budapest in summer 1941 for his family documents, in contrast to my maternal grandfather's successful procurement of papers at a distance. Perhaps it was the anti-Semitic Hungarian military gendarmes or just as likely a random Nazi official who disregarded Hendler's Hungarian citizenship papers because these very documents identified him as a Jew. He was forcibly removed as he was traveling home by train and deported to the east along with Carpathian Jews unable to obtain Hungarian citizenship papers, who were labeled both foreign and Jewish. My mother recalls: "All the poor people in the town, they're the ones who had no papers, they were taken. Bishtine was emptied by 1941" (Vera Slyomovics, interview by the author, Vancouver, Canada, November 27, 2010). In keeping with efficient bureaucratic procedures, a recorded formal notice of Hendler's deportation was delivered to his wife, Malka Hendler, who awaited his return in vain. My mother, then fifteen, tells me she remembers her aunt went crazy. So in love with her husband that no family member could stop her, she raced across the nearby border departing from the Hungarian-annexed Czechoslovakia where they resided, taking the train eastward to the western Ukraine on her rescue mission. She disappeared into the "bloodlands," that part of an Eastern European zone that successively endured Nazi and Soviet regimes responsible for killing more than fourteen million civilians between 1933 and 1945. Among them were Eastern European Jewry but also local populations who died from a variety of Stalinist-induced famines and executions, as well as German starvation and reprisal policies.[42] Word was brought back to the family that the two had found each other. The lovers had been murdered together in the Kamenetz-Podolsk killing fields of the Ukraine.

According to early indictments against the Nationalist-Socialist leaders filed during the postwar Nuremberg Military Trials, it was in the Kamenetz-Podolsk region on August 27 and 28, 1941, that the first large-scale murders of Jews were carried out. French scholars call this early mass murder period in the Ukraine *Shoah des balles*, the "Holocaust of bullets," a two-day period during which some 31,000 Jews were forced to dig their own graves and then were shot, a figure that included local Polish and Carpathian Jews without Hungarian citizenship papers.[43] Among them were the Hendlers, my great-aunt and her husband, whose murders my grandmother ceaselessly documented through her demands for compensation, in deed memorializing them in her fashion and with the means available to her until just months before she died. As she perused her piles of paperwork, my grandmother would cite for me a religious commentary that states as long as a person is talked about, thought about, written about, then her soul is still among us the living.

My grandmother was marked by the Hendlers' deportation and death in concrete ways, focusing repeatedly on how news about her beloved older sister reached the family: a piece of paper, a form, an official notification letter of Avram Hendler's deportation, and, therefore, my grandmother reasoned, duplicated and retrievable somewhere in a government archive. In contrast, her sister's mad rush toward death was forever undocumented, hence not provable. My grandmother's faith in paperwork, carbon copies, archives, files, and procedures, especially those produced by murderous authorities, remained unshaken. Recall that, in the final months of World War II, convinced that liberation and repatriation were imminent, my grandmother felt free to take the first step toward documentation. Sustained by an awareness that underpins the gesture to make demands, she arranged her own written proofs of disposession and family deaths and, in effect, asserted presciently her right to what would unfold in future decades as German reparations to "make good again."

"What Is a Life Worth?"

Financial indemnification programs, even when eliciting financial pain, still confront an implacable unease: managing death and disease as an economic event offends. Even in those cases where blame and punishment cannot be directly assigned to an individual or even to the state, morality and money are linked. Zelizer cites the early history of resistance, especially by women, to the business of insuring their husband's life, seen as deriving profit from the demise of a spouse: "Some women say that life insurance seems to them too much like benefiting by the husband's death. Others feel that if a good man were to die, and the proceeds of a policy should be paid to them, it would seem like accepting 'blood money,' and others say they would not enter any such sordid calculation of his future expectation of life."[44]

Monetary accounting for gross human rights violations, inserted uneasily between victim and perpetrator or mediated gingerly between claimant and commission, is characterized as the apotheosis of commodification and objectification of suffering. In sum, financial reparations are hush money, blood money, tainted, driven by greed, undeserved, unworthy, and insufficient. The 9/11 Fund asked the question, as do many mass tort claims, "How much is a life worth?" Arguments surrounding monetary payments articulate repetitive themes and contradictions that invite limited comparisons. They form part of the "Faustian predicament,"[45] a pact with the devil according to historian Elazar Barkan, who coined the term specifically for Jews taking money from Germans in which contradictory emotional and symbolic statements are articulated: taking money is an affront to the memory of the dead, no amount of money compensates for suffering, it is hush money to replace and impede further investigations, even those perpetrators who acknowledge crimes cannot pay off the debt of genocide and massive human rights abuses.[46] Accusations directed against victims echo the distaste with the legitimacy and legality of equating money to suffering: victims are blackmailing or shaking down governments, they are never satisfied, their lawyers steal reparations, they are manipulated by transnational organizations as intermediaries that pocket the bulk of the money, sufferings are exaggerated, numbers and definitions of the "victim" are enlarged to increase payments.[47]

The pain is incommensurable; it courses alongside the path of money exchanges, leaking throughout the system like bloodstains in the financial body.[48] The actual circulation of money keeps pain alive. Managing victim-perpetrator exchanges are agonizing, financially and medically, even for distinguished and seasoned professionals such as Kenneth Feinberg, the 9/11 Fund tort lawyer. Whenever a third party is interposed, how does any agency, acting on behalf of a sovereign state and in charge of disbursing funds, determine what is called the pain of "noneconomic loss"? Perennial questions faced by truth commissions, reparations boards, and torts cases are, for example, how anyone can put a monetary value on a life and how to predict what the victim would have earned had she or he lived. As legal scholar Richard Abel succinctly puts it, "Tort law gives victims only money damages; it does not elicit apologies, provide care, change risky behavior, or punish."[49] The 9/11 Fund payment schedules did not involve the presence of the perpetrators; they were based on previous cases of death benefits to police officers, a system that offered one template for calculations of noneconomic loss that resulted in $250,000 for pain and suffering per person killed and $50,000 for "emotional distress" for spouse and dependents.

"What could I say about a mother determined to write a dead daughter's future, a future that would never be?" Kenneth Feinberg asked himself in his memoir of fund stewardship.[50] Since the worth of the lost loved one is incalculable, Feinberg noted that, consequently, families were forced to ask for more money. Grieving families were transformed into potential heirs of the 9/11 Fund and found themselves deploying oral testimony to articulate the irreplaceable qualities of a parent, a child—understood, or at best translated by fund managers solely into economic terms. Everyone—survivors, lawyers, fund managers, narrators, and listeners alike—was implicated in telling a story.

In addition to assessing known economic worth (home ownership, assets, current salary, etc.), in order to narrate the value of the absent loved one, another section of the 9/11 Fund claim form gave space "to explain what the numbers could not convey, the uniqueness of the husband, wife, daughter, son or parent,"[51] because, Feinberg avers, many claimants needed to add to the questionnaire. Writing their life story was insufficient, answering questions of economic worth, heartless. During requested hearings by surviving family members of 9/11, a stenographer was present to record the ways in which families narrated orally the story of their dead. Accounts were frequently supplemented by visual images (photographs and albums) and memorabilia supplied by kin. Yet these testimonies and artifacts had no effect whatsoever on financial outcomes because they cannot fit the well-worn templates of calculated cash outcomes:

> Initially described as cool and aloof, he [Feinberg] won over the skeptical and heartbroken by devoting hours of personal face time to hearing stories. He held meetings allowing victims' families to tell their stories and set up a system that allowed nearly anyone to request that he personally hear a claim. Feinberg says he sat through more than 900 hearings. "Don't underestimate listening. Do not underestimate listening," he told interviewer Charlie Rose on PBS.[52]

Feinberg believes that those who chose orally narrated hearings, in addition to the mandatory documented written claims, needed the optional public narration afforded by an official setting to effect what Feinberg therapeutically terms some kind of "psychological closure."

I believe that my mother's ability to accept German money beginning in 1999 was preceded by her recognition of a new and different Germany, one that was worth revisiting. My grandmother took German money but made clear her implacable refusal to set foot in Germany again. As with many survivors of her generation, the ban extended to purchasing German products—no Volkswagen, Mercedes-Benz, BMW, or Audi automobiles. If she could have found a way to boycott Junkers aircraft products, those too would be forbidden to her family. A close friend of my mother's in Vancouver, herself a native German-speaker and Holocaust survivor, refused to speak the German language to her dying day. In contrast, my mother felt the German language was culturally acceptable; it belonged to the Jews too. She kept up her German linguistic skills and loved the language. Why deprive herself of the beauty of Heine, she asked me, as she associatively riffed about her nonboycott of either German goods or even well-known Nazi associates and sympathizers?

> After the war, when I got engaged, it was 1947, your father bought me a beautiful BMW, a two-seater convertible, red leather inside, a long body. With a chauffeur named Tony. Czech Jews, no one we knew, ever considered a boycott of German products. Under Adenauer didn't Germany give Israel buses? I was surprised by Canadian Jews who boycotted German products. I never did. But I do know who requisitioned our BMW once the Communists took over. His name was Novotny, and he was the minister of finance. His nephew, also Novotny, escaped with us from Czechoslovakia in the group that walked over the mountains. We were eleven people going over the Semmering. He escaped with his wife, Lida Barova, a famous Czech actress. During the war, she was a German sympathizer. [Josef] Goebbels [Nazi propaganda minister] fell in love with her. She had been married to Gustave Fröhlich, an Austrian theater actor. Fröhlich confronted Goebbels about the affair, and Goebbels had him shot. The Austrians would have killed Barova if they recognized her. In fact, the nurse in Salzberg recognized Barova, who had dyed her hair red in disguise. I lied for her. She was wonderful with my newborn baby boy. (Vera Slyomovics, interview by author, Vancouver, Canada, August 18, 2010)

For years, sanctions against German products and culture were somewhat tied to what my grandmother and mother insisted was the world's lack of historical understanding and acknowledgment about Nazi Germany's extensive slave labor program experienced by both of them. They believed that Germany's postwar reparations protocols expunged the vast nether-worlds of enslaved populations until the year 2000. The ban on German cultural and material products has long since diminished for many Jews, if not disappearing over time and among successive generations. As for me, I will never buy any Junkers aircraft.

There is no such thing as closure, my mother insists, even if reparations emanate from an apologetic, reunified German state or even a willing 9/11 Fund. Rather, the pain augments annually, the void more palpable for "those left behind"—my mother's term for herself since the age of eighteen in rela-tion to her father murdered in 1944 at forty-two. As she herself grew older, arriving to her forty-second year safely in Canada and believing she was at the height of her mental and physical powers, she often asked me to ponder what her father, the multitalented linguist, might have accomplished had he lived. Forty-second birthdays were met with anxiety and panic until my brother and I successfully passed that ominous benchmark into our forty-third year. When I was pregnant at forty-two, miraculously so according to my mother, there was no question but that my son must carry her father's name in order to acknowledge, onomastically and publicly, my maternal grandfather's potent intercessions in our lives.

Hierarchies of Victimhood

While the 9/11 Fund is considered primarily pecuniary because of the ways it mimics the insurance estimates of the financial equivalence for loss and death of a human being, it also shares with other reparations programs what Feinberg termed a "scale of victimhood measured in dollars." Based on the economic success of individuals (for example, the wealthy stockbrokers in the World Trade Center towers), it not only served to diminish the lives of victims awarded less (for example, the firefighters sent to rescue them) but also meant that high-income earners were equated with higher value, since estimations were based on future earnings as opposed to actions and deeds.[53] Hierarchies of victimhood presuppose that victims are not a homo-geneous group. The terms to describe them vary according to the diverse contexts mentioned so far and encompass multiple legal, historical, economic, and literary identities and categorization. For the word "victim" equally substitutable are survivor, deponent, claimant, plaintiff, militant, political prisoner, resister, witness, heir, mother or family member. All categories produce narratives. Narratives of suffering by victims often determine the amount and duration of monetary outcomes. The complex, dynamic relationship of so many aspects of victimhood to narratives of suffering and to financial reparation partakes of social scientist Pierre Bourdieu's systems of social hierarchization in conformity with the ways in which individual stakeholders within institutions create distinctions. Such narratives also create distinctions among the various cultural or "symbolic capitals" possessed by victims.[54] In turn, the victims' power to narrate self-definitions broadens the way the law and humanitarian organizations think about reparation. This too involves a Bourdieuian struggle for control over history and memory. French historian Henry Rousso delineates clear ideological and practical boundaries deployed by survivors in France after the Second World War: "hundreds of associations were formed establishing what amounts to a veritable hierarchy of suffering: the volunteer resistance fighter did not wish to be confused with the 'racial' deportee; the deportee did not wish to be mistaken for a prisoner of war; the prisoner of war was careful to distinguish himself from . . . the laborer 'deported' to work in Germany for the Reich."[55] My mother augments Rousso's range of French hierarchies with the tale of her camp escape during the chaotic last days of the war. Inside the Markkleeberg women's forced labor camp were some two hundred French political prisoners, described by my mother as parachutists from the Resistance, among them it seems even a French general's daughter held hostage. Although the Frenchwomen had been captured and interned in Markkleeberg, they were housed in barracks separate from the female Jewish slave laborers. Not far from Markkleeberg was another camp to house the *Service du Travail Obligatoire* (STO), the category of paid French laborers working in Germany for the Reich,[56] who redefined for my mother and grandmother the consequences of belonging to the universally recognized and most despised category, namely, the tattooed concentration camp Jew:

> I make friends easily and love meeting new people. So I befriended two French Resistance women who spoke German. They somehow had information about what was going on in the outside world. I don't know how they got it. We Jewish women had no information about anything. They alerted me to the plan of the upcoming death march to Theresienstadt Camp where all concentration camp inmates

would be brought there and everyone blown up at once. Since we marched in lines of five people, they two decided to partner with me, my mother, and Faygie, the Markkleeberg *Lagerälteste*. Beginning in April 1945, 500 women left the camp. We five were marching along and my 80-pound mother became weaker and weaker; the bombs were raining down on us from all three allies—Russian, British, and American. We looked like soldiers from the aerial viewpoint. The Frenchwomen decided the next bombardment would give us a chance to escape since my mother could no longer walk. We hid behind a white fence, let the columns march on, crouching in front of a house. They knew about the nearby French labor camp and brought us there. The leader of the French labor camp made this speech to us in German explaining his hierarchies. He refused to take a chance on keeping us Jewish women in the camp, because, unlike the French-women, we were tattooed. The French panicked when they saw our tattoos. He compared us to the SS who were also tattooed by saying: "You are marked people." Strategically, the French workers told us to go back to the camp, no one would look for us there. The French girls cried when we walked away. It was the French Resistance women. They were the ones who gave me hope in the camp. The hope was survival. (Vera Slyomovics, interview by author, Vancouver, Canada, June 3, 2007)[57]

"Remembrance, Responsibility, and the Future" (*Erinnerung, Verantwortung, Zukunft*)

Since 1996, Henry Rousso's lowest category of "laborer" has emerged to propel a series of Holocaust-related lawsuits that rethink definitions and accord a different set of financial compensations in which "forced laborers" become defined as deportees brought from their home countries to Nazi Germany or German-occupied countries during World War II. Anthropologist Philippe Bourgois wrote about his father, a French former forced laborer, a civilian worker in the French Service du Travail Obligatoire, sent to work in Auschwitz's I. G. Farben petrochemical factory and on whose behalf Bourgois submitted a claim for restitution. What the son calls "worthy victimhood," the kind that receives reparations, was bureaucratically denied to his father in 2004 who fell into the category of "not good enough victimhood."

Bourgois' father supported the claim reviewer's refusal of benefits, insisting, "I don't deserve any compensation."[58]

"Forced laborers" are distinguished from the category of "slave laborers" who were inmates of concentration camps or ghettos. Benjamin Ferencz, a lawyer on the American legal team at the Nuremberg Trials, preferred the term "less than slaves" because, in the 1940s, he could conceive of no words to describe "unpaid workers earmarked for destruction."[59] German historian Ulrich Herbert provides a nuanced characterization of slave labor categories and actual camp conditions in relation to Nazi racial ideologies:

> The workers from western countries were in a worse condition than native Germans, but in a far better position than workers from the East when it came to food rations, the interior furnishings and physical state of living quarters. A hierarchy arose on this basis: French civilian workers ranked above all others, then came workers from southern European countries followed on a lower rung by laborers from Czechoslovakia and beneath them were the Poles. At the bottom of the heap were workers from the Soviet Union—along, since the summer of 1943, with Italian military internees. . . . The concentration camp inmates . . . formed their own special category far beneath the bottom rung of this racist ladder, since their exploitation . . . was not tempered by any sort of treatment ordered [toward] productivity on the job.[60]

Distinctions about forced laborers and concentration camp survivors are part of the "German Law on the Creation of the Foundation 'Remembrance, Responsibility and the Future'"[61] established in 2000 and funded by the German state and a consortium of German private industries implicated in Nazi-era slave and forced labor. The law compensates individual survivors of National Socialist injustice committed by the German Reich during the period between 1933 and 1945.[62] According to its website, the Foundation Law accords indemnities to: (1) "persons held in a concentration camp or place of confinement or a ghetto under comparable conditions and subjected to forced labor"; (2) individuals deported from their homelands into the territory of the German Reich where they were subjected to forced labor; and (3) an open category of victim eligibility pertaining to other situations of National Socialist injustice. Unlike the 1950s postwar German *Wiedergutmachung* program, which took into account biographical data worthy of compensation, such as age, loss of livelihood and family, the year 2000 German Foundation Law avoided the more common indemnification practice of placing a value on the life of the survivor. Its main task is to determine the eligibility of the living, whose numbers are said to diminish ten per cent annually. Such new reparation protocols of the Foundation Law function in radically different ways. There are no medical examinations and interviews. A list of established camps was posted on the Foundation website so that claimants need only prove their presence in recognized "places of confinement." By June 2007, the Foundation "Remembrance, Responsibility and the Future" completed payments to former slave and forced laborers, cash outlays that totaled €4.37 billion to more than 1.66 million people in almost one hundred countries.[63]

These later German reparations definitions entail the complete separation of legal principles of justice from procedural laws because the Foundation follows only procedural codes. This means that, if the Holocaust victim-claimant can conform her experience within the parameters of the Foundation categories and situate herself in the foundation list of camps, then procedurally, financial reparations follow: *ubi ius, ibi remedium* (where there is law, there is remedy). In other words, my mother needed only to demonstrate that she was in Markkleeberg, a priori defined in Foundation lists as a site of forced and slave labor. My grandmother's work paper from Markkleeberg Camp (cf. Prologue) submitted by my mother constituted a rare proof. Thus, the term survivor takes on novel meanings, survivor of camps but also surviving fifty years after the atrocity event, able to make claims and willing to tell the story.

Feinberg's lawyerly attempts at invoking psychological closure for families after legally regulated cash outlays are in striking contrast to the enormous psychological and medical literature on Holocaust survivors and Holocaust families about heirs to reparations but also inheritors to psychological effects with no closure. Indeed, why focus on reparations when considering the destruction of my own extended family? In what way is my understanding of the Holocaust tied to a preoccupation with forms of compensation, no less than the actual lives of aunts, cousins, and grandparents whose physical existence was obliterated? Since my mother wanted no part of German reparations until 1999, instead my grandmother, Gizella Elefant Hollander, inspires this study, first as she undergoes interviews and medical examinations in the 1950s and then as she keeps abreast of the latest reparation initiatives into her ninth decade. Although my grandmother is no longer alive to describe her fifty-year pursuit of reparations, her story belongs to what Art Spiegelman, author of comic-strip tales about his Holocaust survivor parents, calls his "background noise, part of the ambient blur" and "this presence that had been hanging over my family's life, Auschwitz and what it had done to us."[64] My grandmother's account passes through a rereading of German documents in far-flung archives but is also a history I hear from my mother, the consummate teller of tales.

Should there exist a chain of transmission to link three generations of women in my family, my grandmother's legacy to me when I was young was the gift of her Nazi slave labor paperwork that launched this study but also triggered my mother's first reparation request. In 1999, the year my grandmother died, my mother confessed to me that her mother began appearing to her in dreams. At night my grandmother would implore her only child to carry on, to launch independently her own set of procedures against the Germans, and to stake a claim for individual reparation funds. Never mind blood money, my mother was scolded in Hungarian and Yiddish; rather, take payments and give to charity. Blood money, my grandmother argued in my mother's dreams, could be cleansed through pious acts of charitable giving. These numerous mother-daughter dreams permitted alternate ways of thinking about German reparations, instigated by a convincing dream universe of reference, usually the principle repository for ongoing conversations during which the deserving dreamer, my mother, continues to merit connections with her dead parents. All my life, my mother seemed to inhabit two worlds—the one I live in with her and the world to come, *olam ha-ba* in Hebrew, which she conceives of as the afterlife for individual souls. The hinge factor linking the two worlds is the wait, the attentive longing for the reappearance of her murdered family in dreams. When she brings together momentarily the living and the dead, such times become embodied in what psychological anthropologist Douglas Hollan terms the "selfscape dream": "emotionally and imaginally vivid dreams that appear to reflect back to the dreamer how his or her current organization of self relates various parts of itself to itself, its body, and to other objects in the world."[65]

Regardless of the emotional cost, my mother performs the role of conduit by donating to appropriate recipients. The money must be disbursed quickly. Best of all was when she could sign the German check and hand over the very same piece of paper to charity, thereby ridding herself of any physical evidence or contact, as she discounted her appended signature, a fleeting touch of the hand. At first, reparation money was not deposited to

avoid polluting her personal bank account. Inevitably, even viewing and
signing the reparation check became agonizing. She decided to switch to
direct deposit, preferring never to set eyes on the German paperwork. Germany reparation money enables small, preferably anonymous acts of doubly
reparative donations; the same revenue, never cashed, trebles in both value
and meanings as the Germans and my mother, for radically different origins
and outcomes, seem to redeem themselves through giving.

Since January 1, 2000, based on the latest German reparation protocols to
forced and slave laborers, which are amounts symbolically rich but financially
meager, various country's tax codes around the world are in agreement to
characterize these disbursements not as income but in a sense as gifts, hence,
nontaxable. According to Eugene Clay Shaw, Jr., Republican congressional
representative for heavily Jewish south Florida, "the federal government
should not receive a financial windfall from Holocaust payments," estimated at $3 million in lost federal tax revenues for 2012 from 88,000 surviv-
ing Holocaust beneficiaries.[66] In similar fashion, in order not to profit from
the Holocaust, my mother refuses speaker's fees during frequent school lectures about her Holocaust experiences, by stipulating that funds are to be
redirected to a student in need of financial aid. She jokes that each April,
with its officially designated days for Holocaust remembrance, is her "busy
season." As it happens, my mother's acts of charity are individual projects
ritually embedded in religious Jewish, communal practices of *sedaqa*, the
commandment to give charity. To ensure prayers reach God, to mark a personal vow, to give thanks, or to plead for medical respite, prayers are efficacious if recited while depositing money in multiples of the number eighteen
(18, 36, 54, etc., cents or dollars) in a specific charity box called the *pishke* by
many Yiddish-speaking Jews. Eighteen is the magic number. Expressed in
Hebrew letters (*het* and *yod*), it is both a number but also holds meaning
because it spells the Hebrew word "life," *hayy*. When my mother uses the
pishke, as she deposits coins for charity, she apologizes to God in her prayers
if her request is any way related to money.

Marcel Mauss's classic work *The Gift* speculates about the force that in-
heres in the thing given, such that the recipient must give something back.
Even the impersonal character of German reparations to Jewish survivors
compels a response allied to an act of charity giving. The word "gift," possesses
more than one meaning including "poison," and in ancient Germanic culture,
Mauss concludes, a gift may endanger the recipient.[67] Mauss, a French Jew,
lost his position at Paris's prestigious Collège de France during the Vichy era

and the Nazi occupation of France; miraculously, he was never deported to the camps. He maintained that, for societies and individuals to progress toward stable relationships, what was required was "giving, receiving, and finally, giving in return": "It is by opposing reason to feeling, by pitting the will to peace against outbursts of insanity of this kind that peoples succeed in substituting alliance, gifts, and trade for war, isolation and stagnation."[68]

My grandmother's approach, uniquely her own, was to commit gifts of multiples of the number nine, half the designated cash amount of eighteen to charity, with the remainder deposited in the *pishke* money collection box, if and only if her prayers were answered. Outcomes could be negotiated with God, as when my grandmother would sigh and say, "*Raboyne shel oylam*, Lord of the Universe, God, you owe me." My grandmother did not cease to reprimand and bully, fully engaging according to a venerable Judaic disputatious discourse with the divine, practices that she adhered to religiously.

In multiples of eighteen, my mother parcels out German reparation funds. Is my mother's rush to relinquish her reparation check a critique of, an undermining of reparations? Certainly, it compels her to conjure with whom her money must be given as soon as possible, and she does so with some joy at the thought of becoming a potential donor, not merely the actual beneficiary. The risk is never financial but temporal and moral, should funds rest long in her possession. Only in this fashion, as if following Maussian strictures about "gift economies," has my mother come to accept any economic relationship with the German way of dealing with its Nazi past. It is now seen as a gift, albeit tainted and distasteful, whose worth increases exponentially when recirculated, a twist on anthropological explanations about the complex *kula* exchange system in which shell ornaments of Papuan New Guinea islanders endlessly circle among the men of the South Pacific archipelago, accumulating social capital as they pass through the hands of successive recipients. My mother's variation knows similar speedy time limitations for disbursal but permits no return; rather, it is a unidirectional movement from German to Jew, intended toward useful spending down along the chain of anonymously linked partners. Yet for both Papuans and, less benignly, my mother, each enmeshed in their respective exchanges, the system is forever a part of her: "once in Kula, always in Kula."[69]

Since the 1999 death of my grandmother, my mother could no longer rely on her own mother as the designated family representative and recipient of German blood money. My mother was on her own. Seeking reparations was a project to incorporate her dead mother, what the psychological literature understands as a complex process of grieving through which my mother folds into herself her mother's claim on their shared pasts. She absorbs my grandmother's being, opening herself up to the punishment of pursuing financial gain through German reparations. On each succeeding generation devolves some aspect of my grandmother's fierce and implacable command—the Germans must pay for what they did to the Jews—so much so that my mother imagined herself carrying on her maternal legacy when applying for her first reparations claim ever in 1999 by submitting my grandmother's 1945 Markkleeberg slave labor documents, while I follow wherever my grandmother's files lead me, a journey so long postponed.

CHAPTER 2

The Limits of Therapy: Narratives of Reparation and Psychopathology

Reparations touch on aspects of the destruction of the Jews during World War II but fundamentally sidestep the Holocaust. By drawing on ready-made, preexisting economic categories about damages present in the tort system, reparations deal only with those who survived, a remnant minority that cannot represent losses to entire families and communities. To succeed, reparations protocols must construct an image of the universal victim, one that necessarily diminishes the individual in favor of aggregate solutions. Human rights commissions and reparations committees attach conditions to reparation funds they disburse. These conditions are both explicit and implicit. Individual witness testimony is a prime example of an explicit condition directly relevant to the variety of subsequent remedies available or offered through the 1952 West German indemnification laws. For the subsequent 2004 German Foundation awards to North African Jews (cf. Chapter 6), implicit conditions became the norm because witness testimony mattered less than available official documentation of prisoner lists that placed claimants in a bureaucratically recognized internment camp.

Reparations and restitution case studies represent the triumph of two intertwined yet dissimilar notions: financial reparation goes to an individual but is proved through representative template narratives of collective suffering. This chapter explores the ways financial reparation programs for human rights violations under Nazi Germany are not merely about asking "how much?" or primarily "What happened?"—but seek to elicit answers to the question "How does it feel?" The process of directly asking my mother and grandmother intimate questions about their Auschwitz, Plaszow, and

Markkleeberg camp experiences affords glimpses of intractable suffering
and persistent pain, while rendering visible and legible the indignities, injustices, and financial triumphs of their narrated journey through the
worlds of postwar German, Czech, and Hungarian indemnifications. While
the wider socioeconomic, medico-legal, and historical frameworks of postwar German reparations have generated a vast scholarly literature, the narrated experiences of individuals who applied for and received money are
less explored. Lifelong attempts to understand my mother's initial refusal
of German reparations, my precipitating research topic, were influenced
by psychological anthropology's "person-centered ethnography."[1] Despite
a plethora of international Holocaust testimony projects and the reach of
more recent truth commission witnessing, narratives about financial compensation remain private and inaccessible. A person-centered ethnography
provides a cross-disciplinary, context-rich advantage when discussing sensitive money issues, a point underscored by anthropologist Douglas Hollan,
who highlights anthropology's engagement with the consummate human
capacity to respond to interviews through narrating:

> We learn that what people are willing and able to tell us about them-
> selves changes as our relationships with them deepen and evolve
> over time. We learn what part of people's minds and behaviors they
> have conscious access to and what part they do not, and how these
> parts are dynamically related. Not least, we learn what people most
> value, enjoy, fear, or dread in their lives. And how people who can
> look so similar in their overt behavior can be so different from a psy-
> chological or experiential point of view.[2]

Person-centered ethnography shares with ethnography the necessity for rig-
orously applying supervision and methods of clinical psychological training
to ensure some measure of objectivity and cross-cultural comparison. My
approach is informed by aspects of person-centered approach, while lacking
the requisite supervisory protocols to maintain balanced perspectives about
my mother and grandmother. Consequently, I also borrow the term "intimate ethnography," deployed by two anthropologists, Alisse Waterston and
Barbara Rylko-Bauer, who gathered a series of articles grouped around the
theme of anthropologists and life histories of their own family members
caught in the Holocaust:

Although both of us approach these life-history projects as daughters, the anthropologist in each of us is ever present, posing broader questions and looking beyond the personal story. Almost from the outset of the research, there has been interplay of roles: as the daughter chronicles a family narrative, the anthropologist contextualizes the story, situating it in larger history and political economy. And so these personal family narratives have evolved into "ethnographies of discovery"—of our parents' stories, of our own individual stories, and of history writ large. Although these projects may be seen as a form of autoethnography, we have chosen to call our methodological approach "intimate ethnography."[3]

As with many of us engaged in overlapping approaches to Holocaust family life histories using intimate ethnography and autoethnographies by children of Holocaust survivors, in these first chapters, I am aligned on the side of the victim and survivor. Unlike members of my extended family, understandably reluctant to revisit either the past or their individual indemnification negotiations, my mother and grandmother generously and spontaneously reflected on their experiences with German reparations. They approved of my book project, but even more, it was enough that their daughter and granddaughter asked for help. Conversations were turned into a series of extended, open-ended interviews during which I took notes and photographs, read them sections of the manuscript as I wrote, and incorporated their revisions, often rewriting to their satisfaction. Indeed, my mother's ongoing participation is traceable throughout this chapter marked by her subsequent annotations—note interviews dated August 19–20, 2010, in this chapter.

To focus myopically (in a positive sense), to range narrowly, circling obsessively around individual accounts informs not only the content of novels and movies but also nonfictional ethnography, autoethnography, intimate ethnography, life history, person-centered ethnography, and oral history. Narratives about what happened to my mother during the Holocaust emerge from her experiences but also shape how she views herself, as she talks eloquently and unceasingly to me about the painful past since I was a child.[4] From a very young age, I was schooled in her behavioral manifestations and triggers, although less so their root causes, when everyday conditions elicited anxiety and agitated behavior in my mother: thirst, trains, crowds, angry and loud voices, blocked toilets, men in uniform, and barking dogs, especially German shepherds. Traveling with my mother, I learned to carry water and avoid subways. One summer when our family arrived at the Rome airport in 1975 to be greeted by leaping German shepherds sniffing for drugs, my mother reluctantly disclosed her tattooed Auschwitz forearm to sympathetic Italian officials, bypassed custom controls, and was whisked out of the airport in an ambulance:

> It was only until a few years ago that I would take a train because of the clickity click, clickity click, and we could only look out the little windows at the top. And they had nice little games. They would bring water once a day in a trough and we'd all run against it and we'd turn it over. There was a wise man who said, "They will bring the trough, let me start, slowly," so we drank, but it was a most horrible feeling to be thirsty, and I think today thirst scares me more than hunger. If today I'm thirsty on the top of Masada, it should be an event, and it was wonderful, and all of a sudden I got thirsty and then I said, "I've got to have water," and then I learned to take water because it scares me. (Vera Slyomovics, interview by Steven Spielberg Survivors of the Shoah Visual History Foundation, Netanya, Israel, December 11, 1997)

In contrast to my mother, and like many victims of Nazi atrocities, my grandmother chose to articulate publicly her past sufferings constrained within frameworks of an externally assigned role, namely, as a claimant and petitioner for reparations. This occurred during the first decade after World War II, when bureaucratic mechanisms to process reparation claims unfolded with little fanfare. It seemed as if each claimant negotiated in isolation, one on one, albeit with the Jewish Claims Conference organization mediating between North American Jewish victims and German bureaucrats. My mother rejected the role of claimant for reparations but embraced the public performance of witnessing. A large body of scholarly work has emerged about Jewish Holocaust survivors, subsumed under the rubric of "witness studies." Indeed, French historian Annette Wieviorka characterizes the late twentieth century as *l'ère du témoin*, the era of the witness, the century that has accorded the victim of political violence cultural salience and representative characteristics such that an individual may stand both for the collective experience as well as a voice in the public realm.[5] Not until

1961, sixteen years after the war, would German perpetrator and Jewish victim voices come visually and aurally to the attention of a vast audience in the public sphere. Wieviorka locates this watershed historical moment in the landmark trial of Adolf Eichmann, a high-ranking Nazi official charged with the logistics of mass deportation to the death camps, crimes against humanity, and war crimes. Eichmann was kidnapped from his postwar hideout in Argentina by the Israeli secret service and tried in a Jerusalem court from April 11 to August 14, 1961. Unlike the strategy of Allied prosecutors during the 1945 Nuremberg Military Tribunal of the Nazi leadership, Israel's prosecuting attorney, Gideon Hausner, based the state's case on representative witnesses to narrate Jewish sufferings, thereby presenting survivor voices that were aimed less as trial evidence against Eichmann than as an indictment of the Nazi apparatus of extermination. Aided by the global reach of daily television and radio broadcasts, the testimony of 111 witnesses was heard worldwide.[6]

Philosopher Hannah Arendt was present reporting on the Eichmann trial for the *New Yorker* magazine. Although critical of both the preeminent role of witness testimony as Israel's principle legal framework as well as the actual roster of witnesses, nonetheless, she too concluded famously that witness evidence means that

> the holes of oblivion do not exist. Nothing human is that perfect, and there are simply too many people in the world to make oblivion possible. One will always be left alive to tell the story. Hence, nothing can ever be "practically useless"—at least, not in the long run. It would be of great practical usefulness for Germany today—and not merely for her prestige abroad but for her sadly confused inner condition—if there were more stories like [Anton] Schmidt's [German sergeant, who was one of the few Germans to aid the Jews] to tell.[7]

Arendt disputes the possibility of "holes of oblivion" into which twentieth-century history's horrific human experiences of fascism and totalitarianism might have been consigned, absent even a single countervailing voice of "one person left alive to tell the story." What are the implications for storytelling and narrative, folklore and person-centered anthropology in foregrounding the singular, the unique, the one voice left alive? And what to make of Holocaust-era stories by my parents that may be characterized as "true but singular and misleading aspects of what happened," according to

German author Bernhard Schlink in his book *Guilt About the Past*.[8] I ask myself these questions because I wrote this chapter inspired by the following story. On Sunday, June 6, 2010, my mother phoned to tell me that, while scouring a kitchen pot, suddenly she "felt hit by a waking memory": she saw herself descending from a cattle car at the railroad platform. It was Auschwitz, terminus of a three-day journey without food or water packed into the transports that brought her and her parents from the Hungarian ghetto of Mátészalka:

> At Auschwitz, I was seeing that he was there. Rudy Takar. He was a Schwab [so called "Swabian" or "ethnic German"] from our hometown, very handsome, dressed in a SS uniform. I went to school with the younger ones and your Dad with the older Takar boys. His sister was my best friend, and I used to help her with her homework. Then she wanted nothing to do with me and Jews. My father left some of our valuables with them before he was taken away. When [your grandmother and] I returned home to Bishtine [Carpathian Ruthenia] after the war, the whole Takar family was gone. Tears were rolling down Rudy's cheeks, he was crying like a baby. "Is that you *gnädige Frau* [Madame] Hollander? And is that *kleine* [little] Vera," he asked? I had last seen him when he was sixteen or seventeen, and I was eight or nine. Mama said, "That's Vera," and he said, "She's beautiful." Rudy was such a nice guy. His mother asked us to hire him and he worked for us for two summers, then went to Germany and joined the SS. At the risk of being caught, he gave us a huge box of yellow candy, something like *stolverk* [Hungarian for "turd"], looked like taffy. It stuck to the top of your mouth. It was like manna from heaven in that place. (Vera Slyomovics, interview by author, Vancouver, Canada, June 6, 2010)

Then she sighed: "Now that I'm in my eighties, sometimes I think that I wasn't there in Auschwitz. It was a dream."[9] So many of my mother's stories about World War II survival possess magical, dream-like qualities about the goodness of people and God's presence in her life. There were the Ukrainian Baptist missionary priest who risked his life to hide her in his church when her parents were deported; the family's Ruthenian maid, Marika of Shandrif hamlet (in Hungarian, Sandorfalu) who, with little food herself, smuggled provisions into the Bishtine ghetto; and another Jewish family servant who secretly brought them extra food at night to the Auschwitz barracks because she was now the camp cook:

> The cook survived the war and we met up again in Montreal. I remember she made your brother a beautiful sailor suit. That was in 1951. I use to explain that my survival was due to the fact that I could drink their horrible mixture of so-called soup, which was barley and cabbage. It stank to high heaven. I drank it by holding my nose. Your grandmother could never down it. So I gave her my bread and butter. There was always so much soup left over. People couldn't take it. Here in Canada my friends call me "Holocaust stomach," because I could eat anything. (Vera Slyomovics, interview by author, Vancouver, Canada, August 19, 2010)

Even the Markkleeberg Camp *Oberscharführer* (Nazi squad leader), who forced her to clean his quarters, gave her bread and butter for my grandmother unable to stomach camp rations, and the various Nazi guards in the Plaszow Camp exchanged my mother's stolen German military boots for food instead of shooting her. Consider the *choice* (her word, my emphasis) that my mother was given in the Plaszow Camp at eighteen to remain a slave laborer or become a well-fed camp prostitute, or her story of fellow Jewish women campmates in Markkleeberg who concocted her nineteenth-birthday cake resembling, she recalled, the layered Hungarian *sachertorte* with candles made from pooled margarine rations and stale bread, or the gift of bread in this story:

> We were marching in rows, past Mengele, each row five women, a small group of us sent back to Auschwitz from Plaszow, when he spotted my friend carrying bread in her overalls. We had no breasts we were so skinny. My mother and I were selected to live and she was sent to the crematoria. Half way there she turned around, pulled out the bread and threw it to me. She was shot right there on the tarmac. It was a punishment and a warning. This was not unusual. Then we were made to stand there two days naked waiting selection. Why did we leave Plaszow? Because the Russian Army was approaching; it was June 1944. We heard it was D-Day. After we passed the Mengele selection, we were deloused and had our heads shaved again. A Jewish *Kapo* came over and asked me if I am a daughter of a Hollander.

I looked so much like my father, especially shaven. He brought me a beautiful kerchief. As I get older, the kerchief gets bigger and nicer. I was the only one who marched in a kerchief. He looked at me while I was standing there naked. I had put my wooden clogs across my *pundi* [female genitals in Hungarian]. He said sarcastically, *sind sehr elegant*, you look really elegant. Then he told me about my dad and what a good student he was. Dad studied at the famous Pressburg Yeshiva in Bratislava. All my life there has been a helping hand coming out. Even though Mama was deteriorating, as long as she was with me, I was still a little girl. (Vera Slyomovics, interview with the author, Vancouver, Canada, August 19, 2010)

Then there is the Rudy story, new to me in 2010. Days of journeying without food or water, packed upright into wagons without toilets, the train arrival to Auschwitz, the wagon door sliding open to reveal an interior load of corpses, SS guards shouting, whips, screams, dogs barking, the stench of the crematoria—familiar descriptions in memoirs, films, and books depicting the initiation of inmates into Auschwitz. Yet my mother's version elaborates episodes similar to Rudy's gift that, since my childhood sustain her belief in God and the goodness of humankind. Here I call on Hannah Arendt who, relying on court documents from the Frankfurt Auschwitz Trials of 1963–65 that targeted lower level bureaucrats involved in the concentration camp administration, reminds us that

> It is true that there was "almost no SS man who could not claim to have saved someone's life" if he was in the right mood for it; and most of the survivors—about 1 percent of the selected labor force— owed their lives to these "saviors." Death was the supreme ruler in Auschwitz, but side by side with death it was accident—the most outrageous, arbitrary haphazardness, incorporated in the changing moods of death's servants—that determined the destinies of inmates.[10]

For psychologists and anthropologists, my mother's stories of heroes and miraculous donors merely confirm the unreliability of survivors recounting their experiences. My parents' transformation—or repression in the medical literature—of oppressive memories into positive tales has been classified as "happiness psychosis," the opposing pendulum swing of "anxiety psychosis," according to the complex nosological system of psychotic illnesses pioneered by an East German psychiatrist Karl Leonhard (1904–1988).[11] Assuming the existence of this psychosis, I maintain that its narrative expression is eloquence in small doses, terse stories, cryptic utterances, what I sensed as the dam appearing to crack but never actually breaking, merely the relentless drip of anecdotes recounted. My mother believes that the transmission of storytelling is our family's cultural and genetic legacy, tracing it from her father through to me:

> Many, many wonderful memories. First of all he would, the reason I have no fear, and I still don't have any fear, my dad, when I was a child, he went into the fear of darkness, and he explained to me the relationship between the sun and the moon, how the Jewish people view the moon, and he said, "When the sun goes down he shakes hands with the moon and he takes care of you." He had many stories, he would take hours of recounting, my dad was a folklorist, my daughter is now a folklorist I think because of that. So is my husband. Many stories. (Vera Slyomovics, interview by "Steven Spielberg Survivors of the Shoah Visual History Foundation," Netanya, Israel, December 11, 1997)

Similarly, Elie Wiesel, writer and Auschwitz survivor, and apparently a cousin of my paternal grandmother (who died in Auschwitz), characterizes survivor storytelling in this way: "Their sentences are terse, sharp, etched into stone. Every word contains a hundred, and the silence between the words strikes us hard as the words themselves. They wrote not with words but against them."[12] This narrative style also belongs to Henry Krystal, a psychiatrist and Polish Jewish survivor of many camps including Starachowice, Bobrek, Birkenau, Siemensstadt, and Sachsenhausen. He is among the most important clinical practitioners whose writings involve the treatment of Holocaust survivors. In 1947, he immigrated to Detroit, became a psychiatrist, and was interviewed in 1996 as part of the University of Michigan-Dearborn Voice/Vision Holocaust Survivor Oral History Archive. In the interview, Krystal, the psychiatrist, analyzes his own selective narrative techniques, akin to my family, as aspects of his "infantile faith" or the "capacity to regress" and "infantile narcissism":

Do you think that, that there was during the war and continued to be certain kinds of coping mechanisms to, distractions even, that some of the survivors used to get through this?

Well, yeah, I think that there are, depending on the circumstances there were certain talents that were especially helpful and the capacity to retain a kind of infantile faith that things will work out all right. The capacity sometimes to regress. I would sometimes be talking to my mother, especially in Auschwitz I remember.

You mean in your mind you would talk to your mother.

In my mind. But also the ability to receive help and to give help. To relate to others. Not to become insulated.

How do you, is that what you draw from the, the experience? Is that, if you look back on the Holocaust and say what, what, if any, meaning can I give to this, is that part of what comes to mind?

Well, I think that in trying to understand what made a person survive, I still think that it was mostly accidental, a number of accidents. And that many people did things that were potentially self-destructive, but they survived. But uh, I, I think that the ability to maintain a little nucleus of hope was probably the strongest asset. I would call it infantile narcissism, but really this is the way it manifests itself. Against all odds, to be able to, to continue, to struggle and to make a comeback.

Do, do you think this is at all related to talking about it, to telling, the story? You said that at one point you were, you thought if you died that no one would know and no one would have missed you. Some survivors have said that they thought that they would survive because they felt the need that they were going to be the witnesses or at least that's the . . . more folklore.

Well, I know that for many people this is a very important mission. However, I felt keenly already then that we were not just persecuted by the Germans, but I felt that we were abandoned by the whole world. And therefore, it seemed to me that to tell about this to the world was really not going achieve anything. And it turned out that I was right. That the British and the Americans knew what was going on and wouldn't even bomb the trains to Auschwitz, wouldn't even bomb Auschwitz. So, I think that among the most terrible things that happened to us was this feeling of abandonment. And that was why I was more pessimistic about the power of witnessing.

But I think that things have changed, times have changed and we may need the witnessing for ourselves and our people.[13]

My father's wartime tales are no less positive than my mother's. He recounts the years between 1938 and 1945 as a sequence of swashbuckling adventures rather than frantic and despairing dashes undertaken across the continent of Europe steps ahead of the advancing German forces—first in 1938 exiled from his Sudeten Czech hometown of Karlovy Vary to Antwerp; then in May 1940 fleeing Belgium to Paris to be interned outdoors in the vast Roland Garros tennis court stadium on May 10–20 as an enemy alien and a Jew; followed by the fall of Paris to the Germans and his three-week march on foot across France to the Mediterranean port cities of Sète and Gibraltar, there to be evacuated on a British troop ship to England. My father has always been stoic, upbeat, forward looking. As a child, I would hesitantly ask only him, the sole member of my family never to experience the Nazi camps, why my mother screamed every night. He would assure me that everything was okay and that he talks to my mother to make her feel better. What I remember most clearly is his concluding, repeated phrase: she has to "freeze the past." Traumatized children, which in a sense my father was in relation to the camp deaths of his parents and sisters, are said to exhibit a reaction pattern of "freezing." Trauma in infants apparently moves from hyperarousal to surrender and in adults to frozen states of nonverbalization and even disassociation.[14] According to my mother, my father followed his own advice:

In exile in Montreal, your father went so far to freeze the past that these aging Czech actors came to perform in 1948 for the large community of Czech immigrants. One I remembered fondly from my student years in Prague. His name was Jara Kohoutek. Bob Hope had a theme song, "Thanks for the Memories." This comedian had a theme song and I wanted to hear it. I was singing it to your father—"When the Rooster Loves His Hen." I went anyway. Your father refused to go because he said he wants to go ahead and not look back. Pop didn't want to see all the aging exiles reminiscing about the past. He wanted us to mix with Canadians. Anyway your Dad preferred the Czech comedians, Verich and Voskovec, who went to Hollywood and had some success. During the day, Kohoutek was a doorman, *nebukh* [helpless hopeless person in Yiddish] somewhere in front of a

Montreal hotel. I told Dad that he wouldn't come because the man wore an old frayed topcoat and tails. When I got home, he asked whether the coat was shiny. I remember I wouldn't admit it to him but it was so. The first money we had your father bought a black silk suit. Our neighbors, Jewish immigrants who came before the war, were always giving us advice that Dad never followed. They were annoyed when we got a refrigerator too. (Vera Slyomovics, interview with the author, Vancouver, Canada, August 19, 2010)

Only once did he ever acknowledge to me what he left behind: when he was ninety-six, I inquired about his seven-year exile from home and whether he knew what happened to his parents. It was on November 11, 2009, Veterans Day in Vancouver. At ninety-six, as he watched television newsreels of the 1944 Allied invasion of France, in which he had participated as a tank gunnery corporal in the Czechoslovakian Brigade, it wasn't the carnage of war that he mentioned to me. The film images reminded him that, during the landing, he was consumed with anxiety about his parents. He confessed that, at the time, he felt indifferent to bullets; he was in the army, yet all he could think about, once he set foot back on the European continent, was his father and mother, Hayim David and Bluma, unbeknownst to him already murdered in Theresienstadt/Terezín and gassed in Auschwitz respectively. Between sobs, "I knew and I didn't know" was his answer. Immediately, he changed the subject to speak about his Czechoslovakian Brigade comrades who were given the task of guarding the surrendering German soldiers in 1944. He said he still sees Czech soldiers wielding shovels to beat German prisoners of war despite hands held high in surrender: "What tortures me now is that I stood there and did nothing to stop the cruelty."

I have come to rely entirely on a chain of transmission made up of my female relatives who talk and circulate information; we knew not to question our men folk.[15] My father's sister Ida, who survived Auschwitz, recounted to my mother, who told me that my father first learned of his parents' deaths in May 1945. The Czechoslovakian Brigade accompanying General Patton's American Third Army had been halted at the Bohemian town of Plzen (Pilsen), awaiting their triumphal march into liberated Prague. On a weekend army pass, my father, still in uniform, finally traveled home and heard from his sister that their parents had been killed in Theresienstadt/Terezín and Auschwitz. He himself never mentioned it, so my mother's version is what we know:

In Pilsen, there was a holding camp. Lily and Elsa [my father's nieces] told me. Not just Jews but for returning Czechs waiting to go back. Your Dad borrowed a bullhorn and went there calling, "Anyone from the Rutner or Slyomovics family?" He said it in Czech because it was dangerous to speak German after the war. They were there, repatriated from the concentration camps—his sister Bertha, her daughters Elsa and Lily. He rented a house and brought them all to Karlov Vary [Carlsbad]. I met them and your father in the summer of 1946, after I finished a year of medical school. I wanted to know more about the Slyomovics family. Ida especially gave me lots of information. Ida was separated from your [paternal] grandmother [in Auschwitz]. She fought so hard to stay with her. She hit a *Kapo*, they didn't do anything to her. But she couldn't stay and save her mother. I learned from Ida that two sisters, Ethel and Margit, were wealthy and stayed on in Prague. The husband paid off a lot of people and they were called WW, *wirtschaftlich wichtig*, economically important Jews. They never went to Theresienstadt but were shipped off much later directly to Auschwitz. (Vera Slyomovics, interview with the author, Vancouver, August 19, 2010)

A story emerges but in "pieces and snatches," the evocative phrase uttered by psychiatrist Henry Krystal, recorded during his Holocaust survivor oral history interview. Like my father, he too replied when asked "Have, have you told your family any of this story?"

Not in a running narrative, but in pieces whenever I could or whenever. . . .
To, to your children?
Yes.
And you've told your wife?
Also, in, in pieces and snatches. . . .
Um, what, what do you make of this sort of new interest? It's almost chic now to do something with the Holocaust. Schindler's List, the Museum in Washington. How have you thought about those sort of unusual phenomena since 1980 or so?
Yes, I think that, especially some of the other programs are kind of geared to a happy ending. And the survivors are pleased by it in that they can say, "Well, not only did I survive, but I did well, I have

a family, I have grandchildren. I have won." And I think that this is a
kind of a balm to the heart of both the survivors and to their children. Because they can see it in, in their survivor relatives, that this
is uplifting for them to be able to go through this process and say,
"Here I am, I have won." Whereas many things that survivors needed
to experience they would not allow themselves to do so because they
felt that this would be granting Hitler a posthumous victory. You
know if they had a nervous breakdown or if they needed help. So I
think that there is this new trend that the ones that have survived to
now are in two groups. Either they are depressed and they are not
inclined to do that or they feel good about themselves and want to
talk about it. . . .

This sense of victory. Is that the truth?

Well, not entirely, but in relative human terms, yes. Holocaust
survivors have not only survived and had their families, but became
good people and became, give of themselves to good causes and do
everything possible of good things.[16]

In Bernhard Schlink's writings, he asks us to consider whether such
myopic but close-up detailed vignettes that blur distant events—the "pieces
and snatches" that are the prevailing narrative mode in my parent's reper-
toire to their children—are, in fact, misleading: "even if there might have
been a funny moment in Auschwitz, even if there might have been a decent
concentration camp guard, even if there might have been a fairytale element
in someone's rescue from persecution and horror."[17] He alludes to the flood
of fictional representations about the Holocaust, including his own bestselling novel *The Reader*, made into an award-winning film, and similarly
reductive representations of the Holocaust, fictional or not. However, Schlink
cannot know that, as a reader, I chose to disregard his primary theme of intergenerational German confrontations with their unmastered Nazi past.
Instead, my approach to *The Reader* zeroes in on details that specifically illuminate my family's experience in order to extrapolate meanings beyond
my parents' gnomic, cryptic utterances. His book rings true, even as I invert
both the novel and the film to assign the seemingly tangential, all-too-brief
appearance of a mother and daughter pair of Auschwitz survivors to the
lived experiences of my mother and grandmother. In the novel, they have
coauthored a Holocaust memoir, evidence of their Jewish slave labor camp

experience that provides testimony in postwar German courts to convict a Nazi woman prison guard, who was, like Rudy, an ethnic German from my parents region. Near the end of the book, Schlink's narrator will personally convey in his briefcase the woman prison guard's lifetime savings as compensation to the Jewish survivor-daughter now living in prosperity in Manhattan. At first, the daughter refuses the money. Her mother has died in Israel. The German narrator pleads: "Could you not recognize it without granting absolution?"[18] The Jewish survivor-daughter keeps the tin container that held the cash but pointedly suggests a suitable charity for the Nazi prison guard money because "Using it for something to do with the Holocaust would really seem like an absolution to me, and that is something I neither wish nor care to grant."[19] The daughter's recognition of the German perpetrator's reparation in this instance involves accepting the physical object holding the money but not the actual cash.

The Bureaucracy of Reparations

To counteract negative relationships between bestower and recipient resulting from dispensing reparative money, I draw on German philosopher Axel Honneth. His key concept is recognition, meaning the intersubjective recognition that makes possible our engagement with other human beings. Honneth believes that it is only when we recognize that humans *make claims on us* (emphasis added) that we can understand that recognizing another's pain is not enough; we must respond in some way.[20] Christian Pross, cofounder and head of a Berlin center for treating Jewish torture victims, articulates what, by the 1980s, became the broad-based public voice of postwar West Germany and its acceptance of paying reparations to proliferating categories of Germany's National Socialist victims—not only to Jews but also to Roma-Sinti (Gypsies), and forced and slave laborers of many nationalities and religions. If Richard von Weizsäcker's 1985 presidential speech envisioned Germany's May 1945 surrender as the day heralding the beginning of a new Germany, Pross extends that moment of liberation to encompass what he sees as a model of future redemption enacted through decades of Germans paying reparations. He concludes that reparations represent justice for victims, but even more so for the perpetrators forced to commit acts of collective atonement:

> Reparations were among the crucial building blocks for the recon-
> struction of democracy in Germany, establishing legal and moral
> standards that cannot be reversed today. The reparations program
> set the stage for a change in consciousness and for a transformation,
> beginning in the late 1970s, in the way German society dealt with
> the Nazi past. *And, last but not least, it documented the crimes, in
> recorded victims' statements and through numerous witnesses, for fu-
> ture generations.* (emphasis added)[21]

Pross's viewpoint took hold slowly, especially his hope for the redemptive
qualities inherent in the act of documenting reparations about the immen-
sity of Nazi atrocities, precisely because in his work in the 1980s already he
linked money and living victims to victim bodies and testimonies. According to his approach, there is a dynamic relationship between the internal
democratization of German society and the willingness to listen to the victim's voice. Other scholars have emphasized reparations as a way to legitimate
the new postwar German state. Thus, some form of publicly establishing the
truths of victims and survivor experiences based on international human
rights norms ushered in after Germany's defeat in World War II became
integral and necessary to post-World War II reparation processes. In addition, for historian Tobias Winstel, German reparations to Jews were the
"condition, cause or even excuse" for waves of Jewish remigration to Germany after World War II and the subsequent emergence of Germany's current vibrant Jewish communal life.[22]

From the German perspective, granting reparations required documentation that relied heavily on a variety of transnational and governmental,
quasi-governmental, and nongovernmental institutions. Procedures emerged
to hear, process, quantify, determine, and issue reports on reparations based
on testimony. Regardless of the specificity of the German-Jewish case, problems reside in the very nature of bureaucracy. Both pre- and postwar German
institutions shared the characteristics of rational, bureaucratically regulated
societies, according to Max Weber's typology of administration.[23] Therefore, an ordinary human being once placed in an official bureaucrat's office,
following the argument of anthropologist Michael Herzfeld, becomes capable of being transformed by the state into a "humorless automaton": "How
does it come about that repression at every level from that of the totalitarian
state to the petty tyrant behind a desk can call upon the same idiom of
representation, the same broad definition of the person, the same evocative

symbols, as those enshrined in the most indisputably democratic practice?"[24]

Creating a bureaucracy to dispense funds to victims unleashes unexpected outcomes, both positive and negative. Jews made harsh comparisons between a Nazi-German bureaucracy killing Jews and a postwar democratic West German state that disbursed reparations to them, arguing both lacked humanity and made arbitrary rulings. These complaints were echoed in the work of Paul Matussek (1919–2003), a German psychiatrist at the Munich Max-Planck Institute's Research Center for Psychopathology and Psychotherapy. He authored *Internment in Concentration Camps and Its Consequences*, a book first published in German in 1971. His work examined biases inherent in studying concentration camp survivors based on their reparation claims. Since encounters with Jewish survivors took place as a consequence of a compensation request, any such medical interviews were skewed both by the framework of indemnification and more so through attitudes of individual doctors towards psychological illnesses.[25]

It is possible to observe bureaucracies indirectly at work through the ethnography of my family's interactions over decades as they take on multiple, overlapping roles as claimants, witnesses, patients, and narrators. One reason my mother did not apply for German reparations immediately after the war was her fear of interrogations conducted by German doctors in the German language. Zahava Szász Stessel, a Hungarian Jewish survivor of the same Markkleeberg slave labor camp from which my mother and grandmother were liberated, applied for reparations:

> Survivors had to go through painful processes of meeting deadlines, filling out long application forms, and finding witnesses. The questions they had to answer in detail after so many years were very stressful. In some cases we were required to supply the very documents that the Germans and Hungarians had taken from us. Women from Markkleeberg offered to testify for one another, and many discovered their former campmates that way. If claiming health problems or medical conditions as a result of the holocaust, survivors had to bring documentation from their doctors. Then to validate it, we were required to go in front of physicians assigned by the German government! The evaluation and judgment of these German doctors decided the degree of disability and the merit of each claim. The aim of the compensation bureau, of course, was to lessen the extent of the

claimed damages to lower the payment. The office of reparation denied many claims, contending that the survivor's disease was not
connected with the camps but developed from natural causes. When
I was called for an examination and judgment of my request for
health benefits, the German physician involved was unfriendly and
intimidating. He spoke to me sternly in official German. I was petri-
fied and confused. The language and the tone brought back all my
dormant fear and reignited my nightmares. The doctor reminded me
of the SS. His probing questions, loud voice, and harsh expression
left me terrified, as I had been in the camps. My body responded
with stomach problems and weight loss that persisted for months
after that visit.[26]

Even if the claimant encountered a sympathetic postwar German bureaucrat, many inadvertently reproduced aspects of the concentration camp
experience for survivors. Nor could my mother bear any aspect of the process rumored to consist of claimants forced to stand naked yet again in front
of German medical officials during mandatory physical examinations, just
as they had once been selected not for the gas chambers but for slave labor
by anthropologist and medical doctor Josef Mengele, Auschwitz's "Angel of
Death":[27]

I remember Mengele. When we first stood in line, me and my mother,
with my cousin three months pregnant when she caught his eye. He
beckoned to her, put his hand on her stomach, "Oh, you're pregnant."
She was so happy getting pregnant that she admitted, yes. He assured her, "You don't have to work." She was removed to the left, to
the gas chambers. It was rare for anyone to pass Mengele twice because of our substantial weight loss between the occasions. Mom and
I did, the first selection at Auschwitz and the second selection returning from Plaszow to Auschwitz. (Vera Slyomovics, interview by
author, Vancouver, Canada, March 14, 2008)

And it reached a point where my mother and I looked at each other
and we said maybe we should—I should say I was fifteen, you know,
that mother was forty-two because we didn't want to work. We figured we were tired of working and this way we'll have a chance to be
with my grandmother and all my older aunties. And Mengele looked

at the two of us and he says, "You are lying." He says, "You are more than fifteen. You are at least twenty." And you know, I was tall. And he looked at my mother and he says, "You don't want to be with your sister?" You know, he thought she was my sister. She looked very, very young. So we both went on the right side. It was really a flick of a finger. Sent us to the showers. To the real showers and we believed that we both just got into the delousing. (Vera Slyomovics, interview with Robert Krell, Vancouver Holocaust Videotape Project, Vancouver, Canada, ca. 1978)

Bitterly, she commented that Jewish former concentration camp inmates were well trained in obedience to German carceral procedures, especially the frequent command to strip naked and stand outdoors for hours awaiting the routines of the roll call, the torment of the concentration camp *Appell* (roll call) with its meticulous counting off and constant inspections of nude Jewish women's bodies for delousing or diseases. In the event of visible signs of illness, my mother described how the woman was immediately removed from the roll call line and gassed. On August 23, 2002, while we vacationed in Prague, I asked my father why they had refused reparations early on:

It's not worth the money to go through the frustration of the paperwork. It hurts to relive it. Your mother had enough. Right after our wedding [in 1947], she would get up at night screaming, "Don't hit me, don't hit me." I'd wake her up, talk to her, bring her tea, tell her plans. Night after night she was wet, screaming and shaking. In 1960, I sent the three of you on a boat trip, a fancy cruise ship back to Europe. Instead of Peter [author's infant brother] having health problems on the boat we came over as refugees in 1948, I wanted to erase this trip so that she would forget that whole old trip. Instead of a little bed in steerage to sleep on with a sick baby on the way over to Canada, I sent you all back in the top luxury class.

Besides in 1945, there was a program to give restitution to Czechs by the new Czechoslovakian government. But Czech papers listed our mother tongue, which for most Prague Jews was German, and so they couldn't reclaim their property after the war as "Germans." Even a veteran of the Czech Brigade, my niece Etu's husband wasn't successful. He could have cleared it up but the bureaucracy saw "German" and that was the enemy. My Czech papers listed Yiddish as my mother tongue. A Czech Brigade officer asked me in Paris when I signed up: "What's your nationality and language?" "Nationality, Jewish; language, Yiddish." "That cannot exist because there is no such country as Jewish." I answered: "And Czechoslovakia does not exist either and you speak Czech." I did that because I remember my older brother Julius had served in the Austro-Hungarian army in World War I. He was in Italy, his papers didn't show that he was Jewish. After the war we had to hear how Jews were cowards and never went to the army. A third of the Czechoslovakian Brigade in England seemed to be Jewish. Julius survived the Nazi camps and left for Israel in 1948, and died there. That answer got me busted the next day from the Czech officer training corps school down to private. I never applied for my Czech Army pension when I lived in Prague in the 1990s. I could have applied for restitution or reparations for what I lost under the Communists. I owned a fur factory in Jablone Podjescedem and an office and showroom in Karlovy Vary on Stara Louka. Too much paperwork. In 1945 I was too busy. I didn't want to spend time. It's a full time job, lawyers, witnesses, courts. I decided not to lose time. I started off completely new. (Josef Slyomovics, interview by author, Prague, Czech Republic, August 23, 2002)

My mother believes that German bureaucratic mistrust of Jewish Holocaust survivors as beneficiaries of reparations endured for decades.[28] She points to the fact that regularly she is required to prove her existence, attesting that she is indeed alive to receive derisory payments ever since she finally signed on in the year 2000 by mailing in notarized documents to appropriate German bureaucrats. The reparation granting agencies, she feels, do not acknowledge her trustworthy behavior; for example, her return of my grandmother's monthly *Wiedergutmachung* checks that continued to arrive in the mail for ten more months following her death in 1999. On the surface, my mother's bitter critique appears unwarranted. Certainly, American government cash outlays in the form of unemployment checks or welfare disbursements call for similar antifraud identification safeguards.

Helen Epstein, author of a 1979 study on children of Holocaust survivors, evocatively describes her Czechoslovakian mother's reparation visit to a psychiatrist:

The Central Park psychiatrist who examined my mother, among over 1,000 other survivors, was known for his stern, almost martial conduct of interviews. In 1961, he concluded, publicly, that Holocaust survivors, as a group, had a lower rate of mental illness than New Yorkers. "We are confronted with the illogical conclusion," one of his colleagues observed drily," that people's mental health is improved by persecution."

Some examiners were so averse to obtaining details of their patients' experience that their reports glossed over the war and concentrated on early childhood. Others used the restitution interviews to discuss their own suffering under Nazism. . . . Some psychiatrists identified so much with their patients that they were unable to function as therapists. . . .

Few survivors requested treatment, for that implied that liberation had not put an end to Hitler, that Nazism had achieved a posthumous victory. Moreover, many survivors had developed a profound distrust of words, of the futility of trying to communicate their experience to anyone who had not participated in it.[29]

Bureaucracy's taxonomies and hierarchies produced and reproduced feelings of powerlessness and anxiety for the claimant. For a Jew to prove definitively to a German that she is demonstrably, unequivocally alive has been conflated by my mother with decades of interviewers, including German bureaucrats or even sympathetic Canadian psychiatrists, who could not believe what she was telling them. From the onset of the reparation program, the burden of proving disability due to Nazi persecution fell to the survivor. Judging early cases was the purview of German medical experts who were closely tied to the culture of the perpetrator and the medical biases of the era that comprehended trauma by way of scientifically measurable physiological symptoms.[30] Israeli psychiatrist and psychoanalyst Hillel Klein, a survivor of Polish ghettos and Nazi camps, maintains that the tortuous processes of medical examinations and paperwork hurdles, described as additional torture by claimants, sparked subsequent psychotic breakdowns when the first reparation check finally arrived. Both the application procedure and, more so, its successful completion, he noted, "retraumatized" survivors.[31] Survivors who had adapted relatively well to their new postwar lives were vulnerable to periodic setbacks, even psychotic reactions precipitated by specific external events. Klein enumerated three such occasions familiar to therapists by 1968: the 1961 Eichmann Trial, anniversaries of the death of family members, and being examined for or receiving any German reparation money.[32]

Psychiatrists and Survivors, Psychiatrists as Survivors

In the immediate postwar years, sympathetic observations and consistent descriptions of the mental states of survivors had begun to emerge. Indeed, many authors of significant research in the psychological and psychiatric literature of survivors were trained clinicians themselves recently released from concentration camp incarceration, labor camps, or long-term hiding. An extraordinary group of doctors, psychiatrists, and psychologists produced writings that engaged with personal Holocaust-era experiences, among them Dori Laub, Leo Eitinger, Bruno Bettelheim, J. Tas, Emanuel Tanay, Viktor Frankl, Vojtech Kral, Henry Krystal, Hillel Klein, Robert Krell, Peter Suedfeld, Paul Ornstein, and Anna Ornstein.[33] Yet psychiatrist Anna Ornstein, a year younger than my mother, waited until 2004 to publish memoirs of how she and her mother survived Auschwitz together:

> But memories can only be shared with those we expect to listen with respect and understanding. The image of the camps is so appalling that our listeners will suffer a small trauma once they permit the meaning of what they hear to penetrate. People rightfully, naturally and expectedly shut out from their awareness feelings that can, potentially, be disorganizing to them. . . . As we tell the story, resistance to hearing it will come up in many ways.[34]

Emanuel Tanay, a practicing psychiatrist and professor of psychiatry at Wayne State University, authored his first autobiographical article, "On Being a Survivor," in 1991.[35] A Polish Jewish survivor, Tanay recounts that, when he applied to the Michigan Psychoanalytic Institute, the senior interviewer rejected his candidacy: "Someone who survived the Nazi ordeal had to be shrewd and unscrupulous and therefore unsuitable to be a psychoanalyst."[36] Distrust of survivors was pervasive in the psychiatric professions after the war because they had survived at all, an attitude on the part of the interviewing psychoanalyst that gave new life to the idea that the only good

Jew is a dead Jew. To counter such attitudes, Tanay defines himself as a "successful victim," not someone rid of "survivor syndrome."[37] At the forefront of psychologists whose analyses evoked fury in my mother was Bruno Bettelheim, a German Jew imprisoned for eleven months in Dachau and Buchenwald from 1938 to 1939. Throughout the 1960s, my mother was routinely informed by well-meaning readers of his bestselling publication *The Informed Heart* that only the most bestial inmates survived, and that they did so by taking on the values of their Nazi aggressors, emerging from the camps without human connectivity or social supports[38]: "I hated that Bettelheim. Remember when your friend Mindy R. told you, you were little, that your mother had been in prison, was a criminal, had done something very bad? She got this from her parents (Vera Slyomovics, interview by author, Vancouver, Canada, August 19, 2010).

In 1968, a landmark volume appeared titled *Massive Psychic Trauma*, consisting of scholarly papers, proceedings, questions, comments, and discussions by the then-state-of-the-art community of legal and psychiatric practitioners on Holocaust survivors. It was edited by Henry Krystal, a Polish Jewish survivor and psychiatrist, with cocontributors, William G. Niederland, a German Jewish refugee, and Emanuel Tanay. Survivors in the United States had come to the attention of the psychiatric profession because of the confluence of two conditions: Holocaust survivors represented an extreme example of a population subjected to degradation, starvation, terrorization, and systematic destruction. Second, case histories of this group were becoming available in the 1950s and 1960s thanks to German reparation laws that mandated psychiatric examinations to qualify for additional indemnities. What they concluded was that, notwithstanding real hardships in proving psychiatric claims to the German Reparation Board, the numbers of survivors seeking psychotherapy after the initial required psychiatric diagnosis were minuscule, even though, by the 1960s, the Germans began to indemnify psychotherapeutic treatment. During sessions devoted to the principle conference topic, "The Late Sequelae of Massive Psychic Trauma," Tanay described frustrating encounters involving a complex triangulation of survivors, reparation funds, and psychiatry. Most often, survivor responses were to forego reparation for mental injury and claim only physical and material losses. Another prevailing technique he cited was "Let's Cheat the Germans":

> The difficulties in initiating psychotherapy are derived from the essential psychic structure of the traumatic state. It has already been

pointed out that direct requests for treatment are the exception rather than the rule among the survivors. The survivor has to be "seduced" into treatment by the therapist. Some years ago when I first became active in making evaluations in connection with the claims for compensation for damages sustained to health, I was approached from time to time by survivors who have already been given a compensation award by the German government, which usually included reimbursement for treatment. The proposal would run as follows: "They (the Germans) say that they will pay for my treatment. Since I don't need it, why let them get away without paying after all they have done to me and my family? You doctor give me a bill for the treatment and we will split the money." The self-deceptive nature of such requests are transparent, and I would attempt to point out that the individual was, in fact, in need of treatment and was attempting to cheat not the German government but himself. The session would end in an angry exit by the patient, who at times would accuse me of being "on their side." I felt a great sense of frustration since here were people in desperate need of treatment coming to my office and yet I was unable to reach them. This frustration was even more pronounced when I discovered that the great many survivors whom I saw for official evaluation, and whom I advised to seek treatment and referred to carefully selected colleagues, rarely if ever did remain in therapy.[39]

Patients proposing "Let's Cheat the Germans" seemed uninterested in whether money helps financially, pays for therapy, or even what could be purchased with the reparation funds. Such money counterstrategies served to set aside reciprocal professional interactions between therapist and patient because reparation turned both into potential recipients, thereby leveling all exchanges to a shared bond of victimhood. In his 1844 manuscripts, Karl Marx reflects on the power of money to both sunder and resuture new human connections: "If *money* is the bond binding me to *human* life, binding society to me, connecting me with nature and man, is not money the bond of all *bonds?* Can it not dissolve and bind all ties? Is it not, therefore, also the universal *agent of separation?* It is the coin that really *separates* as well as the real *binding agent.*"[40] Is cheating the Germans an expression of revenge in financial terms, a proof of gain, a bond; or can revenge even be bought? As an economic practice, reparation possesses the power to maintain and transform adversely German-Jewish encounters into purely an exchange value or a quest for money, "the bond of all bonds." In sum, a potent constellation of factors contributed to the astonishing fact that survivors reluctantly sought and received psychotherapy. Survivors' resistance to and fear of the discipline and practitioners of psychiatry found their match in German reparation board bureaucratic hurdles. Combined with survivor guilt, victim guilt, psychiatric practitioner guilt, it seemed as if a chain reaction ensued with lethal transference and countertransference intake and feedback, all of which led to a mass "psychic closing off" or inability to feel.[41] In one case presentation during the 1968 Wayne State University workshop, Tanay gave an exemplary account of a women patient, a survivor experiencing a manic episode in the middle of planning a trip to Israel:

> She would stick to a certain specific figure that she would spend on this venture. At one point she said that this is the amount that she "had to spend." When this was followed up, it turned out that *the amount she was about to spend was exactly the sum of money that she had received recently from the German government as restitution.* It was pointed out to her and she had become aware of her guilt from having received some money, an interpretation which ultimately stated that she had been paid for her child's death. Following this clarification, the patient "recovered" from her manic episode, and returned to her usual state of chronic depression. . . . [T]he above patient was unable to accept any money from the German government. This act became linked in her mind with her survivor guilt, which became unbearable when she recognized her feeling that not only had she allowed her relatives and child to die, but that now she was even receiving money from them from the "Restitution" authorities. Obtaining a pension brings identification with the aggressor nearer to consciousness, and with it the guilt over survival priorities. Survivor guilt, the result of universal ambivalence, often makes the acceptance of any compensation a traumatic event for the survivor. Some cannot bear it all because they feel that to become dependent for support on German authorities involves an additional humiliation to them.[42]

There were relatively few cases of survivors for Tanay to treat and present for discussions. Thirty years later during the 1987 University of Michigan-Dearborn oral history project of interviews, he expanded on the uncommon nature of his own multiple roles: he was a survivor, a psychoanalytic patient, and a psychoanalyst:

> So, I consider myself more fortunate than many of the other survivors, but clearly I and every other survivor, is first of all a victim, a living victim, but a victim nevertheless of terrible circumstances. And when you are a victim, you suffer some scars. I have also been in the fortunate situation of having had access to treatment after the war, which many survivors did not. Many survivors actively avoided it even if they had access to it. That's part of the condition of traumatic neurosis, or as it now called post traumatic stress disorder, is to avoid treatment, because treatment is a reminder of the painful experience, so you don't want to be exposed to it.
>
> Do you think that has something to do with why survivors have not been willing to talk more freely?
>
> Certainly, certainly, you know, I'm an example of it myself, you know, during the war, one of my [Pause] one of the forces that kept me was the idea that I will tell the world what happened. That, I, you know, I sort of had a mission, I have to survive because at least somebody has to tell the world what happened. I'm gonna write the book, I even had a name, a title for it. And you know, when I arrived in this country, in the United States in 19 . . . in January '52, I was actively involved right away in some preparation for writing a book about my experiences. And now, [laughs] thirty some years later, I still haven't done it. So, there is the resistance, you know, in doing it, there's a lot of ambivalence about it and fear and difficulty in talking about it. Survivors are reluctant to talk even to each other about these experiences. Because they are, you know, there are certain experiences if I try to tell you about it, I would break down crying. So I won't tell you about it. [laughs][43]

Narrating Holocaust experiences, according to the psychological literature, requires empathetic listeners, often absent in the first postwar decades. Tanay, the survivor and psychoanalyst, who was also analyzed, was exceptional. Albert B. Kerenyi, a practicing psychiatrist at Montreal's Jewish

General Hospital, and present at the 1968 Wayne State University symposium, contributed his experiences in treating my hometown's substantial
postwar Holocaust survivor-emigré population:

> I would like to mention a peculiarity of some concentration camp
> survivors, especially those with major disturbances of reality testing:
> namely their fear and distrust of authority and their ambivalence or
> negative feelings toward doctors. It happened on several occasions
> that such patients developed delusions of persecution against me,
> although I made the most consistent effort to help them while feeling
> and showing a great deal of empathy. Despite the fact that I inter-
> viewed them in Yiddish, whenever they detected a German accent
> on my part, they became suspicious and accused me of being a Nazi
> in disguise; one female patient actually struck me. This type of trans-
> ference became a very difficult resistance to handle.[44]

My mother mentioned only two occasions when she consulted a psychiatrist. In October 1948, mere weeks after my parents' arrival in Montreal
as refugees fleeing the Communist takeover of Czechoslovakia, my mother
was hospitalized. My parents had escaped Karlovy Vary in February 1948
and gone into hiding until the spring snows melted. They made the climb
across the mountains to the American-controlled sector of Austria where
my brother Peter was born in Salzburg in June 1948. My parent's lives re-
volved around an American-run Displaced Persons (DP) camp in Salzburg,
anticipating resettlement to the United States, Canada, or Australia. One of
my parent's favorite stories concerned the unexpected kindness of a doctor
in charge of medical approvals for the Canadian visa. My mother's narrative
of her visits to psychiatrists was embedded in the story of the supremely
generous gesture of a Ukrainian physician, who shared her stateless status.
Her urine sample revealed diabetes, thereby excluding admittance to Canada or anywhere else. The doctor sent my father back to obtain a second
sample, both knowing that my father would substitute his own healthy
specimen:

> After Petie was born [in Salzburg] and we finally came to Montreal,
> there was mild postnatal depression. I was underweight and my
> milk was bad, the color bluish and thin, not creamy. I was also hos-
> pitalized for high sugar counts for eight days. Dr. Mason, head of

diabetes, said he would cure me of diabetes and I never had it again. Your brother was a baby, four months old, underweight and ill from the three-week boat trip over. I was frantic worrying about his health. The doctors were very kind, but in 1948, they couldn't understand what I was talking about. How could Canadians understand Auschwitz? The physicians at the Royal Victoria Hospital recommended me to a psychiatrist. I can't remember his name but I went for one session, then a second session, and I told him about the beatings and torture. He broke down in tears. He started phoning the house all the time. Your father got mad and hung up the phone on him. After two visits, treatment was terminated because he committed suicide. It made me think that my stories could harm and I had been a medical student who wanted to save lives. In Vancouver in 2008—that's almost 60 years later—I went to a psychiatrist because of my dreams. My dreams were becoming worse. I spoke with her for about an hour; I went for no more than a few sessions. The psychiatrist had tears in her eyes. Psychiatrists should not cry. She had just lost her husband and she was telling me her story. I deal with it in a different way, by talking to students, having them touch me and hug me. (Vera Slyomovics, interview by author, Vancouver, Canada, May 22, 2008)

Psychoanalysis and therapy are impossible treatment options for many survivors, rarely undertaken and, it seems for my mother, of no help.[45] She reasoned: "Empathy you don't get from adults, you get from the young. It is such therapy for me to talk to students and see the reactions on their faces" (Vera Slyomovics, interview by author, Vancouver, Canada, August 19, 2010). Like other survivors, she reacted to psychiatry's interventions as a form of "counterfeit nurturing," a term coined by psychiatrist Robert Jay Lifton. Based on comparative work among Vietnam veterans and survivors of concentration camps and Hiroshima, Lifton proposed that these groups experienced a radical disruption of trust in the world that led many to react with suspicion and ambivalence toward the helping professions, especially psychologists, psychiatrists, psychoanalysts, and social workers. The powerful transference and countertransference issues with which patient and therapist must struggle are enduring challenges to treating Holocaust survivors. The following scenario of an enacted transference is summarized by H. Grauer, a psychiatrist at Montreal's Jewish General Hospital:

In the transference the patient relives the concentration camp experience. With the projection of the patient's superego on the analyst,
the therapist quickly assumes the role of the primitive brutal guard.
The alternative is to project the self. The analyst then becomes the
weak and ineffectual inmate exposed to attack. "You could never
understand what happened. I don't see how you can help me, nothing will undo what was done to me." The concentration camp experience seems to block the reliving and repetition of the childhood
neurosis. Pre-war experience and parental figures are idealized.[46]

In addition, most survivors were incapable of trusting the psychiatric
profession's reliance on categorizations of mental diseases according to a
system that my mother felt was inadequate to her experience and all too
reminiscent of the ways in which Nazi anthropology and medicine divided
humanity:

> Maybe the reason is that, in the camps, we were 500 jammed into
> small quarters. People would have nervous, mental breakdowns, people
> would begin to bark. They were taken out immediately and never
> seen again. People were afraid to exhibit any mental symptoms. Only
> the strong and the lucky survived. (Vera Slyomovics, interview by
> author, Vancouver, Canada, August 19, 2010)

Concentration Camp Survivor Syndrome
or *Konzentrationslager* Syndrome

Categories for classifying mental diseases in the first edition of the American
Psychiatric Association *Mental Disorders: Diagnostic and Statistical Manual*
published in 1952 (known as DSM-1) were profoundly shaped by wartime
psychiatry.[47] At the end of World War II in spring 1945, mere weeks after the
British Army entered the Bergen-Belsen Concentration Camp, a report on
conditions appeared in the British medical journal *The Lancet*.[48] The senior
British medical officer, William Robert Fitz-Gerald Collis, described the
physical state of his recently liberated patients: "emaciated apathetic scare-
crows . . . Riddled with typhus and tuberculosis. Gastrointestinal infections
are very common and are probably enteric and very simple gastroenteritis.
Erysipelas, scurvy and starvation disorders are prevalent."[49] Accompanying

Collis were about a hundred volunteer medical students, primarily young English males unprepared for encounters with what the Collis report termed a "Horror Camp." A young volunteer is quoted as characterizing interactions with survivors in accordance with his own "method of survival: to develop more of an interest in the diseases than the people." Given the urgency to rehabilitate their camp charges suffering from malnutrition and typhoid, the strategy of disease-before-people necessarily prevailed.[50] In passing, Collis alluded to pervasive "terror symptoms which are the most terrible aspect of the adult patients' mental state."[51]

In contrast to the fates of other nationals left to languish in camps, the Czechoslovakian government swiftly rescued my mother and grandmother. A state-sponsored bus was dispatched to repatriate Czech citizens interned in German camps, sending the two of them on a tour of the satellite camps of Buchenwald, then on to Leipzig and Berlin. Although my grandmother lived until 1999 and traveled extensively in Europe, her last trip through Germany occurred in May 1945 with my mother. The latter recalled how bizarre it was to travel amid still-burning, wartime German cities in utter ruin, followed by the joyous border-crossing home to Czechoslovakia, a country not physically destroyed by the war:

> In Germany, we saw from the minibus that there were no men. Everywhere there were women clearing rubble by hand, women badly wounded and maimed. I saw that the Germans had suffered too, what had been done to the population. I'll never forget that trip. It took four days. I entered Czechoslovakia in May 1945. As we crossed the border, crowds of Czechs greeted us. They had been without food themselves, yet brought us cakes and hot soups. We were twenty-eight in the minibus, sleeping four nights in the bus. I went to Prague and as fast as I could I resumed my studies with the help of the Czech government. I wanted very badly to be a medical doctor (Vera Slyomovics, interview by author, Vancouver, Canada, January 13, 2008)[52]

> The welcoming of the Czechs was unbelievable. I am a very strong Czech, I am first a Jew, then a Czech. They gave us their last pieces of bread, anything they had, fruits, vegetables, tears in their eyes, "You are our people and you made it." Unbelievable the welcome we received, unlike the other Jews who went to Poland and didn't receive

this kind of welcome. They showered us with everything and anything, and said, "You will never be hungry again." (Vera Slyomovics, interview by "Steven Spielberg Survivors of the Shoah Visual History Foundation," Netanya, Israel, December 11, 1997)

Before taking up medical studies, my mother returned to her hometown, Bishtine in the province of Subcarpathian Ruthenia, soon to be ceded from Czechoslovakia to the Soviet Ukraine, a double loss of a homeland in one decade. Inside the family home, she salvaged items to bring to Prague, her new residence, including a camel suit with a squirrel collar:

The town of Sighet [Romania] had better meat, smoked goose, and turkey, better products than on our side, the Czech side of the Tizsa River. On the day that the Nazis took over [March 19, 1944], it was my eighteenth birthday and I was with my father in Sighet. Sighet was close to Slotina, where we had gone to visit my uncle Eugene. It was just a bridge to cross over. Sighet was always part of Marmorosh. My father had made me a beautiful camel suit with a squirrel collar. When I returned home to Bishtine after the war and the camps, I found the suit. I wore it when I met your father. At that time, Mama wore a bright red dress made from the Nazi flag. Every time they asked her where she got it, she lifted it up and showed the swastika. (Vera Slyomovics, interview by author, Vancouver, Canada, October 20, 2009)

In the summer of her liberation, she traveled from Bishtine to Budapest to complete her Hungarian *matura* examination interrupted by the war. By fall 1945 she was accepted and enrolled in medical school at Charles University in Prague. In her first weeks, she was homeless, sleeping on benches in the Masaryk train station waiting room:

Fayge, the Markkleeberg Jewish *Lagerälteste* came back on the bus with us to Czechoslovakia. During the summer of 1945, shortly after we arrived to Prague, she was arrested. Someone turned her in as a collaborator with the Nazis. I was in Bishtine looking for my father and missed the trial. I left Mom at a sanatorium in the Tatra Mountains and in late summer went to Prague. My girlfriend, Iboyla Simsovics from Bishtine, came to take a train and found me sitting

on the bench. Iboy survived Auschwitz but her mother, sisters, husband, nieces and nephews, more than eighty people wiped out. She
asked me where I was living. "You're standing in my living room."
She said, "I asked you where are you living?" "You're in my home." She
was horrified and took me to her place. I gave her lice. She was so
wonderful to me. I was busy with my first-year medical studies. The
Nazis had suppressed the Czech-language part of the university.
Everything was in confusion and overcrowded in the fall of 1945.
There were five years of a student population kept out during the
war, so some of our medical lectures were held in Prague nightclubs.
For anatomy class, I had the handsomest cadaver, a young, blonde,
blue-eyed, over six-foot-tall Nazi officer shot at the war's end. During
medical school I fell into a deep sadness lasting two months. I still
went to classes, then crawled into bed and lay there. I described it to
others, in Czech *Ja sem tak smutna*, I am so sad, and in Yiddish to
my mother, *sehr trorig*, about my symptoms. Then my mother would
laugh with me. I didn't have the vocabulary for depression. There
were too many of them after the war living in this state of "sadness."
Then I was elected secretary of the entire Charles University student
body. I decided not to look at my past any more. My psychiatry professor kept telling us, "Stop looking behind you because that stops
you from looking ahead of you." Later I heard that Fayge got only
two years in prison; whether she even served at all, I'm not sure. Her
judge at the trial—a Czech, not a Jew—fell in love with her and married her. She was tall and voluptuous. (Vera Slyomovics, interview by
author, Vancouver, Canada, August 31, 2009)

My mother was lucky. Only five months after her camp liberation, she was
in Prague studying medicine (Figure 3). Historically, even though psychological aftereffects began to be documented from the end of World War II,
especially for Jews concentrated in Europe's numerous postwar Displaced
Persons (DP) camps, psychological assistance was inadequate. Paul Friedman, a practicing psychoanalyst appointed by a major aid organization, the
American Joint Distribution Committee, headed a research team to survey
the psychological state of Jewish adult and children survivors into DP camps
in Europe and Cyprus. Friedman was a Polish Jew educated in psychology
and psychiatry in a variety of European universities who had arrived to the
United States in 1938 as a refugee. As the medical community concentrated

on physical rehabilitation, Friedman acknowledged his own inability to listen to survivors' stories, sometimes due to his own state of disbelief but more often, as in the case of many Jewish mental health workers, because the listening professional experienced a sense of guilt:

> How then explain the indifference and even downright opposition on the part of many people to psychiatric aid for the survivors? It was not due—let me hasten to explain—to any lack of devotion or interest. It was rather that all of us—I do not by any means exclude myself—were filled with a sharp and pervasive feeling of guilt toward those very victims we were trying to help. As a defense against this omnipresent emotion, leaders in relief work tended to credit the optimistic stories about the survivors, while at the same time they discounted those describing psychological misery and disorder. We accepted the theory that the very fact of survival was evidence of physical and psychological superiority—without looking too closely at implications of this statement, which dishonored millions of martyred dead.[53]

Friedman's report on the DP camps called for a program of psychological support, not just economic and social measures. Presciently for psychology and psychiatry, he articulated the urgency to recognize survivor experiences as valuable determinants of treatment possibilities: "So the importance of rehabilitating the DP's is much more than that of salvaging one small group of human beings who have suffered. It is a project that has significance for the whole world; it is indeed a reassertion of our belief that civilizing forces in man may yet win to victory. We cannot expect this to happen quickly or easily."[54]

Friedman borrowed the term "affective anesthesia" from the 1946 study by Eugène Minkowski, a French psychiatrist of Polish Jewish origins, to describe a prevailing personality characteristic, one that was the common denominator of the deportee and survivor population, namely, "emotional numbness or shallowness."[55] Other studies published in 1949 and 1950 by French psychiatrist René Targowla documented "deportees' asthenia."[56] By 1954 in Denmark, researchers Knud Hermann and Paul Thygesen, the latter a Danish resistance fighter who survived Neuengamme Camp, were credited with the term "concentration camp syndrome," or *KZ-syndromet*, based on the abbreviation KZ (*katzet*) for concentration camp in German,

Figure 3. Vera Hollander, medical student ID photo, Charles University, Prague, September 1945, five months after her camp liberation. Author's collection.

Konzentrationslager. Their landmark works documented a "photographic similarity" of symptoms and disorders reproduced in the Danish non-Jewish concentration camp ex-prisoner populations, each patient exhibiting consistent and similar pathological reactions: memory problems, nervousness, fatigue, sleep disturbances, headaches, emotional instability, dysphoric moodiness, vertigo, loss of initiative, vegetative lability, and feelings of insufficiency.[57] Another term, "survivor syndrome," was coined in 1961 by William G. Niederland, a German Jewish refugee trained as a psychiatrist and analyst in prewar Germany then relocated in 1940 to the United States.[58] Niederland was influenced by his professional practice beginning in 1953 as a key medical consultant in New York City appointed by the German government to judge Holocaust survivors seeking German reparations. He produced detailed psychiatric reports to delineate the psychic condition of survivors of Nazi persecution.[59] Based on his evaluations, claimants deemed physically and psychologically damaged were awarded financial indemnity. Niederland's reports eventually helped overturn the commonly held views of German psychiatric consultants for indemnification, who focused on physical damage as proof of mental disease. Subsequently, the aims of an immense psychological, psychiatric, and medical literature were to understand consequences to concentration camp survivors, specifically in terms of immediate post-Holocaust effects but also later sequelae derived from prolonged physical deprivation and psychological trauma. At the same time, a Norwegian group headed by psychiatrist Leo Eitinger, a survivor of Auschwitz and Buchenwald, initially concluded that survivor syndrome was in origin "organogenic" (residing in specific organs). He thought that incarceration along with head injuries correlated most closely with both physical and mental symptoms leading to persistent suffering from chronic brain syndrome. Age, social background, and heredity mattered less. Eitinger's later works made him a leader in the field of psychiatric studies of trauma when he focused away from physiological side effects to concentrate on follow-up research relevant to clusters of late-onset psychological symptoms that haunt Holocaust survivors.[60] The move from physiological to psychological analyses and therapies for survivor syndrome took place unevenly, but it began to have an impact on both German indemnification and American psychiatry.

Adding to the difficulties in adequately treating and diagnosing former camp inmates is the fact that medical narratives about the Holocaust are embedded in time passing. My example is my great-aunt Rose Hollander, an Auschwitz survivor who settled in Manhattan after the war. Forced to make innumerable trips to Germany to prove her eligibility, she eventually received her award years after my grandmother successfully pursued her claim. In her case, fighting for reparations for herself and her brother seem to go hand in hand with long-term mental and emotional effects that surfaced at each legal reversal, perhaps leading to belated chronic disorders, especially when denied or repressed. According to my mother, the appeal had been mired in disputes with the German courts, only settled in the early 1960s. Aunt Rose disdained the negotiated reparations between superstructure organizations charged with evaluating and indemnifying Jewish Holocaust victims. She chose to pursue her lonely ordeal through an individual lawsuit against the German government:

> [Roszi] came back angry at the world. She wouldn't marry and looked down on every man who asked her. One man, a wholesale chicken dealer, she said, he smelled like chickens. He was a poor guy from home and she stayed with her pre-war high status. She was paranoid, people were stealing from her. She changed jobs constantly, saying everyone was using her. (Vera Slyomovics, interview by author, Vancouver, Canada, August 19, 2010)[61]

Similar reactions and symptoms, according to J. Tas, a Dutch Jewish psychiatrist and Bergen-Belsen Camp survivor, were ascribed in 1946 "to the fact that abreaction of tensions and aggressiveness was not possible in the camps, a fact which leads to an immense accumulation and encapsulation of emotions."[62] To account for the belated onset of symptoms, a stellar group of international researchers employed a variety of terms such as "symptomless intervals" or "delayed reactions" (*teguvot me'uharot* in the Hebrew language literature) and "late and delayed effects" (*sequelles tardives et retardées* in French). Given the options of assessing whether a patient was relatively symptomless or divining a case of belated reactions, German compensation boards inevitably denied claims during apparent symptom-free intervals. Unless doctors could document and link adequate *Brückensymptome* (literally "bridge symptoms" or consecutive connective symptoms), there was less likelihood of proving unbroken medical manifestations of disability from the time of persecution through currently existing symptoms during persecutees' various trajectories from camp liberation to local repatriation, then on to global paths of emigration and multiple sites of re-settlement.

Furthermore, medical testimony was required to prove that illnesses were *verfolgungsbedingt*, causally related to Nazi persecution. An example of such reasoning is the following claim at first denied (then appealed and eventually awarded by the late 1960s). The wording of the German Compensation Board's refusal makes clear that the reviewer perceived no evidentiary connections between a nineteen-year-old Polish Jew's current mental disabilities and his six years of experiences in numerous camps from 1939, beginning at fourteen until his 1945 liberation:

> The claimant was nineteen years of age when he was first exposed to the procedures of Nazi persecution. It cannot be assumed that their psychic working through in a person of that age can give rise to lasting anxiety symptoms or other psychological manifestations. It must therefore be denied that there are any disturbances in the claimant attributable to the emotional experiences connected with persecution.[63]

Indeed, a condition, first documented in the nineteenth century, was revived by German bureaucrats in the decades between the two world wars: "compensation neurosis" (CN) was defined as symptoms linked either to a real or presumed disability that brings about financial compensation. The German term, *Renten-Neurose* (pension neurosis), is attributed to Johannes Rigler based on his 1879 book *Über die Folgen der Verletzungen auf Eisenbahn* (On the impact of injuries on the railways, particularly spinal cord injuries). To deal with patients who complained of "railway spine injury," an ailment that included emotional reactions of shock and distress based on train accidents for which there were no obvious physical manifestations, Rigler posited pecuniary not psychological causes. Persisting symptoms were thought to derive from the railroad's practice of compensating injured workers: "A Compensation Neurosis is a state of mind, born out of fear, kept alive by avarice, stimulated by lawyers, and cured by a verdict."[64] In other words, when Prussia introduced liability protocols in 1871, compensation practices were responsible for bringing about, even deemed the actual cause of physical and mental complaints.[65] Rigler's position was countered successfully by Hermann Oppenheim, a German neurologist (1858–1919), who, in turn, acknowledged specifically for nervous illnesses such as "railway spine" an etiology that combined the physical and psychological factors of "traumatic neurosis," thereby granting claimants pensions or compensation through recently established social insurance schemes.[66] By 1926, traumatic neurosis was removed as a compensable illness, and Germany reverted in the 1920s and 1930s to a "reencoding of the discourse about nerves in a new language of biological and hereditary stigma," a discourse that matched the Nazi sciences of racial hygiene and blood destiny.[67]

The politics of German reparations for physical and medical sequelae in twentieth-century Germany are not separate from historically determined sociocultural forces such as doctor-patient interactions and the prevailing values of German psychiatry. The postwar German state bureaucracy for reparations enforced strict boundaries, classifying the mental world of Holocaust survivors according to notions about the German state's limits of responsibility. With the German bureaucracy in charge of policing definitions of mental health, especially in the early years, if it could be determined that a survivor was mentally unhealthy before deportation to a camp, any post-camp mental disorders were dismissed. Called to review such cases on appeal in the German court system, German psychiatric experts refused reparations by invoking the category of *durch Anlage bedingt*, "through a preexisting condition." Analogies were made with the ways physical damage was routinely calculated for insurance. Although cross-culturally, bureaucracies are characterized by indifference and fear of responsibility, it became embarrassingly inequitable and certainly unscientific to deny compensation to victims of Nazi camps for the same mental illnesses and disabilities derived from persecution that were recognized and compensated in the cases of Germany's own former prisoners of war. A number of German doctors in the postwar period began to challenge the pattern of denying compensation to survivors, some by pointing to the intersubjective processes between observing German physician and Jewish survivor. For example, they argued that medical diagnoses were supposed to comprehend somatic and psychic aspects of illness and include anthropology's approaches to the patient's biographical illness narrative. Exemplified by the publication of *Psychiatrie der Verfolgten* (Psychiatry of the Persecuted), by 1964 an important countermovement in German psychiatry attempted to comprehend psychological aftershocks for survivors and began to affect changes in the legal opinions related to classifying mental sequelae of the Nazi camps.[68]

In the United States, "concentration camp syndrome" was a recognized category in the 1952 DSM-I, as well as the 1968 DSM-II, including its final 1974 printing, all published under the auspices of the American Psychiatric Association. By 1980, the publication of an expanded DSM-III heralded the new category of post-traumatic stress disorder (PTSD), into which CCS, or "concentration camp syndrome," was subsumed. Yet such a radical change appeared fleetingly in print, with the absence of CCS only manifest through the bibliographical cross-referencing of the DSM-III Index: "Concentration camp syndrome. *See* Post-traumatic stress disorder."[69] Nosological connections between CCS and PTSD were built on foundations by psychiatrists who had contributed their expertise to studying both these conditions. Among them was the Polish-born, Montreal-educated psychiatrist Chaim Shatan, credited with bringing together a core group that included Robert Lifton, William G. Niederland, and Henry Krystal. Symptoms, categories, diagnosis, and compensation had already been operationalized in the research of both Niederland and Krystal (discussed earlier in this chapter), since both were designated experts by the German government to determine Holocaust compensation payments for psychological damage among the survivor community in their respective adopted American cities of New York City and Detroit. Lifton was included in the conference and the 1968 volume *Massive Psychic Trauma* edited by Krystal, contributing his research on Hiroshima bomb survivors around the time he published his highly regarded book *Death in Life*. Lifton's remarkable series of books have continued to compare three seemingly disparate groups, separated by history, geography, and originating atrocity event—Vietnam War veterans opposing the war, Holocaust survivors, and victims of the Hiroshima and Nagasaki bombings— all of whom he deemed a "special contemporary group of 'prophetic survivors' whose 'inspiration' derives not from the Divinity, but from the holocausts they survived . . . who have managed to emerge from their holocaust with similarly regenerative insight."[70] Like Lifton, Shatan was open to the possibility of comparison based on the aftereffects from different wars on Vietnam veterans and Holocaust survivors. Niederland, encouraged by Shatan, delivered a conference paper on "The Guilt and Grief of Vietnam Veterans and Concentration Camp Survivors."[71] By 1970, Shatan and Lifton had formed a network of clinicians involved in group therapy with Vietnam veterans.[72] According to many accounts of the history of PTSD, its origins are interwoven with Vietnam War veterans and their postwar interactions with the medical doctors of the Veterans Administration, along with the working group of psychiatrists for the proposed DSM-III studying what Shatan then termed "post-Vietnam syndrome."[73] Diagnoses of stress and war neurosis had appeared in DSM-I but were not present in DSM-II. Standing in the shadows of the creation of PTSD, which was based on Vietnam veterans' experiences, were decades of studies on "concentration camp survivor syndrome." This is significant because the law—in this case, German compensation law—and money as compensation or for treatment powered much of the evolving underlying logic for classificatory systems concerned with reparation payments to Holocaust survivors. Nosologies, which led to formal diagnoses, in turn were sustained by medical documentation procedures that could also be applied to secure insurance for combat veterans and other worthy victims. In the 1970s, failure of psychiatric diagnoses to prevail in the courtroom or the psychiatric profession to achieve consensus based on psychiatrists' testimony were likened to "flipping a coin," as experts in the legal system disputed each other's findings.[74] What the DSM-III achieved in effacing "concentration camp syndrome" on behalf of PTSD was to infuse the latter with the former's distinctive approach to deemphasize causation in favor of maximizing psychiatric agreement and labeling through developed lists of characteristic symptoms. The large number of Holocaust survivors demanding reparations, swelled by increasing waves of soldiers in distress, called for predictable and consistent, not necessarily valid, diagnoses. Causation was less important, financial disbursements trumped etiology, symptoms and behavior were the building blocks for diagnosis, and the ensuing comparisons across time and place (Holocaust, Hiroshima, Vietnam, and more added) diminished the originating atrocity event. Finally, PTSD acknowledged one of its key events, rooted in "concentration camp syndrome," through the work of Judith Herman, whose feminist-inflected critique enlarges diagnostic models from combat and natural disasters to those who have suffered "the history of subjection to totalitarian control over a prolonged period."[75]

Given my mother's refusal to apply for German *Wiedergutmachung* as an Auschwitz survivor until the year 2000, when she accepted her recategorization as a Markkleeberg slave laborer eligible for work compensation, it makes sense that the two influential thinkers she admires are from the ranks of antipsychiatry thinkers: Thomas Szasz and Ernest Becker. Turning away from psychiatry's categories by deploying philosophical and anthropological perspectives, they attempted to reintroduce the larger social context and relate it to personal experiences. Szasz radically rejected mental illness other than as a "myth" or a "metaphor"; it was never a fact.[76] His argument that mental illnesses were defined through medical professional consensus about clusters of symptoms serves as a critique of the legal-medical classificatory systems, whether these were produced by the German compensation board's effort to determine mental disability or due to psychiatry's ever-evolving diagnostic manuals with shifting categories about mental illness:

> In ordinary life, the struggle is not for guns but for words; whoever first defines the situation is the victor; his adversary, the victim. For example, in the family, husband and wife, mother and child do not get along; who defines whom as troublesome or mentally sick? . . . [the one] who first seizes the word imposes reality on the other; [the one] who defines thus dominates and lives; and [the one] who is defined is subjugated and may be killed.[77]

Ernest Becker was first a student, then a colleague of Szasz in Syracuse, and thereby was granted access to Szasz's psychiatric patients. My mother became closely acquainted with Becker, an American cultural anthropologist and student of psychotherapy, when he moved from San Francisco to Simon Fraser University near Vancouver in 1969, the year my parents left Montreal for Vancouver. Although her medical studies were cut short when they fled Czechoslovakia, she attended Becker's psychology classes until 1974, the year he died of colon cancer at the age of forty-nine. Some of my mother's fondest memories of Becker, tied to her visits to Vancouver General Hospital as he lay dying, became associatively linked to the camps:

> I used to visit Becker often in the hospital his last year. He couldn't eat any more. I got the idea of bringing him a cookbook. I read him the recipes, especially the ones I used to make him, cheese blintzes, potato latkes. They reminded him of his mother and father. I got the idea from the camps. We were starving and with us in Markkleeberg was a woman, Bella, who had the most famous *konditorei* [pastry shop] in Budapest. She created my birthday cake. After the barrack doors were locked in on us, we fantasized about life after the camp. As weak as my mother was, weighing only 80 pounds, she promised to buy me the nicest white bathing suit, she said, to best bring out the

contrast with my beautiful dark hair. Bella described her café spe-
cialty, chestnut purée topped with whipped cream. She described a
pastry, *cremes*, layers of thin flaky *fillo* filled with yellow custard. She
"made" a strudel too, emphasizing that the key was to put under-
neath the dough a warm plate. I had forgotten what a plate looked
like. She said, you have to pull and play with the dough, and she
made the hand gestures, scattered nuts everywhere, and then the
apples. It had to be a special apple. Yonatan apple. She was thirty-
four years old and in the camp, we called her the old lady. (Vera Slyomovics, interview by author, Vancouver, Canada, August 19, 2010)

There was one lady who sort of stayed on the heavy side, so it was so
nice to be hugged by her because it was very cold at night and very hot
in the daytime so we took turns, she would hug us, her body was
warm and was very lovely, we took turns everybody 10–15 minutes,
she was still a bit on the chubby side and we were skinny. The hugging
part, and we talked to each other and told stores, and tried to ease the
hardship going to Markkleeberg. In Hungary, one of the things that
was very nice in the camps, and that persisted, we had, we called them
the old ladies, which were over 32. Some were wonderful bakers,
some of them were famous places in Budapest, and we would cook,
imagine we were cooking cakes and other things, and one gets pretty
good at imaginary cooking, but this I remember. (Vera Slyomovics,
interview by "Steven Spielberg Survivors of the Shoah Visual History
Foundation," Netanya, Israel, December 11, 1997)[78]

In Canada, Becker revised *The Birth and Death of Meaning*, completed
The Denial of Death (awarded the 1974 Pulitzer Prize), and his posthu-
mously published *Escape from Evil*. Like his mentor Szasz, Becker opposed
questionable medicalization and pathologizing of certain life experiences as
mental diseases:

Psychiatry, in sum, is at present little more than a pseudo-scientific
discipline which directively manipulates individuals in the interests
of the social status quo and the personal aggrandizement of the psychiatrists. The definitions of "normal" and "abnormal" that are used
with such facility to pass judgment on largely defenseless patients are
bogus. That is, these definitions have no scientific grounding, and

cannot have. They derive from culturally normative prescriptions for proper behavior. Psychiatry, therefore, has no valid claim to the guise of a science. . . . Its aim has been to fit people back into a social system whose basic values were not questioned.[79]

While my mother does not believe, as Szasz does, that mental illness is a myth, she agrees with Becker that psychotherapy is a waste of time and money in the face of her experiences of Nazi persecution. The treatment itself was the problem for her, especially the ways in which it flattened and domesticated her distress within typical clinical narratives and diagnostic criteria. Empathetic-like interventions by psychiatrists in relation to many survivors were unrecognized, remained unwelcome, and were tinged with deep-seated, implacable ambivalence and resistance. As anthropologist Jason Throop indicates, empathy into the subjective life of another person is not cross-culturally interpreted as a positive and valued social practice. Indeed, even locating empathy primarily within the limits of dialogue and narrative, so characteristic of psychotherapy, is a gross misperception of what is needed for understanding.[80] Instead, Henrik Hoffmeyer, a Danish psychiatrist involved with the circle of researchers in Denmark who contributed in the 1950s to the use of "concentration camp syndrome" for psychiatric vocabulary, proposed "therapeutic optimism": "*L'optimisme thérapeutique* [therapeutic optimism] is the golden rule with all medical acts. Even with the case of camp syndrome, chronic and lesional, there might be a chance of success in the sense of relief from suffering. It's necessary to let therapeutic optimism act on the larger scale in which all parties are outlined, schematized."[81]

As for my mother, resolutely not in therapy, she finds comfort in the internalized routines of prayer, regular attendance at Vancouver's Orthodox Jewish synagogue, charity giving, speaking to high school students about her camp experiences, and volunteer social work, as well as physical touch, symbolic gestures, cooking, and gently voiced, familiar comforting phrases uttered in the presence of her close family and friends.

CHAPTER 3

The Will to Record and the Claim
to Suffering: Reparations, Archives,
and the International Tracing Service

This is the space of the . . . archives, where truth claims
compete, impervious or fragile, crushed by the weight of
convention or resilient in the immediate threat of the
everyday; where trust is put to the test and credibility
wavers.
—Ann Laura Stoler, *Against the Archival Grain*, 24

Quod non est in actis non est in mundo
[What is not in the records is not in the world]
—Latin proverb

An archive may be an actual space—a physical depository designated to store the artifacts and documents that record history. Many such archives are housed in architecturally purposeful edifices, as if the materiality of the concrete building underwrites not merely the acts of preserving records but also the claim to constitute data as definitive sources to past events. Archivists are increasingly cognizant of power relations that govern what, when, and how evidential and historical information are present in the archive, to the extent that archive keepers speak of repositories shaped by and producing collective memory and identity formation.[1] Between a tangible document lodged in a government archive and the living person, the construction of identity is so vital and seemingly unbreakable that history regularly provides cases of riots or resistance activities deliberately targeting archival holdings or examples of natural causes destroying identity papers to the relief of multitudes. During the 1871 Paris Commune uprising, fires were set deliberately to burn registers of civil status in the Paris region. Demonstrators targeted for destruction the official buildings of the Palais de Justice and the Hôtel de Ville where birth, marriage, and death certificates are housed. For a time, Parisians were at liberty to fabricate false documents and create new identities. The 1906 San Francisco earthquake and fire destroyed the city Hall of Records, enabling many Chinese immigrants to forge new identities based on now nonexistent paperwork or even take on identities of already legal immigrants whose paperwork was lost. Relatives once barred from entering America due to Chinese quotas were called "paper sons." In the Netherlands under Nazi occupation on March 27, 1943, resistance groups attacked "documentary nerve centers" to stop German conscription of forced laborers by destroying the population registers and records of the Dutch Bureau of Vital Statistics in Amsterdam.[2] Palestinians destroyed their documents in 1967 when Israel first occupied the Gaza Strip, "fearful what might be done with the information contained."[3]

Invasions, displacement, and the plight of refugees are so much a characteristic feature of contemporary history that provisions have been put into place to create substitutes for lost, destroyed, or missing paperwork. My parents fled Czechoslovakia in 1948, arriving in Canada with only my father's British military passbook that demonstrated he had served in the Czechoslovakian Brigade from 1940–1945 and two years of my mother's Charles University transcripts and student ID photos from 1945–1947. My mother recalls:

> We arrived to Canada [in 1948] with minimal documentation. Nothing more, no marriage or birth certificates. We had married in the Altneue Synagogue in 1947 but had to marry again in the Prague city hall, and we could never get a marriage certificate. I used to joke to Dad that he could leave me whenever he wanted since I had no marriage certificate. When we were escaping from Czechoslovakia, we were so afraid that I concealed the papers on top of my pregnant stomach just where the baby was. On the basis of sworn testimony about who we were, we were granted Canadian citizenship. (Vera Slyomovics, interview with the author, Vancouver, Canada, August 20, 2010)

In my family's account about their civil and marital status, oral testimony sworn before a Canadian judge on behalf of my parents was transformed into certificates whose physical existence, fortunately for the bereft identity seeker, elides its own shaky oral provenance. Archives subtly acknowledge orality, while they efface it to render testimony, court transcripts and speech into acceptable written form such as that which created the paper trail for my undocumented, refugee parents. Moreover, the successive cataclysms of fascism and communism in Europe that brought my parents to North America meant that prewar papers and photographs were precious and few and in need of oral history.

While an archive may consist of physical books and files, rarely are its workings, organization, and multiple potential points of entry to holdings transparent to the researcher. According to philosopher Jacques Derrida, the archive reveals its own acts of archiving as a system of intertextual organization in which texts refer to other texts, thereby becoming "the place of the originary and structural breakdown of . . . memory." Although his book *Archive Fever* promotes the concept of the "archive" as an immaterial transgenerational memory and history of culture, Derrida sets out questions pertinent to Holocaust studies pursued through the data recorded and preserved in a variety of German archives. In relation to the history of psychoanalysis, he asks, "In what way has the whole of this field been determined by the state of the technology of communication and of archivization?" While meditating on the role of the archive in the work of psychoanalytic ideas about memory and mourning, Derrida coins the term "archivization" for entwined processes of forgetting and remembering engendered by the never simple act of recording data. In particular, his term could apply to Nazi-era documents hidden or absent since World War II that might commemorate millions of the civilian war dead:

> the archiving, printing, writing, prosthesis, or hypomnesic technique in general is not only the place for stocking and for conserving an archivable content of the past which would exist in any case, such as, without the archive, one still believes it was or will have been. No, the technical structure of the archiving archive also determines the structure of the archivable content even in its very coming into existence and in its relationship to the future. The archivization produces as much as it records the event.[4]

Derrida's term "archivization" is relevant to the acts of Nazis preserving records of murdered Jews no less than the production of painful accounts that emerge from Nazi records. What one finds in an archive is potentially dangerous and traumatic beyond the contentious issue of archives that withhold information through difficulty of access. Moreover, in the waning decades of the twentieth century, as actual physical archives disgorge information, Derrida sees that their contents render readers and users ill and anxious:

> The *trouble de l'archive* stems from *mal d'archive* [archive fever]. We are *en mal d'archive*: in need of archives. . . . It is to burn with a passion. It is never to rest, interminably, from searching for the archive right where it slips away. It is to run after the archive, even if there's too much of it, right where something in it archives itself. It is to have a compulsive, repetitive, nostalgic desire for the archive, an irrepressible desire to return to the origin, a homesickness, a nostalgia for the return to the most archaic place of absolute commencement.[5]

Holocaust researchers and survivor families seeking information about the Nazi era in a variety of archives strive to become not the *hypo*mnesiac bearers of weak memory, but rather Derrida's opposite, the *hyper*mnesiac drowning in painful memories of the past. Much of my family reparations histories depend on Nazi and German-held documents that engender a return to the "compulsive, repetitive, nostalgic desire for the archive." Not only does the archive hold out the possibility for knowledge about the demise of my extended family under the Nazis, but there is another benefit linked to the archives: the proof it offers the demand for reparations to compensate for murder.

Despite omissions and Nazi euphemisms in need of decoding, documents were long assumed to be more objective and trustworthy sources for historians of the Holocaust than subjective memories and testimonies of aging and frail survivors. Indeed, the sheer volume of paper, philosopher Hannah Arendt believed, obviated the need for personal memory and testimony:

> the secrets of the Nazi regime were not so well kept by the Nazis themselves. They behaved according to a basic tenet of our time, which may be remembered as the Age of the Paper. Today no man in an official position can take the slightest action without immediately starting

a stream of files, memos, reports, and publicity releases. The Nazis left behind them mountains of records that make it unnecessary to confide the slaking of our thirst for knowledge to the memories of people who were in the main untrustworthy to begin with. Nor could it have been otherwise. Hitler's great ambition was to found a millennial empire and his great fear, in case of defeat, was lest he and his fellows go unremembered in centuries to come. Red tape was not simply a necessity forced on the Nazis by the organizational methods of our time; it was also something they enthusiastically welcomed and multiplied, and so they left to history, and *for* history, type-written records of each and every one of their crimes in at least ten copies.[6]

The International Tracing Service and the International Committee of the Red Cross

A preeminent archive that preserves a partial record of Nazi crimes is the International Tracing Service (ITS) in Bad Arolsen, Germany. Its value is based on a treasure trove of personal names. A Central Name Index (CNI) of more than fifty million reference cards, catalogued according to sur-name, first name, and date of birth, serves to identify 17.5 million people's records in the form of 26,000 meters of physically aging lists of persecutees, deportees, internees, prisoners, concentration camp inmates, and displaced persons from World War II.[7] Initially the ITS was administered through the International Committee of the Red Cross (ICRC) for purposes of tracing missing persons after World War II. It may be that this small archive formed during the war will represent one of the foremost, enduring early projects of humanitarian documentation and intervention. This is despite the Red Cross's sullied reputation, according to my family, earned on their visits to various concentration camps. For example, on June 23, 1944, the Danish Red Cross arrived at Theresienstadt/Terezín, sixty miles from Prague. As part of the *Verschönerung*, or "beautification," of the camp and ghetto in preparation for the Red Cross visit, seven transports with more than 17,000 Jews were sent to Auschwitz, including a last one in May 1944 that carried my paternal grandmother and aunts to the gas chambers (cf. Prologue). In September 1944, three months after the Theresienstadt/Terezín visit, the Red Cross famously inspected Auschwitz shower rooms, failing to see their function as gas chambers.[8] My mother and grandmother's sole encounter with Red Cross inspectors took place after they arrived as slave laborers to Markkleeberg Camp outside Leipzig:

In Auschwitz, I never saw the Red Cross. In Markkleeberg, they came in February 1945. They told me that me and Fayge are in the best shape in the whole place. The Red Cross representative, I think they were Swiss, asked me why and how come I didn't look emaciated, and was I getting special food? Fayge refused to be interviewed because as the *Lagerälteste* she had access to special food. The Nazis always treated these *Lagerälteste* very well. I told them it was a matter of discipline. We received soup, like cows I'm sorry to say, in a trough, and the soup stank. It had rotten cabbage and lots of barley which was more nutritious than the one slice of bread and bit of margarine per day, which I gave my mother. They kept it there for a few hours. You could have as much as you wanted because nobody could eat or digest it. Every half hour I took another bowl, held my nose and drank it. So I suggested this method to my grandson forty years later when he had bitter medicines to swallow. Discipline, I told him, make yourself drink it, since that's how I overcame hunger. The nasty soup filled you up. (Vera Slyomovics, interview by author, Vancouver, Canada, December 15, 2010)

The postwar ITS archive is said to have originated as a depository of files confiscated from concentration camps by Allied forces, who then stored them in a former SS school and barracks in the town of Arolsen, Germany, a town later renamed Bad Arolsen (Arolsen baths), for touristic reasons. Arolsen was chosen because it suffered no war damage, and the excellent telephone and telegraph lines from the SS complex were intact. The town was strategically situated in the American sector of a divided, postwar Germany near the geographical juncture of the French-, British-, and Russian-controlled zones. An *Auskommando*, or external satellite slave and forced labor camp of Buchenwald nicknamed "Arthur," had been located inside Arolsen's SS training school, and that very building became the first site of the ITS.[9] Of the twenty-two wartime Nazi concentration camps and more than one thousand *Auskommandos*, the ITS possesses complete documentation only for Buchenwald and Dachau, with other camps partially represented or not at all. Certainly, no professional archivist at the ITS would claim that the current organization and classification system of the ITS emerged in any obvious or organic fashion from the vast amount of materials and files collected by the Allied forces, which largely consisted of lists—concentration camp inmate transport lists, individual prisoner cards and death certificates, inventories and registrations of the deceased, infirmary lists, and so on. Instead, the ITS archive uses a categorization system of the Name Index developed in the London offices of the British Red Cross in 1943, where it was created exclusively for victim names of Nationalist Socialist persecution.[10] The ITS task was defined in general terms as "the will to meticulously record, if possible, all stages of the persecution" and, in particular, "to provide for humanitarian purposes to the individuals directly concerned any and all personal information extracted from its archives and documents."[11] For Jacques Derrida, the Holocaust (he prefers the Hebrew *Shoah*) was an attempt to erase the proper name of the Jew, "as if the names were really the very thing that the extermination was aimed at."[12] The individual first and family name of each victim, enshrined in the Central Name Index, was transformed into a comprehensive "card-indexed person," a type of Derridian "proper name of the Jew," who endures as the heart and soul of the ITS archive:

> The origin of this Index is the registration of the Displaced Persons, after their liberation in the DP camps, on so-called DP-3 cards. All subsequent registrations of the names in the actual documents or from the correspondence (card-indexing of inquiries) of more than half a century are united in one place here. The Central Index of Names thus consists of a certain part of original registration records as well as of reference cards written by the ITS itself, which have the same paper format.[13]

"The protection of the records of occupied territory had to be acknowledged by the conqueror as a kind of moral obligation," wrote Ernst Posner, a distinguished German Jewish archivist interned in Sachsenhausen Concentration Camp before arriving as a refugee to the United States in 1939.[14] Posner had a stellar career at the Prussian State Archives before securing a professional position as an archivist and historian at the National Archives in Washington, D.C. His arguments about the importance of archives is said to have greatly influenced both President Roosevelt and General Eisenhower to implement the protection of records and cultural objects as European sectors came under American Army jurisdiction or administration.[15] According to ITS personnel, Americans were seriously engaged with archive maintenance; to this day, ITS personnel gratefully cite the Americans for exemplifying excellent postwar archival practices, along with their use of high-quality paper materials. Since 1998 the files have been digitized, although variant spelling of surnames—the key to the files—proliferate. For example, the ITS archive webpage cautions that there are 849 variations of the name Abrahamovitsch,[16] while our family surnames of Slyomovics and Hollander appear with several distinctly different orthographies and accent marks. The ITS point of departure, as with my own research, began with the names of the survivors, those who lived past the era of National Socialism and whose whereabouts are deemed traceable.

For archives created by dictatorships since transformed into human rights archives, and the ITS is among the original models, the individual's name still stands at the heart of any process to unravel the fate of thousands of those forcibly disappeared, illegally incarcerated, and tortured as documented by a bureaucracy. The name is the constitutive tracing element, according to Trudy Huskamp Peterson, the archivist who has worked with truth commissions. Archival standards must ensure that the original organization and nomenclature of all documents created and filed by the perpetrators are retained, as is illustrated here in the case of Guatemala:

If you are trying to figure out what happened to a disappeared person, you start with his name and locate his *ficha* [identity record] and one of the numbers on the back of it will refer to a *libro* [oversized ledger that indicates when charges—or *denuncias*—were filed against suspects] and the *libro* will give you the file number of the *denuncias*, so you go to them and examine the nature of the charges, and so forth. That's why we want to keep the document types together; with all the *fichas* in one group and the *denuncias* in another, and the radiograms and reports and correspondences in their own sets—all within the Detective corps. That's how the police filed the documents themselves.[17]

At the ITS archives in Bad Arolsen, the names of the known dead are mingled with the living. Files about murdered victims are joined to the names of their survivors and those seeking information about victims and survivors. This is because the ITS also maintains correspondence files, called the

T/D or Tracing and Documents, created when an individual or institution mails in a written request for information. Filled with letters from a variety of applicants, the T/D files contribute to the growth of ITS holdings decade by decade. These archived inquiries at the same time provide updated information (current whereabouts, date of death) about individuals already found in the CNI. Even as reparation claims rise, spike, or crest depending on the most recent German reparation laws, inquiries from new generations in search of family members and their itineraries during the Nazi period are increasing. There have been approximately 2.3 million T/D case files since 1946, and recent success rates for positive ITS replies hover at 50 percent. In November 2007, application forms to learn about missing relatives became accessible to researchers and survivor families online, and these too augment T/D holdings.[18] What pleases me about the T/D filing system is the incremental family history of requests it has produced, including inquiries that unite our three generations of names: my grandmother's several reparation claims from 1956 and 1968, my mother's slave labor claims since 1999, and my 2007 correspondence with the ITS citing reasons of family memory. Our three generations of women are filed together, bringing familial sorrows into the ITS and thwarting what Max Weber characterized as the best practices of bureaucracies to suppress: "the more completely [bureaucracy] succeeds in eliminating from official business love, hatred, and all purely, personal, irrational, and emotional elements which escape calculation."[19]

Literature produced by the ITS underscores the trustworthy nature of the organization's own knowledge of names and documentation practices, pointing to its origins as an entity constituted under the auspices of the ICRC. Citing the impartial and neutral nature of the parent organization, the longtime former director of the ITS, Charles-Claude Biedermann, emphasizes unique aspects of certification operations:

> In connection with the issuing of information to the persons concerned, the seal of the ICRC warrants the neutral quotation of the information from the documents preserved at the ITS. Without certification by a lawyer, the confirmations are acknowledged worldwide by the pension authorities, the numerous foundations, funds, associations, and organizations.... As the confirmations and the excerpts from Documents of the ITS with the seal of the ICRC are acknowledged worldwide without certification by a lawyer, an ITS-

employee must have had the original in his hands at once before duplication and subsequent inventory-taking. Only few third offices
[non-ITS organizations] are willing to give originals out of the house
for the purpose of duplication, which is why the task is chiefly fulfilled on the spot and therefore requires traveling.[20]

What this means is that frequently an original document residing in the ITS
cannot be seen by the petitioner but is cited as one of a series of references in
a concise list, or as a brief response in the formulaic question boxes filled in
by ITS personnel, information whose authenticity and veracity are backed
by the weight of the organization's seal. Proof for reparation claims is duly
noted through the bureaucratic device of the ICRC seal, sidestepping the
legal-notarial procedures requiring additional lawyer certifications. Each
ITS-produced summary bears the title "Certificate of Incarceration and
Residence" and includes the following statement in German, French, and
English: "It is hereby certified that the following information is available
in documentary evidence held by the International Tracing Service." But
where exactly is the documentary evidence, and what does it look like?
    Prior to my 2008 site visit to the ITS archive, the fate of my paternal
grandfather had been confirmed for my family through a certificate issued
by the ITS in response to my 2007 letter, which was explicitly couched as a
request in the interests of memory and not for the purposes of indemnification. Whether for historical memory or reparation, as it turns out, ITS responses are identical. I was uncertain whether my grandfather had died in
Theresienstadt/Terezín or had been deported to Auschwitz and killed with
his wife months later. Dated October 26, 2007, the ITS response form swiftly
arrived in my mailbox, an example of its newer "short processing" system to
provide speedier, albeit abridged answers to my specific question (Figure 4).
In 1994, to shorten the time of response, the ITS had relinquished the quest
for "complete processing," its original mandate of evaluation. Thus, the form
I received, labeled "Excerpt from Documents," provided my grandfather's
name, with a variant spelling of our surname as Chajim Slomovits, born
August 8, 1873. The rubrics for nationality, religion, profession, name of parents, marital status, and date of arrest and reasons for arrest were filled out
using these two words: "not indicated." His last known residence was given
as Zlatnicka 11, Prague. He was imprisoned in "Ghetto Theresienstadt" on
July 20, 1942, by the Geheime Staatspolizei [Gestapo] Prague, sent there as
part of Transport "Aas." His "category" was listed as *Jude* (Jew). Under

| Notre Réf.
Our Ref.
Unser Az | T/D | - 2 217 047 | Votre Réf.
Your Ref.
Ihr Az | | Bad Arolsen, | 26th October 2007 |

EXTRAIT DE DOCUMENTS	EXCERPT FROM DOCUMENTS	DOKUMENTEN - AUSZUG
Il est certifié par la présente que les indications suivantes sont conformes à celles des documents originaux en possession du Service International de Recherches et ne peuvent en aucun cas être modifiées par celui-ci.	It is hereby certified that the following indications are cited exactly as they are found in the documents in the possession of the International Tracing Service. It is not permitted for the* International Tracing Service to change original entries.	Es wird hiermit bestätigt, daß die folgenden Angaben den Unterlagen des Internationalen Suchdienstes originalgetreu entnommen sind. Der Internationale Suchdienst ist nicht berechtigt, Originaleintragungen zu ändern.

Nom Name Name	SLOMOVITS-/-	Prénoms First names Vornamen	Chajim-/-	Nationalité Nationality Staatsangehörigkeit	not indicated-/-
Date de naissance Date of birth Geburtsdatum	08.08.1873-/-	Lieu de naissance Place of birth Geburtsort	not indicated-/-	Religion Religion Religion	not indicated-/-
Noms des parents Parents' names Namen der Eltern	not indicated-/-			Profession Profession Beruf	not indicated-/-
Dernière adresse connue Last known residence Zuletzt bekannter Wohnsitz	Praha, Zlatnicka 11-/-			Etat civil Marital status Familienstand	not indicated-/-
Arrêté le Arrested on Verhaftet am	not indicated-/-	à in in	not indicated-/-	par by durch	not indicated-/-
Emprisonné Confined Eingeliefert	in Ghetto Theresienstadt-/-			No de détenu Prisoner's No Häftlingsnummer	not indicated-/-
Le On Am	20th July 1942-/-	venant de coming from von	not indicated-/-	par by durch	"Geheime Staatspolizei" Prague (Transport "Aas")-/-
Catégorie Category Kategorie	"Jude"-/-				
Transféré Transferred Überstellt	not indicated; died in Ghetto Theresienstadt on 11th February 1944. (Cause of death not indicated)-/-				
Indications complémentaires Further indications Weitere Angaben	none-/-				

| Remarques du SIR
Remarks of the ITS
Bemerkungen des ITS | none-/- |

Gabriele Liepe

G. Wilke
for the archives

Bianka Geißler

B. Geißler
for the archives

A-143.1   *Explication du SIR. *Explanation of the ITS *Erklärung des ITS
Grosse Allee 5 - 9, 34444 Bad Arolsen, Bundesrepublik Deutschland, Tel.: (05691) 6290, Telefax: (05691) 629501, www.its-arolsen.org

Figure 4. International Tracing Service (ITS) short form certification mailed to the family about my paternal grandfather. Author's collection.

"Transferred," I learned "not indicated: died in Ghetto Theresienstadt on 11 February 1944, cause of death not indicated." Of the 140,000 mainly Czech Jews transported to Theresienstadt/Terezín, approximately 33,000 died in the camp-ghetto. Others, such as my paternal grandmother and her family, were transported to various concentration camps. At age sixty-eight, moved from Theresienstadt/Terezín to Auschwitz-Birkenau to form the separate "Czech family camp" (known as *Famillienlager Theresienstadt* or *Familienlager* BIIb), she was exterminated along with aunts, cousins, and the extended family on my father's side.

Although I knew that tangible pieces of paper lived on somewhere in the precincts of the ITS in Bad Arolsen, not even copies of documents were forthcoming. Instead, ITS certification and certificates resemble the circulation of bills based on the public's trust that paper money is backed somewhere by genuine gold bars or at least by governmental fiduciary responsibility. The intertextual interdependence among such a variety of paper and paperwork—first, the documents necessary for reparation, then the applications for reparations funds, and, finally, successful outcomes in the form of paper money and bank deposits—highlights for me the preposterous condensation and extraction methods intrinsic to both archives and money as units of account and accountability for redress.

Research at the International Tracing Service: Bad Arolsen, June 2008

The ITS collection of Nazi documents was made available to the general public for the first time in 2007, following the 2006 agreement to ratify access by all eleven countries that governed the archive—the United States, Britain, France, Germany, Italy, Belgium, the Netherlands, Greece, Israel, Poland, and Luxembourg. Open access to the archive had been held back due to Germany's strict privacy laws, as well as the requirement to send copies of the archive files to each signatory country. Arguments in favor of an open archive included the aging population of Holocaust survivors, the ITS backlog and wait time for responses, the need for new sources of financial support after sixty years, and striking a balance between privacy laws and the needs of survivors and their families for information.[21] By 2007, the ITS was in search of new paradigms for reclassifying and rethinking research uses for its colossal name index. Accordingly, in the summer of 2008, I traveled to Bad Arolsen as part of a group of international scholars sponsored and funded by the Center for Advanced Holocaust Studies of the U.S. Holocaust Memorial Museum in Washington, D.C. We were invited to determine the scholarly potential of the collection for future research projects and to consider proposals for more intensive cataloguing and standardized finding aids.

We were warmly welcomed by Dr. Irmtrud Wojak, a historian and then head of research, along with Udo Jost, head of the archive, and the entire ITS staff. On our first day, Jost led us on a tour of the ITS complex. As we moved through several of the buildings, he told us about changes in wording introduced in 2006, already in use for the forms that I had received from the ITS in 2007: "Evacuated to the east" was now "deported," while "died" (*gestorben*) was changed to "murdered" (*ermordet*). The ITS had inherited and extended the life of Nazi categories and terminology, analyzed by Hannah Arendt in 1961 in relation to the language of high-ranking Nazi official Adolf Eichmann during his trial. "Rigid language rules" and euphemisms, she noted, served to mask the project of mass extermination of European Jewry:

> The prescribed code names for killing were "final solution," "evacuation" (*Aussiedlung*), and special treatment" (*Sonderbehandlung*); deportation—unless it involved Jews directed to Theresienstadt, the "old people's ghetto" for privileged Jews, in which case it was called "change of residence"—received the names of "resettlement" (*Unseidlung*) and "labor in the East" (*Arbeitseinsatz im Osten*) . . . for whatever reason the language rules may have been devised, they proved of enormous help in the maintenance of order and sanity in the widely diversified services whose cooperation was essential in this matter. Moreover, the very term "language rules" (*Sprachregelung*) was itself a code name; it meant what in ordinary language would be a lie. . . . The net effect of this language system was not to keep these people ignorant of what they were doing, but to prevent them from equating it with their old, "normal' knowledge of murder and lies.[22]

Archivists, librarians, and users are not always in agreement with efforts to unmask and redress euphemisms by updating terminology. Archives prefer the evidence itself to reveal what was thought and carried out during that murderous era. Perhaps the Nazi elements of bureaucratic organization over time may pass away. When I graduated from Simmons College School of Library Science in 1974 and began my first job as a cataloger at the Brooklyn College Library, I encountered the contentious subject of racist and ethnic nomenclature and categorizations. My copy of *Revolting Librarians* (title an intentional pun) included an essay by my then boss, Joan Marshall, who along with Sanford Berman, argued to overturn biased, ethnocentric, and racially prejudicial Library of Congress subject headings, a most important access point in the decades before computer retrieval and search engines allowed instant availability via keywords.[23] The adoption in 2006 of new terms by the ITS indicated clearly its laudable intent to provide open and speedy access to new publics who were not archivists and researchers. It also signaled a shift away from archival practices that retained contemporary Nazi vocabulary, and toward semantic drifts more in step with our current politics of memory, and the "majority reader" of the archive, a potential nonacademic user in search of reparation and family history.

Another change settled on by the ITS was the use of the term "prisoner" (*Häftling*) to cover typologies of persecution found in their archive. "Prisoner" more closely approximated the terminology used by the immediate postwar organizations my mother joined after my parents fled Czechoslovakia in 1948 to Montreal. At that time, "survivor" was not yet current; "concentration camp inmate" was preferred. In later decades, "victim" and "survivor" became terms favored by my mother, never "prisoner." "Prisoner" was also the Nazi term for my mother when she came under so-called Nazi "protective custody" (*Schutzbehaftbefahl*) in the camps. Although ITS paperwork listed both my mother and grandmother under the rubric *rotter winkel*, "red triangle" wearers, my mother told me she wore no red or yellow triangle in the Auschwitz, Plaszow, or Markkleeberg camps. Instead, the yellow star was first encountered in high school prior to her deportation:

My first yellow star was in high school. In Khust [Carpathian Ruthenia, Czechoslovakia] around 1944 or maybe 1943 when I was a high school student. Out of a thousand pupils, maybe twenty-five were Jews. The Hungarians enforced *numerus clausus* [quota system for Jews] from 1939. I never wore it. I was advised by my math teacher not to wear it. He was *Nyilas*, the Arrow Cross Hungarian Nazi party. He liked me a lot and wanted to hide me. His name was Professor Pásztory and Bela Bartók was his brother-in-law. He was my protector. (Vera Slyomovics, interview by the author, Vancouver, Canada, August 20, 2010)

Udo Jost has been the head archivist for more than twenty-four years. He described his workplace to our group of visiting scholars as the "bureaucracy of the devil," acknowledging that, when mired in routine paperwork, he returns to delve into the files for a few hours to remind himself about the archive's contents. For example, to interpret an oblique reference to gassing human beings, he would turn to the files surrounding the construction of gas wagons and the calculations necessary to "remove shipments." In this way, he was forced into the archivist's knowledgeable role. For a segment of *60 Minutes* originally broadcast December 17, 2006, Jost recounted the meticulous nature of Nazi record keeping: "[Correspondent]: The Nazis couldn't have disease spreading among slave laborers. 'You can see he was a perfectionist. He even put down the size of the lice. Large, small or medium-sized lice,' Jost comments about the Nazi lice inspector."[24]

As we toured the buildings, Jost recontextualized that story in terms of the miracle of archival holdings. It happened that same list of lice-infested prisoners was instrumental in providing rare written proof for one particular survivor. One louse placed his name on a list preserved at the ITS and thereby situated him in a camp. The link between Jews and lice under the Nazis was foundational to the violence of their self-authorized power in which the operating binary was the Jew as animal, even insect. The texts of Nazi record keepers are close to Giorgio's Agamben's reflections on "bare life" published in *Homo Sacer* in 1995, in which "the life of *homo sacer* (sacred man) who may be killed yet not sacrificed" is sacred in the sense of being at the mercy of anyone, the lowest ranking human, exemplified by the Jew in the concentration camp: "the Jews were exterminated not in a mad and giant holocaust but exactly as Hitler had announced, 'as lice,' which is to say as bare life."[25] In this system of total, utter management over the life of Jews, one verminous Jew is counted, named, somehow lives, and a single louse attached to his name permits the postwar German reparations system to disburse payments.

At the ITS, I became aware of the existence of a Children's Tracing Archive (*Kindersucharchiv*) whose files cover the cases of around a quarter of a million children. A "child," defined by the cutoff birth year of 1927, was two years younger than my mother when she was deported into the Nazi system of ghettoes and camps in 1944 at eighteen. ITS documents at Bad Arolsen that I was able to view directly showed that my mother, born in 1926, lied about her age, giving her birth date as 1925 (or nineteen) when she arrived in Auschwitz, knowing that anyone under eighteen or over forty went to the gas chambers. At the other end of the age spectrum for survival, my grandmother made herself five years younger: her birth date on German documents was listed as 1910 instead of a possible 1905. It is noteworthy that my grandmother has never committed herself to an actual birth date, all her life hinting at an earlier year of 1902 or sometimes 1904.

Having received the ITS "short processing" dossier in the mail, it was a revelation at the archives to handle tangible paperwork referred to but never seen, yet relevant to my family. Recourse to original papers was not mandated for making claims for reparations, and the ITS could not process requests quickly if it included all the documentation required for a system of trustworthy referencing. Nonetheless, the contemplation of an original document leads to insights beyond its circumscribed content. There is, for example, the shock of recognition at seeing a familiar signature, the immediacy of the pen stroke in the formation of the personal name. Experts maintain that handwriting recognition software cannot match the perceptual capabilities of the human brain. When faced with the cursive loops of a signature in which an actual name has been more or less fixed in handwriting and is uniquely recognizable, the computer's ability to read human handwriting drops. Indeed, an individual's signature may vary little during a lifetime, unless physical infirmities change what the hand can produce. My mother and grandmother wrote in a distinctive German cursive often illegible to me. "Print block letters," I would beg them whenever they wrote letters to me. Their signatures closely resemble the Sütterlin script introduced in Prussia in 1915 for offices and schools that subsequently spread to their region of the Austro-Hungarian Empire. At the ITS, I perused and made colored photocopies of documents, each one recounting the bureaucratic steps they two underwent entering the slave labor camp as prisoners: their Prisoner's Personal Card (*Häftlings-Personal-Karte*), the Women Card (*Frauen-karte*), the Card of Personal Effects at Buchenwald Concentration Camp (*Effektenkarte des Konzentrationslagers Buchenwald*), and the Prisoner's Personal Sheet (*Häftlingspersonalbogen*) (Figure 5).

The Card of Personal Effects enumerated what presumably the regular female prison inmate in the German carceral system might have registered but had to give up to the "Effects Administrator": her suitcase briefcase, package; pair of shoes (loafers), pair of shoes (heels), pair of shoes (house slippers),

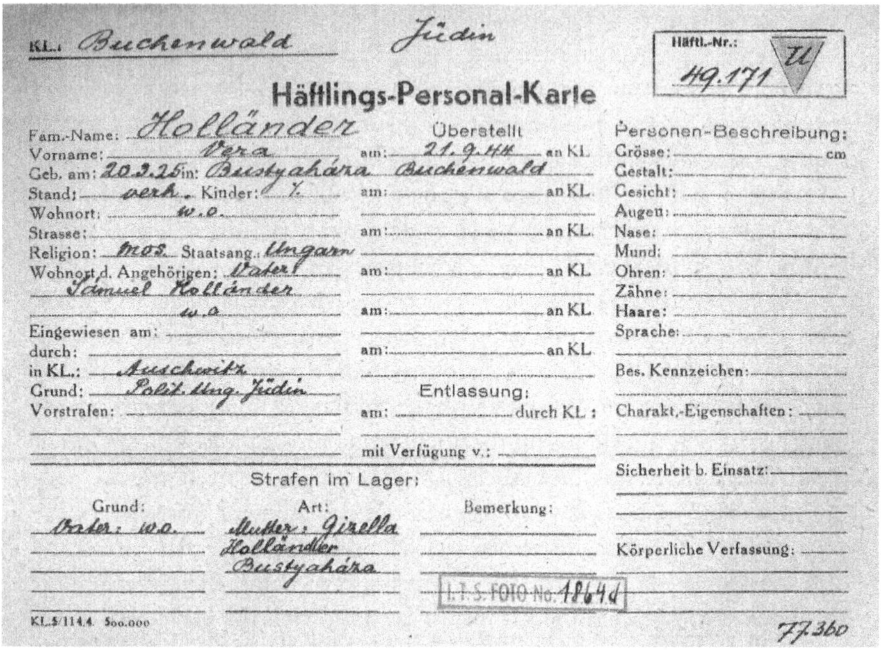

KL.: Buchenwald Jüdin

Häftl.-Nr.: 49.171 U

Häftlings-Personal-Karte

Fam.-Name: Holländer
Vorname: Vera
Geb. am: 20.3.25 in: Bustyaháza
Stand: verh. Kinder: 1.
Wohnort: w.o.
Strasse:
Religion: mos. Staatsang.: Ungarn
Wohnort d. Angehörigen: Vater: Samuel Holländer w.o.
Eingewiesen am:
durch:
in KL.: Auschwitz
Grund: Polit. Ung. Jüdin
Vorstrafen:

Überstellt
am: 21.9.44 an KL. Buchenwald
am: an KL.
am: an KL.
am: an KL.
am: an KL.
am: an KL.

Entlassung:
am: durch KL.:
mit Verfügung v.:

Personen-Beschreibung:
Grösse: cm
Gestalt:
Gesicht:
Augen:
Nase:
Mund:
Ohren:
Zähne:
Haare:
Sprache:
Bes. Kennzeichen:
Charakt.-Eigenschaften:
Sicherheit b. Einsatz:
Körperliche Verfassung:

Strafen im Lager:

Grund:	Art:	Bemerkung:
Vater: w.o.	Mutter: Gizella Holländer Bustyaháza	

I.T.S. FOTO No. 1864d

KL.5/114.4. 500.000

77360

Figure 5. My mother's *Häftlings-Personal-Karte* (Prisoner Personal Card), Markkleeberg Auskommando, Buchenwald. Author's collection.

pair of shoes (galoshes); pair of stockings (wool), pair of stockings (silk), pair of socks; shirt; undergarment, bra, panties (silk), panties (wool), panties (cotton), bodice, corset, garter belt, slip; blouse, dress, skirt, house dress, apron with pockets, handkerchief, sweater, training suit, coat (cloth, leather, fur), jacket (cloth, leather, fur, embroidered), hat, cap, shawl; pair of gloves (wool), pair of gloves (leather), pair of gloves (cloth); purse, wallet; mirror, knife, comb; ring, watch with chain, wristwatch, necklace, bracelet, choker; effects pouch; disability card number, disability receipt; workbook; photos; and, finally, writing paper. In sum, enumerated was an average woman's life and possessions. This same formulaic list existed for my mother and grandmother's personal effects, but all entries were left blank. Transported from Auschwitz to Markkleeberg in October 1944, they arrived with only the prisoner's striped uniform on their backs.

Nonetheless, the Prisoner's Personal Sheet required each inmate to affix her signature at the bottom right corner, despite her dearth of personal effects, and my grandmother's stood out even within the square confines of the handwritten, half-page card. The capital "G" for "Gisella," in my grand-mother's first name, loops grandly and in three circles, a large balloon for the top of the letter leads to a middle flourish ending in a long sinuous tail for the below line section of the "G." The letter "H" for Hollander similarly flows strongly with circles at the top and middle of the letter, preceded by a dramatic rightward horizontally thrusting hand movement to initiate the midline flow that links the two vertical bars of the letter "H." Although the lines of penmanship are shaky from hunger and her weight loss down to eighty pounds, each letter stands confidently upright, an idiosyncratic sig-nature evoking tears as I imagined traces of her inside the metal archive drawer—my grandmother with coiffed blond hair, dark blue eyes, 5'10" stat-ure, her robust laugh: a signature I immediately recognized, the same one that punctuated loving letters and birthday cards with lipstick kisses, that dispatched signed checks for my college expenses and paid for my Berkeley doctoral hood and robes. I believe that my grandmother and mother's sig-natures, filed one after the other, although imposed on them bureaucrati-cally on entry into the Markkleeberg slave labor camp, preserve not only a rare moment of individual human identity but one that proved that they were still alive and together.

What Is the Archive Worth?

From the point of view of the victim, reparation claimant, survivor or fam-ily member, what does it mean to call on the ITS archive resources? Does one have to become a user to grasp imaginatively the workings of survivor memory? Does using the archive help or cause disquiet because it retroac-tively legitimizes the documents of an enemy, rogue state? Historian Ken-neth Waltzer, a member of our 2008 group of invited scholars to the Arolsen site of the ITS, questions the value of its archive for survivors and their families:

> What does it mean to Frieda Jaffe in Miami to learn that her late uncle was sent from Buchenwald to Schlieben? What was Schlieben? What occurred there? What does it mean to child survivor Sidney Finkel of Chicago to learn that, despite what he wrote in his fascinat-ing memoir, *Sevek*, he arrived after child slave labor in Polish factory camps in Piotrkow and Czestochowa at Buchenwald in December

1944, not January 1945, and was in block 23, not block 66? What does it mean to child survivor Mikki Schwartz of San Diego, to discover that after arrival from Auschwitz at Buchenwald in May 1944, his name was on a transport list to infamous Dora, Hitler's "super weapons complex," where Hungarian Jewish boys and also Gypsy boys died quickly from terrifying labor? But his name was scratched off the list, and he was placed in children's block 8. Access to the documents is a first step that often demands more investigation.[26]

My response begins with a document I discovered through archival research at the ITS of Bad Arolsen: a typewritten, single-page report, dated May 12, 1945. My mother rarely knew the names of her torturers and guards and usually only the first names of her fellow camp inmates. The thrilling tale of her joint escape from what she called the "Death March" with my grandmother, their doubling-back return to Markkleeberg Camp, and liberation by American troops, as described in previous chapters, always ended with the words of the Yiddish-speaking U.S. Army chaplain using his bullhorn: "Have no fear, we are your people." The document I found in the ITS revealed his identity as Chaplain Robert S. Marcus, who addressed his report to "Headquarters in Tactical Air Command, Office of the Chaplain":

On May 8th I visited the Leipzig area in order to trace the Jewish women who had been kept at the Concentration Camps of Markleeberg [sic] and Schoenefeld-Hasaag and Schonau. I found to my dismay that the camps had been evacuated before the Americans arrived. I was able to trace the evacuees from Markleeberg until Wurzen where I lost their trail. These latter totaling approximately 1700 women of whom 1300 to 1500 were Jewish were evacuated on April 15th, two days before the Americans came in. I found approximately 40 women at Markleeberg who escaped into the woods when the forced march began. Of these 17 were Hungarian Jewesses.[27]

Marcus's memorable encounter with my mother and grandmother has been repeatedly recounted to me and remains outside the parameters of the conventional military report. His meticulous list of names included my grandmother and mother, alphabetized one following the other and next to the column for hometown: "Hollander, Gizi," and "Hollander, Vera" from "Bustyahaza." Research about him became my entry into an extraordinary life, shaped by his role as a rabbi in the American liberation forces. He was among the first to enter Dachau, Bergen-Belsen, and Buchenwald, and he stayed to work with the children in Buchenwald.[28] Finally, I know a name, a biography with which to honor the formerly mysterious figure of the savior.

A list begets more investigation. While a rich array of descriptions, testimony, documentation, and writings has been produced about Auschwitz, even the all-women's Markkleeberg Camp, with its small population of French prisoners of war and Jewish slave laborers, is the subject of written accounts. These works flesh out the ITS archive, although they lack the immediacy of Chaplain Marcus's report. Several Holocaust memoirs by women survivors describe their enforced sojourn in the Markkleeberg Camp, operational from August 31, 1944, to its "evacuation" beginning April 13, 1945. One such rich and beautifully researched book is by Zahava Szász Stessel. Like my mother, she was transported to Markkleeberg from Auschwitz but, in her case, at age fourteen and accompanied by a younger thirteen-year-old sister. Stessel launched her study after a visit decades later to Buchenwald where she came upon the Markkleeberg prisoner transport lists featuring her own and her sister's names. This encounter with Nazi paperwork resulted in her 2009 book *Snow Flowers: Hungarian Jewish Women in an Airplane Factory, Markkleeberg, Germany*:

> Looking carefully at the old and dusty document, I saw the names of my fellow inmates emerge. They were there—the girls and the women—with whom I shared life in the camp. I heard their voices and I knew I had to let them speak. (p. 11) . . . Yet seeing the site did not touch me as much as reading the transport list of prisoners brought to the camp. The register contains the names of 1,300 Hungarian Jewish women, who worked in the factory as slave laborers and 250 French women political prisoners. The names listed were those of my comrades, sharing the train ride, the living quarters, the work, the death march. They were the girls with whom I stood in the five-person line in *Appels* (roll calls). I see them and I see myself with short hair and gray uniforms, standing with no coats, barefoot in wooden sandals in the snow.
>
> The transport list is a lifeless document, a dust-collecting inventory, until a name is identified. Then it miraculously becomes real, the people alive, their stories unfolding. The list provides the name, age, place of birth, profession and prisoner number. The transport

list is a fading trace of Hungarian Jewish history. Cities and towns listed as birthplaces of the inmates document the locations where Jews lived in Hungary before the Holocaust. Today there is no Jewish community in most of the provinces mentioned.

The family names in the transport list relate to the memory of our parents, who went directly to the gas chambers; little account remains of their existence. As the survivors of the camp in Markkleeberg married, they changed their last names, leaving the transport list a slim record of their Hungarian past.[29]

Stessel delineates the ways specific research difficulties emerged and what she made of them when perusing the names of those sent to Markkleeberg: the duty to remember each one, the problems of resurrecting Jewish life in Hungarian towns cleansed of Jewish names, and even tracing her fellow prisoners' names, who, like herself, married and took on spouses' surnames. An earlier and shorter Holocaust memoir by Miriam Porat includes a section on Markkleeberg and was published in 1982 in Hebrew as *Le-lo shihrur* ("Without Liberation" or "Not Liberated"). One chapter details Markkleeberg living conditions after she was transferred as slave labor from Bergen-Belsen Camp. I have quoted a lengthy passage because she includes the contingent of Carpathian Jewish girls, speaking not only Hungarian but Czech and Yiddish, that describes my grandmother and mother's trajectory:

We were brought into the camp. Again we found ourselves in awe: the houses were built from concrete, with windows, glass, and electric lighting. They were divided into rooms, and, in each room, there were about ten or twelve bunk bed frames, each frame had a jute cloth mattress filled with straw and two blankets. We had yet to settle on our beds when one of the girls gleefully entered and informed us that, down the hall, there is a normal toilet, in four separate stalls with possibility of shutting the door from within. Next to the toilet, there is a sink with a faucet, where water flows regularly. . . . A guard shows up, a women SS soldier, neither her appearance nor her behavior gave the impression of any good. Her form of language and her personality in general projected hatred and malevolence. . . . The guard continued and said that we would rise each morning at 5.30 AM and lights will be out at 8.30PM. She added the barracks would be locked during the night and that we were brought here for work, and those women who will not work properly will be sent to another camp.... The next day was a Sunday, a day of rest. The girls from previous transports came to visit us and told us about the place where we had arrived. The following facts were clarified by them: we work in a factory that manufactures parts for "Junkers" airplanes. The factory is situated in an old fabric factory confiscated from a Jew. Work goes on twenty-four hours a day, spread between three shifts.... Some of the girls that were already in the camp came straight from Auschwitz, those were the more veteran girls, and some of the girls came from a camp that was a passage between Auschwitz and Markkleeberg called Plaszow. They have been told that conditions are better here than Auschwitz, but the prison guards are a group assembled of sadists, Jew-haters, and women who most probably in the Middle Ages would be burned as dangerous witches.... The female prisoners who visited us were dressed in a dark-grey overall uniform.... The camp commander called for us to be his soldiers in his army, and, in uniform, we looked more like soldiers. We didn't have gloves, and, as we walked across the camp, we put our hands into the overall's pockets. But God forbid if we would meet a German and would not pull our hands from our pockets and stand straight. As long as we were addressed by a prison guard, we had to stand straight with our hands outside. The guards would make us stand in formation inside the rooms, and even on Sundays or other rest days, we could not lay down covered in these cold rooms; the blankets had to be folded accurately on the beds and next to them the cup and food bowl, all organized in exemplary military order. While standing in formations, we stood straight, each by her bed, like soldiers, each barrack had a little stove made from black metal and next to it would be a box with coal. But the stoves were not connected to pipes of the chimney in the wall. These pipes were kept away in closed storage. Apparently, the factory management has provided coal for the heating of the barracks, both ours and the guards, but the supply was not high so the SS decided that they would be warmer if they would not share the coal with us. The coal was kept in our barracks for storage purposes only, and we had to fill large containers and carry them to the SS barracks; our barracks, of course, remained without a heater in the cold that sometimes reached during the winter between below 15 to below 20.[30]

Stessel published her book in English in 2009 and Porat in Hebrew in 1982. A third memoir in the form of poetry in Hungarian appeared shortly after the war in 1946. The author Erzsébet Frank managed to write a manuscript somehow concealed while in Markkleeberg Camp.[31] Both Stessel and Frank were incarcerated with their sisters and, as with my mother and grandmother, formed caring, life-sustaining dyads.

Material Claims to Physical and Psychological Suffering: The *Wiedergutmachung* File of Gizella Elefant Hollander

Does the archive lie? My question understandably annoys most archivists for whom the notion of truth in the archive is to be subsumed under more important considerations, such as what the archive tells us about informational layers from bygone eras that contribute to the formation and organization of each archive's holdings. Perhaps, archivist Verne Harris's notion of the archival sliver explains best what my family understands by the archive that lies to us:

> in any circumstances in any country, the documentary record provides just a sliver of a window into the event. Even if archivists in a particular country were to preserve every record generated throughout the land, they would still have only a sliver of a sliver of a window into that country's experience. But of course in practice, this record universum is substantially reduced through deliberate or inadvertent destruction by record creators and managers, leaving a sliver of a sliver from which archivists select what they will preserve. And they do not preserve much. Moreover, no record, no matter how well protected and cared for by archivists, enjoys an unlimited life span. Preservation strategies can, at best, aim to save *versions* of *most* archival records. So archives offer researchers a sliver of a sliver of a sliver. If, as many archivists are wont to argue, the repositories of archives are the world's central memory institutions, then we are in deep, amnesiac trouble.[32]

One ITS caveat is that, due to lost, misplaced, or deliberately destroyed documents, "the ITS can take no responsibility for the accuracy and completeness of entries in the documents nor is it permitted to correct misspellings or mistakes which might have occurred."[33] Interviewed in the late 1980s,

Elie Cohen, a Dutch Jew who worked as a prisoner physician in Auschwitz, reflected on his experiences with medical record keeping there, where perpetrators were presciently aware of their need to distort camp conditions in the event documents were not destroyed:

> The sense of guilt that I suffer at having survived is made all the more acute by the memories of those things. The things we did were insane by any standards. We had to keep records of medicines administered, though in fact none were—there were none to be had. Perhaps the SS sought to cover their tracks, in case there should ever be a Red Cross inspection, or should they be unable to destroy their records in the event of defeat.[34]

The human element, Elie Cohen's first-hand knowledge of nonexistent medical care and the Nazi cover-ups, could have fallen away if not for oral histories conducted soon after the war. What if Nazi record keeping depicts certain facts, but the living witness asserts something else? My main example concerns my mother, who commemorates annually the *yortsayt*, the actual date of her father's death on December 8, 1944 (the twenty-first day of the Jewish month of Kislev). She lights a memorial candle to burn for more than twenty-four hours at home because "the soul of a human being is a candle of the Lord" (Proverbs 20:27). She prays in the synagogue and gives more to charity. Even in the camps, she kept close to the Jewish calendar, maintained prayer times, and especially followed Jewish fast days, despite her own state of starvation:

> [Vera Slyomovics]: I don't remember if it was in Yom Kippur, I remember that they called us stiff-necked Jews for fasting and refusing what little provisions we were given. I just remember that.
>
> [Interviewer]: What do you remember about Yom Kippur that year?
>
> [Vera Slyomovics]: We prayed. And we, there were women who were graduates of a seminary, in New York, and my daughter is actually, I had to put that in, in a Jewish seminary in New York. And most of them knew their prayers by heart we follow with them, I don't know every word. People observed. We passed it, 24 hours, with the little provisions we got.
>
> [Interviewer] Do you remember what you thought then about religion and God?

[Vera Slyomovics]: Religion and God was tremendously debated
in the camps. Some people, total disbelief, especially the brighter
ones. I think I belong to the stupider ones. The brighter ones were
saying that God gave us the Torah and made us the chosen people;
they asked Him what guarantees were made. He said children. He
gives us children and throws them from the third, fourth floor, a few
million. So how can you believe that God is there? On the other
hand, we felt that there are no atheists in the trenches if you know, if
you start believing in God. My belief in God got stronger. I believed
that there must be something better, something good would come
out of this horrible calamity that had befallen us, and it's been suggested that the state of Israel was our reward. On the other hand the
Israelis felt that this is not so, the Israelis they didn't wait for the
Messiah, and thought to establish a state. So Jewish people are divided on the opinion of God. I will say to you that as I get older I get
more religious. I find that many things in my life I should be grateful
for. I thought that I couldn't have children, my menstruation was lost
for two and a half years. I have two wonderful children who have
given me the greatest pleasure. (Vera Slyomovics, interview, Steven
Spielberg Holocaust Survivor Testimony Project, Netanya, Israel,
December 11, 1997)

For Holocaust survivors and their offspring, the widespread Jewish custom of lighting the candle at the deceased gravesite is impossible for our
family, but time and date of death are miraculously available:

After the war on the train from Budapest to Prague, I met Isidore
Kleinman, my father's best friend. He was the manager of a large
lumber company back home. Kleinman had been with my father in
Mauthausen Camp, in *Auskommando* Melk. He said to me, "I held
his hand until the very moment he died. Remember the date December 8 for his *yortsayt* [anniversary of a death]. I marked it down for
your sake." By the time he said, "Your father died," I was unable to
hear any more. When someone dies young in a normal fashion, even
then it is dangerous to name the next generation after them. But those
who died in the camps, as martyrs, *kiddush ha-shem*, they should be
remembered through naming in the next generation, already through
my son, my grandsons, but even unto my great-grandsons. (Vera

Slyomovics, interview by author, Vancouver, Canada, January 1, 2008)

I learned that every death must be matched with documentation leading to the death certificate. In 2007, the ITS mailed me what it possessed in the archives pertaining to my maternal grandfather, Samuel Sandor Hollander, which consisted of (1) a list of arrivals to Austria's Mauthausen Camp from Auschwitz on June 13, 1944; (2) a copy of the Mauthausen death book with handwritten lists of names that gives his time of death at precisely 7:50 A.M. on November 20, 1944, and another column on his cause of death, "Phlegmon on left leg, general sepsis"; (3) a typewritten list by the administration of Mauthausen Camp, titled "Notification of Changes" (*Veränderungsmeldung*), 306, for November 24, 1944, number 30, listing a Hungarian Jew, Hollander, Samu [*sic*], prisoner number 72848, born May 17, 1902, died (*verstorben*) November 20, 1944, in the Melk quarry, "Quarz, Melk"; and, finally, (4) a typewritten notification of death (*Todesmeldung*) with the same information. Each of the four pieces of Nazi documentation recorded the paper trail to his death on November 20, 1944, a date that corresponds in the Hebrew lunar-based calendar to the fourth of Kislev 5705. This is not the same date that my grandfather's friend Kleinman told my mother to commemorate, namely, December 8, 1944, or seventeen days later. My mother repeats her correct date: "Kleinman especially marked it down so I would know the *yortsayt*. He was there at the last moment, held his hand, comforted him, and to me that's important because he comforted me" (Vera Slyomovics, interview by author, Vancouver, Canada, August 20, 2010).

Archivists weigh the relationship between provenance and pertinence, meaning that, although the Nazis created these documents that recorded the date, time, and cause of my grandfather's death (that is provenance), these data are contradicted by pertinence, or Kleinman's physical presence during the last precious moments of his life. Two information regimes coexist uneasily. For the purposes of compensation claims, my mother submitted her father's ITS paperwork, the gold standard proof of persecution and murder in a Nazi slave labor camp. In contrast, and following my mother's lead to commemorate the dead, our family chooses personal witness and testimony, regardless of the data recoded in quadruplicate in Nazi archives created by Nazi bureaucrats or their prisoner-overseers for whom my grandfather's life and death held no importance. In order to receive the official death certificate, ITS personnel requested that I return a form including my grandfather's birth certificate and wedding certificate, neither of which had been salvaged after the war. Any paperwork that referred to a prewar normal life of birth, photo albums, and marriage had long since vanished. Besides the impossibility of furnishing the requested documents, it seemed unnecessary for us to obtain a death certificate given extensive ITS paperwork revealing my grandfather's name buried among the rows of handwritten and typewritten names of Mauthausen's murdered. Furthermore, we reasoned, who wanted a death certificate with an incorrect date of death that would affect our observing rituals of mourning? Oral testimony and my mother's annual prayers have long since sanctified the Hebrew date of 21 Kislev matched calendrically to the year 1944 and the day of December 8.

Like a detective, for years I have tracked down my grandmother's reparation dossier. I found no evidence of paperwork from the various Jewish organizations in Canada and the United States designated to process and maintain records about Jewish claims. Records at certain United Restitution Offices in North America had been moved, lost, destroyed in a fire, or simply could not be easily retrieved by the current librarians. Thanks to an officer in New York City's Jewish Claims Conference, I contacted my first set of German authorities, the *Amt für Wiedergutmaching*, the Restitution or Redress Office, the main government compensation offices located in Saarburg, Germany.[35] I successfully provided proof that my grandmother Gizella Hollander had died, my mother Vera Hollander Slyomovics was her daughter, and I was my mother's daughter. Tracking three generations of women on paper, I mailed a sheaf of papers to the ITS offices that consisted of my grandmother's 1999 Israeli death certificate, her lawyer's copy of the last will that named my mother and me as executors, my mother's Czechoslovakian papers, and my Quebec birth certificate that named her as my biological mother. Each piece of paper attested to an inherited legal right to access. For my mother, this paperwork served to rebuild three generations of women and make them genealogically unchallenged to an imagined adversarial German bureaucrat. Throughout their concentration camp experience, my mother told me she was forced never to call her mother "Mama" (*anyuka* in Hungarian), an appellation that could kill, since my grandmother, barely forty years old, teetered at the brink of old age for slave labor and was otherwise slated for extermination. They two passed for sisters.

In 2006, my grandmother's claims for reparation, her file, arrived in the mail from the Amt für Wiedergutmaching, requested as a direct result of the 2000 German reparation protocols that not only granted my mother a first lump sum payment for her slave labor but also opened the possibility of viewing my grandmother's file. The accumulated paperwork my grandmother produced to shore up reparations claims had now returned to her family, thereby making possible new readings more than fifty years later. For the first time, the German reparations correspondence tracked for us my grandmother's peregrinations across continents and over decades. This is because until 1951 the ITS was subordinate to the International Refugee Organization (IRO), which transferred documents concerning "former civilian persecutees of the National Socialist regime." In addition, the ITS was a repository of originals and copies of lists—registration lists (for example, of displaced persons camps), repatriation lists from the Hebrew Immigrant Aid Society, and emigration lists:

> In summary, the collection of personal documents of the ITS is subdivided—depending on the type or category of persecution—as it is shown by the following illustration. One and the same persecutee may well have belonged to several of these categories or have gone through various stages within one and the same category. All pieces about the persecution available at the ITS are important for the provision of evidence by the persons concerned. Considered from this point of view, a valuation of the different categories is not possible. The large number of post-war records, however, are of special significance, because, in addition to the actual evidence, they also furnish the proof of having survived at the end of the war. This represents above all the basis of any promising and thus sensible investigations regarding the further fate, in the course of which an odyssey through several countries, or even continents, has often not been unusual.[36]

A stream of documents was filed in support of my grandmother's reparation claims. Some were notarized copies she herself provided, which the Amt für Wiedergutmaching had then checked against existing Red Cross and ITS lists. I now possessed two sets of documentation from two separate organizational entities, the multinational ITS and the German government Amt für Wiedergutmaching. Amt paperwork is barely reflected in the ITS archives: all that is there is a log in which only the requests to verify my grandmother's claims are duly noted. Thus, the contents of her reparation requests are not in the ITS archive. Minus any financial accountings between

Germany and my grandmother, they are found in the Amt documents sent to me, as follows. An early set of documents consists of photocopied pages of the Czechoslovakian passport issued May 11, 1948, jointly to my grandmother and her second husband, appended to which is a transit pass through France that leads to a Cuban entry visa, dated May 30, 1948. Unlike the Nazis who had kept my mother and grandmother together throughout the war, the postwar Communists of Czechoslovakia forced my mother and grandmother to separate when they left their homeland. My mother recounts that, as she fled on foot with my father illegally to Austria, climbing the mountains out of her native land, her mother traveled by train and ship legally with her second husband, Martin Hollander, a first cousin of her murdered husband. They had encountered each other again among the survivor community reconstituted in Prague during the immediate postwar years, where so many former camp inmates, unwilling or unable to return to their home villages, met and remarried. Postwar survivor marriages happened immediately on liberation from the camps. Yael Danieli, a practicing clinical psychologist whose patients are Holocaust families, describes the choice of a spouse:

> "I am lonely and have nothing: you are lonely and have lost everything and everybody; let's get married" was a proposal made by the majority of adult survivors after a short acquaintance (from as little as a week to three months). Even a remote connection of the chosen spouse to the survivor's past was sufficient for this decision. These marriages of despair disregarded differences in prewar socioeconomic status, life style, age or other ordinary criteria for marriage. Recreating a family was a concrete act to compensate for their losses, to counter the massive disruption in the order and continuity of life and to undo the dehumanization and loneliness they had experienced.[37]

My step-grandfather survived Auschwitz and was freed by Soviet Army liberators. He had been left there to die with the old and sick, while his still healthy fifteen-year-old son was forced to depart on the Death March west from which he never returned. His first wife, clutching their eleven-year-old daughter in her arms, was immediately dispatched to the crematoria, as were most children with their adult caretakers. Among the hierarchy of losses enumerated by postwar Jewish survivors, my step-grandfather figured among the most unfortunate (*imgliklikhe* in Yiddish), the profoundly traumatized parent who survived his children's murders. Since he was my biological grandfather's first cousin, no one wanted to call him *zayda*, grandfather in our West Carpathian Yiddish. My brother and I followed my mother's example with "Uncle Martin" in Hungarian.

Official papers necessarily make no mention of my family's brief, failed attempt to rebuild lives in Czechoslovakia between 1945 and 1948, as survivors were buffeted by twentieth-century Europe's political earthquakes: liberation from the Nazis became flight from the Communists in Czechoslovakia, accompanied by another loss of homeland and possessions, poverty, separation, and dispersal to a widening circle of distant, exotic locations—for my parents, it was first to nearby Austria, then to Montreal; for my grandmother, it was to France and Havana and, after my parents, to Montreal. The psychological literature terms these reluctant and proliferating trajectories "retraumatization" through immigration.

Another form in her German reparation file marks my grandmother's entry to Canada on August 11, 1949, to join her daughter in Montreal. Between 1947–50, Canada lessened stringent prewar immigration policies to bring in 98,000 refugees. Louis Rosenberg and Saul Hayes, the latter a prominent Jewish leader whom my mother would revere and count as a friend, served as the longtime head of the Canadian Jewish Congress. To demonstrate discriminatory quotas for the numbers of Jews admitted, they pointed to Canadian immigration policies that classed Jews under the category of "race" rather than as nationals of a specific country.[38] Their exemplary labors on behalf of postwar refugees, coupled with demographic pressures to increase Canada's population through immigration produced by October 1947 Canadian government approval to admit five hundred furriers (and over two thousand tailors) under an Order-in Council 2180. Missions were sent to Displaced Person camps in Germany and Austria, especially the British and American controlled zones; at a DP camp in Salzburg, Austria, my father, trained as a furrier in prewar Leipzig, answered the call to settle in Canada. In 1948, the year my parents arrived, 11,000 Jews, the majority Holocaust survivors, were also admitted. My grandmother's movements were tracked in the German reparations paperwork through her complex correspondences, legal notarizations, and documents in several languages, as she voyaged from postwar Prague to

Havana to Montreal to Brooklyn, and to her final resting place in Netanya, Israel.

Reparations Paperwork

A second sheaf of my grandmother's documents is part of her first claim for German reparation, translated below into English from the original German (which appears in Appendix A):

Declaration under Oath In application for reparation

To: **Gizella HOLLAENDER, maiden name Elefant, widow to Hollaender**
(First and last name, women include maiden name)
Pending under: **Mainz 13388**
(Reparations authority or court, file number)
Witness: **Applicant: see above**
Birth date and place: **July 6, 1905 in Buchtina (C.S.R.)**
Marital status: **married**
Current address: **Montreal, Queb. (Canada) 286 Villeneuve St. W.**
ID provided (picture mandatory): **C.S.R. Passport 4430** issued on: March **14, 1948** in **Prague**
Citizenship—cannot be determined
Only for witnesses: Not related to applicant, also not related by marriage—the applicant is (explain nature of relationship): **Not applicable**

My own reparation application is/was submitted to: **Not applicable**
(Reparations authority or court, file number)
I have not applied for reparation.
Admonished to the truth and knowing the significance of the oath, particularly that intentional or carelessly false statements under oath are punishable by law, and having been informed that claims for reparation containing knowingly or recklessly false or deceptive information about the reason or extent of the harm, will be rejected, I declare the following:

When the war began, I lived in Buchtina, C.S.R., and in April 1944 when the Germans marched in, I had to wear the Jewish star and perform forced labor.
To be signed only after the reading and approval of the explanation
In April 1944 I arrived in the Matisalka ghetto and remained there until May of 1944. Then I was brought by way of Auschwitz concentration camp to Plaszow concentration camp, where I remained until the end of July [September is crossed out] 1944.

There I worked in the rock quarry. At the end of July 1944 I was again brought by way of Auschwitz to the Markkleeberg concentration camp near Leipzig, where I remained until May 1945. I worked in the munitions plant of the Junker factories. The director was Engineer WITT. A few days before liberation, after the German guards had fled, I left the camp and was liberated a few days later by the Americans. After liberation I went to Prague, was married in 1948, and emigrated with my husband to Cuba in May 1948. In October 1949 we immigrated to Canada. I declare, specifically, that on January 1, 1947, I was in Prague and was registered with the police authorities there.

[In English:] I certify that I have seen the number A19459 on the left arm of Mrs. Gezella Hollaender.

According to the entry by the Canadian immigration authorities in my passport, I immigrated to Canada in October 1949 and I have had my permanent residence in Montreal, Canada, since then.

Deposition Under Oath
Today, the 13th of May 1956, Mrs. Gizella HOLLAENDER, born Elefant widow to Hollaender, appeared before me, Charles ?? [illegible].
Occupation: [left blank] residing at: Montreal, Que. (Canada), 286 Villeneuve St. W.
The identity of the person appearing was confirmed by the notary by way of identify card number 04774, which contains a photograph and a signature in her own hand.

The person appearing before me declared:

I would like to give a certified deposition for the purpose of claiming a reparation payment according to paragraphs 71–75 of the Federal Law for Reparation to the Victims of National Socialist Persecution of September 18, 1953 (BEG).

I know that a false deposition under oath is punishable by law and that according to paragraph 2 of the law named above can disqualify me from receiving reparations. In addition, I am aware of the punishments for giving a false declaration under oath in the country where I currently reside.

With this knowledge, I declare as evidence of the claim in accordance with paragraph 71 BEG and in fulfillment of the other conditions, the following:

I. Personal Data

My name is Gizella HOLLAENDER, born on July 6, 1905 in Buchtine (CSR), living in Buchtine CSR. Prior to the National Socialist persecution.

II. In the Case

1) The reasons for which I had to flee my home country or did not return to my home country after the National Socialist persecution were the following:

Because of my anti-communist views, I am not willing to return to my former homeland.

2) After I became a refugee, as defined by the Geneva Convention of 28 July 1951, and emigrated to Canada on October 25, 1949, I did not seek renewed residence in my home country.

3) In reference to the exclusion of political prisoners in Article 1 F of the Geneva Convention of 28 July 1951, I guarantee

a) that I have not committed any civil disruptions, war crimes, or crimes against humanity as defined in international agreements that have been reached to define these crimes;

b) that I have not committed any severe non-political crimes outside of the country to which I emigrated before I was accepted as a refugee there;

c) that no actions can be attributed to me that go against the goals and principles of the United Nations.

4) I have been a citizen of CANADA since 1956.

Before acquiring this citizenship I had citizenship in Romania.
I have not yet received citizenship of ————, but possess proper immigration papers.
5) No state or intergovernmental organization has provided me with financial assistance due to the harm suffered as a result of the National Socialist persecution and I am not currently receiving any such allowance.
I am Jewish and descend from Jewish parents.
I confirm under oath the truth of the foregoing declaration and sign of my own free will in the presence of a qualified official.
I, the undersigned official confirm that the claimant made the declaration under oath in my presence and executed the signature.

————

As I perused my grandmother's reparation claim, specific sections seemed to epitomize a counterexample to the ITS system—which I understand as certification devoid of any attached and evident back-up proof. Especially so was the notarization system alluded to above by a Montreal lawyer. Dated May 13, 1956, the legal notarial seal included this statement: "I certify that I have seen the number A19459 on the left arm of Mrs. Gizella Hollander." Of the Hungarian Jewish transports that began arriving to Auschwitz in May 1944, approximately thirty thousand Jews were registered by tattooing as part of the "A" series,[39] and thereby each person whose arm bore this letter is traceable to a list in the German archives. The lawyer's testimony translating my grandmother's tattooed forearm as trustworthy documentation was accorded the same weight for the purposes of authentication as the original tattoo it represents. The lawyer had created another document of secondary evidence, given that no copying process can reproduce her tattoo's physical characteristics—imagine submitting a photograph, a xerography, a carbon copy of the arm? As my grandmother aged, the flesh expanded and wrinkled, the ink faded, the tattoo stippled. Instead of the original, namely, my grandmother's arm, her "notarized" form of the tattoo becomes a successful example of authentication. I have no comparative data to ascertain how common such lawyerly testimony was. My grandmother's sister, my great-aunt Hani, was immediately shipped from Auschwitz to Buchenwald and never tattooed, which did not prevent her from obtaining German reparations. Was this my grandmother's innovation? That remarkable woman, who translated her slave labor into a German work certification (see

Prologue), certainly had the imagination and bureaucratic savvy to transform her tattoo into its acceptable paper version.

My grandmother's second reparation claim was filed in 1965, this time
as a request for additional funds to compensate for psychological trauma.
It too yielded astonishing insights into the fifty-year dispute between my
grandmother's claiming her right to German reparations and my mother's
refusal to do so (see Appendix B for the original German):

Mrs. GISELLA HOLLAENDER, residing at 414 Elmwood Ave.,
Brooklyn 30, N.Y., appeared before me—the undersigned notary—
today and presented the following personal declaration in support
of her own claim for compensation before the reparations authority
[*Wiedergutmachungsamt*], after she was apprised of the legal consequences of a false statements in a deposition.

I lived in Buchtina, Czechoslovakia, until the start of the persecution and was completely healthy until this time. In the course of
the Nazi persecutions I was sent to the Matisalka Ghetto in April
1944 and from there, by way of the Auschwitz Concentration Camp,
I was brought to the Plaszow Concentration Camp. In all of these
places I was housed under the well-known unhygienic and inhuman
conditions, suffered from hunger, was sent out in all weather conditions without the necessary protection, and was forced to do the
most physically demanding forced labor. I worked in rock quarries
and had to lift heavy loads far beyond the capacity of my strength,
such that I thought I would collapse. I was pushed to do this work,
which was exceptionally difficult for me, by the guards, who badly
mistreated me every day. After this, at Markkleeberg Concentration
Camp, I was also forced into difficult labor, this time in a munitions
factory of the Junkerswerke, and there, too, I was repeatedly subjected to severe abuse. I was hit in the head and back until I collapsed
unconscious—once in Auschwitz and again in Markkleeberg. During this period of persecution my health suffered terribly because of
the horrible conditions and because of the fear of the repeated mistreatment as well as the fear of a final liquidation. Especially after the
abuses to my head and back, I was plagued by severe headaches and
dizziness, suffered from back pains, and due to the exposure to bad
weather had pain in my joints, particularly in both knees and hands.
I frequently had crying attacks and could not sleep. The nourishment

provided to us was inadequate and consisted mostly of food substitutes, causing me stomach pains and the symptoms of colic, including alternating diarrhea and constipation. In addition to my headaches and dizziness, I also had ringing in my ears. After liberation I was a physical and emotional wreck. My first husband was killed by the persecution by the Nazi murderers. Although to this day I receive constant medical treatment for the suffering I endure as a result of the persecution, I have not been able to restore my state of health. The continuing symptoms of these illnesses make a normal life impossible for me. In addition, I have nightmares in which I reexperience the horrors, mistreatment, and humiliations to which I was subjected during the Nazi period, and following which I fall into deep depression. During such periods I lose all interest in my surroundings, can accomplish nothing, and have thoughts of suicide.

[Signature of my grandmother]
Subscribed and sworn to before me
This 3rd day of December 1965.

My mother and I reviewed my grandmother's second reparation claim for the first time in 2007, eight years after she died. I recall my mother's initial shocked reaction: "She stole my symptoms." Over decades, the family consensus had always been that my grandmother exhibited little psychological effects from the camps compared to my mother, who suffered nightmares, panic attacks, depression, and not a few breakdowns. Neither had ever considered suicide, a question routinely raised in Holocaust testimonies by a variety of interviewers. My mother answered this very question during her 1978 videotaped interview with Vancouver psychiatrist Robert Krell:

[Dr. Robert Krell]: Did you think about killing yourself? Did you think about putting an end to it?
[Vera Slyomovics]: Funny. Really I didn't, you know. We watched people, you know, running to their-to their-the electric gate. And electrocuting themselves. But you see you must remember that I had my mom with me. That was a tremendous help. We had each other, I mean. She's a very very beautiful character as far as strength. More strength than many people there. And so I had her, whenever she was down, I put her up. And whenever I was down, she put me up.

Physically, I was stronger. Emotionally, she was stronger. (Vera Slyomovics, interview with Robert Krell, Vancouver Holocaust Videotape Project, Vancouver, Canada, ca. 1978)

My mother feared that my grandmother's affidavit describing post-
concentration camp psychological trauma would prove to the Germans that
Jews lied and that, therefore, we were untrustworthy plaintiffs in making
claims for reparation. My mother considered her mother's paperwork a fab-
rication at worst and, more charitably, the vengeful postwar propensity of
my grandmother to make the German's pay for everything she suffered—
the deaths of husband, sisters, parents, along with material losses, multiple
forced emigrations, loved ones relocated throughout the globe—most of
which did not fall under the initial German reparation protocols of the
1950s. I recall when a relative died in the 1990s and their children did not
intend to inform the German bureaucracy so as to continue receiving *Wiedergutmachung* payments, my mother successfully urged them not to do so.
She would marvel to me about those a generation removed, wealthy and
North American-born, who felt justified in claiming victimhood through
financial channels. While much social science literature on humanitarianism reflects on the need of the sufferer to tailor testimony to changing templates of reporting requirements,[40] the work of Didier Fassin and Richard
Rechtman reconceptualizes "the moral economy of trauma" to remind me
that it is "the product of a new relationship to time and memory, to mourning and obligations, to misfortune and the misfortunate."[41]

My mother asked me to exclude my grandmother's second application
for psychological trauma reparations from the Germans from this chapter. I
believe my grandmother, profoundly and vocally convinced that my mother
was wrong to refuse German reparations, decided to incorporate her daughter, as if to embrace her and to articulate suffering publicly for both of them
in the face of my mother's refusal to deal with postwar Germany. Even if it
meant taking on her daughter's psychological symptoms, my grandmother
pursued claims through her own documentation efforts, despite her perception of my mother's seemingly stubborn and willful resistance, successfully
maintained until after my grandmother's death. My grandmother immersed
herself in the culture of trauma, her monthly German payment proudly
discussed and lovingly disbursed, while my mother, in turn, carried her
righteous refusal to be "paid off" for their remaining five decades together.
My grandmother died in 1999, unaware of my mother's decision to apply,

for the first time ever, for compensation that same year as a slave laborer. I was able to argue convincingly to my mother, with the result that this chapter could be written and published, that my grandmother's 1965 reparation claims for psychological trauma embodied her own physical and material losses to which she felt obliged to add the configuration of her beloved daughter's mental sufferings—tinnitus, headaches and dizziness, insomnia and nightmares, panic attacks and depression. For the purposes of reparation, my grandmother lovingly incorporated her only child into her own self-presentation of not only physical and material losses but also psychological trauma, precisely because her daughter would not admit to psychological aftereffects nor seek psychotherapy or indemnification for physical and psychic wounds. On paper and for the Germans, my grandmother and mother are intertwined once again—not as mother and daughter Holocaust survivors, nor disguised as two sisters who were slave laborers, but instead as one single suffering self.

CHAPTER 4

Canada

Vos der erd dekt tsi, mis men fargessen
[What the earth covers, we must forget]
—Yiddish proverb from my father

To conjure riches and plenty in buildings abundantly stocked with food and goods, *Das Kanada* was the name given by Auschwitz-Birkenau inmates to the vast storage warehouses located near the gas chambers. After the latest arrivals were forcibly herded from packed transports onto the infamous concentration camp ramp, everything they brought with them was confiscated for processing to Germany and deposited in *Kanada*. It was an imagined paradise run by *kapo* overseers, "well nourished themselves, having bacon and tinned foods in supply, chocolate, as well as good clothes and woolens, leather gloves, and their exquisite boots standing beneath their bunks," so well recorded by writer Hans Günther Adler in his book *Panorama*:

> All of this is booty from possessions of the newly arrived lost ones, this only a small part of the untold thievery that doesn't benefit the collaborators and the regular lost ones, but rather the conspirators, whose most loyal members need to be compensated a little for the great service they provide the Conqueror. . . . This is why huge storehouses have been built here, which are referred to as "Canada," they being full of gold and jewels, clothes and shoes, bedding and handbags, watches and perfumes, children's clothes and toys, all of which had been quickly and carefully packed by the clueless, they who had readied themselves for the journey to Pitchipoi, since for such a journey

they took their very best things, often carrying their most expensive items in the hope of using them to trade for necessities or to save for future times, only to have everything taken away on the ramp or in the room where they disrobed before entering the gas chambers, or remaining behind in the big sauna, where after awhile they end up in the storehouses, albeit not as items recorded as tremendous losses. Instead announcements are made that say the wares have been confiscated as stolen or fenced goods, the will of the Conqueror having been fulfilled, for which many people are thankful, though often they have no idea what they should be thankful for, since the countless owners of all these goods have long since been consumed by the flames.[1]

"Pitchipoi," another infamous place name Adler mentions, was an imagined safe destination for deportation located somewhere in the east, a locale invented by French Jews awaiting the wagon trains to the death camps.[2] Auschwitz possessed the perverse secret to signify the imaginary *Kanada* lurking behind the reality of a site that was the commercial lifeblood of the camp. *Kanada* was a terrifying and lethal workplace described in the memoir of Rudolf Vrba, who would eventually settle in Vancouver and join the city's small community of survivors to which my mother belongs. His book *I Cannot Forgive* details his existence as a slave laborer sorting the mountains of confiscated Jewish wealth and food, the poisoned gift of a brief life in *Kanada* for those who inhabited the "dangerous paradise where men died violently after barely sipping its nectar. . . . in Canada you live on the edge of a precipice." For starving inmates, the paradise of food, clothes, and goods insinuated additional layers of violence among Jewish *Kapos*, "prepared to do anything for food," and Nazi overseers monitoring the confiscation process through overwork and beatings until death:

We dumped out trunks and cases and rucksacks on a huge blanket in the store. Immediately they were ripped open or burst open with a sledgehammer and food, clothes, toilet equipment, valuables, documents, pathetic family pictures were emptied out. Specialists fell upon them segregating them, pitching men's clothes to another blanket, women's to another, children's to a third until half a dozen blankets were piled high. The suitcases and trunks were whisked away and burned with all documents. More porters descended on the blankets and carried them away to the women who would classify them by quality and pack them away in the warehouses; and all the time, while the experts sweated and we donkeys galloped to and fro, Graff and Koenig were beating, searching, punishing and bellowing their signature tune: Los! Los! Faster, you bastards, faster! *Karacho! Karacho!* [quickly].[3]

This chapter abandons Auschwitz's heinous and macabrely nicknamed *Kanada* to explore the genuine postwar richness of my parents' new lives in the actual country of Canada. From 1948 to 1969, they resided first in Montreal, where I was born and raised, and then moved to Vancouver, where my father died on January 5, 2011, and was buried in the city's Jewish cemetery. My mother was involved successively and successfully in Montreal's Concentration Camp Ex-Inmate Association, Vancouver's Holocaust Centre, the Vancouver Videotaped Testimony Project, and the 1980s trials of James Keegstra from Eckville, Alberta. While the disciplines of political science and law are concerned with institutional forms and state practices of reparatory justice aimed at redress, my extended family, through their everyday lived responses, quietly made individual choices whether to accept or reject reparations. If a key aspect about restorative justice is to empower victims to define what matters most,[4] to my mother, resettled in Montreal, it was her right to refuse the 1950s era, German *Wiedergutmachung* for surviving Auschwitz and then, decades later in Vancouver, to accept Germany's slave labor reparations in the year 2000 for building Junkers airplane engines in Markkleeberg Camp. Between those two moments, separated by fifty years and marked by contrasting decisions about reparation, were decades of my mother's communally based activities and joyful, creative participation in innovative projects she considered more worthy of her Holocaust experience.

There is a radical perspective suggested by Paul Chodoff, a practicing psychiatrist and clinical professor of psychiatry at George Washington University, to account for the affective sources of her activism: that the continuous and long-term psychological depression and anxiety of concentration camp survivors are forms of memorialization to murdered families.[5] By giving a positive cast to negative and sometimes pathological emotions of survivors, Chodoff's position realigns inner psychological terrors with behavior that is also manifest through positive social, cultural, and collectively made gestures and events. One can grieve and organize. To memorialize, following Chodoff, one may partake of survivor guilt yet also allow for symbolic reenactments as ways to deal with the past. In contrast to restorative processes that seek to measure victim satisfaction, psychiatric perspectives on financial reparation emphasize that, regardless of money received or refused, there are psychic processes, especially survivor guilt, that may also obstruct, postpone, and suppress the desired outcome, which psychologists believe is to complete mourning. My mother articulated few feelings of survivor guilt during her videotaped interview in 1978 with Vancouver-based psychiatrist Robert Krell:

[Dr. Robert Krell]: There are people who have as you well know, who have written about survivors and some of the consequences of-of having been at a camp, and one of the major features that survivors share are nightmares. And it said that there is another major feature of survivors and that is all of them have guilt about surviving. Do you share that feeling?

[Vera Slyomovics]: Never. Never have guilt for surviving. I never have guilt for surviving. I always felt that it's a special privilege for me to live. I questioned whether those who hadn't survived were better than I was. And I questioned, my very closest friend that I grew up with was certainly a better person than I. In many ways, more religious, much more deeply religious, and I question that.

[Dr. Krell]: *You mean you think he should have survived instead of you?*

[Vera Slyomovics]: *No, with me* [my emphasis]. I guess I have a very healthy wanting to live even now.

[Dr. Krell]: So you don't agree with the fact that all [survivors] live only with guilt about—

[Vera Slyomovics]: No. No. I don't, I really don't. I don't think I feel-I would love you to call or talk to my mother. I don't know if she would agree to, but I think you should. Without me. You know? Because I never-

[Dr. Krell]: To ask her if you are a guilty person?

[Vera Slyomovics]: Yeah, which I never did. I always felt that, oh God, I did my utmost and with the last of my strength many times. I gave it my very best. But maybe that sounds very conceited. But many a times I would be very tired. . . . I don't think that-we have a right to be tired, certainly, but I don't feel guilty. Really. (Vera Slyomovics, interview with Robert Krell, Vancouver Holocaust Videotape Project, Vancouver, Canada, ca. 1978)

My mother's "very closest friend" refers to Imy, the nickname for her seventeen-year-old boyfriend, Emerech Schwartz, who chose to accompany his father into the gas chambers, even though his father did not tell him to. Krell inquires, "You mean you think he should have survived *instead* of you?" My mother's reply is a moving rebuttal: Imy should have survived *with* her. She rejects a zero-sum game with its demonic echo of Nazi extermination practices obsessed with increasing the number of Jews eradicated. There are documented instances throughout survivor memoirs to tell of a child or parent's life substituted for another as long as the kill quota, or slave labor battalion body count, retained the projected number of murdered Jews. Imy's choice of holding on to his father's hand is the Holocaust version, as my mother has always recounted to me, of the *Akedah* biblical story in which God asks Abraham to sacrifice his son Isaac. Her emphasis is on the Hebrew *hineni* ("Here I am"), God's words repeated by Abraham to indicate a readiness to be present, proof for my mother that God's speech to Abraham is about divine presence, despite the call to sacrifice what is most precious to a parent. *Hineni* is her signature, sacred word to mean she is alive, survived, and must attend to an obligation to be there for others. My mother's bedrock belief is in her actions as a moral and believing Jew who makes choices. She transmits this through often-repeated vignettes whose narrative core remains relatively fixed but with an ever changing, indeed dizzying, array of contexts and applications to give new meanings to instruct her offspring.[6] A series of discreet tales are strung together to delineate step by step, choice by choice, her unwillingness to abandon parents to save herself. A first step was when she surrendered her church hiding place to join the ghetto to which her parents had been deported:

> My dad paid the Hungarian Gendarmerie before being deported to Mateszalka, to save me and not to take me. They knew more or less that I was hidden in a church, a Ruthenia Baptist church in Bishtine. They left the elderly behind including my grandmother [Pearl Elefant]. She stayed at home and, when I heard she was going to be deported, I left the church. I couldn't stand it there anyway. It was terrible isolation all by myself in the church attic. By then, everyone from our town was deported to the nearby ghettos, to Tecso. At that point our personal physician, Dr. Pauli Davidovitch, was hiding in the Carpathian Mountains and he said, "I'll take you alone," but he

couldn't take my grandmother. He was able to save his wife and two daughters in the mountains. The Rusyn peasants took them in; they knew him as their doctor. He was from the mountains, originally from Rachovo, and they knew him well. So I went to the Hungarian Gendarmerie. They were afraid I would denounce them for taking bribes from Jews. I was ready to do it and they knew that I knew. I insisted on joining my parents in Mátészalka. "Don't worry, we'll escort you all the way." They were so nice. There were two who came for the trip, five, six hours by train. My grandmother and I got off the train in Mátészalka and my father was crying when he saw me: "Why did you come? Why did you come?" He knew what was happening. The head of the Mátészalka ghetto would eventually escape from Mátészalka. When I arrived, he told me, "You're the most beautiful girl in the ghetto; I'm glad you came." He asked me to escape with him but I stayed with my parents. (Vera Slyomovics, interview by author, Vancouver, Canada, September 3, 2010)

But I always felt good that I was with them in the ghetto. And I loved my dad, they would have a young person in the ghetto, and basically when I got there I did help them, I was very pretty and everybody was very disheveled, they stayed in their ghetto. And the commandant, the Jewish commandant of that ghetto, I was able to get a better job for my father. He was doing work not as hard, just cleaning latrines and boilers, and that I helped him and got him out from the attic and into a room, and a little of that helped. (Vera Slyomovics, interview by Steven Spielberg Survivors of the Shoah Visual History Foundation, Netanya, Israel, December 11, 1997)

In Plaszow, my mother refused Nazi "invitations" to become a camp prostitute or privileged female work leader (*Blockälteste*). She encountered Oskar Schindler in the Plaszow Camp, who informed her that she was "ineligible" to work in his factory unless she agreed to be separated from her mother:

[Interviewer]: How big was the [Plaszow] camp?
[Vera Slyomovics]: With the Polish and Jews together, about 25,000. It wasn't a big camp.
[Interviewer]: Did people go out to work?

[Vera Slyomovics]: There were the Schindlers. And he would visit and come and ask for young people that he took out. I wasn't eligible because I wouldn't leave my mom.

[Interviewer[: He asked for people from your group?

[Vera Slyomovics]: Yes. He wanted Hungarians. (Vera Slyomovics, interview by "Steven Spielberg Survivors of the Shoah Visual History Foundation," Netanya, Israel, December 11, 1997)

My grandmother never ceased to remind me that she would not have returned from the camps without my mother by her side. Applying for reparations so late in my mother's life bore no relation to her ability to forgive, as she replied to a group of Canadian high school students, some of whom publicly avowed Ukrainian descent and family histories as perpetrators of crimes against Jews:

I made up my mind that in order to function I had to forgive. So I forgave you. But I'm not so sure I can speak on behalf of six million others. I don't know if they do. If my Dad is in heaven, which he probably is, he would forgive you. He told me if you hate, a little bit falls on you, then you hate yourself. My forgiveness comes from him. (Vera Slyomovics, interview by author, Vancouver, Canada, September 3, 2010)

As for me, I meditate on events during the early, heady days of their April 1945 liberation in Markkleeberg and the activities of my two remarkable female forebears: my grandmother as she obtains her "work certification" from the civilian German engineer in charge of the slave labor battalions and my mother as she testifies to his kind treatment, thereby assuring his release from prison. Many camp survivors expressed anger toward my mother for this gesture, the act of a Jew instrumental in freeing a German. My mother distinguished between the civilian German engineer and the members of the SS who ran the camp.

My mother's willingness to forgive derives from multiple yet mysterious sources. Anthropologist Esther Herzog notes the capacity, as well as the cost, to do so. Her own mother's approach is to humanize the demonic Nazi other. This became her mother's prevailing coping mechanism in the face of Auschwitz memories because to forgive, Herzog concludes, is to become the heroine of one's own narrative:

In the positive statements about the Germans and in her words, "They were also human beings" my mother finds, perhaps, a way to alleviate the memory of the past as a total horror, inhuman and impossible to grasp. Thus she humanizes the Holocaust and the perpetrators. Her insistence on remembering the events through positive thinking (of good-heartedness, self-sacrifice, help with the weak, luck and so on) indicates the way in which she copes with memories, organizes and processes them in the present. The anthropologist, at long last, should be satisfied as the journey that passed through unpleasant, undesired, suspicions regarding beloved informant's accounts, ended well. Ambiguous, self-contradicting pieces of information gained sense and coherence by drawing a complex portrait of the person's life story. Thus, every informant becomes, through suspicious observation and loving analysis, a hero/heroine of his/her narrative.[7]

Forgiveness is hard and was not always the case with the immediate postwar settling of accounts that overtook American soldiers, overwhelmed by encounters with the extermination camps. What happened when camps were liberated is the subject of films, scattered testimonies, and a few comparative studies: American soldiers liberating Dachau slaughtered the guards; in Bergen-Belsen, British soldiers used SS guards, who subsequently died of typhus, to bury corpses in mass graves, while surviving inmates killed over 150 Jewish *Kapos*:[8]

They got rid of the old and children in the Czech family camp [in Auschwitz] and put our transport from the Mateszalka Ghetto there. K. and her two sisters were my childhood girlfriends from our town. K. became a Jewish *Kapo* over the women. She was asked for some of her extra stores of food, and she refused. She said that she was put in charge and could not play favorites. After the liberation of Auschwitz, she was found killed in the camp. She had two sisters who survived and we were all in Prague after the war. Her middle sister M. was beaten up badly by people who thought she was her sister K. the kapo. M became a recluse and wouldn't have anything to do with us. She and her sister left for Israel. When I was there in 1960, her husband, a wonderful man, came to me and said, M. would only see you, and begged me to come. We had a nice time, reminisced about

Bishtine, my father, never the camps. I still can't believe K. did what
she did. (Vera Slyomovics, interview by author, Vancouver, Canada,
November 28, 2012)

In Markkleeburg Camp, an American soldier handed my mother his gun
and urged her to finish off the Nazi guards, who were cowering among the
former inmates:

We saved his life [Markkleeberg civilian engineer], he was arrested
and I told them how helpful he was, we testified on his behalf. The
overseers and the Germans, I never saw again. One of the things that
might be good and might be bad. There were lots of SS hiding in
Markkleeberg in our camp after the Americans came in. But they
were also tattooed under their arm. The Americans were so angry,
and they came up [with guns], and I was in a group with my friends,
and they said, "Here, shoot them, you'll feel much better." But I
couldn't take a life. I always wanted to be a medical doctor. I always
felt strong. I don't know, I'm happy that I haven't got any human
beings' blood on my hands. (Vera Slyomovics, interview by Steven
Spielberg Survivors of the Shoah Visual History Foundation, Netanya, Israel, December 11, 1997)

The psychological and medical literature enfolds us in the framework of
developmental sequelae of trauma across multiple generations, and healing
is held out as a possibility through "creative reparation and memorialization."[9] Victor Frankl, a doctor, clinical psychologist, and concentration
camp survivor, foresaw the emergence over time of innovative responses
and acts that reflect back on the experiences of having once been a concentration camp inmate and forever a Holocaust survivor:

The experiences of camp life show that man does have a choice of
action. There were enough examples, often of a heroic nature, which
proved that apathy could be overcome, irritability suppressed.
Man can preserve a vestige of spiritual freedom, of independence of
mind, even in such terrible conditions of psychic and physical distress. We who lived though concentration camps can remember
the men who walked through the huts comforting others, giving

away their last piece of bread. They may have been few in number, but they offer sufficient proof that everything can be taken from a man but one thing: the last of the human freedoms—to choose one's attitude in any given set of circumstances, to choose one's own way.[10]

In Canada, my mother eagerly participated in a variety of charitable, activist, and educational outreach projects described in this chapter. Her activities stand as a series of creative memorializations linked to the determination, held onto until the year 2000, not to accept German reparations.

Montreal

My parents departed from Europe in October 1948 on the *SS Scynthia*, a ship chartered by the International Refugee Organization and the Canadian Government to bring refugees from Bremerhaven, Germany, to Montreal.[11] They were first housed outside Montreal in former army barracks, a place that reminded my mother of the camps:

> I was very unhappy in those barracks. I was traumatized. Jews were coming to the barracks to find their *landsman*, mainly Polish Jews, never anyone from Czechoslovakia. A Mr. Horowitz came and was so happy to encounter Dr. Weinfeld. Horowitz had a duplex on Ball Avenue in Montreal. So Dr. Weinfeld said, "We won't take anything unless we can take Mr. and Mrs. Slyomovics and little Peter." We each had a bedroom and shared the living room, bathroom, and kitchen. Then we had to buy stuff. We didn't have money to buy sheets. So we doubled the sheets as tablecloths. There was only one bathroom and often Mr. Weinfeld would go into dreams there and we had to remind him to leave. We had no refrigerator so we put everything out on the cold balcony. One November night we put all the coke bottles on the balcony, it was cold in Montreal in winter. And they expanded and started exploding and Genya [Mrs Weinfeld] exclaimed that she thought World War III was starting. She took to bed, that's how she took it. We were still panicky from the war. Next door we had wonderful neighbors, French, Mr. and Mrs. Halpennie [?], and they

planted tomatoes in their garden, and they would invite us and we didn't speak French or English so we had an evening making hand gestures.

It was a beautiful relationship. We cooked together. Genya taught me how to make Polish stuffed cabbage, sweeter than our version. We washed clothes and dishes together. She taught your brother Polish songs. We never spoke Yiddish, always German. It was a wonderful experience for me to live with them. Peter loved Dr. Weinfeld. Once they tested Peter who he would crawl to first and your brother hesitated and only finally went to his father. Dr. Weinfeld's brother had immigrated before the war and had a big job in Washington, D.C. He had degrees in law, economics, a wonderful knowledge of Talmud. When he came, our Passover *seders* were the most beautiful ever. After thirty years apart, the two Weinfeld brothers sang in perfect harmony. (Vera Slyomovics, interview by author, Vancouver, Canada, September 12, 2010)[12]

My mother found a home in two Canadian cities, each possessing a rich Jewish cultural and religious life. Throughout centuries of Jewish existence in the diaspora, far-flung places were anointed as a new "Jerusalem." Lithuanian Jews of Winnipeg called their city the Jerusalem of Canada, reflecting on Jewish Vilna's reputation as the "Jerusalem of Lithuania," while, in another Canadian city, Rabbi Jacob Gordon declared Toronto the "Jerusalem of Canada" in 1919.[13] Rooted in nostalgic memories of my insular youth, I share with the scholar David Roskies the conviction that only my city, Montreal, considered "home to the third largest proportion of Holocaust survivors in the world," truly deserved the appellation "Jerusalem of Canada":

Montreal was a city of survivors. Everyone knew who these were, not because of their tattooed numbers (which marked very few) because they were so active in communal affairs and because they gathered each year in public mourning. There was the citywide commemoration in the spring and the smaller gatherings of Bundists (members of the Jewish Labor Bund) and the *landslayt* (people from the same town or region) on the dates on which their ghettos had been "liquidated." My parents, who escaped the Holocaust by a hairbreadth, lit memorial candles on August 16 for Bialystok and on September 23 for Vilna, to honor all their family whose actual death dates would never be known. And we, the youngsters, were called upon to recite poetry, sing ghetto songs, and light the six candles. There was no conspiracy of silence, no stigma. We could see adults crying in the synagogue or school auditorium, and sometimes we cried too. What made the survivors special in my eyes was that they were at least a decade younger than my parents and most of my teachers.[14]

Montreal was also dubbed the "Jerusalem of the North," second only to New York City in North America, due to the central role of Yiddish culture and language in the city's educational and political life.[15] By the 1950s and 1960s, the Jewish population of my hometown outstripped Toronto, a statistical predominance since reversed and directly related to the watershed year 1976 in which an election victory brought the separatist bloc, the *Parti Québecois*, to provincial power. During my childhood, Jewish Montreal's residential patterns and communal activities were noticeably segregated not only from anglophone Montreal but more so from the majority of francophone Montreal, creating my city within a city. From 1953 when my parents moved to Ville St. Laurent, until we all departed in the early 1970s, the local Jewish population in my suburb soared from 100 to over 10,000 inhabitants. Moreover, the linguistic and social stratifications of the postwar Montreal milieu in which my parents landed, with separate religious and language-based school systems for francophones and anglophones, produced schools and enclaves arranged according to language distinctions, further subdivided by religion for Jews, Catholics, and Protestants. Given concentric circles of exclusion, not only was the majority of our family's circle of friends Jewish, but we knew many Holocaust survivors. Based on these institutional infrastructures and geographical boundedness, my father sardonically characterized our world as the only Polish-style ghetto in North America. He depicted Jewish space as linguistically and religiously excluded from the bedrock of Quebec society that had hitherto maintained an uneasy accord between French Catholic and English Protestant identities. My father explained to me why he went to Montreal, the city of my youth that I still compare to Beirut, Belfast, or Nicosia for its sectarian patchwork of neighborhoods[16]:

I had a newborn baby boy and a sick wife. Your mother was eating entire bowls of sugar in one go. We were convinced in the spring of 1948 that the Soviet Union would overrun Austria too and we would be trapped in Salzburg. Like they did Czechoslovakia. And there was the Berlin airlift. Palestine was at war. I was willing to go anywhere just to get far from Europe, anywhere, Canada, Australia. They were looking for furriers in Canada. In Carlsbad I had lived like a European in public, a Czechoslovakian citizen with Czech friends and business associates, and I was a Jew in private. In Montreal, I found myself back in a nineteenth-century Polish ghetto. I tried to send you to French schools, like your mother who graduated from the best Catholic convent [Maria Theresa] in Budapest. There they agreed to let the Jewish students out of religion classes. But the French priest in Ville St. Laurent wouldn't agree. Jews, he said, had to attend Catholic religion classes. (Josef Slyomovics, interview by author, Vancouver, Canada, summer 1996)

Despite the conversation between my father and the local priest that occurred around 1955, non-Catholic children could not legally attend Catholic schools in Montreal until 1969. Even by 1977,

If, already exemption from Roman-Catholic teaching was difficult to obtain for children of non-believing Catholics, one can imagine how a non Christian child would be treated in schools who pursued in their curriculum a "Christian educational project." For these reasons, very few Jewish children non eligible to English education entered Catholic French Canadian schools.[17]

As Czechoslovakian Jews, my parents were not part of the rich *landsmanshaftn* network of hometown associations created or revived by the influx of Montreal's large Polish Jewish community after World War II. Instead, they attended events such as the annual Czechoslovakian Ball that mixed newcomers, regardless of religion, arriving in 1945 or later in 1948, and who, like my parents, had fled the Communist takeover of their country. In addition, our family was tied to local Jewish institutions, many within walking distance of our house: Beth Ora Orthodox synagogue, my Hebrew afternoon school Talmud Torah (while my brother commuted daily downtown to Adath Israel Hebrew school), and my various suburban and B'nai B'rith youth groups. Until midway through high school, when I switched to the province's rare nonsectarian St. George's School, my interactions with non-Jews, whether suburban Anglo-Protestant or rural Franco-Catholic, were minimal. During summers from 1959 to 1966, I traveled from one rigidly divided ethnic world to an intensified two-months' version for vacations at the religious, Zionist, Hebrew-speaking enclave of Camp Massad, located in Quebec's Laurentian Mountains. Consider the bilingual Hebrew-English booklet, self-published by Rabbi Aron Horowitz, a founder of Camps Massad in Canada, who articulated the camp movement goals:

> It is no secret that even graduates of day schools were not trained to SPEAK Hebrew. Although they studied all the Judaic subjects in Hebrew, speaking Hebrew in school and especially out of school was not stressed. Furthermore, the Ashkenazi pronunciation was in vogue at the time, while we were determined to use the Sephardic pronunciation even in prayers. (It is noteworthy that the Calgary Hebrew School was the first to introduce the Sephardic pronunciation in North America!) . . . The underlying principle of Massad, as of its parent organization the Keren Hatarbut, was to serve "K'lal Yisrael," the total Jewish community. We were going to cater to people of all religious and political ideologies. . . . Our common denominator was Zionism in its broadest meaning and the revival of Hebrew as the spoken language of the people.[18]

As I peruse his booklet, I marvel at the grainy black-and-white photographs, the author's unflagging boosterism for his project to revive the Hebrew language in the Quebec forests, the impressive listings of fellow campers' adult accomplishments, and the incongruities of this radically divergent lifestyle from our surroundings, as if I were an alien aberration excluded even from Quebec's famous "two solitudes" that set the English and French communities against one another. Linguistic ruptures with my refugee parents were exacerbated according to the educational pathways and possibilities then open to Montreal Jewish youth, or so it seemed to me whenever I compared the experience of my cousin and age mate growing up American in the Bronx. I learned Parisian-inflected, not Québecois,

French from Swiss, Haitian, or Moroccan non-Catholic teachers; spoke Hebrew pronounced the "Sephardic" way; and studied Spanish. My parents
speak Yiddish, Hebrew pronounced the Ashkenazi way, German, Czech,
and Ukrainian (Rusyn dialect). Growing up in the 1950s and '60s amid
Montreal's Jewish neighborhoods that formed a self-contained world with
rich social activities, religious schools, and summer camps populated by a
high percentage of Jewish survivors, Eastern European refugees, and their
offspring, I assumed that most adults were marked in some way, perhaps by
their accent but especially with concentration camp tattoos. From the age of
twelve in the early 1960s, I recall meetings of the "Organization of Concentration Camp Ex-Inmates" in our suburban Ville St. Laurent home. I can
still summon memories of one session devoted entirely to their anguish
about the Jewish *kapo*, in which I conflated all tales about evil into one such
villain named Hilevitch, my private name for a bogeyman. My mother attended these meetings as early as 1951, barely three years after my parents
landed in Canada:

> Right away in Montreal we were called the concentration camp in-
> mates, it was a very big [organization], [elsewhere] nobody wanted
> to talk about it. Most survivors didn't want to talk about it in those
> years. In 1951 it was a rarity, and we tried to form the first organi-
> zation. I have two cousins who survived with me, in Europe, and
> they never talked about it. I have a friend, never spoke about it.
> (Vera Slyomovics, interview by "Steven Spielberg Survivors of the
> Shoah Visual History Foundation," Netanya, Israel, December 11,
> 1997)

In contrast, my mother speaks openly about her concentration camp experiences. She could even pinpoint her earliest experience as a Holocaust
educational speaker that came about through a friendship with Mrs. Murphy, my beloved Gardenview elementary school teacher, whose first name
I never knew. Mrs. Murphy was tall and skinny with short, graying hair,
coiled pageboy style. She wore pleated skirts, had kind eyes, introduced me
to the treasures of the school library and the idea that a book could be
checked out and brought home. One winter some time between 1959 and
1961—since I was her pupil for three years in a row in the fourth, fifth,
and sixth grades—my mother approached Mrs. Murphy to request an ab-

sence of ten school days for me to spend the Christmas holidays in Miami Beach:

> Mrs. Murphy asked me, "Why do you want to go away to Miami; it's a family holiday?" I told her, "We have no family; even the Jewish holidays we go away. (Remember, Susan, to kosher hotels in the Adirondack Mountains?) Don't think I run away from Christian holidays, I run away from Jewish ones too. Listen, I'm a survivor of Auschwitz." She was shocked and I showed her my tattoo. She said: "We always have ten to twelve teachers at lunch, can you come and speak to us about World War II? So many of our teachers are ignorant." She introduced me with these words to the other teachers: "You are going to hear something that you probably have doubts about." I was there for an hour and a half, and she told me that I made such a big impression. (Vera Slyomovics, interview by author, Vancouver, Canada, October 20, 2012)

In Montreal, my mother joined B'nai B'rith Canada, a Jewish volunteer service organization founded in 1875 and was elected to the presidency of her Ville St. Laurent chapter in 1964. Throughout high school, I received rigorous training about the ways in which to write about loss, when my brother and I became her speechwriters:

> My closing speech as chapter president was at Ruby Foos [Montreal restaurant]. I can see your father laughing during my speech. I was talking and getting emotional about being an immigrant, a refugee, an Auschwitz camp inmate, from no English and starvation to finding a home and friends in Montreal. You and your brother sat next to him; it was a gala affair and dinner. He told me later you two kept arguing, your brother saying, "This is my page," and you saying, "No, it's my page." But you typed my speeches, not him, so you had the final say. You were always telling me, "Mother, you're getting too emotional, too hokey, tone it down." When we teased you and called you our "cool Canadian," you called the three of us "you refugees." We laughed a lot together, I was happy in Montreal. In 1960 when the three of us took a fancy boat trip back to Europe, your brother asked me if now he could call you a refugee. I said, no, your sister

would always be Canadian. (Vera Slyomovics, interview by author, Vancouver, Canada, December 1, 2012)

Perhaps the first immigrant and certainly the first survivor to be so honored, she was formed and honed by an apprenticeship in the 1950s and 1960s within a variety of local Jewish organizations. From training acquired through the Jewish women's benevolent association movement, she committed herself to Canadian Holocaust educational initiatives on the national level, including the courtroom as a novel venue for instruction.[19]

The James Keegstra Affair of Eckville, Alberta

In April 1985, the crown prosecutor (the public prosecutor in the Canadian legal system) of the province of Alberta, brought to trial a high school history teacher in the town of Eckville, Alberta, by the name of James Keegstra. He was accused of public incitement and willful promotion of hatred by a student's mother, who complained to the local school board after reading her son's anti-Semitic history notes. The Canadian definition of a hate crime was invoked: "a criminal violation motivated by hate, based on race, national or ethnic origin, language, colour, religion, sex, age, mental or physical disability, sexual orientation or any other similar factor," violations of former section 281.2(2) of what became sections 318 and 319 of Canada's Criminal Code:

> *Public incitement of hatred*
> 319. (1) Every one who, by communicating statements in any public place, incites hatred against any identifiable group where such incitement is likely to lead to a breach of the peace is guilty of (a) an indictable offence and is liable to imprisonment for a term not exceeding two years; or (b) an offence punishable on summary conviction.
> *Wilful promotion of hatred*
> (2) Every one who, by communicating statements, other than in private conversation, wilfully promotes hatred against any identifiable group is guilty of (a) an indictable offence and is liable to imprisonment for a term not exceeding two years; or (2) an offence punishable on summary conviction.[20]

During the years Keegstra taught history, between 1978 until he was dismissed in 1982, the Canadian Legal Information Institute enumerated his pedagogical biases:

> Mr. Keegstra's teachings attributed various evil qualities to Jews. He thus described Jews to his pupils as "treacherous", "subversive", "sadistic", "money-loving", "power hungry" and "child killers". He taught his classes that Jewish people seek to destroy Christianity and are responsible for depressions, anarchy, chaos, wars and revolution. According to Mr. Keegstra, Jews "created the Holocaust to gain sympathy" and, in contrast to the open and honest Christians, were said to be deceptive, secretive and inherently evil. Mr. Keegstra expected his students to reproduce his teachings in class and on exams. If they failed to do so, their marks suffered.[21]

Keegstra's 1985 trial, the preliminary hearing in 1984, and even the initial 1982 complaint, were well publicized in the Canadian media. He lost the mayoralty election in October 1983 and his teaching permit in January 1984 and spent more than a decade enmeshed in and impoverished by lengthy legal battles. His first July 20, 1985, trial ended in a guilty verdict, a fine of $5,000 and six months in jail. In 1988, the Alberta Court of Appeal overturned the conviction based on arguments by his lawyer Doug Christie in favor of Keegstra's right to freedom of expression and the unconstitutionality of antihate laws.[22] The case returned to Alberta's Court of Appeal and was reversed again. Keegstra was brought to trial in 1992, found guilty by a second jury, and fined $3,000. In 1996, based on another appeal, he was given a one-year suspended sentence, one year of probation, and two hundred hours of community service instead of the $3,000 fine and instructed that "he must not attempt to preach hatred of the Jewish people to anybody, including hatemongering that is thinly disguised as historical research," while a judge summarized the prevailing position on hate crimes:

> Promotion of hatred of discreet groups is a crime in Canada because widespread hatred of discreet groups is the antithesis of democracy. Democracy is all about the right of every person in our society to equal respect and dignity. A democracy is not the happiest society for a zealot, a person who thinks he knows all truth and is so certain

of his knowledge that he would suppress all opposition as wrong and therefore evil. A democracy is a happier place for a tolerant person, who may have equally strong beliefs about what is right and what is true but who is willing to treat with respect those of a different mind, and use only rational persuasion to correct their thinking. Mr Christie [Keegstra's lawyer] before us commented upon the paradox of a law that, in the name of free speech, forbids some speech. But the greater paradox is offered by the argument that the principle of free speech justifies freedom for those who would end free speech. In any event, there is no great paradox about a hate law as a bulwark of a free society so long as we keep in mind that group hatred is the enemy of freedom. When people in society hate a group, they tend to tolerate scorn and disrespect toward the members of the group, who thereby become social outcasts and the victims of all manner of indignities, including the loss of a voice in public debate. In short, although they never go to prison, the victims of hatred lose their freedom. The hate law seeks to preserve their freedom. The Canadian hate law condemns hatred of groups defined by race, gender, religion, or ethnic origin simply because in the recent history of western society these are the kinds of hatred that have led to persons ceasing to have civil rights in any meaningful sense. It is not, sadly, a complete list. But it is a list of occasions for irrational hatred that our society has rejected as essential if democracy shall be preserved. There have been few charges laid in Canada under this law, but we do not have to look too far beyond our frontiers to be reminded how easy it is in this age to stir race and religious hatred to the murderous level that destroys civil society. In sum, in Canada the right to free speech is not an absolute right.[23]

Canada's hate speech laws share features with other democratic countries that prosecute Holocaust denial. Various European states, obviously Germany and Austria as former perpetrator states, possess Holocaust denial prohibitions.[24] In contrast, American legislation, rooted in First Amendment speech protections, permits articulating the falsehood of denying the Holocaust, even when intentional. Enforcement in Canada derives from several considerations: first, the public nature and forum for statements inciting hatred, similar to the German law of *Volksverhetzung* or "incitement of the people"; second, targets of hate speech are "groups defined by race,

gender, religion, or ethnic origin," as noted above; and, third, hate statements threaten violence ("likely lead to a breach of the peace"). Alan Davies,
called to the trial as an expert witness on anti-Semitism, recalled that "Keegstra spoke freely, and revealed a great deal about himself in the course of
cross-examination. He convicted himself entirely out of his own mouth."[25]
Nonetheless, based on Keegstra's diminished penalties and lack of jail time
after the lengthy appeal process concluded, a hate crime as defined in Canada
underscores the judge's sober assessment that "there have been few charges
laid in Canada under this law."

For my mother, her desired outcomes were achieved when two verdicts
upheld Keegstra's removal from teaching and the permanent loss of his
teaching license. In 1983 while his trials were beginning, under the auspices
of the Canadian Jewish Holocaust education projects directed to high school
students, my mother visited Eckville at the behest of the Canadian Jewish
Congress or CJC, which was the main organizational umbrella group for
Canadian Jewry for over ninety years until 2011 when it was disbanded and
renamed. Eckville's earliest Holocaust education event was reported by Ben
Kayfetz, the director of CJC community relations for over four decades:

> High school students in Eckville, Alberta, listened seriously, some in
> tears, as three Holocaust survivors explained the reality of the mass
> extermination of Jews during World War II. The three, Aba Beer, 61,
> and Lou Zablow, 59, both of Montreal, and Vera Slyomovics, 57, of
> Vancouver, travelled thousands of miles at their own expense to talk
> to the students about the unprecedented tragedy. The principal of the
> school agreed to have them talk to the students. Their former teacher,
> James Keegstra, who has been discharged from the school system,
> taught over a period of years that the Holocaust was a hoax. One of
> the students, Brad Andrews, 17, said, after listening to the three Ho-
> locaust survivors, "They sure opened our eyes to what happened."
> One student broke into tears watching a one-hour film on the Holo-
> caust which Beer brought with him. The three survivors related their
> stories in methodical fashion. Mrs. Slyomovics, from Czechoslovak-
> ia, recalled carrying her 80-pound mother from an Auschwitz death
> march under the cover of an Allied air raid.[26]

Both Lou Zablow and Aba Beer were survivors and activists working on educational outreach through the CJC and its National Holocaust Remembrance

Committee formed in 1973. Zablow (1924–2005) was the founding president of the Association of Survivors of Nazi Oppression in Montreal, created in 1960 by members of the city's survivor community for the purpose of combatting neo-Nazi movements in Canada. This organization was credited as an important pressure group that brought the first antihate bill before Parliament.[27] At the time of the Eckville trials, Aba Beer, the second speaker, was the national chairman of the Holocaust Committee of the Canadian Jewish Congress. My mother's Holocaust education activities were similarly tied to the CJC committee. As the third speaker, my mother recalls that Keegstra himself was present during the time she spent in Eckville:

> When you drive into Eckville, there is a big welcoming sign, "Eckville—a wonderful place to live." Keegstra was also a mechanic and fixed all the kid's bikes. He endeared himself to the students, never charged anything. Keegstra heard my talk to the high school students. After the talk, he came out to the main area, following along with me and the Eckville High School students. He pointed at me and yelled, "Does she look like she went through a concentration camp?" A compliment, I always remember. (Vera Slyomovics, interview by author, Vancouver, Canada, Vancouver, May 8, 2012)

Vancouver

> But I stayed on the train all the way through the Rockies to Vancouver. This is my home now. My uncle's confident prediction that I would soon join them [in San Francisco] was misplaced. I was still on the Polish quota and still a long way down the list [for entry into the U.S.]. But it didn't matter for I'd found an incredibly beautiful country where the people were warm and friendly, and where I had as much right to walk on the sidewalk as anyone else. (Leon Kahn, *No Time to Mourn*)[28]

For Vancouver's survivors and refugees, according to historian Jean Gerber, "memorials were the first reaction, gratitude the second."[29] The first manifestation of a Holocaust tribute in Vancouver is believed to have taken place on July 25, 1943, when a gathering mourned the destruction of the Warsaw Ghetto and commemorated the courage of Jewish fighters. For more than forty-two days, beginning April 19, 1943, Warsaw's Jews resisted the German troops, tanks, and airplane bombardments sent to liquidate the ghetto population. Within two months of the Warsaw Ghetto's annihilation in the summer of 1943, at Vancouver's Orthodox Schara Tzedeck synagogue, rituals of prayers, speeches, and mourning for the dead were pronounced by the community

> to express, as a group, the admiration which each holds in our heart for the Polish Jews who have been sacrificed to the hatred of Hitler. It may seem superfluous to suggest that any organized tribute should be paid by our small Jewish community in Vancouver when each of us knows that our thoughts are ever with these people who have contributed all that life can give.[30]

From the war years onward, Vancouver benefited from a variety of overlapping commemorative streams and organizations: individuals or families of Polish Jewish survivors; the Vancouver section of the United Jewish Peoples' Order (UJPO, a Canadian Jewish left-wing, Yiddishist association founded in 1926 in Toronto with unofficial ties to the Communist Party of Canada); Vancouver's Yiddishist I. L. Peretz School's annual memorial evenings to the Warsaw Ghetto beginning in 1948; and the city's rabbis who, as early as 1952, inserted calendrically based ritual mourning days in spring to incorporate the Holocaust dead. Research by scholars such as Jean Gerber, Barbara Schober, and Myra Giberovitch attests to the critical importance of survivors to the enrichment of postwar Canadian Jewish communities, just as historian Hasia Diner's study similarly chronicles the impact of the survivor population on American Jewry:

> The survivors who came to America functioned as more than recipients of American Jewish aid or as abstract symbols of Jewish survival. The Jewish women and men who made their way to the United States after the Nazi catastrophe created organizations, participated in Jewish communal life, and told their stories, and in those ways made an impact on the American Jewish scene. Their words and actions entered into the communal culture. Survivors associated with particular religious and communal organizations, Zionist groups, Hadassah chapters, synagogues, and the like addressed audiences and spoke about their Holocaust experiences. This fact stands in

direct contradiction to the often repeated, nearly universal accepted assertion that the survivors of the catastrophe came to the United States and refused to talk about their experiences. According to the dominant narrative, American Jews cajoled the "new Americans" into keeping quiet, demanding that they remain silent about the horrors that had befallen them.[31]

In 1969, my parents moved to Vancouver, currently Canada's third largest city also in terms of its Jewish population. Compared to Montreal's substantial survivor population, no more than four hundred ever resided there.[32] After twenty years as Montreal residents and familiar with the possibilities of cross-Canada Jewish organizational life, my mother quickly found equivalent communal institutions: membership in the Schara Tzedeck (Orthodox) synagogue and active involvement in two long-established Zionist organizations, Hadassah-Wizo and "Friends of Hebrew University," who performed local and Israel-centered charitable fundraising and good works. Around 1976, my mother became involved in Holocaust education for western Canadian high school students with the inception of an annual symposium for high schools that continues to prosper and grow in outreach to this day. As part of her ongoing Holocaust education projects on behalf of British Columbia high school seniors, she followed up with additional sessions, for example, one held on May 26, 1983, in Vancouver in which several Eckville students participated.[33] Following a brief presentation of her own concentration camp experiences, she continued with her preferred extended format, which was to field questions, however random or personal, from the students:

> In 1976 when I first began talking about my Holocaust experiences in Vancouver, I always spoke to high school seniors. I saw in them, in their faces, all my friends who had perished. One was Imy, another Marta, Pauli, I transposed my dear schoolmates, cousins, family, and age mates on these Canadian children. In this way, I received so much back from being able to talk to them. (Vera Slyomovics, interview by author, Vancouver, Canada, March 14, 2008)

> I don't know if this belongs to it but when I talk about the Holocaust, I have a lot of [German and Ukrainian] parents calling me, a lot of

guardians calling me, asking me could I help out because the children are very angry at them, and could I try to help them, they were young and they were 16, 17, 18, and they were forced into the army, and they were not SS, they were . . . , so I come and help them out, and I do that. I tell the children, some of them never want to see them again, they're very anti-German those youngsters. I tried to speak to my rabbi who is a Harvard graduate and he is a very big help to me. I say, "How can I help these parents?" "You tell them," and my rabbi is the most fantastic human being, he says, "Vera, you tell them, honor your father and mother above everything else, you have no right to be judgmental." So now I am doing that. I believe that we have to go on, with my daughter, she speaks Arabic, she teaches Arabic literature, and she belongs to [organizations like] Peace Movement Now, which wasn't very popular, but to me a life is very important, more so than territories. We might disagree; it is a little, thank you. So I am not either. I love my rabbi, I adore them. I love what they are doing, making peace, I adore them. Can I say that? (Vera Slyomovics, interview by Steven Spielberg Survivors of the Shoah Visual History Foundation, Netanya, Israel, December 11, 1997)

Kit Krieger, a Vancouver high school teacher long involved in the city's annual symposium on Holocaust education to students, informed me that my mother was among their most effective speakers:

In the end, it comes down to revealing your humanity, and there is the narrative. Students always wanted to touch her, kiss her, kiss her tattoo. Vera wanted no honorarium for speakers. She talked about her belief in fate and destiny, how society may not prevail but individuals might, and how it was possible for good to exist in that world. How do you get kids over the abyss and define evil without going into the abyss? She would say to them, "Don't be afraid to ask questions." (Kit Krieger, interview by author, Vancouver Holocaust Education Centre, Vancouver, Canada, March 14, 2008)

In recognition of my mother's outstanding achievements, one of Canada's prominent national government honors, the Governor General's Caring

Canadian Award, was bestowed on her in 2002. Since the governor-general of Canada often represents Queen Elizabeth II, who is also queen of Canada, my mother jokes that we could henceforth address her as "Lady Vera."

Vancouver Holocaust Testimony Audiovisual Projects

Although my mother never hid her concentration camp past from me, a vast literature by and about children of survivors details the more common, opposite experience of parental silence within pervasive postwar social contexts similarly characterized as a "conspiracy of silence."[34] An example is Leo Lowy, my mother's fellow Vancouver Holocaust educator, who with his sister Miriam survived the infamous Dr. Mengele's Auschwitz experiments on twins. He spoke out for the first time at the seminal inaugural April 27, 1976, Vancouver symposium on the Holocaust: "The inner feeling was that I had a story to tell, and for one reason or another, I never told my children. They knew that I survived the camps. We never discussed it. . . . I relived my life to the point that I didn't realize the impact that it had on my psyche. . . . I just had to go back to describe to these kids the emotions, the feelings, the behavior that I had at the age."[35]

The first 1976 Vancouver Holocaust Education Committee high school symposium was produced by a stellar and overlapping group of survivors, academics, high school teachers, and community activists. Jews and non-Jews convened under the cosponsorships of Capilano College, Vancouver City College, the Canadian Council of Christians and Jews, and the Canadian Jewish Congress. Although many contributed to make the event successful (and a proper account of the annual symposium awaits its historian), among those who helped organize it were Robert Krell (University of British Columbia psychiatrist and a child survivor), Graham Forst (Capilano College English professor), Robert Gallagher (Department of Religious Studies, Capilano College professor), and William Nicholls (chair of Religious Studies, UBC).[36] Along with my mother, there were other survivors who were speakers, for example, Rudolf Vrba and Leon Kahn, authors of published memoirs in 1963 and 1978 respectively.[37]

Individual Holocaust witnesses during the educational symposium inspired the creation of permanent testimony records in the form of videotapes to disseminate to schools and preserve aging survivors' words, according to guidelines written by Krell:

The author [Robert Krell] has been taping eyewitness accounts of the holocaust since 1977. It was obvious even then that such materials were urgently needed for historical and educational purposes.

Survivors in the community had already been teaching classes of high school students in Vancouver and participating in the annual Vancouver symposium on the Holocaust.

To bear witness in front of five hundred students is no easy task, however necessary. Audiovisual tapes can ease the burden of survivors who teach, by occasionally using their own videotapes.

In the foreseeable future, the numbers of such accounts will die with the survivors. They must be captured on film for future generations.

Students of the future, or for that matter, the present, will listen to audiotapes. The visual world of contemporary education requires that survivors be heard and seen.[38]

On the stage during the 1976 symposium were several speakers who went on to become the first group of survivors interviewed on film by Robert Krell in 1978. Krell, a Dutch Jew born in 1940, survived, hidden by a Christian family.[39] He was reunited with his parents at war's end, and they immigrated to Canada in 1961 where he trained as a psychiatrist. He has conducted extensive, long-term psychological research on Holocaust survivors, child survivors, and children of Holocaust survivors.[40] My mother served as his first informant in 1978 for the Vancouver initiative to videotape survivors and appears in his 1979 article on the configuration of the "Holocaust-family children" that quotes my personal correspondence with my mother:

It is the fate of the Holocaust-family children to share the trials and hardships and memories of the parents. But not infrequently, they stand to benefit from the wisdom gained through their parents' intimate encounter with suffering and death. The strengths demonstrated by survivor parents in adjusting to new lives in new places and succeeding against incredible odds inspire many children. In the words of one such child to her mother, ". . . in this letter, dearest Mom, I wish to write to you that whenever I become depressed, exasperated, feel confined and frustrated, I remind myself that I am the daughter of a mother who has been in Auschwitz and can still give to her daughter on her fourteenth birthday a book with the title, *The Diary*

of Anne Frank, with the words 'I believe in the goodness of humanity' underlined."[41]

My mother's openness to talking and thinking aloud about her Holocaust
experiences is articulated in three videotaped interviews (1978, 1981, and
1982, which are part of the Vancouver Holocaust Education Centre archives),
all moderated by Krell:

> [Dr. Robert Krell]: Some survivors prefer not to ever mention the
> camps again. Not to ever tell their story. What do you think about
> that?
> [Vera Slyomovics]: I think it's wrong. It really is wrong. It's not in
> the Jewish tradition. There's so much solace in sharing. Um, If some-
> one, if I could get a phone call, uh: I haven't been dehumanized. This
> is my story. I feel. I am not cold. I am not frozen. I feel these people
> have not let themselves—they have surrounded themselves with an
> armor and I think that it's a great disservice um, to other people. I've
> never allowed—I've never committed a crime, I'm not a murderer. I
> could never kill, I have never killed. I have no blood on my hands.
> I've never gone under revenge. I think the Jewish people have suf-
> fered throughout the centuries and I've always looked at Joseph So-
> loveitchik. I take a great deal of solace in the fact of learning from
> my son who has got a tremendous Talmudic knowledge, my daugh-
> ter. And Soloveitchik says that we zigzag through history because by
> zigzagging we are not a target. We cannot be shut down. We are al-
> ways here to tell a story. I went to a debate with [Arnold] Toynbee.
> He called us fossils, and I don't believe we're fossils. But there are
> survivors who feel that way.
> [Dr. Krell]: He called you. . . .
> [Vera Slyomovics]: He called the Jewish people fossils.
> [Dr. Krell]: Fossils of history, yes.
> [Vera Slyomovics]: I don't buy that. And I don't believe that the
> survivors are fossils. They are human beings, flesh and blood. And
> just like we were optimistic and we had that hope pulling us
> through. We have to go on again. (Vera Slyomovics, interview with
> Robert Krell, Vancouver Holocaust Videotape Project, Vancouver,
> Canada, 1978)[42]

The Vancouver project undertaken by Krell joined other archives on the Holocaust located in local museums and libraries throughout North America that have systematically attempted to amass audio recordings and videotapes of survivor testimony from within their own local communities. An early influential 1979 project to film Holocaust survivors began in New Haven, Connecticut, by the grassroots organization Holocaust Survivors Film Project, Inc., and included television specialist Laurel Vlock, Yale professor Geoffrey Hartman, and Dori Laub, psychiatrist and child survivor. Laub emphasizes the psychological importance of video testimony for facilitators, audience viewers, and survivor witnesses, no less than future historians:

> Video testimonies of genocidal trauma are a necessary part of the larger historical record as well as of the individual's release from entrapment in trauma. The experience of survivors may be the *only* historical record of an event that has not been captured through the usual methods of historical record and public discourse. The event can literally be recreated only through a testimonial process. The process is a method of registering, perceiving, knowing, telling, remembering, and transmitting historical information about genocide that varies from traditional methods of academic historiography to a considerable extent.[43]

By 1981, the New Haven project was integrated into Yale University's library system as the Fortunoff Video Archive for Holocaust Testimonies.[44] In 1985, the Vancouver Holocaust Centre Society for Remembrance and Education (VHCS) was incorporated, followed by the creation of a physical center in 1994, with Krell spearheading audiovisual testimonies that henceforth had a public, accessible repository home:

> It was clear that the most powerful instruments of education were the eyewitness accounts offered by survivors. We personally "recruited" survivors to join us. We began to tape audio-visual testimonies in 1978. The first two accounts were Vera Slymovics [*sic*] and Leon Kahn. As a national vice-president of CJC [Canadian Jewish Congress] I proposed at the 1980 national meetings that we tape Canada's holocaust survivors. Aba Beer, the National Holocaust

Remembrance chairman, structured a committee under the direc-
tion of Stan Urman, which secured a large Multiculturalism Grant.
In 1982, we taped the accounts of about 80 survivors across Canada.
In 1983, I began the local audio-visual testimonies project, and with
Ernie Forrai as its volunteer coordinator, we taped about 100 accounts. Copies were sent to Yale University as a permanent collection in the Fortunoff Video Archives of Survivor Testimony.[45]

Film sessions of the Fortunoff Video Archive took place in a studio, interviewers were heard but rarely seen, and the focus remained on the survivor
as the "talking head and embodied voice," a format that initially involved
"irritating camera work," according to Hartman:

> Wishing to project the act as well as the narrative of witness, we
> often sought what one of the project's founders, adopting a legal
> term, called "demeanor evidence." The result was excessive camera
> movement. The supposedly "imperturbable" camera (Kracauer's
> word) zoomed in and out, creating Bergmanesque close-ups. Even-
> tually we advised that the camera should give up this expressive po-
> tential and remain fixed, except for enough motion to satisfy more
> naturally the viewer's eye.[46]

These camera techniques and interview styles are familiar to me from the
"Steven Spielberg Shoah Visual History Foundation" interview with my
mother (cf. Prologue). Literary critic Lawrence Langer offers his characterization of teleological chronologies after viewing the Fortunoff videotapes:

> virtually all videotaped interviews begin in the same way, innocently
> conspiring to establish an atmosphere of familiarity: tell us every-
> thing about your childhood, family, school, community, friends—
> that is, about the normal world preceding the disaster. And most
> of them end in the same way too, implying a severance between the
> camp experience and what followed: tell us about your liberation
> (and your life afterwards).[47]

Similarly, the Spielberg archive's questionnaire, divided into three parts—
idyllic prewar period, Holocaust years, and postwar rebuilding of lives—
shaped my mother's responses on December 11, 1997. There were other

factors inhibiting this specific interview, unknown to the cameraperson and interviewer for an expected single event with what was supposed to be a mother-daughter session. As I review the videotape, I note the camera panning across my grandmother's apartment in Netanya, Israel, with its familiar furnishings of Czech crystal ware and the framed, embroidered artworks fashioned by Marika, their Ruthenian maid in prewar Bishtine, precious items retrieved after 1945 that followed my grandmother wherever she resided. At the time of this interview, my grandmother was too ill to participate, while my mother was miserably aware of her mother's failing health just steps away in the next room. In addition to the Spielberg interviews, my mother was the subject of several one-time, two-hour interviews; for example, she was part of a comprehensive project of the Canadian Jewish Congress titled "Canadian Jewish Congress Holocaust Documentation Project." Their documentary film *Voices of Survival* excerpted testimony from seven survivors, one of whom was my mother.[48] According to CJC interview methods, "a standardized interview structure" is sought that resembles many Holocaust testimony projects. Although, the CJC project hoped to film family members of survivors, particularly "children who may have insightful comments to contribute,"[49] my mother and grandmother have never been interviewed on film together, to my great regret, nor has any member of my family been part of any videotaped interview session with my mother.

Many Holocaust videotape projects are interviews filmed in a single sitting, a snapshot capturing one random day in the long life of a survivor. After being the subject of much videotaping, my mother can articulate criteria on how to produce a meaningful interview:

> Much depends on the interviewer, her voice, the sound of compassion. She's like an artist who plays the piano. The piano is only as good as the person who plays it. This is a topic that cannot be done by anyone. With Rob Krell, I had a friendship, a teaching commitment in common. (Vera Slyomovics, interview by author, Vancouver, Canada, November 18, 2012)

Although Robert Krell of the Vancouver Holocaust Videotape Project prepared questions for my mother, he willingly followed wherever her thoughts led. Unlike the lone survivor headshot characteristic of many projects, Krell is in the picture, he and my mother in comfortable rapport, seated in facing

Figure 6. Screenshot from the videotaped interview of Vera Slyomovics by
Dr. Robert Krell, dated February 18, 1981, Vancouver Holocaust Testimony
Project. Videotape copy belonging to Vera Slyomovics.

armchairs at the University of British Columbia (Figure 6). It is either 1978
or 1981, and Krell's hair is longish, he sports side-whiskers and aviator
glasses, while my mother is fashionably attired in bell-bottom pants and the
ever present, oversized designer sunglasses to shade eyes suffering from Sjo-
gren's Syndrome, and unable to withstand strong lighting. The picture quality possesses great clarity, more so than other videotaped interviews of my
mother, perhaps because the best equipment then available was utilized
(black and white ¾ inch tape), and studio conditions were made available,
courtesy of the Department of Psychiatry at the Faculty of Medicine at the
University of British Columbia where Krell conducted his research. When I
spoke with Krell some thirty years after he began the videotape project, he
wondered, "Was it even possible to fit a survivor—whose stories deserved
three days and three nights to listen to, whose accounts could fill a book—
into two hours?" (Robert Krell, interview by author, Los Angeles, January 3,
2008).

   Later interview projects arranged different protocols relying on multiple
interviews shaped by life history approaches in some ways closer to my

privileged lifetime position as the daughter and granddaughter of survivors. We, her offspring, have long since concluded that my mother knows no boundaries in her willingness to reminisce, perhaps because early audiences were family in informal settings. We are either the best or worst listeners, trained since childhood to hear, filter, digest, and respond to her unfolding processes of memory over time. We are her intimate, emotionally intertwined, uncritical, nonobjective partners for life, partly fulfilling a definition proposed by Shoshana Felman and Dori Laub of Yale's Fortunoff archives: "For a testimonial to take place, there needs to be a bonding, the intimate and total presence of the other—the position of the one who hears. Testimonies are not monologues. . . . The witnesses are talking to somebody, to somebody they have been waiting for, for a long time."[50]

Given diminishing numbers of Holocaust survivors alive into the twenty-first century, a younger, articulate generation of child Holocaust survivors has emerged—my mother, age eighteen in the camps in 1944, is on the cusp of these two categories of adult versus child survivors—who do not want to be anonymous informants but named and honored witnesses. Ongoing projects to record Holocaust survivor testimonies shape but also have been shaped by immigrants from genocides in Rwanda and Cambodia newly arrived in Montreal. Deploying newer, extended protocols, survivor testimonies for proposed profiles have been undertaken through the "Life Stories of Montrealers Displaced by War, Genocide, and Other Human Rights Violations" project at Concordia University:

> Researchers are devoted to a multiple, life story interviewing approach that privileges spending time with interviewees, building trust, and sharing authority within the interview space and throughout the research process. As part of the project, over eight months, a team of interviewers met with eighteen Holocaust survivors who give testimony in public settings, wanting to understand survivors' motivations for doing so; what they learned from recounting publicly; how they transformed their memories into narratives that could be adapted to various settings; and what they thought was missing in Holocaust education. This was a significant sample, given that there are only about thirty men and women in Montreal who do this work. All of our interviewees were of Ashkenazi origin and all were affiliated, to varying degrees, with Montreal's main-stream Jewish community.[51]

Videotaped Holocaust testimony projects do not capture my mother's improvisational, associative, free-flowing responses, whether elicited by student questions in the classroom or spontaneously evoked by her family in daily life. Key moments preserved on film, in turn, are extracted for documentaries, excerpted for television, screened for pedagogical purposes, and ethnographically redacted for this book. Perhaps Vancouver's more ephemeral, performative gatherings and educational outreach programs, initiated in 1976 on behalf of Holocaust education, stimulated communal Jewish institutional building. Vancouver's survivor testimonies found a home in 1994 within the outward-looking, interfaith, secular-minded Vancouver Holocaust Education Centre. These survivor acts of public witnessing, enshrined in museums and centers, live alongside the Jewish community's prior internal, religious rituals to remember the Holocaust dead through synagogue worship. From the time when services first marked the annihilation of the Warsaw Ghetto and its Jewish inhabitants in 1943, prayer, mourning, and commemorative synagogue rituals have never ceased.

Ritual and Reparative Acts

In 1987, a Holocaust monument was unveiled in the Vancouver Jewish cemetery, where the name of my maternal grandfather is commemorated. There are some twenty similar monuments to the Holocaust in Montreal Jewish cemeteries, with the earliest erected in 1952 by the Adath Israel Congregation in the Baron de Hirsch cemetery.[52] Regardless of the year of installation, postwar immediacy or decades later, these monuments possess shared iconographies that may comprise a list of names of the dead, reburied ashes brought from the Auschwitz crematorium, a poem, and explanatory plaques. In the 1980s, my mother paid to add the name of her father and his brother to the Holocaust memorial inside the Bet Marmorosh synagogue of Tel Aviv, where they joined a long list of names on the wall under the column devoted to their home village of Slotvine (Slatinska Dole in Czech, in Hungarian Slatina). Although my maternal grandfather's name was first inscribed among his hometown association's *landsman* in Tel Aviv's Bet Marmorosh, my mother would always say to me, "There are hundreds of names. In Bet Marmorosh, he is between his own people and his brother, not among strangers. But Dad never liked crowds. He didn't like stones; he loved roses." This may account for my mother's unshakeable belief that her beloved father has accompanied her as she made her way to Canada. Like Moroccan Jews now residing in Israel who believe their saintly rabbis once entombed in Morocco have tunneled underground across North Africa in order for them to reestablish shrines as followers who immigrated to Israel,[53] so too my mother has arranged for her father to be "buried" in the Jewish cemetery among the roses of Vancouver, her home for the past forty years. On April 26, 1987, in Vancouver's Orthodox Jewish cemetery, the community dedicated a monument to the six million Jewish dead on Holocaust Memorial Day. In front of the sculpture is a large plaque inscribed with names, each name related to and paid for by a family member. In 1987, the cost of commemorating a murdered ancestor's name was $200. In my photograph taken during family visits to the dead, my mother gestures to her father's name, Samuel Hollander, while immediately behind her are our three family cemetery plots that face him and look upon his name. My maternal grandfather's grave is nowhere on earth, yet his name is inscribed everywhere my mother resides.

In turn, according to my mother, my grandmother bought cemetery plots wherever she alighted, each time imagining her temporary residence as permanent. Her global post-World War II peregrinations and successive displacements can be tracked through a list of purchased plots. It began with the hometown family cemetery in Bishtine, former Czechoslovakia, where generations of Hollanders, Shreters, and Strulevics from our genealogy were interred up to 1943. Only once did my mother succeed in dissuading her mother from buying a plot, and that was during their brief postwar stay in Prague from 1945 until 1948. It helped that my grandmother viewed the picturesque, medieval Jewish ghetto cemetery behind the Pinkas Synagogue, a resting place beloved of tourists to this day, as unkempt, crowded, and dirty. Instead, she would go on to purchase plots in Budapest, Havana, Montreal, Brooklyn, and, finally, Netanya, Israel, pointing to clear grounds to determine the excellence of a burial site. My mother told me:

> Brooklyn was the best, your *bubbe* said. She spoke about the cemetery's beautiful view, nice neighborhood, elegant and well taken care of gravestones, situated among very important scholars, and that the land was part of their Marmorosh *landsmanshaft* [hometown] association. (Vera Slyomovics, interview by author, Vancouver, Canada, August 20, 2010)

In Israel, my grandmother lies next to my step-grandfather (her second of
three husbands). My mother notes that my grandmother liked to shed years.
She persisted in presenting herself as younger than her actual age, a mysterious number to her family, albeit a practice that my mother claims saved her
life when my grandmother lied to make herself younger as she passed
through Auschwitz's selection process, as has been mentioned previously:

> In Israel gravestones go up early. After her second husband died,
> your grandmother ordered her stone and it was placed in the ceme-
> tery next to his. Over the years I would say to her, "Mama, you have
> to have your birth date and year on your gravestone." She would toss
> her head and say, "*Raboyne shel oylam* [Master of the Universe]
> knows my age and that's enough for me. (Vera Slyomovics, interview
> by author, Vancouver, Canada, August 18, 2010)

My mother's unfulfilled wish is to order a Torah scroll with her parents'
name inscribed on the covering to donate as a gift to her Vancouver synagogue. When she investigated costs in the 1980s to pay the ritual *sofer* or
scribe, the price was $30,000, too expensive on her limited income. She was
first introduced to the idea in Montreal, when three times each year, as a
reward for excellent elementary school grades, my brother and I were taken
to a restaurant meal in Montreal's Van Horne neighborhood, followed by a
stopover at Rodel's, the store for Jewish traditional gifts, filled with Torah
scrolls awaiting a home. When I asked her why this particular philanthropic
act, she replied that, every week when the Torah scroll was unfolded to be
recited during the synagogue service, those were the precise moments her
deceased parents would listen, and maybe they would *mitnemen*, or "take
her along" with them to heaven (Vera Slyomovics, interview by author, Vancouver, Canada, October 22, 2010). This follows a legend that circulates
among ex-inmates of Nazi concentration camps. My mother's version recounts that, whenever a Holocaust survivor dies, each one will be lifted up
to heaven attired in the striped camp uniform. There, my mother believes,
her father, family, and friends are waiting for her; it is they who have abandoned her, not the reverse. In the meantime, this world possesses purpose
and meaning. She is confident about a teleology that both presupposes God's
ultimate and benign purpose but also assumes events possess *beshert*, a
term many Yiddish-speaking Jews extend to all that is destined, fated, what
God wills:

When we returned from Plaszow to Auschwitz, everyone began running around to join other groups. I wouldn't. I go where *beshert* tells
me. Rumors circulated that there were transports that would go to
Germany, a better place. It turned out that they were sent to Russia,
a much worse fate. I waited. I remember standing in front of the crematoria, which was burning bodies round the clock. There were
never any birds at Auschwitz. Maybe that's why I love birds. I waited
and didn't run. I don't want to go against the wishes of *Raboyne shel
oylam* [Master of the Universe]. (Vera Slyomovics, interview by
author,Vancouver, Canada, August 29, 2010)[54]

Beshert traditionally refers to a soul mate, one's intended in marriage, a concept tenuously based on Talmudic reference in which forty days before the
fetus is formed, in heaven the decision is rendered who is destined to mate
with whom.[55] Mark Dvorjetski, a doctor and a survivor of the Vilna
Ghetto and Auschwitz, who chronicled survivors post-concentration camp
physiological aftereffects, alluded to widespread expressions involving
beshert: "Camp inmates believed in 'blind fate,' predestination (*vas beshert
is beshert*)."[56]

The Dreamer

Adaptive and maladaptive practices are said to be the hallmark of Holocaust
families, the accepted term for possessing at least one parent-survivor. To
my opening paragraphs of this chapter citing psychiatrist Paul Chodoff's
pervasive states of depression as forms of memorialization, I add literary
critic James Young's useful notion

> to distinguish a memorial from a monument only in a broader, more
> generic sense: there are memorial books, memorial activities, memo-
> rial days, memorial festivals, and memorial sculptures. Some of these
> are mournful, some celebratory: but all are memorials in a larger
> sense. Monuments, on the other hand, will refer here to a subset of
> memorials; they are the material objects, the sculptures and installa-
> tions used to memorialize a person or a thing. A memorial may be a
> day, a conference, or a space but it need not be a monument. A mon-
> ument, on the other hand, is always a kind of memorial.[57]

There are the roles to be played by specific, culturally shaped practices that may serve to commemorate, reproduce, replace, supplement, or complement the horrific past with its monumental losses of people, things, and places. To find the way back to families and places from the past when all is discontinuous and ruptured, recourse has been to monuments and memorials such as museums, Holocaust testimony, synagogue rituals, photography, charitable works and donations, storytelling, and the most intimate expression of interior states of anguish—the dream. Are these discursive and alternative nondiscursive ways to compensate and rehabilitate?—in other words, to "perform" restitution and reparation individually and locally in ways that bear little relation to official reparation protocols enacted by governments, states, psychologists, and rabbinical authorities? If one refuses reparations for over forty years, as my mother did, are rituals and beliefs an emotional compensation? The burning issue for my mother remains the ways in which it is possible to remain in constant and close touch with martyred relatives, while waiting to rejoin them in the world to come. Along with educational activities, synagogue prayer, and cemetery visits, her conduit is the dream. That the dead have agency to erupt into our lives through dreams is well documented in medical and anthropological literature. So, too, is it a common occurrence among Holocaust survivors.[58] After my grandmother died in 1999, my mother would visit her grave in Netanya, Israel, to consult with her in Hungarian. My mother credits dream visitations by my grandmother as the prime influence to move her toward her own separate, first claim for reparations from the Germans in 1999:

> At night I dreamed with her your grandmother and she said, "I want you to go ahead and do everything. You're not well and you're not young. Never mind blood money." She was always so upset with me that I didn't apply for *Wiedergutmachung*. I was trying to lose weight. I dreamed she was knocking at the door saying, "Don't you ever do that again." Skipping a meal always made *Bubbe* angry. (Vera Slyomovics, interview by author, Vancouver, Canada, November 16, 2004)

Indeed, the dead possess the power to travel long distances. My maternal grandfather does not merely symbolically inhabit his monument in the Vancouver cemetery as a name on a list of Vancouver survivor family's murdered ancestors. Since his 1944 death in Austria's Mauthausen-Melk concentration camp and my grandmother's 1999 burial in Netanya, both her parents have followed my mother throughout her life in dreams, even to the distant reaches of western Canada. Dreams, she informs me, are a privilege, a defense, and a weapon:

> As much as I'm an optimist, it's wonderful to retreat back into the world of dreams. The dream was the safest place to be. Reality was difficult. *Geshenkte yorn* means the gift of years. Anything past the seventieth birthday, Jews consider a gift. There is the opposite, a life cut down too early. The opportunity to be with the dead, ask for advice, for support, that continues through dreams. (Vera Slyomovics, interview by author, Vancouver, Canada, August 20, 2010)

> I have, it shows you how mentally I am still strong, when somebody hurts me badly, even somebody now after many years of war, I have a tendency to go to bed and put them in an SS uniform, that person. So I remember when I was at the university, I had a teacher, he had a very slick way, I said, "You better watch out, I'll put you in an SS uniform," and he says, "How do you do it?" I say, "In my dreams I can do it." He laughed about it. But I do have that. I still dream about being in camp, about running, the gathering of the Jews, my father and mother tried to escape that night from the house before they took us away to the ghetto. (Vera Slyomovics, interview by Steven Spielberg Survivors of the Shoah Visual History Foundation, Netanya, Israel, December 11, 1997)

Dreams link dead family members with the living, provide warnings, and reward good deeds. They are operational in this world, intruding in the here-and-now by trespassing from the dream world to alter the course of our everyday life. The most convincing proof is the story of Julius, my father's oldest brother, a concentration camp survivor, who had been drafted to serve in the Austro-Hungarian Army during World War I. The whole Slyomovics family, according to my mother's tale, could recount the precise dream that kept him alive during the worst battle:

> I interviewed your Uncle Julius in Carlsbad [Karlovy Vary] in 1947. Whenever he came to Carlsbad from Prague, he stayed with us. His wife and young seven-year-old boy died in the camps together, but

he did not, two daughters and a son survived. I asked him, "Yehiel-baci [Uncle Julius], how did you survive, how did you survive the trenches [of World War I]?" He said, "There was a poor man in Vermi-ziv, and every Friday I would visit the old man who lived alone and I'd bring him food for *shabbas*." Yehiel lay in the trenches for a few days and the Allied forces were coming closer. This was the Italian front, on the Battle of the Piave River [June 15–23, 1918]. Bombs were every-where. He was exhausted and fell asleep. All of a sudden he felt a tap on his shoulder. This same old man shouted, "Get up, get up fast, and run." So he got up and ran. Within a few minutes, a bomb exploded, the trench was in flames. No one survived but him. In 1948, while we were in hiding in Bratislava [Czechoslovakia] before we crossed the border illegally [to the American sector of Austria], my father came to me in my dream and said, "Shortly you'll find freedom." I woke up your father and told him. Two days later we were given escorts to cross the mountains. A week later, people were shot using the same route. Although your father screams and cries in his sleep, he says he never dreams. But he believes in my dreams. (Vera Slyomovics, interview by author, Vancouver, Canada, August 19, 2010)

The ease with which my dead grandparents visit my mother regularly in her dreams—over twenty years ago my mother informed me that her father, the linguist, learned to converse in English—exemplifies for me the inter-rupted search for closure that, for example, Kenneth Feinberg in charge of disbursing the 9/11 Fund hoped reparation protocols would bring about but do not. Researchers Hanna Kaminer and Peretz Lavie contend that a marked decrease in recounting survivor dreams reveals long-term adjustment to trauma.[59] My mother disagrees, as do many Native Americans, for whom dream visits from the ancestors are honored; the more she dreams, the bet-ter she says she feels. If my maternal grandfather, Sandor Samuel Hollander, does not appear regularly in my mother's dreams—which I interpret as a good sign because she is made happy by narrating them to the family—she becomes anxious. She always begins, "I dreamed about my father. He spoke to me in Hungarian and said, 'I am here. I watch over you. Don't worry.' He always made me feel so good" (Vera Slyomovics, interview by author, Van-couver, Canada, August 24, 2010). When I'm not near her, many of our phone conversations begin with a dream retelling, which I only began to write down in the past few years:

In my dream I said, "Please Dad, talk to me, I need you. I used to see you so often." He answered, "I'm busy." I had asked his help for your father's financial deals. "You are not to worry, sweetheart, you'll always have everything. I watch over you." You notice he didn't make specific promises. I told him I fell. I had to tell somebody. "Throw away your slippers. Don't be so tight." Actually it was my fault. I was so sleepy I put the right slipper on the left foot and vice versa. (Vera Slyomovics, interview by author, Vancouver, Canada, October 17, 2009)

Dreams recounted to me continue like an inexhaustible stream, but unlike her spoken and videotaped Holocaust testimonies, which understandably retell events I have heard repeatedly over decades, her dreams always surprise me with fresh visions. Psychoanalyst Heinz Kohut, a Viennese Jew who experienced the trauma of forced immigration in 1939, devised the term "self-state dreams" to account for images of trauma in dreams not easily open to talk or free association, yet to the listener appear eminently interpretable because they so obviously relate to the dreamer's current state and preoccupations.[60] There was one my mother narrated to me in October 2012 that concerned Alois Knittel, the *SS Oberscharführer* in charge of Jewish women slave laborers in Markkleeberg Camp. My mother never knew his name because, like many camp inmates, she was familiar only with her tormentors' faces. Nor did she see him again after Markkleeberg Camp inmates were dispersed into the Death March of April 1945. After the war, attempts were made to indict him in German courts, but he was able to maintain sufficient legal confusion about his identity. Knittel died in West Germany in 1962, never serving time in prison.[61] But in dreams begin possibilities:

We were the first to escape—*Bubbe*, me, Fayge, and the two Frenchwomen from the Death March, leaving Markkleeberg. The Frenchwomen were prisoners of war and they said that the *Oberscharführer* was nice to them, didn't make them work like us. He said he wouldn't take them on the Death March but release them in some city. They all spoke German beautifully. "Vera," they said, "we know exactly when we leave camp." "Good, I'm ready." "Speak to Fayge as our third." "I have so many friends in this group. Can't we take them instead? "We only know Fayge and you from the Jewish women. We're afraid to take chances. What if your friends change their minds? Then the two of us would march alone and if we're not five marching, the Nazis will notice and catch us." I liked them [French women] very much, especially the general's daughter who had no legs. They gave me their addresses in France to stay in touch but in the spring of 1945 all I could think of was finding my father. I lost so many good people. Remember, I told you all about the *Oberscharführer*, the one that beat me and gave me food for *Bubbe*? He never searched for us after the five of us escaped from the line of marchers, even though he was in charge of organizing the Death March. I am suspicious. I wonder if he realized we were gone. I dreamt about him last night for the first time [October 19, 2012]. I saw him so clearly. The *Oberscharführer* was no longer wearing the SS uniform. He said to me, "I am now doing social work. I try to make up for all my sins." In my dream, you know. (Vera Slyomovics, interview by author, Vancouver, Canada, October 20, 2012)

CHAPTER 5

Children of Survivors: The "Second Generation" in Storytelling, Tourism, and Photography

The Holocaust comes to me not only through my mother's dreams and anecdotes or because I am the namesake of my murdered paternal grandmother, but through additional family rites—the pursuit of reparation claims, visits to actual cemetery headstones, memorial plaques with no bodies beneath, found and created photographs, and, always, by means of truncated stories whose chronology and horror I imaginatively smooth over even as I reconstruct them. Anthropological conventions about reflexivity relate the ethnographer's background (that is, positionality) to her research projects, but, in writing about Germany's Holocaust reparations, I note that emic categories of the postwar Jewish community already label me "second generation," the term to designate the offspring of Holocaust survivors. Since the 1960s, we are numbered intergenerationally according to parental experiences in much the same way sociological research characterizes the first, foreign-born immigrant generation reproducing their native-born, second-generation immigrant children. It is easy for most native-born Canadians and Americans to slough off the label immigrant, especially a second-generation one; this is not so for the "second-generation" child of a Holocaust survivor parent. Although many of my Montreal childhood friends shared my background of survivor and refugee parents, I was introduced to the category "children of Holocaust survivors" and the acronym COS, "children of survivors," in New York City when I was a graduate student at the Jewish Theological Seminary and the 1975 issue of the journal *Response*, titled "The Holocaust: Our Generation Looks Back," came into my hands.[1]

It started slowly and then became a flood of articles and books, meetings and conferences that debated and discussed the second generation of COS, just when we reached adulthood and began to speak for ourselves and to research findings by psychiatrists and psychologists. In 1977, the year I graduated from the Jewish Theological Seminary, writer Helen Epstein, daughter of Czechoslovakian survivors, published "Heirs of the Holocaust: The Lingering Legacy for Children of Survivors," a cover story in the Sunday *New York Times Magazine* that resonated to many like myself in Canada and the United States. That article became a book, published by Epstein in 1979: *Children of the Holocaust: Conversations with Sons and Daughters of Survivors.*[2] After moving to Berkeley in 1977 to pursue graduate studies, I responded to a student-newspaper announcement of a meeting of the "second generation." Convened by a mental health specialist, the gathering included about a hundred people, whose tales of parent survivors widened my own narrow definitions of my family and tattooed concentration camp Jews. Each one recounted their COS story, reminding me of the transcription published in the 1975 issue of *Response*, "Five Children of Survivors: A Conversation," with its measured conclusion about the efficacy and importance of those early meetings in the 1970s:

> We have seriously questioned the merits of such an article [transcription of COS meeting]. Have we anything unique to say? Are we truly representative of survivors' children and therefore qualified to speak for them? Are we over-attributing our personal concerns and dilemmas to the horrors our parents survived? The answer to each of these questions is, we believe, a qualified "no." We neither think we have offered profound illuminations on the conditions of survivors' children, nor do we claim that what we said can speak for all who share our backgrounds. But we and future generations will have to consider the continuing effects of the Holocaust and the influence it has had on our lives. The reflections in this article represent our attempts to come to terms with the very personal responses we have necessarily made to the Holocaust.[3]

Another important benchmark occurred on November 4–5, 1979, when a large conference was held in New York City on the topic of the second generation, featuring Helen Epstein as keynote speaker, supplemented by panels with psychiatrists Leo Eitinger, Hillel Klein, Vivian G. Rakoff, William Niederland, Henry Krystal, and Yael Danieli. Ambivalent, emotional responses by COS audience members were directed against the panels of mental health professionals, some of whom were conference presenters as well as Holocaust survivors and parents.[4] Soon more international conferences were convened, and the second generation formed local and national organizations. Such research and conferences yielded no uniform conclusion, and even some disagreements about the burning issue that preoccupies children of Holocaust survivors: the transmittal of intergenerational trauma from survivor parents to COS and from the "second generation," the COS who become parents, to their own children, who are labeled the "third generation."[5]

Many early pioneering investigations into second-generation COS characteristics were done in Montreal by Montreal-based psychologists and psychiatrists on the Montreal Jewish community. This has implications for findings given the uniqueness of that city's survivor-refugee population. Although early researchers rarely highlight the city's high postwar demographic concentration of survivors, one exception is the article published in 1966 by psychiatrist Vivian G. Rakoff, who notes the unusual profile of Montreal's immigrant patients:

> it has been my experience—similar to that of "other psychiatrists"—that I am seeing more adolescents than one would expect whose parents are survivors of the holocaust. . . . It could be argued that the population I encounter is unique; perhaps because I work in Montreal, which is one of the immigrant cities of the post-war world, I encounter more rootless refugees than in other cities. But the parents, the actual victims in these cases, are not conspicuously broken people.[6]

Based on a 1978 survey of heads of households conducted in my hometown, sociologist Morton Weinfeld concluded that fully 20 percent of Jewish Montrealers self-identified as Holocaust survivors. Relative to the American Jewish population where they constituted barely two per cent, Weinfeld foresaw a greater impact and legacy for the Holocaust survivor community.[7] By the 1980s in Montreal, there were an estimated 30,000 survivors and descendants, constituting close to a third of the diminishing numbers of the Jewish community.

I am most interested in Canadian studies by Robert Krell, the University of British Columbia professor of psychiatry my parents and I know personally,

John J. Sigal, professor of psychiatry at McGill University, and Vivian G.
Rakoff when he was a psychiatrist at the Jewish General Hospital in Montreal, because their studies included participants drawn from my two home
communities, Vancouver and Montreal. Moreover, Sigal's frequent coauthor,
McGill University sociologist Morton Weinfeld, is well known to my family
(see Chapter 4). In 1982, John J. Sigal summarized the 1960s-era, Montreal-
based research findings produced by himself, Vivian G. Rakoff, Nathan Epstein, and Bernard Trossman:

> From two different centers in Montreal, the Jewish General Hospital
> and McGill University's Student Counselling Center, came the first
> reports of a special, psychologically unhealthy quality of the relation-
> ship between survivors and their children, which resulted in difficul-
> ties for the children. Rakoff, later joined by Sigal and Epstein, two
> psychoanalysts, reported an unusual degree of mutual involvement,
> an enmeshment between parent and child. The children were ex-
> pected to share in the unyielding intensity of the parents' mourning
> and to complete the interrupted lives of dead members of the family.
> They were not only expected to replace dead relatives, but to become
> the idealized, perfect version of them. Any suggestion of an unwilling-
> ness to share the parents' experiences of suffering, victimization, or
> suspiciousness of the surrounding world, any hint that they wished to
> lead their own lives or to follow their own ambitions, was met with
> protest and outrage by the parents, as if it were a betrayal or an aban-
> donment. As a result the children were reported to be guilty and de-
> pressed, and to feel alienated from the community. They were also
> observed to be rebellious and, if there were more than one child in
> the family, to demonstrate an excessive degree of rivalry with each
> other. Trossman, observing young university students, noted that
> their rebelliousness sometimes took the form of dating non-Jews, in
> one case even a student of German extraction.[8]

Actually, Sigal's example of adolescent COS rebellious behavior is misclassi-
fied as dating a German girl, when, in fact, the rebellion concerned an angry
young girl who failed all subjects at school except German.[9] Given that so
many of us grew up hearing and often learning Yiddish at home, it is possible that doing well in German, a cognate language, exemplifies linguistic
familiarity, even continuity with our parent's past. Yet, for Trossman, the

student who did well in German is "conflicted in seeing the irrationality of his [sic] parents' attitudes yet being aware of the suffering that resulted in these attitudes. Often his [sic] only solution is to become mistrustful and paranoid like his parents."[10] Their study population was formed by culling respondents with Jewish-sounding names from the 1971 electoral lists in Montreal census tracts with Jewish majorities. They cautioned: "In the areas examined here, and in the areas of autonomy and ties to the family (Sigal and Weinfeld 1984) there is, fortunately, a lack of evidence for the transmission to the majority of the second generation of the negative effects documented for the first generation that survived prolonged, excessive stress."[11]

COS stories, including mine, for I was certainly a rebellious adolescent during the 1960s, are often described in terms of Freudian allegories pointing to our survivor-parent heritage, while the psychological literature remains silent about the confusing and conflicting dynamics of our Montreal contexts: a revolutionary push for Quebec separation from Canada with consequences feared by Montreal Jewry framed by the larger cataclysmic sexual, artistic, and political movements of the 1960s that further distanced my generation from that of our parents, regardless of immigrant, refugee, or Holocaust background.

Critics of such early studies were well aware of problems endemic to most clinical studies in psychology: participants are drawn from groups of students or adolescents who sought therapy and, therefore, constitute self-selected and nonrepresentative samples. A study of 1,116 Jewish orphans under eighteen, young Holocaust survivors from European displaced persons (DP) camps brought to Canada in 1948 and resettled in thirty-eight communities across eight provinces produced a very different picture. Many of the adoption placements involving European Jewish youth recently emerged from camps were not successful; however, the fears of the Canadian Jewish Congress War Orphans Rescue Movement that the youth would present massive psychic wounds occasioned by multiple and traumatic processes of survival, displacement, and immigration were not confirmed, according to a review of the resettlement project fifteen years later:

We were warned that, because of the background of these youths, we could expect mental breakdowns and that we would mortgage this generation to pay for the upkeep of many of these young people who might have to spend the balance of their days in asylums or under other protective institutions. Indeed at one point we began to wonder whether there was any purpose in transferring the afflictions of these people from Europe to Canada, since in the new country they would not be able to escape the impact of the old. Fortunately, we took the counsel of a few psychiatrists, who held that such a depressing prognosis was buncombe, and how right they were! Of the 1,116 children who were brought to Canada under the War Orphan Plan, less than a score were subject to mental breakdowns. In fact, we were correctly informed, as it turned out, that there would be no more cases of juvenile delinquency and mental troubles among any given one hundred refugee children than there would be among one hundred children of the highest income group living in Canada.[12]

Clinical observations based on individual case histories are inevitably at odds with large randomized samplings. Evidence for "second generation" psychopathologies runs throughout clinically based studies but diminishes when data are correlated and compared with Jews who are not survivors' children and with non-Jews of the same age. There is significant research in the literature that contradicts the effects of survivor parents on COS as suggested in the early studies. "Holocaust families," the accepted term for possessing at least one parent-survivor, did not uniformly manifest aberrant behaviors that were derived from frameworks in search of developmental trauma across multiple generations. As I report, transcribe, and describe my family's consciously articulated feelings, attitudes, reminiscences, and dreams—the very stuff of ethnography—I too, question the unconscious connections between my parents' experience and mine. I find more resonance with the views of Eva Hoffman, who was raised in Vancouver and whose book *After Such Knowledge* probes her membership in what she prefers to call the "hinge generation," because of our deep and organic bond to our parents and grandparents:

> The second generation is the hinge generation—the point at which the past is transmuted into history or into myth. It is in the second generation, with its intense loyalties to the past, that the danger of turning the realities of the historical experience into frozen formulae of collective memory is the greatest, but it is also in that interval that we have the best opportunity of apprehending history in all its affective and moral complexity. . . . Paradoxically, I believe that if we are to guard it well, then we need to achieve a certain thoughtful separa-

tion from received ideas as, in our personal lives, we need to separate ourselves thoughtfully and with sympathy from our persecuted
parents.[13]

As the daughter and granddaughter of Holocaust survivors, I felt most
implicated in my family's reparation protocols based on an acute awareness
of their financial instability, especially because my grandmother's monthly
Wiedergutmachung payments helped fund my undergraduate college tuition.
As a direct second-generation beneficiary of my grandmother's German
reparation money (in relation to her reparations, am I simultaneously third
generation?), I would visit her each month in Brooklyn to receive her generous contribution from the German check to help pay my Barnard College
tuition. When I obtained my doctorate, she insisted on buying me the expensive doctoral cap, gown, and hood of a University of California, Berkeley
graduate, because her granddaughter should never have to rent but must
own prestigious garments of achievement, a fact I recall each time I don
them, with my tears.

COS: Appropriation, Restoration, and Postmemory

Intergenerational COS memories find a literary form in the subgenre of
mother-daughter memoirs to which anthropologists contribute their share.[14]
When writing about my mother and writing as an anthropologist, I consider *Das, was geschah* (that which happened), poet Paul Celan's words to
refer to the Holocaust and to what language finds difficult to name and say
aloud.[15] Some COS engage in oral history of our elders, search archives for
the fates of destroyed families, name children for the murdered departed,
and tour European sites relevant to family histories. These expressive acts,
according to the theoretical writings of theater critic and performer Richard
Schechner, are subsumed under his idea of the "restoration of behavior,"
which he succinctly states is what is " 'out there' distant from 'me' ":

Restoration of behavior is living behavior treated as a film director
treats a strip of film. These strips of behavior can be rearranged or
reconstructed; they are independent of the causal systems (social, psychological, technological) that brought them into existence. They have
a life of their own. The original "truth" or "source" of behavior may be

lost, ignored or contradicted—even while this truth or source is apparently being honored or observed. . . . Put in personal terms, restored behavior is "me behaving as if I am someone else." But this someone else may also be "me in another state of feeling/being." Performing my dream, re-experiencing my childhood trauma, showing you what I did yesterday. Also social actions: the enactment of events whose origins can't be located in individuals, if they can be located at all. Sometimes these events are attributed to collective individuals like the Books of Moses, the *Iliad* of Homer, the Mahabharata of Vyas; sometimes they belong anonymously to folklore, legend, myth. Restored behavior offers to both individuals and groups the chance to become someone else "for the time being," or the chance to become what they once were. Or even, and most often, to rebecome what they never were.[16]

Applying Schechner's theories means being attentive to the stages of performative events, recognizing reflexively my place in all this as well as larger sociocultural contexts, yet remaining alert to reinventions, whether they are touristic reenactments or familial adaptive strategies to the painful past. Schechner's metaphor of restored behavior encompasses cinematic, visual, and ritual performance practices that illuminate the public ways in which my family passed on the Holocaust to me in the forms of storytelling, photography, visits to former hometowns, names given to offspring, and more evolving rituals of remembrance.

I am named, for example, after my paternal grandmother who was part of the Czech family camp deported from Theresienstadt/Terezín to be gassed at Auschwitz, while my brother carries the names of both paternal and maternal grandfathers killed in Theresienstadt/Terezín and Mauthausen-Melk camps respectively. Were I to begin with the names of my grandparents, I would skip over obvious generational links that assign their names to my brother and me, since naming children after deceased family members is certainly not unique to Jews or Holocaust survivors but cross-culturally a vibrant practice.[17] My parents share the belief that the dead live on partly through our names, evoked each time they call out to us. My mother defines my brother and me, her three grandchildren, and, so far, four great-grandchildren as the best evidence and living proof that Hitler failed. She adopted influential writings by Toronto-based philosopher Emil Ludwig Fackenheim, whom she heard speak on several occasions. Fackenheim's thesis elaborates practical theological responses for the post-Holocaust Jew not to hand Hitler a "posthumous victory." My mother freely borrows his concepts to live her life also in "revenge against Hitler," by surviving, prospering, having children, and practicing Judaism.[18] In turn, my grandmother, looking back at her eventful life, including being three times widowed— her first husband was my grandfather killed in Mauthausen-Melk Camp, the second was a cousin of the first and a Holocaust survivor, and the third, a survivor of the Rudolf Kasztner trainload of rescued Hungarian Jews[19]—elaborated to me her version of Fackenheim's thesis, an insistence that she was never bitter: "I never lost a father or a child and from that one daughter now I have five. And each time I married, I got a better husband."

Names of the Holocaust dead are carried over into the next generations, sometimes in translation or sometimes evoked simply by a shared initial consonant. As visible and viewable artifacts, my paternal grandparents' names appear on the wall of Prague's Pinkas Synagogue, opposite the main nave devoted to Bohemian and Moravian Jews: "Slomovits Chajim 8. VIII 1873–11.II 1944 Blima 1.II 1875–18.v 1944" (Figure 7). Between 1954 and 1959, Czech painters Václav Boštík and Jiří John inscribed 77,297 names of murdered Bohemian Jews, followed by birth and death dates. After 1968, the year of the failed Prague Spring, the synagogue building was closed for decades, supposedly for repairs, and the names were said to have disappeared. After the fall of Czechoslovakia's Communist regime, the project to rewrite the names and reopen the Pinkas Synagogue to the public was completed by 1996, however, with this caveat by Jewish Museum curators:

> The text of the inscriptions was compiled from card indexes, which were drawn up shortly after the war on the basis of extant transport papers, registration lists and survivor's accounts. The names of Holocaust victims, together with their dates of birth and death, are inscribed on all the interior walls. Where the precise date of death is not known—which is generally the case—the date of deportation to the ghettos and extermination camps in the east is stated instead— this is usually the last information we have on the victims.[20]

The Pinkas Synagogue adjoins the ancient cemetery of Prague's Jewish ghetto. The former synagogue took on a cemetery function relinquishing the role of a place of organized Jewish prayer to become a monumental, albeit

Figure 7. Paternal grandparents names inscribed on the Pinkas synagogue wall, Prague. Photo by the author.

partial indoor gravestone that memorializes the dead, because no genuine headstone may be erected absent physical remains. Wall inscriptions are replete with errors, misspelled family names, and wrong death dates. No matter. My mother and I went with my son as if paying a visit to our dead in the cemetery. It was for us to bring together the scattered pieces: their names inscribed here before us, their bodies burnt in Auschwitz and dumped sixty miles from where we stood in Theresienstadt/Terezín Camp. Although names were freshly repainted a mere two years before our visit in the 1990s, already an aura of sanctity reigned with candles, piped-in synagogue music, and signs prohibiting photography. I was compelled to photograph my grandparents' names, so my mother obliged by distracting the guard with queries in Czech. The flashing camera bulb elicited outraged cries, as if precious painted images of a representation of a symbol of annihilation were threatened with extinction by my acts of photographing. A Czech museum guide leading Spanish tourists reprimanded us in English for breaking the holy silence of the place. My mother replied to him (and incidentally to the wide-eyed Spaniards caught in our crossfire) that this place belonged to us, not him, and that we were paying our respects to our murdered family. This place was not a Christian church, she told him in Czech, and we were Jews engaged in our noisy mourning rituals.

I mailed out the image, first enlarging and enhancing my paternal grandparents' names, to descendants and relatives of their ten children, namely, my father's seven sisters and two brothers—among whom were two sisters killed in Nazi camps, my father and one brother who escaped through their Czechoslovakian Brigade service, two of the youngest sisters who entered Palestine clandestinely, and four siblings who survived various internments in concentration camps. These photographs were understood by recipients as mnemonic devices to be displayed in domestic interiors, an acknowledgment of absence and loss. They are artifacts derived from "postmemory," the term used to characterize COS memory mediated through photography or family testimonies, following definitions proposed by literary critic Marianne Hirsch:

> Postmemory is distinguished from memory by generational distance and from history by deep personal connection. Postmemory is a very powerful and particular form of memory precisely because its connection to its object or source is mediated not through recollection but through an imaginative investment and creation. . . . Postmemory characterizes the experience of those who grew up dominated by narratives that preceded their birth, whose own belated stories are evacuated by the stories of the previous generation shaped by traumatic events that can be neither understood nor recreated. I have developed this notion in relation to children of Holocaust survivors.[21]

Photography is the preeminent medium to discover encounters with familial losses because, as Roland Barthes informs, photographs possess the strongest indexical relationship to their referents. There is the incontestable actuality of a human in a photograph being once alive and no possibility to "deny that *the thing has been there*."[22] Critic Susan Sontag concludes that those "robbed of their past seem to make the most fervent picture takers, at home or abroad."[23] In a famous passage about her childhood, Sontag reveals a divide in her life brought about by viewing photographs of Nazi death camps:

> One's first encounter with the photographic inventory of ultimate horror is a kind of revelation, the prototypically modern revelation: a negative epiphany. For me it was photographs of Bergen-Belsen and

Dachau which I came across by chance in a bookstore in Santa Monica in July 1945. Nothing I have seen—in photographs or in real life—ever cut me as sharply, deeply, instantaneously. Indeed, it seems plausible to me to divide my life into two parts, before I saw those photographs (I was twelve) and after.[24]

It is difficult for me to view photographs or films by others about the Holocaust. Writing, not visual depictions, is my preferred medium. When I was eight, a textbook from my third grade Montreal Yiddish class recounted the adventures of young Serele and Berele in drawings. While my French class taught that same year followed mundane adventures of Jeanne and Pierre, children teaching children the vocabulary of Parisian fruit and vegetable markets, our Yiddish class learned about Serele and Berele who celebrated the Jewish holiday of Hanukah despite starvation in Majdanek Camp. My childhood nightmares began with opening the eggshell-blue cardboard covers of the Yiddish text to enter their world, the prison universe of simple line drawings, emaciated stick figures in black-and-white striped uniforms, haunting sketches foreshadowing the graphic style of Art Spiegelman's masterly *Maus*.

Observations by Marianne Hirsch and Susan Sontag, however, hold true for picture-taking projects in which I rephotograph when and what I can to create a variety of my own images as substitutes for this much-lamented loss: when my mother was deported to the Mátészalka Ghetto with her maternal grandmother, Pearl Shreter Elefant, she filled much of the space inside her single allotted suitcase with photographs. She mentioned the elegant, wine-colored album lovingly captioned in Hungarian by her father that documented her life in images from birth in 1926 to schoolgirl pastimes abruptly cut short at eighteen in 1944. Had my mother left her album at home in Bishtine, she believes she would have found her prewar photographs intact on her return visit, immediately after the camp liberation in search of her father:

Our house was completely emptied. The local people dug up our basement but missed one thing, a ring my father bought me in Budapest before the war, which I gave you. I had gone back with *Bubbe*, and I kept saying, let's get out of here. They were looting everything. I was a little afraid. We had already heard about Magda; her husband and brother came back alive from the camps. Then they went back home to Hungary, there was $10,000 in the cellar, and they were both shot because of the money. So I went off to Prague and sent my mother to Bucharest to her sister, your great-aunt Hani. (Vera Slyomovics, interview by author, Vancouver, November 27, 2012)

Once members of my family disembarked together at the Auschwitz train platform, the camp procedures of separation began: the stripping away of family, belongings, suitcases, and photograph album, and the ensuing nakedness and selection process that my mother recounted to the Spielberg Holocaust project interviewer:

I have a grandmother and her name was Pearl Shreter Elefant. In those times a grandmother was supposed to be little but she was 5'9" tall, and was very scholarly and very history minded. She came from Transylvania and married my grandfather [David Elefant], and I stayed with her when everybody left town, for nine months. I was hiding still, I was hiding and then I left my hiding place and came to stay with her. I had wonderful memories. One of the memories I will always remember is her walking down the paths and orchards. And she went to the crematorium, but she didn't know, and she was holding her little grandchildren in both hands [Ruth and Oskar], and was taking both of her grandchildren and walked straight with enormous pride, no tears. I have the most wonderful memories of my grandmother. (Vera Slyomovics, interview by Steven Spielberg Survivors of the Shoah Visual History Foundation, Netanya, Israel, December 11, 1997)

Place and Origins

Seeking the safety and richness of my prewar family history in Europe, I was encouraged by my parents in my childhood fascination with folklore collecting, especially legends of the hometown miracle-working rabbi, Rebele Mordkhele Leifer, whose surname was also confusingly pronounced or spelled Laufer. His gravesite, still a place of pilgrimage, is located in my mother's birthplace of Bishtine. To search out the ways in which my family and the Jews of my parent's ancestral villages struggle within the structure of continuous reminiscence, storytelling, and selective suppression of memories, I called upon my mother, who helped me interview her fellow survivors and interpret their words from Hungarian and Czech wherever they resided in England, Canada, the United States, and Israel. Although in 1998 my father chose to return to western Czechoslovakia and Karlovy Vary/Carlsbad, where he moved with his family in 1922 to spend his youth and young adulthood, in fact, my parents' background connects me to a different place in East-Central Europe, a region designated in different ways by the various ethnic and linguistic groups who live there as Subcarpathian Rus, Carpathian Ruthenia, Zakarpatya, or Marmarosh (Yiddish), while other names are Tschechische (Czech) Marmarosh, or (Romanian) Maramures. Place names in my family's ancestral province have been inflected in many tongues, depending on shifting linguistic allegiances of speakers and listeners. *Marmarosh*, the Yiddish pronunciation of Hungarian Marmaros, had been the northeasternmost district or province of the Austro-Hungarian Empire, straddling the eastern range of the Carpathian Mountains. This crossroads location ensured that, after World War I, the several newly formed yet geographically indeterminate nation states of Czechoslovakia, Romania, Hungary and the Soviet Ukraine would contest possession of its territory.[25] Accordingly, Marmarosh inhabitants changed nationalities the way other people change shirts. In a popular joke, a man tells his listener: I was born in Austro-Hungary, I grew up in Czechoslovakia, I have lived in the Republic of Carpatho-Ukraine, Romania, and Hungary, I resided in the Soviet Union, and now I am a citizen of the Ukraine. The listener replies, you must have traveled a great deal. No, the man answers, I never moved, I'm from Marmarosh.[26]

Chauvinist histories explain the shifting boundaries of the pre-1918 Austro-Hungarian Marmarosh province on the basis of parochial, nationalist agendas. According to Hungarian irredentists, for example, Marmarosh (like present-day Transylvania, now part of Romania) is a lost Hungarian-speaking territory. Indeed, the Republic of Carpatho-Ukraine was the shortest-lived state in history. Overlapping with sections of northern Marmarosh province, it existed a mere twenty-four hours, declared independence from Czechoslovakia on March 15, 1939, and one day later, was formally annexed by Hungary.[27] At war's end in 1945, northern Marmarosh was taken over by the Ukraine under the name of the Transcarpathian Oblast (district), as Soviet historians heralded the region's reuniting with its ancestral Slavic motherland. Since 1918, the province of Marmarosh, divided among Czechoslovakia, Romania, Hungary, and the Soviet Union, has ceased to exist as a political entity but lives on in the collective memory of its former Jewish inhabitants currently residing in New York City, Tel Aviv, and the present-day Transcarpathia region of independent Ukraine. Among surviving Jews, the pre-1918 Austro-Hungarian idea of an intact Marmarosh Province is sustained through organizations and institutions that continue to represent a place that exists primarily by way of a collective will to remember.

Until 1989, I had never seen this region with my own eyes. I confected a social construct of geographically nonspecific tales recounted by parents, relatives, and the larger circle of former inhabitants who would meet at the *landsmanshaft*, or hometown society meetings organized by exiles in Tel Aviv and New York City. Jews from Carpathian Ruthenia/Marmarosh encountered abroad would speak to me because I was not only an ethnographer, but also the daughter of Vera Hollander of Bishtine and Josef Slyomovics of neighboring Vermiziv (Urmezo in Hungarian and Ruske Pole in Czech and Rusyn), or because they wanted their story told to one of their own, or because they believed in scholarship, or even because they loved my mother and would do what they could to help my project, though it meant letting loose the suppressed anguish of decades. But more than that: my mother accompanied me at my request because, at first in the 1980s, I could not bear to research the Holocaust and the destruction of my own particular extended family without her physical presence, a literal hand-holding that enabled me to return to both a communal and an individual past through narrative, photography, and memory with her by my side. Until May 1989, interviews and oral narratives far from the Carpathian region were the only possible sources concerning the subject of my inquiries. Other American Jews had regularly visited ancestral villages in Poland or Hungary. I could not go as a tourist to what had been, during my parents' time between the two world wars, the easternmost Czechoslovak province of Subcarpathian Ruthenia. After World War II, the Soviets annexed the districts of the former Hungarian county of Marmarosh that lay north of the Tisza River to the province of Transcarpathia. Then only the district capital of Uzhgorod (Ungvar in Hungarian), 150 km from my parents' villages, was accessible to travelers on restricted and expensive tours by Intourist, the foreign visitor service of the Soviet Union.

Geographical place, the inhabited locale of corporeal experience, may be lost through the uprooting and dispersal of entire populations by war, systematic persecution, or the redrawing of national boundaries. A "topology of the remembered,"[28] a memory of place expressed in complementary narrative and ritual forms, has arisen among Jews to compensate for the loss of place and people. I too, was entirely dependent on articulated memories by others. My own ethnographic study seemed intertextually focused on ethnographic writings, such as Jewish *yizker bikher* (memorial books) or other forms of self-published folk histories, diaries, and pamphlets, as well as oral narratives.[29] The opposition between memory and narrative, on the one hand, and physical return to a geographical location, on the other, informed both my method and my responses to those who choose either to return or not to visit Marmarosh. Memories narrated by and about my family were difficult to hear (and for them to narrate), whereas traveling alone to what was then Soviet Transcarpathia in 1989 was a carefree, enjoyable adventure that neither enhanced nor negated the vividness of representations conveyed to me through decades of storytelling. With no localized place associations whatsoever, I tramped the Carpathian foothills intrigued by their striking resemblance to upstate New York's Adirondack Mountains. I waded in Bishtine's Terebla River and later ventured further eastward to the nearby towns of Aknaszlatina (now Solotvyno) and Técső (now Tyachiv), home to both sides of my family lineage. I was guided to stretches of the upper Tisza River, where Romania is visible on the other side of the riverbank across wide currents that arise in the nearby Carpathian Mountains to flow over six hundred miles southward across eastern Hungary and into the Danube River. I did not know what I was seeing or if there was anything left from my parent's generation to see. The impossibility of visiting both their villages until 1989 predetermined the primacy of storytelling, narrative, and memory, normally complementary aspects of the experience of place, over the physical reality of my own eventual touristic pilgrimage.

Parenthetically, even now that visits are possible, many of my parent's generation avoid the trip back home. The day of my departure from New York to Budapest, I stopped to visit my great-uncle Jack Brandstein, a camp survivor. He maintained that the recollection of past destruction brings only bitterness so intense that treading on the identical earth and dust where atrocities against Jews took place is unthinkable, "to go there and have pleasure is a sin" (Interview with Jack Brandstein, Forest Hills, New York, May 17, 1989). His wife, my great-aunt Hani, survivor of Bergen-Belsen, informed me that, if I write about their hometown, please credit her husband's name in quoted interviews. I asked if I could write his name as Yankel or Yakov: "No, we're in America. His name is Jack here. We don't go back to Europe"

(Hani Elefant Brandstein, interviewed by the author, Queens, New York, May 17, 1989). My mother's childhood comrade, Peter Iszo Hilman, who immigrated to London after his camp liberation, dated his nervous breakdown to a brief visit back to this birthplace. He undertook the journey "to eradicate certain places from my mind," but remains blessed or cursed with detailed photographic recall and cartographic memory (Peter Iszo Hilman, interview by author and Vera Slyomovics, London, December 15, 1990). The association of a geographical return with ensuing madness or with overpowering memories of persecution and murder, perhaps combined with the fact of long decades of Soviet travel restrictions, served to eliminate for Jews of the Carpathians the possibility of even a transient refreshment of memories in formerly inhabited places. My departure date of May 17, 1989, my maternal grandfather's birthday, was labeled a blessing and good omen for the journey.

Landsmanshaft (Hometown) Cemeteries

What have been the expressive and performative ways for Marmarosh Jews currently living in Tel Aviv and New York City to replicate, commemorate, and represent Marmarosh the place and its murdered Jewish population, numbered at more than sixty thousand? How are images and recollected knowledge of a destroyed past transmitted by ritual performances? Do specific cultural performances do the work of reparation or even reparative justice? How closely bound together are Jewish claims for German reparations and my mother's repertory of ritual acts? Alongside unspoken struggles to apply and receive reparations, I maintain that this particular Jewish and Holocaust-haunted diaspora community has responded not only through narrative and storytelling but also by means of a physical recreation of lost Marmarosh territory that replicates elsewhere what was ineluctably physical, namely, the unvisitable Jewish cemeteries of Marmarosh Province. In New York City, reclaimed Marmarosh takes the form of a *landsmanshaft*-owned cemetery, while, in Tel Aviv, it inhabits the synagogue with its Holocaust memorial, the latter standing in for cemetery rites. In contrast, the remaining Jews in Marmarosh during my visit in 1989 were too few to form the *minyan* of ten adult Jewish males required to conduct full prayers. Although they live in present-day Transcarpathia of the western Ukraine and possess what is lost in New York City and Tel Aviv—the geographical space

with its crucial sites of burial—the narrative is ruptured; instead, the cemetery has become the place of prayer, since all synagogues and other Jewish
spaces were taken over after the war and locally repurposed into sports halls
or private residences.

I begin the topic of recreated cemeteries minus actual bodies with a
description of the diaspora community of New York City. It was first organized in the form of two hometown associations or *landsmanshaftn*, the
Federation of Marmarosh Jews in America, founded in 1924, and the all-
male First Maramaros Young Men's Aid Society, founded in 1912. The two
survived because they preserved and expanded one of the hometown society's original functions as a *khevra kadisha,* or burial society for those
members who died either in New York or during the Holocaust. The *landsmanshaftn* bury and commemorate the American and the Holocaust dead
by maintaining three cemeteries for the former and by honoring in annual
ceremonies the Marmarosh Jews who perished in the Holocaust and received no burial. In the late 1980s, when I was able to attend meetings in
Manhattan, a Marmarosh society member, eighty-six-year old Dovid Katz,
told me to visit the cemetery in Queens because, he declared, that is where
the true history of the American Marmarosh *landsmanshaftn* is inscribed.
When I attended the seventy-fifth reunion weekend in 1987 held at the Con-
cord Hotel in the Catskill Mountains, another member explained the continued importance of the societies' functions despite the notable absence of
a new generation. He recounted the following joke with its rhymed Yiddish
punch line: When a famous Jewish artist had died, the burial society of his
fraternal organization arranged the customary modest ceremony. A delega-
tion of his famous artist friends (presumably non-Jewish or nonpracticing
Jewish artists) protested the lack of fanfare or eulogy, and they claimed such
a famous man belonged to the universal realm of art. The president of the
Jewish burial society replied to the artists: "You may have thought he belonged to art (*kinz*), now you know he belongs to us (*inz*)": *Der man gehert zu
der kinz, aber hister gehert er far inz.*

Belonging is defined by the community as the act of dying, during
which time you publicly announce with whom you will die, the place where
you are to be buried, and who will speak the funeral eulogies. The importance of this communal public identification was emphasized during one of
the bimonthly Marmarosh *landsmanshaft* business meeting held at the
Workmen's Circle building that I attended in March 1987. A senior member, a distant cousin named Haskel Klein, angrily castigated his fellow

Marmarosh brothers for not attending the recent funeral of a member of
the society:

> Even though the funeral took place in Spring Valley, a suburb of
> New York City which is a long distance from most members' homes
> in the city, even though the funeral was on a Monday, a working day
> for the members, even though the funeral took place on the worst
> snow storm of the year and transportation was impossible—if you
> cannot be buried with your *landslayt* around you, what is the point
> in living with them? (Haskel Klein, interview by author, New York,
> March 1987)

Klein's furious rhetorical question reinterprets secular American geography
(a cemetery in Queens) as a shred of Marmarosh territory sanctified by the
presence of the Jewish dead who demand the *mistvah*, the commandment of
mourning rituals. Perhaps only when someone dies and a body is placed in
the ground are claims both to spatial ownership and communal identification finally settled for Marmarosh Jewish immigrants in America.[30]

Bet Marmarosh in Israel: Cemetery and Memorial

For Jews in Israel, where geography is conceived as entirely Jewish, the cemetery that articulates Marmrosh terrain is located within the architectural
space of a Tel Aviv synagogue. Marmarosh House (in Hebrew *Bet Marmarosh*) was dedicated on April 29, 1973 as a central meeting place for the
remaining Jews of Marmarosh in Israel and the Diaspora. The three-story
building's exterior facade is adorned with a mosaic of a six-branched cande-
labrum, symbolizing the six million dead, and a sign states that it is both a
synagogue (*bet knesset*) and a memorial house (*bet zikaron*). The iconography of Holocaust mourning and memory adds to the traditional decor of the
Jewish synagogue. The first floor combines contrasting themes of sacred Judaism and secular Marmarosh. While the eastern wall is furnished with
ritual objects characteristic of a house of prayer, including the ark containing the Torah scrolls, a fixture unusual in a synagogue stands opposite. It is a glass painting in folk style depicting the map of the pre-1918
Austro-Hungarian province of Marmarosh, bounded by the names of the
Carpathians, Bukovina, Satmar and Hungary hand-painted in Hebrew

script. A second glass painting represents the main synagogue in the town of Over Viso, located south of the Tisza River, in former Marmarosh and current Romania. As the congregation prays, it faces the Holy Ark containing the Torah scrolls. Behind their backs is the map of Marmarosh, the artistic representation of their European-based brotherhood. This is an unusual instance of Jewish devotional practice backed up literally and figuratively by a parallel and competing religion of secular memory. It is unconventional to decorate the actual prayer room of a synagogue with drawings and maps, especially if they commemorate a former homeland. When such folk paintings are found in diaspora synagogues, they usually depict an imaginary Jerusalem and Holy Land. Reversing the customary iconography which equates the Promised Land with the Holy Land for most diaspora communities, Marmarosh refugees and immigrants to Israel choose to picture the paradise lost of Ukrainian Transcarpathia or Czechoslovakian Subcarpathian Ruthenia or Austro-Hungarian Marmarosh in their synagogue. While in exile in Marmarosh, Israel was the yearned-for object; once attained, it has not eliminated a countervailing dynamic that appears to engender the reproduction of endless structures of remembered exile.

Another heterodox feature in the layout of the synagogue is the memorial room, *heder hazikaron*, which I maintain functions as the equivalent of the cemeteries that the people of Marmarosh are unable or unwilling to visit. The memorial room is a small square space kept perpetually dark except for small eternal lights. In the center is a large black tombstone engraved with the one hundred and sixty names of Marmarosh villages and districts. Around the walls, district by district, further subdivided village by village, are memorial plaques etched with names of the dead. The room functions at once as a metaphorical cemetery, because there can be no corpses, and as an actual cemetery, due not only to the presence of recreated gravestones but also because it is opened to the community during the commemorative *yizkor* prayers and *yartsayt* anniversary occasions in accordance with rituals of mourning. While Bet Marmarosh shares some of the iconographic features of the Holocaust memorial at the Yad Vashem Heroes and Martyrs Memorial Authority in Jerusalem, it is functionally a synagogue for study and prayer into which a cemetery has been incorporated. As a synagogue and a cemetery, the building serves as a site of tourist pilgrimage during the spring "memorial season": "Marmorosh House in Tel-Aviv considers itself a center for Marmorosh Jews in Israel and elsewhere in the world. Many tourists of Marmorosh extraction visiting Israel find an opportunity to come to Marmorosh

House. Yearly ceremonies in commemoration of the Holocaust victims originating from Maramorosh are held there."[31]

The Memorial Book: Indigenous Processes of Narrative Memory

Survivors from Marmarosh clearly articulate the ordering in time of place and space in which their communal memorial tombstone precedes written narratives. Other Jewish hometown societies made it their first priority to commemorate the history of their demolished communities by writing and publishing memorial books immediately after World War II, but the Maramarosh *landsmanshaftn* were clear about the primary focus of their cultural memorializing. In the preface to their *yizer bukh* (memorial book) published as late as 1980, the authors state,

> Once the project of the erection of Marmoros House had been brought to successful fruition, there resurfaced the idea of publishing a Book of Marmoros. In the years preceding the construction of Marmoros House, the committee members had been unable to agree as to which project should be attended first. What was more important, first to put up the house or first to publish the Book of Marmoros? So now the building had arisen, they proceeded to the second project.[32]

Certain features of the Marmarosh *yizker bukh* depart from the typological description offered in Jack Kugelmass and Jonathan Boyarin's moving collection of memorial books in translation, *From a Ruined Garden: The Memorial Books of Polish Jewry.*[33] For example, the *Marmarosh Book* was written in Hebrew with an English preface, not in Yiddish, perhaps reflecting its Israeli origins and the fact that Hungarian, not Yiddish, was a primary language for many Jews from the region. Also *yizker bikher*, according to Kugelmass and Boyarin, reverse the traditional order of Jewish mourning practices, whereas the Marmarosh synagogue-cemetery-memorial house orders correctly the two mourning injunctions: first to bury and then to remember. Unlike a *yizker bukh*, the Marmarosh synagogue, with its adjoining recreated cemetery, allows Holocaust victims to receive their proper burial at last and to permit mourners their visits and prayers over gravesites. Finally, the Marmarosh synagogue-cum-cemetery is a private, independent, spontaneous commemorative gesture that may be construed as a series of ritual acts and icons set up to complement, supplement, or stand in quiet opposition to the Israeli state-built and organized civic Holocaust memorials such as Yad Vashem. The people of Marmarosh in Israel may or may not participate in Yom Hashoah, Israel's nationally mandated Holocaust Day, or other activities sponsored by Yad Vashem, the national memorial site to the Holocaust.

Their Marmarosh memorial book is an official record of an entire region's past, not of an individual *shtetl* or town. Privately, many friends, relatives, and other subscribers to the *Marmarosh Book* have voiced reservations concerning its emphasis on historical figures drawn largely from a religious, orthodox, or Hasidic past at the expense of a more textured, secular history. In response, other writings overlap and flesh out the official record. Alexander Kraus chose to author a personal, self-published history of his natal village titled "Bustino as Remembered," which he began writing in 1980. He dedicates it to "our descendants, wherever they may be in the world, who have only heard, or may only hear about Bustino," and quotes Deuteronomy 32:7, admonishing us to "remember the days of old, think of the generations long ago, ask your fathers to recount it, and your elders to tell the tale." Biblical verses frame a life-long project of recreating in writing a detailed topography and history of his town. Though Kraus told me he chooses never to walk again where he once lived, his first chapter, "A Guided Tour Around Bustino," takes us on an imaginary tour of the village in which "such a walk would have taken three hours and one would have seen everything worth seeing."[34] Kraus explained why writing books is more meaningful than return visits: "Books are always crying. I do not cry. I write about things that were, not things that are dead and gone. I write through the eyes of a child with sweet memories who left in 1927 and only returned summers until 1933" (Alex Kraus, interview by author and Vera Slyomovics, London, December 15, 1990). Not just memory, but written memorialization becomes the means by which to discover an emotional truth hidden in childhood experiences about a world that no longer exists.

Similarly, Kraus's choice of a drawing over photography for his proposed book cover uncovers an unconscious understanding of the myth of photographic truth. In the years before World War I, many Bishtiners who had emigrated to Palestine or America received an emblematic postcard from their hometown (Figure 8). In the foreground, a tiny, almost imperceptible, dark figure is moving diagonally across the postcard. He has just passed my maternal grandmother Elefant's store. It is winter in the Eastern European hamlet, and a light coating of snow dusts the landscape, the houses, a fir tree, and the shadowy distant Carpathian foothills. Two kinds of writing appear on the postcard: superimposed on the picture, Hungarian words caption the name of the street, Utca Részlet, and also greetings from the sender, *Üdvözlet Bustyházárol*, "salutations from Bustyahaza." The only writing within the streetscape that identifies location is the sign on my grandmother's store bearing her family surname of Elefant. Rather than use the well-known photograph, Kraus decided in 1982 on a visit to Israel to commission Alfred (Israel) Gluck (whose wife Marta Kraus comes from Bishtine) to produce a cover drawing that would be based on the famous postcard from prewar Bishtine. Gluck's black-and-white line drawing cropped the photograph, thereby eliminating internal and external writing and replacing it with a large hand-printed street sign, "Our Village," which continued its lettering down to the lower right-hand corner, forming the completed title, "as remembered by Heimus fin Bishtine" (Figure 9). From photograph to redrawing, the tiny human figure has been enlarged, moved into the center and paired with a second figure. Two figures are to be read as cultural representations of the religious Jew and the Carpathian Rusyn peasant. As Kraus relates it, Gluck is a Viennese urban Jew imagining village Jewish life in the remote Carpathian Mountains. Nonetheless, both for Kraus, the folk ethnographer, and Gluck, the artist, photography can no longer remind them of what they once looked like. Photographs, which are presumed to offer an immediate, transparent reproduction of reality, are insufficiently connotative in Barthes' sense—they are not invested with a culturally determined meaning.[35] Writing and its iconic analogue, a line drawing, are preferred over a photographic copy of a world that no longer exists. The photographic reproduction, unlike writing, cannot cry, in Kraus's words, nor can it mourn.

Storytelling: Tales of Rebbele Mordkhele

When my mother was a child in the 1930s in Bishtine, her mother's store, depicted in the postcard, marked the main crossroads of the village. One road led westward to the towns of Khust (Khist in Yiddish)[36] and Munkács (the Hungarian name of the Slavic Mukachevo). A second north-south street curved toward the cemetery that was then on the periphery of the village. By the time I arrived to Bishtine in 1989, a city of 30,000 inhabitants, the cemetery was located in the center of the town. Just as the Bishtine cemetery, once

Figure 8. Postcard from Bishtine, circa 1908. Author's collection.

Figure 9. Drawings of Bishtine by Alfred (Israel) Gluck for Alex Kraus's *Bishtine As Remembered*. Copy courtesy of Israel Gluck and Alex Kraus.

located on the periphery of town now served as the center of Jewish burial, so too the legends of the rabbi have supplanted pilgrimage as a ritual of commemoration. I entered the town with outdated information, guided by the prewar postcard and a 1908 map of Austro-Hungarian Marmarosh purchased in a Budapest bookshop. I had recorded legends about the rabbi's gravesite and pilgrimage from Marmarosh *landslayt* in New York City and Tel Aviv. Their stories linked narrative and memory (alive and familiar) to geographical place (utterly unrecognizable) by justifying my actual pilgrimage and providing me with a historical personage around whom everybody had a story to tell. For Jews in Israel and the United States, narratives provide partial recourse for the loss of the genuine ancestral gravesites located in Marmarosh. The cemetery in Queens and the "cemetery" in the Tel Aviv synagogue have created structures of mourning that are not based on the modalities of memory and writing but rather focus on territorial recreations and place representations.

In what follows, I foreground legends concerning Rebbele Mordkhele, the miracle-working rabbi of my mother's town of Bishtine, in the light of earlier descriptions concerning the recreated cemeteries of New York City and Tel Aviv. In particular, for local Jews as well as descendants living elsewhere, the cemetery with Rebbele Mordkhele's grave at its center is the sole surviving locus for Jewish pilgrimage, prayer, ritual, and tourism (Figure 10). Rebbele Mordkhele of Bishtine was a descendant of Rabbi Mordechai Leifer (1824–1894), known as the Nadvorner Rebbe whose Hasidic dynasty originated in eastern Galicia, currently in the Ukraine. His ancestor's genealogical and scholarly lineage was distinguished: he was a great-nephew of Rabbi Meir of Przemysl, the latter a disciple of the Baal Shem Tov, founder of the Hassidic movement. Rebbele Mordkhele's own rabbinical authority derived from Rabbi Israel of Rizhin (1796–1850), the great-grandson of another notable Hasidic rabbi, the Maggid of Mezeritch. Rebbele Mordkhele of Bishtine was the son of Rabbi Isamar of Bishtine, the grandson of the son of Rabbi Yissachar Dov Ber (Bertche) of Nadvorna-Satmar. He was part of an influential migration of Galician rabbis and religious practices that traveled southward across the Carpathian Mountains. For my family, his religious affiliations were ambiguous because he is thought to have headed south into the mountains either to disseminate or to flee the Frankists, a powerful offshoot of the heretical Sabbatean movement opposed to rabbinic Judaism. Indeed, according to scholar David Weiss-Halivni, my Talmud teacher at Barnard College and a native of the region, Carpathian Jews whose surnames,

Figure 10. Rebbele Mordkhele's gravestone, Bishtine cemetery, with
candles lit by author. Photo by the author.

like mine, comprise a Hebrew name plus the Slavic patronymic *vich*, "son of," are frequently descendants of Frankists who settled in the mountains to escape persecution for their heterodox Jewish beliefs.

Rebbele Mordkhele was thought to have extraordinary powers and abilities to perform miracles. By several accounts, he was one of three famous rabbis of Carpathian Ruthenia and by many deemed the strangest.[37] Men and women, Jews and non-Jews patronized Rebbele Mordkhele during his lifetime and later flocked to his Bishtine gravesite where he is buried. According to my father's tales, he was known for making the high low and the low high, the rich poor and the poor rich. He could "make and break families" (*zebrekhen a mishpokhe, makhen zay groys*). My great-great-grandfather, Melech Elefant, was reputed to have lost his lumber business because he did not pay proper homage to Rebbele Mordkhele, whom he visited only after praying at the court of the rival Szigeter Rebbe. Rebbele Mordkhele sternly rebuked my ancestor with words that foretold financial failures of subsequent generations: "I am not a toilet for you to stop at on the way back. I want you to make a special trip to see me. You will pay dearly."

Rebbele Mordkhele was said to be equally peremptory toward man, God, and the illnesses visited by God on man. A story from my father concerning Rebbele Mordkhele's bout with rheumatism begins with the rebbe's physician prescribing the customary cure of taking the waters at the mineral springs of Varhegy, located several kilometers into the Carpathian Mountains. Patients were expected to follow the customary efficacious thirty-day cure, during which period family entourages camped near the springs in order to immerse themselves once each day in the restorative, sulfurous springs. After delaying his cure for months, Rebbele Mordkhele arrived with his entourage of *shoykhet*, *gabbay* (ritual slaughterer, deacon), and Hassidic followers in thirty wagons loaded with cooking utensils, food, and books. In the afternoon, he and his followers prayed *minkha*, then *maariv*, awakened next morning, and prayed again. Then Rebbele Mordkhele entered the mineral baths. He immersed himself thirty times in a single day, exited the baths, and prayed addressing God in these often recounted phrases: "Lord of the Universe, I have done my part; now you do yours" (*raboyne shel oylam, ikh hob getin mans, di tin dans*). He packed everything and told his followers to break camp (Josef Slyomovics, interview by author, Vancouver, November 3, 1989).

There are numerous tales of the miracles he performed during his lifetime and even after his death. My relative, Hayim Shreter, had a wife who could not conceive. Shreter was told by Rebbele Mordkhele to buy enough white linen cloth to cover the entire cemetery, then to cut up the material in pieces, to distribute them to the poor, and then his wife would become pregnant. His wife eventually bore him a runty, half-witted child. Though mentally deficient, the child, called Mendi, was considered to bear a charmed life. One story recounted how Mendi was reported to have miraculously escaped the gas chambers at Auschwitz-Birkenau by climbing out a narrow opening in the gas chamber window. After the war, when he settled in Montreal, Mendi once again escaped through iron-barred windows, this time in the psychiatric ward of Allen Memorial Mental Hospital. Other versions of how Mendi's life was saved in Auschwitz also show the continued working of the rebbe's blessing in Mendi's life: a *Kapo* was (so they say) enamored of young Mendi and altered the tattoo number on his arm that would have sent him to the gas chambers. This explained how Mendi magically possessed two concentration camp numbers burned into his flesh.

In 1985 in Israel, my mother and I encountered two doctors originally from a town in the vicinity of Rebbele Mordkhele's grave. They claimed that the rebbe was currently known for miraculously obtaining exit visas from the former Soviet Union for Jews and non-Jews. They related how a dozen Jewish doctors applied to leave Soviet Transcarpathia and how they had been refused the right to emigrate for twelve years. On the advice of his father, one Soviet doctor and a friend decided to visit, pray, and light candles at Rebbele Mordkhele's grave. Within a month, only those two were granted the long-awaited exit visas from the Soviet Union to Israel. My favorite childhood tale about Rebbele Mordkhele encodes an ambivalent view of the miracle-working rebbe's efficacy. In Bishtine, a man challenged a friend to stick a pole into the grave of Rebbele Mordkhele at midnight. The man who agreed to perform this impious act to win a bet was wearing a long caftan. When he stuck the pole into the grave, unaware that the pole had become entangled in his coat hem, he died of a heart attack on the spot, believing Rebbele Mordkhele was pulling him into his grave. My father concluded that the question preoccupying both Marmarosh atheists and believers was whether this man was punishing himself for desecrating a grave—or was it indeed Rebbele Mordkhele "calling him to the other side" (*der rebbe hot im gerifen*)?

Most narratives about Rebbele Mordkhele were recounted to me in Montreal and Vancouver by my parents or in New York and Tel Aviv, but not by the handful of Jews who continue to reside near Rebbele Mordkhele's grave. Gedalia and Faygy Itskovitch were eighty years old, or more, when they hosted me in Bishtine in 1989. He was the caretaker of the gravesite, and his wife baked challahs for the small community every Friday. Neither could remember stories about the rebbe. Until 1977, when Shabbse "the shoemaker" (*der shister*) Berukhovitch and his six sons emigrated to Brooklyn, a minyan of ten Jewish men could be found to pray Friday nights in front of Rebbele Mordkhele's well-maintained grave in the cemetery. In Bishtine, I encountered elderly Ruthenian women who spoke German to me and remembered better lives when their region was part of Czechoslovakia before annexation to the Soviet Union in 1945. At a gathering on June 2, 1989, my fieldnotes describe my German flowing fluently thanks to vodka, homemade wine, and cakes, as local women recalled my grandmother fondly once I mentioned her maiden name Elefant. They spoke of her selling goods behind the counter in the only store in town, and they directed me to her former house and store. Writer Aharon Apelfeld's experiences were the opposite of mine. When he returned in 1996 to visit his hometown Czernowitz, now in the southwestern Ukraine of the Carpathians, he found derelict Jewish cemeteries and gravestones, as he sought the mass grave where his murdered mother was buried. Apelfeld quotes the current rabbi of Czernovitz about the locals and their memories of former Jewish inhabitants: "Ruthenian peasant women come to him to ask not only for advice and a blessing but also for forgiveness for what the Ukrainians did to the Jews. In Czernovitz, we had found many church candles placed on the graves of famous rabbis. It seemed that even though no Jews remained in the city, their spirits wandered about everywhere, and must be appeased."[38]

It appeared to me then in 1989 that the few Jewish families were newcomers who had resettled in Bishtine after the war and lost access to the stories, though they still possess the geographical site. The local Ruthenians and Ukrainians knew about the miracle-working rabbis. I believed then that it could be said with certainty, while Rebbele Mordkhele is *buried* in Maramarosh, in fact, he *lives on* in New York and Israel. I was wrong. The story is not over as if historical events, however feebly and haltingly, realign and overlay new narratives. Beginning May 1, 1989, tourism was permitted in the Soviet Ukraine outside of designated provincial cities, thereby enabling my visit. Officials specifically targeted Jewish pilgrims who could bring in hard-currency dollars. Since the formation of an independent Ukraine after 1989, several categories of tourists have appeared in recent years, each group focusing in distinctive ways on the miracle-working rabbi's burial place. Soviet Jews who emigrated from the district in the 1970s are returning to visit family and friends, introducing their American-born children to their

former towns. During my 1989 visit, I encountered three of the Berukhovitch sons on holiday with their mother. They videotaped their journey,
prayed at the cemetery, and took the famous water cure of the mountains.
At the time, the youngest son partnered with the local Ukraine government tourist offices in the hope of establishing a tourist business for
American Jews traveling to Carpathian mountain resorts. He dreamed of
attracting another group of Jewish tourists, those with no ties to the area
but lured for health reasons by mountains and mineral springs. In addition, groups of Nadvorner Hasidim residing in Israel and the United States
have embarked on pilgrimages to Rebbele Mordkhele's grave.[39] For the
first time since 1917, in 1989, one thousand Bratzlaver (Breslov) Hasidim
from Brooklyn were permitted to fulfill their founder's request to spend
Rosh Hashanah at the tomb of Rebbe Nahman of Bratzlav (1772–1810) buried in the Ukrainian city of Uman. Some traveled to Rebbele Mordkhele's
site along the route. As of this writing in 2013, the annual pilgrimage to
Uman numbers 25,000 followers. There are plans to construct a 22,000-
seat synagogue near the site.[40] My mother counts an additional "return" exemplified by her granddaughter, a secular Israeli, who went on pilgrimage to
Uman and consequently became a "returnee" (Hebrew, *baalat teshuvah*) and
follower of Hasidic Judaism.

Stories featuring Rebbele Mordkhele have moved in a geographical triangle among storytellers in Israel, the United States, and Carpathian Ruthenia and now make the rabbi a narrative presence among Jews in New York
and Tel Aviv, while pointing to an absence in most places of origin where
Jewish communities were eradicated. Memory and narrative, rather than
complementing place, are in opposition; the result is disequilibrium. Using
a model based on figures of speech, the relationship of memory and narrative to geographical place wavers about the formal rhetorical tropes of syn-
ecdoche, metaphor, and mimesis. Synedoche substitutes the part for the whole,
as in the example of Rebbele Mordkhele's actual gravesite standing for his
person and his legend, and, in fact, for the entirety of destroyed Jewish life
in Marmarosh. Mimesis pictures and mirrors, ultimately mimicking what it
presents, as in the synagogue and cemetery of Bet Marmorosh in Tel Aviv.
Third, the metaphor in America of a *landsmanshaft* asserts an identity as
opposed to a likeness. The triad of representational tropes all carry within
themselves the regretting difference from that which they represent, thereby
provoking a desire for that which is absent and lost. One may speak of loss of
place versus loss of memory and narrative. If it is the case that one must al-

ways rediscover loss, then every story and narrative retold, every plaque and headstone inscribed and installed, effectively presents the loss of place that occurred in a past no longer accessible to us. It seems that one conclusion is we must then live within the structure of continuous reminiscence, one that produces the flood of synecdochic memory books, commemorative texts, folk ethnographies, my book, ritual headstones, and academic articles that compete successfully with oral narrative. By means of the public manifestation of writing, one way to make a pilgrimage to Rebbele Mordkhele's grave without actually traveling to Eastern Europe is by exposing the framing effects of memory so that we can refashion geographical setting into narrative texts. Perhaps this is because no one else in my immediate family has evinced any interest in visiting the actual geographical locales of Bishtine or Auschwitz.[41] I alone traveled to their former village hometowns of Khist, Bishtine, Techu, Vermiziv, Slotvina—the Yiddish forms of place names that in my youthful imaginings rivaled Paris and Prague in importance.

Performing a one-time pilgrimage to my family's ancestral Carpathian Ruthenian villages highlighted the many ways that German reparation modalities and pragmatics provide me with additional, compelling ways to track my mother and grandmother's post-Holocaust worlds. German reparations that began in the 1950s are ongoing, while my family's life in Carpathian Ruthenia ended abruptly in 1945 when the region was ceded to the Ukraine. While my parents never returned to visit their ancestral Carpathian villages of Bishtine and Vermiz, my mother did make a swift, one-day trip on August 6, 1998, to Markkleeberg, a suburb of the German city of Leipzig, from our vacation spot in the Czech spa town of Jachimov near the German border. My parents last saw Jachimov in 1947, when my father sent my mother to take the waters the year before they fled Czechoslovakia. This trip to Germany was her first return visit to that country since 1945 when a Czech bus was dispatched to Markkleeberg to bring their newly liberated citizens home. This time my mother was the sole passenger in a chauffeured Czech taxi, and she arrived without warning to the Markkleeberg city hall. The mayor and staff warmly welcomed her, and they toured the neighborhood around the camp location. Much of the Markkleeberg Camp no longer exists, but, on the site, a memorial plaque, placed there a few months earlier on June 13, 1998, during a commemoration ceremony attended by remaining women survivors, marks the former places of incarceration.[42] Each year around Christmas time, she is cheered when cards, calendars, and letters from the Markkleeberg municipality arrive.

I did not accompany my mother to Markkleeberg in 1998. After my 1989 trip to my parents' villages in Carpathian Ruthenia, I knew I was researching my own present and future, not their European pasts, despite Walter Benjamin's famous admonition:

> It is well known that the Jews were forbidden to look into the future. The Torah and the prayers instructed them, by contrast, in remembrance. This disenchanted those who fell prey to the future, who sought advice from the soothsayers. For that reason the future did not, however, turn into a homogenous and empty time for the Jews. For in it every second was the narrow gate, through which the Messiah could enter.[43]

When I asked my mother what she felt on returning from her Markkleeberg visit, I received her briefest ever reply: "I'm glad they remember us."

CHAPTER 6

Algerian Jews Make the Case for Reparations

Once my mother entered the German reparations program in the year 2000, I began to monitor the website of the German Foundation Remembrance, Responsibility, and the Future (Stiftung Erinnerung, Verantwortung, und Zukunft), the entity charged with new categories of claimants and victims worthy of compensation. Their avowed goals were to indemnify individual survivors of National Socialist injustice committed by the German Reich during the years between 1933 and 1945 based on new parameters.[1] Consequently, Germany continues to add to compensable victims, notably slave and forced laborers, that go beyond the first 1952 German Federal Compensation Law on behalf of European Jewry, known as "Bundesentschädigungsgesetz" (BEG). Funding for the Foundation comes from the German state based on the year 2000 German Law for the Creation of the Foundation "Remembrance, Responsibility and the Future" (henceforth, Foundation and Foundation Law) supplemented by a consortium of German private industries implicated in Nazi-era slave and forced labor. The underlying purpose of the Foundation fund was to cover all further claims by forced laborers from the Nazi era, specifically those hitherto excluded from reparations. In April 2004, after Germany launched an official supplemental compensation program extending Foundation Law for Jews interned in an approved list of World War II camps located in the Maghrib, North African Jewry was counted among the later groups to be covered by Germany's sustained redress program. My decades-long personal connections to the disbursement of German reparations suddenly encompassed the plight of Algerian Jews during World War II. As an anthropologist of North Africa, I began to research the ways in which a specific German reparation program illuminates histories of Maghribi Jews, but structured by novel themes that extend the study of Jews under French colonialism in Algeria:

[H]istoriographic tendencies, inherited from colonial scholarship, have been found to be academically alluring to a body of scholarship generated from within the field of Jewish Studies that has marched, teleologically, toward the "inevitable" exit of North African and Middle Eastern Jewries with the ascendance of anti-colonial, independence, and national movements in the middle twentieth century. This vein of literature is constitutive of a larger story of Jews in North Africa and the Middle East that is undergirded by a "neo-lachrymose" orientation—scholarship that paints a dismal picture of Jews' place within Muslim majority societies and that builds towards the triumphant ascendance of Zionism. Scholarship on Algerian Jewry has often been marked by the related tendency to focus narrowly on the history of anti-Semitism. To some scholars, anti-Semitism has appeared an undeniable telos of North African Jewish history: to others (including certain voices represented here), it appears a phenomenon that must be carefully contextualized, for example, with the rise of European fascism and its efflorescence in French settler colonial Algeria during the interwar and Vichy periods. Nor can anti-Semitism be understood without considering the varieties of prevailing "anti-Muslim" racism, the latter term itself part of the colonial nomenclature that typologized native Algerians according to religion.[2]

Additional cultural and political debates, internal and external to the Middle East and North Africa, frame and often distort reparation histories of Algerian Jewry in Israel, France, and North Africa. In Israel, one debate calibrates lesser Sephardic suffering during World War II versus the majority Ashkenazi Jewish Holocaust.[3] Another layer of debates surrounds the role of Arab regimes during the Holocaust (or whether there was even a Holocaust in the Arab world).[4] Yet a third approach, one that draws on North African immigration to Israel, exploits the notion of population exchanges: Palestinian expulsion and indemnification claims are linked to the large-scale immigration of Jews from Arab lands to Israel and their claims for financial indemnification.[5] Complicating all these considerations is that Jews constituted a small number, an estimated 10 percent of those interned in camps across North Africa, and that most Algerian Jews were sequestered in their own Jewish camps for "racial" reasons, the latter term being the justification for the eventual 2004 German reparation. In what follows, I explore the consequences of their internment that exemplify the vastly different routes to reparation and apology taken by post-World War II governments of France and Germany beginning with my interviews at the Foundation fund headquarters in Berlin.

A Visit to the Foundation "Remembrance, Responsibility, and the Future"

If pilgrimage is a physical enactment of remembrance and memorialization when it transforms and redirects the seeker's life journey, my April 2006 visit to the Berlin offices of the Foundation was the pilgrimage that helped launch this project by stimulating the pursuit of comparative frameworks for reparations. I spent an afternoon at the Foundation offices, hosted by Hans Otto Bräutigam, the German diplomat who was head during the period 2000–2006. He spoke with me at length to clarify the new, "relaxed" forms of evidence and proof required of former forced and slave laborers concerning their individual camp internments. Such approaches considerably downplay victim testimony in favor of swift acknowledgment and small payments whenever claimants can be documented within the parameters of known, listed, and acknowledged places of confinement. Around a conference table, I then spoke with additional members of the Berlin Foundation staff: Dorothee Lüke, Jens Schley, Kathrin Janka, Stefan Gehrke, and Ulrike Vasel-Coulibaly, the latter my email correspondent, always available to respond efficiently to my many inquiries about the 2004 Foundation reparations in relation to North African Jews. I was fifty-six when we met and had conducted fieldwork for decades as an anthropologist of North Africa. They were a generation younger, most in their thirties. East and West German divisions seemed to align neatly with gender: the men were *Ossis* ("Easties") and the women *Wessis* ("Westies"), yet all seemed driven to account for the fact of individual, forced labor despite the variety of proliferating categories, anomalous conditions, political pressures, time constraints, and a complex network of partner organizations contracted to deal directly with claimants. What to do about camps in Serbia, for example, where women and small children did not work yet were systematically starved to death and appeared on no BEG camp lists? How to account for atrocities by the puppet regimes of Vichy France, Slovakia, or Croatia, each of which had exercised direct or indirect racial discrimination against Jews, Roma, and Sinti in relation to the newly minted criterion of "German instigation"? How to deal with insufficient information about the Italian Fascist camp for Libyan Jews at Giado, added to the list for the 2004 indemnification, that produced close to five hundred claims comprised of two hundred requests with no documentation, one hundred with claimants writing a few sentences and one hundred with slightly more details?

Simultaneously, Foundation staffers were charged with overseeing random audits of their disbursing partner organizations. The impetus to give away money is always institutionally counterbalanced by the opposing bureaucracy of angst to uncover fraudulent abuse, inevitable perhaps with such large sums at stake. As of 2012, the FBI was investigating the New York office of the Jewish Claims Conference (JCC), where, allegedly, some staffers have bilked the main partner organization for Holocaust survivors in America since 1993 through the device of creating fraudulent claims and fake victim identities totaling over $12 million.[6] Whenever German Foundation staffers follow through with inquiries and questionnaires concerning the payment processes via their intermediary partner organizations, how much was received and when, they are castigated with, "We can never forget," "You bastards," "Why don't you trust (Polish, Jewish, etc.) organizations?" and "The amounts are ridiculous for so much suffering." For the most part, although with exceptions, the Foundation remains a superstructure organism that deals with suffering abstractly by establishing lists and databases, aggregating data, vetting documents but rarely seeing victims' faces. Staffers pushed me to consider important questions that they ask themselves: what is the sense of what we do here? Is the end of the Foundation the end of compensation? What would be the profile of a future fund and its relation to victims? Can we remember without survivors? Is what we do here a model for compensation elsewhere? Drawing on scholarship relevant to Holocaust studies, anthropology, human rights, and the legal histories of remedies and redress, my encounters with the Foundation bureaucracy inform this chapter and the next, which deal with histories that both influenced and resulted from Germany's postwar compensation to European Jews.

Algerian Jewry Make the Case for German Indemnification to European Jews

According to the latest international protocols, reparation includes restitution, compensation, rehabilitation, and satisfaction, as well as guarantees of nonrepetition. Acknowledgment of the United Nations definitions[7] by sovereign states are partly exemplified by France and Germany, countries whose restitution and compensation projects respectively, apply and distinguish between the implicit goals of French restitution, which was to return the victim to the financial conditions *prior* to violation, and German financial attempts to assess harm as a *consequence* of the violation. Although the right to reparations as they are construed between states was established as a principle of national and international law in the early decades of the twentieth century,[8] the plight of Jews during and after World War II was understood to be administratively anomalous and legally exceptional.

As early as 1944, Nehemiah Robinson, a Lithuanian Jewish jurist living as a refugee in New York City, concluded in his landmark work *Indemnification and Reparations: Jewish Aspects* that indemnities benefit all parties, not solely the targeted beneficiaries: "Indemnification for damage Jews suffered in consequence of exceptional measures taken by the Axis and because of war activities must be effected in the interest of all concerned as an elementary rule of justice."[9] Consequently, when restitution was impossible—in the sense of restoring conditions exactly as they once were before inflicted losses—then compensation, he concluded, became the principal and most just means. Due to difficulties in determining individual and private actors who could be held responsible for indemnification (in contrast to public and organizational ones), Robinson inclined toward the necessity of a state-administered indemnification plan:

> The state [is] the organization responsible for the action of its apparatus (in the Axis countries) and also empowered to effect some sort of equal distribution of losses by compensating the damaged individuals at the expense of the rest of the nation. Compensation by the state is thus not only just (since there is no reason why the damage in non-Axis nations should fall upon certain nations only and not the totality of citizens, nor why the Axis states should avoid their responsibility), but also necessary.[10]

Nehemiah Robinson and his brother Jacob are both credited with key conceptions related to the successful implementation of postwar reparations to European Jews. This was explicitly articulated in 1964 shortly after Robinson's death, when Nahum Goldmann, head of the World Jewish Congress, delivered a moving eulogy to highlight the origins and striking originality of the reparations project:

He [Nehemiah] and Jacob [Robinson] were primary among those who
conceived the very idea of demanding from Germany payments for
indemnification and restitution. It was a revolutionary idea. In no
previous case in history had a State paid indemnification directly to
individuals, most of them not even its own citizens. Countries paid
indemnification when they were defeated in war; the fact is as old as
human history itself. But that a government should pay for crimes
committed, not only to its own citizens, which was unusual enough,
but to hundreds of thousands of non-citizens, or to another state, the
state of Israel, which was not even in existence at the time the crimes
were committed and had no legal claim to anything, was truly a revolutionary idea. I don't say that Nehemiah and Jacob were the only
ones who conceived the idea, but it was worked out and elaborated
by them. During the war, when I first proclaimed this demand before
the World Jewish Congress, the merit was not mine; it was their idea
and we stated that fact at the time.[11]

Post-World War II German reparative measures were first and foremost
for the benefit of European Jews. Therefore, granting reparations on behalf
of Algerian Jews from North Africa involves the history of German indemnification superimposed on a prior history of French restitution. For Franco-
Algerian philosopher Jacques Derrida, this complex, entangled chronology
is best subsumed among the injustices of French colonial politics:

In what had been, under French law, not a protectorate but a group of
French departments, the history of the foreigner, so to speak, the history of citizenship, the future of borders separating complete citizens
from second-zone to non-citizens, from 1839 until today, has a com-
plexity, a mobility, an entanglement that are unparalleled, as far as I
know, in the world and in the history of humanity.[12]

Moreover, while postwar German reparations since the 1952 BEG indemnification laws continue to be rooted in ongoing vibrant debates about coming
to terms with Germany's Nazi past (*Vergangenheitsbewältigung*), France's
attitudes and policies toward the Vichy past in France and Algeria foreclosed
French financial responsibility to Algerian Jews (or for that matter Algerian
Muslims) for what Frantz Fanon called a "just reparation" for the crimes of
colonialism.[13] Consequently, addressing indemnification histories relevant

to the case of Algerian Jewry and what happened to the community from the beginning of World War II through Algeria's 1962 independence and into the era of their settlement en masse in France draws on Holocaust studies, postcolonial studies, Algerian Jewish diasporic history, the dynamic unfolding of French-Algerian decolonization, and the history of Germany's post-World War II indemnification programs that seem as though they will never end.[14]

Discussions in Jewish circles about reparations, already underway as early as 1940 when the outcome of the war was still uncertain, emphasized the singularity of Nazi state policies that targeted Jews first for despoliation, then extermination.[15] By 1943, the German term *Wiedergutmachung* (to make good again, to make amends) was adopted for Jewish claims against Germany, despite its historical origins in the Nazi juvenile penal code of the same year as a way "to give young people the opportunity to pay for the damage they had done with good deeds rather than by serving a jail sentence."[16] As Nehemiah Robinson in New York City investigated reparation precedents while World War II raged, he came upon a little known contemporary wartime example that conformed to his two conditions: first, restitution and reparation were instigated by the state, and, second, such remedies were applied specifically to Jews. This was an early case study concerning collective spoliation and discrimination suffered by the Jewish communities of North Africa, especially Algeria's Jews subjected to the direct rule of Vichy France beginning in 1940.[17]

While Germany's post-World War II European Jewish victims remain the starting point for discussions about reparations, also pertinent to the situation of North Africa's Jews was the context of French colonialism and imperialism beyond Europe's borders. Vichy France actively collaborated with Nazi laws, but their enforcement in Algeria was rendered more complicated given the relations among Algeria's populations—or to use the terminology of the time, its Muslim native majority (*musulmanes, indigènes*), its Jewish minority (*français israélites d'Algérie*), and the French settler-colonizers (*pieds-noirs*). Therefore, in considering the laws governing postwar restitution to Algerian Jews, additional factors such as citizenship, religion, and the right to a French education were inextricably linked in the immediate years of liberation from Vichy rule. By 1943, although the experiences of Algerian Jews under Vichy came to be articulated through the lens of compensable victimization endured during World War II, it was only belatedly mapped onto Holocaust memory and postwar Jewish compensation programs. Thus,

overlapping histories of genocide and colonialism continue to intersect with
the aftermath of Vichy collaboration in Algeria into the postwar era.[18]

Vichy Legislation in Algeria

After the German defeat of the French during World War II, conquered
France was divided between the Nazi-occupied zone (two-thirds of the country, including Paris) and the so-called unoccupied free zone to the south,
headquartered at Vichy. Despite the bifurcation of the country, scholars
such as Michael Marrus and Robert Paxton conclude that France was that
rare country in Europe—another exception was Bulgaria—to hand Jews
over to the Germans even from territory not directly occupied by the Germans.[19] France did so in Vichy and Vichy-ruled Algeria. Between 1940 and
1943, the flood of Vichy's economic, legal, and educational directives, decrees and orders imposed a cascading series of deprivations and hardships.
By the end of 1940 in both France and France's overseas department of Algeria, a series of anti-Jewish laws defining who is a Jew went into effect.[20] In
Nazi-occupied France, according to orders published in the official journal
of the German military government, *Ordonnance relative aux measures con-
tre les Juifs* (Ordinance concerning mesures against Jews) of September 27,
1940, a Jew was defined by religion or by at least two Jewish grandparents.
Vichy's Statut des Juifs (Jewish Statute) of October 3, 1940, defined the Jew
as a person with three grandparents "of the Jewish race," or with two Jewish
grandparents if the spouse was Jewish. Since German law was not in force in
1940 Vichy France, these definitions of the Jew that evolved were peculiar to
Vichy. Other discrepancies between Nazi German and Vichy French law on
Jews concerns the plight of Russian Karaites, as well as Georgian and Central Asian Jews settled in France since the 1917 Russian Revolution. The
Nazis exempted these three groups from the category of Jewish identity,
hence, from anti-Jewish racial laws, while in contrast Vichy initially designated them *juif*, eventually retracting it under Nazi pressure.[21]

The Vichy Jewish Statute of October 3, 1940, defining a Jew was followed
by the law of October 4, 1940, ordering foreign Jews to be placed in special
camps or under house arrest. As Jews were singled out and foreign Jews targeted for special abuse, legal strategies unique to Algeria came to under-
mine the legal foundations of the Algerian Jewish community put in place
by the French colonial regime. Within days of the Jewish statute, the law of

October 7, 1940, abrogated the Crémieux Decree that, since 1870, had granted Algerian Jews French citizenship. Once stripped collectively of their status as French citizens, Algerian Jews were subjected to additional discrimination hitherto reserved for foreign Jews. Vichy laws and the abrogation of the Crémieux Decree undermined the existence and identity of Algeria's Jewish minority as French citizens. To borrow Benedict Anderson's approach in the French version of *Imagined Communities*, he describes Algerian Jewry's established allegiance to French culture and citizenship by the time of World War II as an agreement to "remember that they forgot."[22] Granted French citizenship through the Crémieux Decree, the majority of Algerian Jews by World War II had relegated their origins as autochthonous Arabic and Berber-speaking Jews to the past, while maintaining forms of remembrance and allegiance to North African Jewish religious practices.

Moreover, unique to the Algerian context were laws eliminating any possibility for Algerian Jews to request French citizenship in ways made contingently possible to Algerian Muslim *indigènes* since 1919, notably through service in the French armed forces. Through enactment of the law of October 11, *Journal Officiel* of October 13, 1940, Vichy jurists swiftly revoked these possibilities specifically for the Jews of Algeria, many of whom had served in the French military during World War I. Furthermore, a list of names of Algerian Jews residing in France who had protested their loss of French citizenship was given to the Nazis.[23] The fates of French Jews, foreign Jews, and Algerian Jews residing in France were the same. Approximately 75,000 were deported and died in various Nazi camps. Based on a survey of North African Jewish surnames and places of birth— in an effort to reconstruct even an incomplete list of Algerian-born Jews that does not include their French-born children – the estimated numbers are approximately 1,500 Algerian Jews transported to Nazi extermination camps beginning in 1942. Few survived. Yet, in stark contrast to France and to neighboring Italian Fascist-controlled Libya, no Algerian Jew was deported from Algeria.[24]

Vichy France's racial laws against Jews created additional hardships when applied in Algeria. There, Xavier Vallat, first head of the Commission Général aux Questions Juives enacted a second, harsher Jewish Statute in the law of June 2, 1941. Consequently, Jews in Algeria were prohibited from a long list of jobs and restricted to a small fixed number (*numerus clausus*) in the classroom and the professions, removed from the civil service, and expelled from banking. Vichy officials, zealously exceeding their Nazi overlords, did not bother to formulate laws—even ones eventually defined in the postwar restoration of Republican France as "acts said to be 'laws' of the de facto authority claiming to be the 'government of the French State'."[25] Inspired, so to speak, by Nazi decrees, many Vichy functionaries in Algeria (often members of the European settler population) were notorious for virulent anti-Semitism of more than one variety: they were both anti-Jewish and anti-Muslim Algerian.[26]

Jacques Derrida and Educational Losses

"French culture is not made for little Jews,"[27] was the phrase uttered by his French school teacher to Franco-Algerian Jewish philosopher Jacques Derrida:

> Perhaps one of the many things that made me sensitive to law is that I belonged to a minority in a colonized country. The Jewish community in Algeria was there long before the French colonizers. So on one hand, Algerian Jews belonged to the colonized people, and on the other they assimilated with the French. During the Nazi occupation, there were no German soldiers in Algeria. There was only the French and the Vichy regime, which produced and enforced laws that were terribly repressive. I was expelled from school. My family lost its citizenship, which is a legal event. Even when you're a child, you understand what it means to lose your citizenship. When you're in such a marginal and unsafe and shaky situation, you are more attentive to the question of legal authorization. You are a subject whose identity is threatened, as are your rights.[28]

As one casualty of Vichy anti-Jewish educational quotas, Derrida would write more than fifty years later about his permanent removal from an Algiers high school between 1942–44: "they expelled me from the Lycée Ben Aknoun in 1942, a little black and very Arab Jew who understood nothing about it, to whom no one ever gave the slightest reason, neither his parents nor his friends."[29] Derrida's confusions were based on Vichy's illegal application of already existing Nazi directives about Jewish quotas. Derrida expresses the child's viewpoint of memories under Vichy, reminiscences he resurrects in the 1990s to evoke his humiliation and bewilderment. As Vichy Algerian educational bulletins circulated, their odious provisions determined, for example, that, if a class of thirty-five students had attained the 14 percent *numerus clausus* figure and the mathematical result was 4.9 Jews, only four Jewish children were permitted because "nine-tenths of a Jew does not equal one Jew."[30]

Another source of information about Vichy's discriminatory educational practices is the writings and activism of the de facto Algiers Jewish community leader, Maurice Eisenbeth, the Ashkenazi and French-born grand rabbi of Algiers. Eisenbeth describes anti-Jewish directives and laws frequently not published, focusing on the ad hoc nature of practices implemented without official notifications. He took various actions to oppose the situation of Jewish exclusion prior to the first weeks of the 1941 school year. In response, General Weygand, governor general of Algeria, announced expanded restricted percentages for Jewish school attendance to include primary school education when initially directives were aimed at only Algerian Jews at the high school and university levels. In 1945, Eisenbeth published his aptly titled chronicle *Pages vécues, 1940–43*, filled with documents that encapsulate his experiences as couched in the words of the Vichy Algerian bureaucracy. Page by page, he compiled the catastrophic consequences of Vichy's legal and bureaucratic apparatus that reduced Algerian Jews to penury and fear by means of official memoranda, letters, decrees, circulars, orders, bulletins, and telegrams deployed against all Jews.[31] Eisenbeth's book, arranged as a diary, reports his verbal exchanges with various Vichy leaders beginning June 18, 1940, the date of France's surrender to Germany, and ending October 20, 1943. On August 17, 1941, Eisenbeth conversed with Xavier Vallat, then visiting Algiers in his role as Vichy's first commissioner in charge of Jewish affairs. A few weeks later, on September 3, 1941, he records speaking with General Yves C. Chatel. Both French Vichy functionaries assumed that Jews, like Muslims, were educated in religious schools. When they each demanded that Rabbi Eisenbath list the Jewish religious schools (*écoles confessionelles*), he had to confront their ignorance with the lived reality that Algerian Jews possessed no Jewish religious schools because, in accord with their rights as French citizens, all were educated within the French system. Eisenbeth writes his reply:

> I recall our protests against abrogating the Crémieux Decree and against the Laws on the Status of Jews. We submitted to these laws but do not accept them and we will never accept them. . . . Racial theories come from across the Rhine; why do you not say to us that the

restoration of France demands the sacrifice of the Jews? Faced with such frankness, we would accept any sacrifices for the grandeur of France. Algerian Jews are treated as foreigners, although they are autochthonous to North Africa. In front of tomorrow's uncertainties, France has no interest in alienating 130,000 faithful citizens of the Jewish faith, she might have need of them one day, all the more so that Jews give no credence to irredentist and dissident ideas. We protest against collective measures.[32]

Eisenbeth positions the Algerian Jewish community as the native (*autochtone*) bulwark against the imminent threat of Algerian Muslim independence as well as loyal French citizens prepared to sacrifice, if only they were asked. Xavier Vallat reportedly replied, "I am a state anti-Semite not a passionate anti-Semite."[33]

Given his exclusion from French education with Jewish schools as his only alternative, Derrida chose not to participate in the collective educational punishment of the Jewish community. His radical solution encompassed a double refusal: expelled from the French school system, he refused to attend the Jewish schools set up during Vichy-ruled Algeria, ambiguously declaring, "So that, thus, expelled, I became the outsider, try as they might to come close to me, they'll never touch me again."[34]

Roger Azoulay and the Internment of Algerian Jewish Soldiers

In addition to loss of citizenship, expulsion from the education system, and the spoliation of property, a small number of Algerian Jews were subjected to confinement in camps.[35] Algerian Jews were a minority in the North African camps predominantly populated by a variety of other groups labeled by the Vichy regime as "undesirables" and "criminals." Algeria's wartime imprisoned population included the overlapping categories of Spanish Republicans (both families and soldiers fleeing Franco's Spain), foreign and local Communists, union leaders, Algerian militants (for example, Messali Hadj and his political adherents in the Parti Populaire Algérien), fighters from the International Brigades deported to North Africa, freemasons, and a flood of European refugees (including German antifascists). An estimated three thousand Jews were placed in Algerian internment camps by 1942 (including foreign Jewish refugees) alongside political prisoners of various nationalities to form an approximate prisoner population of twenty thousand people.[36]

One group, singled out by the March 27, 1941, *circulaire* for internment camps (*camps d'internement*), signed by General Odilon Picquendar, was Algerian Jewish males of conscription age, the only group to be interned in all-Jewish camps. By April 1941, the first Algerian Jewish soldiers arrived at Bedeau Camp, a location in Algeria's western department of Oranie, slated for Moroccan and Algerian Jews, while another camp was set up in Telergma (Constantine Department) for Tunisian and Algerian Jews. At a third camp, Chéragas near Algiers, internees were formed into units called *Pionniers Israélites* (or young Jews involved in the French Scout movement.) Young Algerian Jews, who should have been mobilized for army service during the period 1938–1942, instead were "demilitarized" as soldiers and shipped out as laborers to form the *Groupes de travailleurs israélites* (groups of Jewish workers, or GTI). According to memoirs,[37] and based on my interview with Roger Azoulay, a former Algerian Jewish conscript turned internee who has resided in Israel since 1948, not only camp conditions but also the prospect of an eventual deportation to Germany led him to describe Bedeau as a *camp de concentration*.[38] Descriptions of camp conditions would feature prominently in eventual allocations of French and German benefits to former internees, since German reparation authorities, unlike the French, acknowledged and compensated the disciplinary regime of penal servitude, forced labor, and administrative detention. The GTI was a category specific to Algerian Jews, legally and administratively preceded by the French law creating the *Groupes de travailleurs étrangers* (Groups of foreign workers, or GTE) in France for foreigners (based on the Decree of November 29, 1940). In France, GTEs entirely composed of Jews were called *Groupes palestiniens* or *Groupes juifs homogènes* (Palestinian groups or all-Jewish groups) and, by August 1942, were way stations to deportation and death in eastern concentration camps.[39]

Azoulay, born in 1923 in Oran, chose to volunteer in February 1940 for the French Army in advance of his call-up date, only to find himself under Vichy rules and the Picquendar military circular that mandated his internment in Bedeau and mistreatment as a civilian detainee in 1940–43 during Vichy-era Algeria.[40] Once Algeria was liberated by the Allied forces landing in North Africa in 1943, he would go on to serve with distinction as a much-decorated soldier and radio-technician in the Third Algerian Infantry Division (DIA, or Division d'Infanterie Algérienne) reconstituted in 1943 as a fighting force that participated in the liberation of Tunisia and then Italy.

During my interview in the presence of his daughter, the philosopher Ariella Azoulay, he spoke at length of his military career from 1943 but very
little about his time in Bedeau. Many Algerian Jews saw themselves as French
patriots eager to serve in the French Army who experienced personal, social, and political humiliation because of their treatment. For Yehouda Léon
Askénazi, noted rabbi, educator, and son of the last chief rabbi of Algiers, his
internment in Bedeau Camp helped instigate first a rupture, then the abandonment of his identity as a "français d'Algérie de religion juive":

> We were mobilized as foreigners, particularly in the Foreign Legion.
> The vast majority of Jews mustered in the Legion camp thought that
> this was the vicissitude of history and that the time would come when
> French citizenship would be returned to us. I was in Bedeau Camp
> between 1943 and 1944; then I was a soldier in the war in the Colonial
> Army, a regular corps in the French infantry. What I lived through
> during this period certainly affected me deeply, and the moment I
> encountered the Israeli reality, it was all naturally settled. Fundamen-
> tally, if I had to live in the diaspora, I would have been seen more as
> an Algerian Jew of French culture than as a French Jew of Algerian
> culture. Algeria later became an Arab country, and I could not con-
> sider myself an Arab.
>
> Even today, I cannot comprehend how North African Jews con-
> sider themselves French. Aside from the anti-Jewish and anti-Israel
> character of Arab countries, it does not occur to them to consider
> themselves Arabs but as French. This attitude springs from racism. It
> can be explained by the fact that Jews consider the mark of French
> culture superior to the mark of Arab culture. Objectively this is non-
> sense because cultures cannot be measured by the same criteria. But
> there is evidence for a Jew who has lived in an Islamic country: the
> difference between Jew and Arab is not only according to religion, it
> is also national. This double difference does not exist in relation to
> the European. This explains the continuity of the diaspora in a Euro-
> pean milieu.
>
> After the fact, it was a very enriching experience for me to know
> the milieu of the Foreign Legion, but we were not organized as Jews,
> in order for us to develop a national conscience. We considered our-
> selves as a kind of minority of the diaspora type. Religious life in the
> camp was very intense and it was there perhaps that I began to un-

derstand the condition of exile, which I have completely rid myself of on becoming Israeli.

I felt that I was not at home and, consequently, that I had no rights I could claim. I could only attempt, through a strategy of submission, to obtain favors.[41]

Roger Azoulay and Jacques Derrida represent unusual cases of post-World War II Algerian Jewish destinies that differ from the majority of Algerian Jewish trajectories. Most of the community settled in France during the 1960s to escape Algeria's imminent independence from France. In contrast, Derrida and Azoulay left in the late 1940s. Derrida, who missed out on a few years of his schooling during the Vichy era, would leave Algeria by 1949 to enroll in the Paris Lycée Louis le-Grand and obtain his French baccalauréat, while Azoulay, a member of an Algerian Zionist youth group, emigrated in 1949 to be part of the establishment of the State of Israel. Despite the example of Azoulay's singular decision, historians continue to disagree about the importance of Zionism to Algerian Jews. Michel Abitbol writes that Algerian Jewish communities were "indifferent" to Zionism in the modern cities of Oran and Algiers; what little support there was, came from religious traditionalists in the conservative centers of Constantine and Tlemcen, where urban Jews viewed the movement as a defense against assimilation to French culture.[42] In contrast, Keren Rouch argues regarding Zionist identifications linked to "Algerian Jews [who] had not forgotten their recent experience under the Vichy regime, during which they were stripped of their French citizenship and excluded from every institution affiliated with the French state."[43] Nonetheless, Azoulay, a Jew from Oran, was a statistical anomaly, figuring among a mere 8 percent of North African Jewish immigrants, and even fewer Algerian Jews, to depart for Israel in 1948 as opposed to the subsequent decade's rising numbers. By 1957, North Africans were 86 percent of Israel's entering population, primarily Moroccans and Tunisians, with Algerian Jews still constituting a tiny proportion.

Although choosing radically different destinations, Derrida and Azoulay, respectively, elided their Maghribi backgrounds for decades in favor of French linguistic and cultural attachments. Ariella Azoulay recounts in a moving essay about her father, titled "Mother Tongue, Father Tongue," that, in reply to a question by an Israeli bureaucrat about his birthplace, her father stated, "Oran, in France, of course." Indeed, Ariella Azoulay wonders, "who would want to be from North Africa in late 1940s Israel? . . . When he was spoken of as Algerian, he felt taunted, when he was spoken of as French, he felt flattered."[44] Research on North African Jewish inmates of Vichy-era camps in the Maghrib is influenced by many considerations, especially the implacable experiential hesitations and silences of those interned, such as Roger Azoulay. Some remain unwilling to speak about a past that was both shameful personally as well as a national disgrace to France and their French allegiances. Azoulay was unaware of the German reparations that had expired at the time of our interview but said he would have applied had he known, regardless of the derisory sums. For Ariella Azoulay, in the post-1948 Israeli context characterized by social, economic, and cultural erasures of the large Jewish community from Muslim-majority countries (known as *Mizrahim*) dominated by the minority of Jews of Eastern European origin (known as *Ashkenazim*), her father's reticence was interpreted as a lie to efface a Maghribi, hence Mizrahi identity that her father could not and did not embrace as his daughter does.

French Restitution: 1943

As early as October 4, 1941, while in exile in Brazzaville, General Charles De Gaulle wrote to Rabbi Stephen Wise, president of the American Jewish Congress, saying that Vichy laws were illegal and illegitimate, indeed an injustice directed against France's Jewish citizens. His subsequent November 22, 1940, statement to the American Jewish Congress stated,

> Be assured that since we have repudiated everything that has been falsely done in the name of France after June 23, the cruel decrees against French Jews can and will have no validity in Free France. These measures are no less a blow against the honor of France than they are an injustice against her Jewish citizens. . . . When we have achieved victory not only will the wrongs done in France itself be righted, but France will once again resume her traditional place as a protagonist of freedom and justice for all men, irrespective of race or religion, in a New Europe.[45]

A subsequent letter by De Gaulle, dated September 23, 1943, delineated forthrightly the wrongs to be righted, declaring that, once the laws of the French Republic were reestablished, reparations for Algerian Jews and the restoration of the prewar legal situation of their French nationality could also be envisioned.[46] Thus, restitution to the Algerian Jewish community was to be preceded by the reinstatement of their French citizenship, which meant abrogating the abrogation of the Crémieux Decree. Despite De Gaulle's declaration, restoring Algerian Jews' French citizenship was not immediately undertaken once American troops landed in Algeria. Indeed, on March 14, 1943, some four months after liberation, General Henri Giraud, French high commissioner, voided all Vichy legislation for France but retained the abrogation of the 1870 Crémieux Decree for Algeria, reasoning that the decree itself was a racially motivated edict that instituted distinctions between the native Muslim and Jewish inhabitants that should have never been propagated. In other words, abrogation of the Crémieux Decree, despite its Vichy pedigree, was an important step in returning the native communities to their shared status under French colonial rule. In contrast, Hannah Arendt pointed to the abysmal continuities between Vichy Algeria and liberated Algeria concerning the status of the Jews and the decree's non-nullification:

> General Giraud, instead of abolishing the Crémieux decree, had extended French citizenship to all natives prepared to accept French civil law. . . . General Giraud pretends to have nullified the Crémieux decree because it caused inequality among the natives and gave a privileged position to the Jews. Actually, he has acted as an agent of those French colonials who always wanted to bring under their "dictatorship" the only part of the Algerian population that so far escaped their arbitrary and selfish rule. The French colonials, in other words, took advantage of France's defeat and of their freedom from control of the mother country to introduce into Algeria a measure which they would have never been able to obtain through legal means.[47]

In Algeria when the Crémieux Decree was eventually reinstated on October 21, 1943, by the Comité Français de la Libération Nationale (French Committee for National Liberation), the text left open possibilities for additional future legal changes affecting the two indigenous communities, Muslim and Jewish.[48] In France after the republic was restored, many officials were reluctant to reproduce Vichy and Nazi-era laws designating Jews as a group. Although restitution was to be framed as the return of law and legality to the French Republic by 1944, historian Claire Andrieu makes clear that at that time, people did not distinguish between different degrees of suffering caused by the war as they do today. Jews, resistance fighters, and victims of bombings all had the same entitlement to restitution and compensation. Their claims against the state were treated relatively uniformly as cases of war damage. Since 1997, however, policy has been entirely informed by the remembrance of the Holocaust. This is chiefly a moral and emotional and only secondarily material.[49]

In Algeria, according to French law, Jews were unavoidably singled out for restitution because they had been singled out for spoliation as a group. In both France and Algeria, however, restitution was framed according to an individual claim, regardless of the collective nature of Jewish losses and suffering. A special commission was created to deal with disputes arising between original Algerian Jewish owners and Vichy-appointed bureaucrats who were charged with the economic crime of "Aryanization," achieved through outright confiscation, liquidation sales, and transfer of Jewish assets (*Journal Officiel*, June 22, 1943). Nehemiah Robinson's early and prescient case study (referred to above) on French processes of indemnification in North Africa summarizes the series of measures and decrees dealing with Algerian Jews and the principles of financial restitution and restoration of job and material assets that began in 1943 and continued until 1957. In particular, he cites an early case for restitution brought by a Tunisian Jew in which the courts produced a rare moral statement attached to their ruling: The Civil Tribunal of the First Instance in Tunis (April 24, 1944) followed by the Court of Appeals of Tunis (July 4, 1944) in *re Saveur Campubello v. Consorts Gandus* ruled that the intention of post-Vichy laws and commissions was "to repair totally and without delay" the injustice done to the Jews by anti-Jewish measures.[50]

France's compensation began in Algeria in 1943 in the form of restitution for material losses and was purely a French program throughout the early post–World War II decades. To understand the specificity of these historical processes from the vantage point of hindsight, it is worth considering the report, five decades after World War II, by the 1997 French government's Commission pour l'Indemnisation des Victimes des Spoliations (Commission for the Compensation of Victims of Spoliation),[51] known as the Mattéoli Commission after its president Jean Mattéoli, a hero of the French Resistance. The commission provided extensive reports that include an index of each French law in Algeria that rescinded Vichy era legislation and a list of archives relevant to Algerian spoliation documents in France's National Archives. The Mattéoli Commission was instrumental in working toward the establishment of a second Commission pour l'Indemnisation des Victimes de Spoliations Intervenues du Fait des Législations Antisémites en Vigueur pendant l'Occupation (known as the Commission Drai after its president, Pierre Drai) in charge of compensation to individual victim-claimants.[52] Nonetheless, no mechanism for restitution to Algerian Jews as a collectivity was put in place due to the mass exodus of the majority of Algerian Jews to France after Algerian independence in 1962.

This departure caused Algerian Jews to be recategorized alongside Algeria's European settler colonialist population as the "repatriated" (*rapatrié*), as if they were "returning" to France, never the place of their origins. There are other examples from post-World War II Europe of massive population transfers in which forced migrations are mislabeled "repatriation" to an ancestral homeland. To this day, debates continue about who counts as German as opposed to native Polish, Slovak, Hungarian, or Czech from among the vast "ethnic German" populations of Eastern Europe once slated for successive waves of *Aussiedlung* to Germany.[53] This term possesses multivalent uses and geographical trajectories: its literal meaning of "resettlement" or "evacuation," referring to the massive postwar "expulsion" of "ethnic Germans" into Germany, was also euphemistically applied by the Nazis to the mass deportation of Jews to camps in the east. Greeks deploy the term *palinostisi* (coethnic return) to describe ethnic Greeks, for example, from the former Soviet Union, arriving as migrants to Greece.[54] The State of Israel's "Law of Return" extends the lifelong privilege of immediate Israeli citizenship to diasporic Jews as well as to people of Jewish ancestry wherever they reside.

An overwhelming number of Algerian Jews, estimated between 100,000 and 120,000 from a total population of 140,000, were "repatriated" to France and, for the purposes of a separate series of indemnities, bureaucratically assimilated to the category and financial fate of Algeria's settlers of European origin (*pieds-noirs*).[55] Historically speaking, few Algerian Jews could be considered *pieds-noirs*; rather, most were either of Sephardic origin arriving during the expulsions of Jews and Muslims from Spain or predated the medieval era as part of the native population. Once assimilated in France to the appellation *pied-noir*, Jews benefited from a series of reparations funds disbursed to both groups united bureaucratically in France after Algerian

independence as a single entity. A French indemnification law was passed
on July 15, 1970, modified in 1974 to increase payments, further amended
January 2, 1978, with additional amounts, and yet again in 1984.[56]

German Restitution for North African Labor Camps

In the context of France's Vichy-era constellation of internment camps,
labor camps, and concentration camps, the lowest category of "laborer" has
emerged to propel a series of Holocaust-related lawsuits, resulting in complex restitution programs that rethink definitions and accord a different set
of financial compensations: "forced laborers" are currently defined as deportees during World War II from their home countries brought to Nazi
Germany or German-occupied countries. "Forced laborers" are opposed to
the category of "slave laborers," who were inmates of concentration camps
or ghettos. Distinctions between survivors would play a role in Germany's
indemnification program for North African Jews as part of the year 2000
German Law on the Creation of the Foundation "Remembrance, Responsibility and the Future." The Foundation Law applied indemnifications to North
African Jews who were in concentration camps or other places of confinement under comparable conditions and subjected to forced labor.

   Foundation funds bestow recognition and acknowledgment, thereby
pointing beneficiaries to find value in the symbolic content, not actual amounts.
Actual cash awards since 2000 are meager: compensation is nominal in the
legal sense rarely exceeding $5,000 per victim. The disequilibrium between
low cash payouts and official government recognition for wrongs committed dogs other international reparations protocols. In what way does reparation speak to the representation of rights, and are demands for compensation
and financial payouts about rights vindicated, rights narrated, or rights established as a matter of record? Unlike postwar German *Wiedergutmachung*
programs of the 1950s to European Jewry that took into account biographical data worthy of compensation such as age and loss of livelihood and family, the subsequent 2000 German Foundation Law indemnifications and its
2004 addition of North African Jews avoided the common practice of placing a value on the individual life of the survivor. Its main task was to determine the *eligibility* of the living whose numbers were said to diminish 10
percent annually. Thus, the terms *survivor* and *witness* took on new meanings, not only having survived the camps but also having survived at all,

lived fifty years after the atrocity to become a witness able and willing to make claims and tell the story.

Designating additional camps and detention centers in a default catch-all category as "other places of confinement" became possible under new 2004 Foundation Law criteria: inhumane detention conditions similar to a concentration camp such as insufficient nutrition, lack of medical care, and any indications that all detainees, or at least some of them, were subjected to forced labor. To determine the category "other places of confinement" (*Haftstätten* or "detention sites"), the foundation turned to the Conference on Jewish Material Claims Against Germany (or the Claims Conference). Originally established in 1952 to deal with the *Wiedergutmachung* claims and payments made to European Jewish victims of Nazi atrocities, the Claims Conference was charged with conducting research on living conditions and forced labor in North African places of confinement submitted for recognition. On May 18, 2005, the Claims Conference announced that, following discussions with the German government, Jews who had been incarcerated in North African internment camps in Morocco, Algeria, and Tunisia for at least six months were now eligible for compensation.[57]

According to my interviews in April 2006 with the Berlin office of the German Foundation "Remembrance, Responsibility and the Future," recognition for Jews in North Africa and their "places of confinement" went to thirty-six camps in Algeria, twenty-seven in Tunisia, twenty-four in Morocco, and one in Libya. In many North African camps, researchers noted that both Jewish and non-Jewish inmates were interned together, with Jews constituting a minority of inmates. Algeria was exceptional in that there were all-Jewish labor camps for Algerian Jewish male soldier-conscripts. Despite Jews as a minority of internees, Foundation Law recognized indemnities for Jews only as a people persecuted because of their "race" and only during the Vichy period defined by Germany from October 1940 until November 1942 in Algeria and Morocco and additionally from November 1942 until May 1943 in Tunisia.

The Foundation possessed little information about living conditions in these camps and turned to the expertise of outside researchers. The final list of camps established was based on the research team at the American Claims Conference headed by free-lance historian and researcher Marc Masurovsky and in Germany by "Facts and Files," a historical research company.[58] In my interviews and correspondence with Masurovsky, he stated,

We—the Claims Conference [U.S.-based] research team—pressed hard for acceptance of the North African camps, and obtained rulings via the Claims Conference from the German government to extend the settlements to include a number—not all—the camps in North Africa. The Algerians fared the best, the Tunisians, the worst—in terms of recognized slave/forced labor centers.[59]

Establishing the fact of forced labor in North Africa faced obstacles. American and German researchers repeatedly mentioned resistance among European Jewish Holocaust survivors who themselves were administrators at the Claims Conference offices. Providing compensation to Jews in North African camps was not an obvious case because it was believed that their suffering did not match European Jewish suffering. Financial reparation programs for human rights violations in Morocco, Algeria, and the Foundation cases in North Africa were not asking "How much?" or primarily "What happened?" but rather eliciting answers to the question "How does it feel?" These latest reparations draw on individual survivor testimonies and memories not only to reconstruct a historical absence but also to ensure eligibility for payments. Due to lack of archival evidence concerning the degree of suffering in the North African camps, survivor testimonies establish the places and the very grounds for the right to reparation.[60]

For the German Foundation researchers collecting data in American, German, Israeli, and French archives, another difficulty that arose concerned the issue of deportation as the criterion for forced labor. Algeria was then a department of France; therefore, could transfers from French camps in France to those in Algeria be considered deportation? Moreover, France has a long history of deporting common criminals and political prisoners to Algeria since 1830 and the advent of French settler colonization. In France, the hundreds of Vichy-era camps do not qualify for German indemnities, even for Jews, except for a list of the top worst; in contrast, in Algeria, all Vichy-era camps were included as long as the claimant was Jewish. Italian camps were deemed less awful and not included, except Giado, an all-Jewish camp in Libya. Bizerte in Tunisia was included because it was more German than Italian. In sum, criteria for inclusion and exclusion to the list of camps recognized for financial indemnities are based on evidence and testimonies collected from inmates and witnesses over decades through letters, memoirs, and oral interviews.

By 2004, the Germans recognized some thirty-six camps in Algeria as places of confinement for financial indemnification, including Bedeau, the internment camp for Algerian Jewish soldiers. In contrast to Germany's response, in 2007, the French National Assembly again underscored its refusal to assign Algerian Jewish interned conscripts under Vichy the status of bearers of a political internee card (*carte d'interné politique*) as determined by the Office National des Anciens Combattants et Victimes de Guerre (National Office of Veterans and Victims of War). Official French government recognition of "political internee" status bestows a variety of financial and symbolic benefits: increased pension, additional indemnifications, the bearer's right to wear a medal, the ceremonial right to have the French tricolor flag drape the coffin, and more.[61] As with Germany, France's determination rested on camp conditions and establishment but its conclusions were the opposite. Since Algerian Jewish conscripts were not placed in genuine prisons or internment camps, but instead as it was claimed, "regrouped" in labor units (*unités de travailleurs*) at the behest of the chief of the French armed forces on March 27, 1941, any and all indemnification and recognition as internees were refused:

The State Secretary at the Ministry of Defense in charge of veterans, wishes to clarify to the honorable Parliamentarian that the situation of former soldiers, originally from Algeria and of the Jewish faith, who were directed toward "Jewish workers groups" pursuant to a decision of March 27, 1941, has given rise to a number of opinions from the National Commission of the Deported and Political Internees. However, the members of this commission have always considered that these soldiers were not interned in the sense of the status under the internal code of military disability pensions and war victims but as regrouped, until the liberation of their [conscription] class, in workers units in Bedeau and the forests of Bossuet (Algeria), pursuant to a decision of the Chief of Staff of the Armed Forces in March 27, 1941. Under these conditions, these people cannot lay claim to the title of political internee, as defined by articles L. 288 and R. 388 of the aforementioned code, under which this title is awarded to any French or French national resident in France or in a country overseas country having been the object of an internment. Concerning North African territories and in particular Algeria, only those recognized are persons detained in prisons or "monitored residence centers" created by the decree of November 18, 1939 and imposed in Algeria by the decree of November 21, 1939, modified and completed notably by the

laws of September 3, 1940 and November 15, 1941. These texts had
established a procedure for an administrative order providing for the
internment of "persons dangerous to the national defense and public
security."[62]

Algerian Jews en masse received reparations for material losses only
after they left Algeria for France, where they were recategorized not as indigenous Jews but as settler colonialists "repatriated" (*pieds-noirs rapatriés*)
to a homeland that was never historically theirs but subsequently did become so. Similarly, Algerian Jews who served in the French Army, as did
Roger Azoulay during World War II and the post-Vichy 1943–45 years, were
granted the same veterans' benefits as French citizens.

Not So for Algeria's Muslims

Algeria's "Muslims," to use the terminology of the time, interned in Vichy-
era camps for political activities (often categorized as criminal acts) were
not recognized by German indemnities because Germany reasoned that Muslims, unlike Jews, were not imprisoned on racial grounds. Nor is it conceiv-
able that Algerian Muslims and their sojourns in a variety of Vichy-run
Algerian camps, or for that matter internment during the lengthy French colonial era, will ever be a matter for official French government acknowledgment. For Algerian Muslim military veterans, as well other soldiers from the
colonies, minimal pension and benefits for their exemplary service in the
French Army to the Allied war effort constitutes a separate shameful history.
Allocated 3–30 percent of their fellow French combatant pensions, the situation began to be rectified in 2001 for the surviving 40,000 still living in Algeria. During the 1939–40 "phony war" (*drôle de guerre*) ending in the fall of
France, military statistics show that 5,400 North Africans were killed (from
a total of 85,000 men who died). In addition 1,800,000 French Army soldiers
were taken prisoner by Germany, as enumerated by Algeria's governor-general
Yves Chatel, among them 90,000 Algerian Muslims, sixty thousand Algerian
pieds-noirs and Jews, eighteen thousand Moroccans, and twelve thousand Tunisians.[63] Some 120,000–150,000 Algerian Muslim soldiers fought heroically
in 1942–45, as part of the 235,000 Muslims from the Maghrib in the French
Army who suffered 52 percent of casualties (killed, wounded, and missing in
action).[64] Among demands made by the returning World War II Algerian

combat veterans conscripted into the French Army was full citizenship. On May 8, 1945, in Setif, Algeria, the day of Germany's surrender to Allied Forces in Europe, an estimated forty-five thousand Algerians (European historians put the figure at between fifteen and twenty thousand) died in a series of raids, reprisals and crackdowns after a victory parade turned into protests and then uprisings by Algerians in opposition to French colonial rule.

In *The Wretched of the Earth*, written before Algerian independence was achieved in 1962, Frantz Fanon foresees and presumes the successes of political independence for French-colonized Algeria. More interestingly, he carries his argument past the inevitability of national self-determination and sovereignty to envision the next stage of relations between the former colonizer and colonized. Fanon argued, as early as the 1950s, for a "just reparation" for the crimes of colonialism, one that he insisted should be marked by a "double realization": on the one hand, the colonized must articulate that reparations are their rightful and just due; on the other, colonizing capitalist powers must acknowledge the requirement to pay, to indemnify the colonized:

> The imperialist states would make a great mistake and commit an unspeakable injustice if they contented themselves with withdrawing from our soil the military cohorts, and the administrative and managerial services whose function it was to discover the wealth of the country, to extract it and to send it off to the mother countries. We are not blinded by the moral reparation of national independence; nor are we fed by it.[65]

Thus, while independence and self-determination were defined as mere moral forms of reparative justice, Fanon considered centuries of colonialism and its attendant despoliation of land, people, and resources compelling and justifiable claims for financial indemnification:

> The wealth of the imperial countries is our wealth too. On the universal plane this affirmation, you may be sure, should on no account be taken to signify that we feel ourselves affected by the creations of Western arts or techniques. For in a very concrete way Europe has stuffed herself inordinately with the gold and raw materials of the colonial countries ... Latin America, China, and Africa. From all these continents, under whose eyes Europe today raises up her tower of opulence, there has flowed out for centuries toward that same Europe

diamonds and oil, silk and cotton, wood and exotic products. Europe is literally the creation of the Third World. The wealth which smothers her is that which was stolen from the underdeveloped peoples. The ports of Holland, the docks of Bordeaux and Liverpool were specialized in the Negro slave trade, and owe their renown to millions of deported slaves. So when we hear the head of a European state declare with his hand on his heart that he must come to the aid of the poor underdeveloped peoples, we do not tremble with gratitude. Quite the contrary; we say to ourselves: "It's a just reparation which will be paid to us."[66]

Reparations That Never End

During World War II, the crime of colonialism, to borrow Fanon's term, was intensified and exacerbated by French and German fascism with the result that the preexisting French colonial disciplinary regimes of prisons, *corvée* (forced labor) for the natives, camps, and other forms of internment were mobilized against Algerian Jews who were French citizens. Reverberations for these forms of confinement continued for decades afterward to assert the French colonial state's seemingly never-ending control over Algerian bodies, both Muslim and Jewish. The postindependence Algerian state founded in 1962 never asked for reparations from France according to available avenues through which one state may raise claims against another state. However, when France attempted to pass the 2005 law mandating colonialism's positive features and its civilizing mission to be taught in the French secondary school system, Algerian president Abdelaziz Bouteflika swiftly demanded an official state apology—but not reparations—from the French government for the "crimes of colonialism." In the end, French president Jacques Chirac vetoed this law, but no apology was forthcoming. In practice, individual Algerian Muslim citizens have used the French court system with varying degrees of success to make claims for individual reparations, for indemnification, or for veterans' benefits for spouses and children. Conflating World War II and the Algerian war of independence, these demands rely on accusations of French torture and rape by the French military or France's forced conscription of Algerians as soldiers in its various wars.

Algerian Jews, specifically former Vichy Algeria camp internees currently residing in France, have continued to demand recognition and compensation from France for Vichy-instigated confinement in Algerian camps during World War II to no avail. In contrast, pensions, certainly French military pensions, are perceived as the citizen's right for services to the nation and are allocated according to transparent, systematized schedules of payment. Once France belatedly recognized financially its World War II colonial army in the second millennium, the French state retained colonial practices that distinguished between the price of blood shed in war by French citizens as opposed to the price of blood shed by its colonial conscripted subjects. France reinscribed the colonial state by continuing to deny pension payments to widows and children of fallen Algerian Muslim veterans, the latter, if alive, finally paid at parity sixty years later in 2007 with their fellow combatants who were French citizens. Yet when claims for human rights abuses during the colonial era are in fact recognized and money disbursed, as were German Foundation Law reparation protocols, beneficiaries are not seen as heroic and deserving combatants but rather as victims or survivors who nonetheless insist that reparative sums are insufficient.

It is significant that Algerian Jews as French citizens "repatriated" to France after 1962 had access to indemnities because they were considered to be like the former *pieds-noirs colons* (European settlers) by both the French colonial rulers in Algeria and in post-1962 France. Conversely, they had access to German indemnities because they were not considered settlers but rather *indigènes* (natives) by Vichy authorities in power from 1940 to 1943 in Algeria. In the first, French case, indemnity was dispensed after Algerian independence because they were included in the colonizing social body of lost French Algeria once they arrived in France and, in the second German case, because they were excluded during Algeria's Vichy era when the Crémieux Decree was abrogated returning Jews to their pre-1870 status similar to Algeria's Muslim "natives." These reparations decisions merit a rethinking of the Crémieux Decree, usually interpreted as the legal and juridical mark of the emancipation of the Algerian Jews. Within the colonial setting of French Algeria, the decree also functioned to fix the boundaries of the Arab-Berber Muslim indigenous other in opposition to European settlers and Algerian Jews. According to historian Lorenzo Veracini, the Crémieux Decree initiated settler colonial Algeria by constituting the separate spheres of settler and indigenous collectives. Prior to the decree, Algeria was configured as a classic colonial system: metropolitan France in charge with all the other communities subjected to its rule, including the community of European settlers. After the Crémieux Decree, a settler colonial system sets up communities construed as exogenous outsiders (European *pieds-noirs* and Algerian Jews) at the top of the hierarchy, and the various Arab and Berber communities, labeled indigenous, are subordinated.[67] The power of the Crémieux Decree is overturned in 1962, when Algeria gains its independence and the communities considered "native" become the rulers. Therefore, the European settlers along with the Algerian Jewish community depart en masse because leaving Algeria is made possible by French acknowledgment that their home is France, even for native Algerian Jews.

Both German and French reparations are targeted as payments for the settler colonizer to compensate for the end of colonialism. Reparations were never for the native, even the Algerian Muslim native relocated to the metropole, a conclusion made clear in the case of the *harkis*, or Algerian Muslims who departed for France after Algerian independence because they sided with the French, including through military service, against their Algerian compatriots. *Harkis* (estimated at 85,000 auxiliaries with families plus 55,000 privileged Algerian Muslims) were granted lesser compensation, indemnifications, and subventions.[68] Therefore, it is worth emphasizing this point: there is a remarkable degree of consistency between French and German practices— *neither compensates the colonized.* From the perspective of settler colonial studies, the life and fates of an individual are determined by one's place in the settler colonial hierarchy. North Africa's Jews under French colonialism, according to Tunisian Jewish writer Albert Memmi, uneasily shifted categories between colonizer and colonized: "I was sort of a half breed of colonization understanding everyone because I belonged to no one."[69] The mutability and dispensability of Algerian Jewry in the settler colonial context of French Algeria transformed the indigenous North African Jews from native to French Jewish citizens of Algeria to *pied-noir* settlers repatriated to France, thereby opening up the space for various indemnifications from the French government that will lead to their ultimate disappearance as Jews native to Algeria through absorption into the French metropole.

CHAPTER 7

Compensation for Settler Colonialism:
Aftermaths and "Dark Teleology"

Revenge

is not what you're after you're after what
you cannot name but names you

Revenge is after you
After you

words be my body
lick my ears against revenge

—Fady Joudah, "Revenge"

Two fundamental questions are posed by post-World War II German reparations in relation to monetary recompense—how much is an individual life
worth, and who counts as human? By effectively broadening legal and economic constructs for human rights remedies in the aftermath of the Holocaust, Germany's approach to its European Jewish victims became a starting
point for scholarly studies of postwar reparative protocols. Since 1952, Germany's *Wiedergutmachung* attests to the seminal roles that Jewish experiences of Holocaust reparations play in ongoing considerations of reparations
worldwide. "The Holocaust," Hungarian author Imre Kertész affirms "is a
value, because through immeasurable sufferings it has led to immeasurable
knowledge, and thereby contains immeasurable moral reserves."[1] Through
the lens of torts and rights, the measurability of immeasurable Holocaust
suffering is articulated in the 1948 Universal Declaration of Human Rights

(UDHR), a document that was itself an outcome of World War II's genocides and regimes of slave labor. As principles of the UDHR compensation for gross violations of fundamental human rights attain global endorsement and application, so too do reparations evolve from past to future-oriented claims and, therefore, from past war-related violations to encompass state-sponsored violence of many types. As anthropologist Barbara Rose Johnston attests,

> "reparations" has come to mean the struggle as well as the end result and refers to those efforts to voice social injustice, demand account-ability, and seek remedy not only for violations of human rights and humanitarian law that occur during time of war, but also for those violations that occur as a result of state-sponsored violence against its own citizens in the name of colonial expansion, economic devel-opment or national security.[2]

Incommensurable suffering is atoned for through a counterdynamic of quantifiable, assessable measurability. Even at the individual microsocial level, interactions between my family and the postwar German reparations bureaucracy are profoundly influenced by measurable amounts of money transmuted both quantitatively and qualitatively through the passage of time. Between my mother and Germany, each side makes decisions about their re-spective, sometimes opposing preferences, while both are subject to dynamic and reciprocal recalibrations concerning the nature of reparations: beginning in 1952, my mother refused to have any part of German reparations ex-changes; in turn, Germany increasingly enlarged the categories of beneficia-ries until it arrived at my mother's acceptance in the year 2000 of her designation "slave laborer."

Based on family experiences, I conclude that, between perpetrator and vic-tim (or, in neutral terms, between a bestowing agent and a recipient), repara-tions remain an incomplete and unstable process because they are part of a dynamic mechanism in which money is not the sole determinant. Economists are cautioned to take into account individual visceral reactions, dominant feel-ings, and religious beliefs in the face of economic exchanges commonly labeled "repugnant markets." For example, economist Alvin Roth examines resis-tances to monetizing certain activities, such as legalizing kidney sales and es-tablishing a kidney exchange bureau, noting the potential for change over time once society no longer deems them "distasteful, inappropriate, unfair, undig-nified, unprofessional."[3] For my mother and Roth, society's capacity to correct glaring disparities surrounding economic remedies is linked to the dimension of time because only with the passage of decades might recipients' repugnance to monetizing suffering diminish in the face of reparative remedies.

Over sixty years have passed since West Germany enacted the Federal Indemnification Law, known as the Bundesentschädigungsgesetz (BEG) for reparations to European Jews. Are reparations ever finished? Germany continues to expand possibilities for claims beyond the 2000–2004 slave and forced labor categories acceptable to my mother by adding new indemnifications for Nazi-instigated Jewish sufferings. In 2007, the German government's Social Security administration revamped the "Ghetto Work Fund" to provide a one-time payment of €2,000 to Jewish survivors of Nazi-era ghettos. Created to acknowledge a category of ghetto survivors previously rejected for German social security payments, the fund accommodated my mother's 2009 application for months spent in the Mátészalka Ghetto where she worked without remuneration in what passed for a medical clinic (cf. Chapter 1).[4] On November 12, 2012, the year marking the sixtieth anniversary of the historic 1952 BEG, a ceremony brought together representatives from Germany (unified with different postwar boundaries), Israel (established after World War II with the largest Jewish survivor population), and the Jewish Claims Conference, the prominent American partner organization and conduit for reparation disbursements in North America. Even as the numbers of Jewish *Wiedergutmachung* recipients decline precipitously and in inverse ratio to new and proliferating categories of victim inclusion, German delegates publicly affirmed additional open-ended, financial home-care support agreements for elderly aging survivors. Whatever the complex, varied forces propelling these latest, ongoing reparation initiatives—the international Jewish community, the United States government, and Germany's own internal considerations—the 2012 ceremony foregrounded a salient feature of reparations: the human capacity to continue to give money when sustained by institutional frameworks that maintain the flow of funds from German to Jew for payments on behalf of psychological trauma, time in the ghetto, slave labor remuneration, and more. Stuart Eizenstat, in attendance as an American lawyer and "special negotiator ambassador," reminded audiences

> of the work that is still to be done. All is not finished. The Claims Conference and the international Jewish community call upon Germany to finish out this critical process. After enduring the worst that humanity could devise, these elderly victims—many frail, many more

destitute—deserve in their final years to receive the best that humanity can provide. . . . We are inspired that Germany has committed to ensure that Holocaust survivors, in their final years, can be confident that we are endeavoring to help them live in dignity, after their early life was filled with such tragedy and trauma. Let us help them not to be forgotten again.[5]

For financial reparations to succeed, the reparative motion to give away funds must be sustained, just as philosopher Georg Simmel counseled that money itself must keep on moving:

> There is no more striking symbol of the completely dynamic character of the world than that of money. The meaning of money lies in the fact that it will be given away. When money stands still, it is no longer money according to its specific value and significance. The effect that it occasionally exerts in a state of repose arises out of an anticipation of its further motion. Money is nothing but the vehicle for a movement in which everything else that is not in motion is completely extinguished.[6]

A version of economist John Maynard Keynes's multiplier effect will occur when currency, in this case a strong German euro earmarked for *Wiedergutmachung*, multiplies its symbolic meanings and financial worth whenever Holocaust recipients disburse these awards. In addition to the known benefits of pumping money into the nascent Israeli economy during the 1950s, German reparation to my grandmother in the form of checks automatically deposited each month in an Israeli bank, continue to move around the world, gathering momentum and velocity with her own individual benevolent transactions and gifts to her family. Each successive German reparation payment, both monthly and lump sum since 1952, marks the role of time passing and enhances sixty years of economic exchanges between Germans and Jews, and, in so doing, I claim, opens new ways of giving and receiving money.

My historical and anthropological investigations about my family as *Wiedergutmachung* recipients give me a window into worldviews about the content and outcome of a variety of reparations since World War II. Although my grandmother and mother's experiences do not inherently lead to the necessity for new compensation programs to be put in place, my lifelong exposure to detailed individual narratives of suffering by my mother and grandmother has pushed me toward constructive advocacy, thinking about reparations informed by empathy, the movement of money, and the necessity for financial remedies that return to haunt givers and receivers.[7] My mother's World War II stories about goodness, altruism, silent resistance, and choice under extreme circumstances, which she repeats and recontextualizes throughout my life, provoke human and humane responses in her listeners, whether family or generations of her high school students, because they should. Altruism is humankind's baseline normative behavior, avers anthropologist David Graeber, in agreement with my mother:

> The very existence of altruistic behavior is considered a kind of puzzle, and everyone from economists to evolutionary biologists has become famous through attempts to "solve" it—that is, to explain the mystery of why bees sacrifice themselves for hives or human beings hold open doors and give correct street directions to total strangers. . . . If one were to assume altruism were the primary human motivation, this would make perfect sense: The only way they can convince themselves to abandon their desire to do right by the world as a whole is to substitute an even more powerful desire to do right by their children.[8]

Through family talk (and their anguished decision making) about taking and receiving German reparations, I have come to understand how *Wiedergutmachung* reaches well beyond purely utilitarian and instrumental aims. My attachment to reparative remedies parallels a family history of Holocaust payments, which I view as a potent gift, in contrast to my mother and grandmother's perceptions of a poisoned gift. My grandmother's relentless demands for reparations resulted in something accidental and extrinsic to her own life story, as knowledge about her claims, narrated down our female line, produced a vibrant discourse of human rights and an innovative model with which to rethink contemporary reparative economies. My grandmother's active quest for reparations throughout her post-World War II migrations, matched by my mother's refusal of them for most of her life, have meant that I, a second-generation child of Holocaust survivors, am the third generation caught in the web of financial indemnities, if only as the indirect recipient and intimate onlooker touched by the promises of reparations. German reparations is a gift insofar as the process created a sense of obligation in me to advocate for reparations for others, despite the fact that I was born and raised in Canada, educated in prosperity and freedom in the United States, and, therefore, am reliant on postmemories of inherited narratives about traumatic histories I myself never underwent. Marcel Mauss's insights in *The Gift* are relevant to me, but never to my Auschwitz survivor grandmother and mother whose anguish is bottomless, when he inquires, *"What rule of legality and self-interest, in societies of a backward or archaic type, compels the gift that has been received to be obligatorily reciprocated? What power resides in the object given that causes its recipient to pay it back?"*[9] In other words, my grandmother took reparations, my mother refused them, and I advocate for paying them back by bestowing reparations in contemporary cases of redress.

In this chapter, as an indirect recipient of reparations, my self-appointed task is to think about repayment by moving away from cases of recognized claimants such as my family members, who are free to accept or reject reparations. I extend reparative categories to include potential beneficiaries, those awaiting their right to reparations and to becoming partners in exchanges of redress. If German reparations to European Jews arising from World War II Holocaust claims are past-oriented, then I consider reparations that are future-oriented—in dispute, in process, misnamed, nonpurposeful, indirect, accidental, hoped for, emergent, and still to come. These are ongoing social projects that draw on prior reparative protocols, notably the *Wiedergutmachung* as a preeminent model for reparations, but address what Johnston categorizes as contemporary "injustices that fall into the culpability gap," for which my examples are the "crimes of colonialism" (Frantz Fanon's term) and ethnic cleansing.[10] In contrast to Holocaust reparations that are commemorative, symbolically rich processes to repair the past, following sociologist John Torpey's typology, claims for reparation involving the historical injustices of colonialism are extrapolated, forward looking, and futuristic, "transforming the current conditions of deprivation suffered by the groups in question, and are more frequently connected to broader projects of social transformation than are commemorative projects."[11]

Dark Teleology: The Holocaust and Settler Colonialism

As with many mass tort claims and truth commission payouts throughout the murderous twentieth century, the fundamental question—how much is a life worth?—looks backward to past crimes to trigger a variety of reparation programs that repaired crimes of the National Socialist German regime held responsible for the destruction of European Jewry. Since money emerged as one among a constellation of remedies to restore justice, with reparations by Germany to European Jewry, it is crucial to determine what precisely is the breach in need of repair through German financial indemnifications.[12] During World War II, Germany ripped to shreds the divide that separated European colonizers of the metropole from what they did to their colonized subjects somewhere off in the peripheries of the empire. The result was the confluence of the anti-Semitic genocide of Jews within Europe and the racist genocides of colonized groups outside Europe. Explicit links between the Holocaust and colonialism, as integrally intertwined for the twentieth century, are found in the writings of Martiniquais poet and politician Aimé Césaire in his classic 1955 *Discours sur le colonialisme*:

> Yes, it would be worthwhile to study clinically, in detail, the steps taken by Hitler and Hitlerism and to reveal to the very distinguished, very humanistic, very Christian bourgeois of the twentieth century that without his being aware of it, he has a Hitler inside him, that Hitler *inhabits* him, that Hitler is his *demon*, that if he rails against him, he is being inconsistent and that, at bottom, what he cannot forgive Hitler for is not *crime* in itself, *the crime against man*, it is not the *humiliation of man as such*, it is the crime against the white man, the humiliation of the white man, and the fact that he applied to Europe colonialist procedures which until then had been reserved exclusively for the Arabs of Algeria, the coolies of India, and the blacks of Africa.[13]

Césaire is a proponent of dark teleology, in which colonialism, unleashed on the European continent against Europeans, is directly linked to the emergence of Nazism. A straight line runs from the brutal racist worlds of prior centuries of European colonialism hidden abroad to post-World War I fascism in Europe. Colonialism, he argues, was the necessary forerunner to the Holocaust:

> First we must study how colonization works to decivilize the colonizer, to brutalize him in the true sense of the word, to degrade him, to awaken him to buried instincts, to covetousness, violence, race hatred, and moral relativism; and we must show that each time a head is cut off or an eye put out in Vietnam and in France they accept

the fact, each time a little girl is raped and in France they accept the
fact, each time a Madagascan is tortured and in France they accept
the fact, civilization acquires another dead weight, a universal regres-
sion takes place, a gangrene sets in, a centre of infection begins to
spread; and that at the end of all these treaties that have been violated,
all these lies that have been propagated, all these punitive expeditions
that have been tolerated, all these prisoners who have been tied up
and "interrogated," all these patriots who have been tortured, at the
end of all the racial pride that has been encouraged, all the boastful-
ness that has been displayed, a poison has been distilled into the
veins of Europe and, slowly but surely, the continent proceeds toward savagery. And then one fine day the bourgeoisie is awakened by
a terrific boomerang effect: the gestapos are busy, the prisons fill up,
the torturers standing around the racks invent, refine, discuss.[14]

Like his mentor Césaire, Frantz Fanon teleologically connects Nazism
and colonialism: "Deportations, massacres, forced labor, and slavery have
been the main methods used by capitalism to increase its wealth, its gold
and diamond reserves and to establish its powers. Not long ago, Nazism transformed the whole of Europe into a veritable colony."[15] These analyses by
Fanon and Césaire, based on clear continuities of a brutal empire inexorably
paving the way to modern forms of Nazi atrocities, explain the ways colonial racial hierarchies were subsequently and teleologically inflected for Europe during the Holocaust. My point is that their views are opposed in every
measure by Germany's reparation programs when determining who is compensable and who is rejected. As long as postwar German compensation
constitutes the Nazi German era as a historical anomaly (which I claim is
the way *Wiedergutmachung* operates), then Germany must repair the ways
in which the Holocaust breaches geographical, racial, and moral divides by
treating Jews, Slavs, and other targeted groups, hitherto considered white
and European, as if they were colonized blacks and Arabs. This explains
why Germany stands consistent in refusing responsibility for the crimes of
colonialism in Vichy French Algeria. Germany, exceptionally and only as
late as 2004, acknowledged discrimination against Algerian Jews, who had
been transformed by the Crémieux Decree of 1870 from colonized native
into colonizing French citizen of Algeria, while it ignored histories of the
fate of Jews in Algeria where they were subjected to the multiple frameworks
of colonialism, settler colonialism, fascism, and imperialism from beyond

their borders. In specific historical and genealogical ways, Algerian Jewry helped make the case for indemnification to European Jews in the 1940s precisely because they were perceived as nonnatives and Europeans (cf. Chapter 6). In contrast, Algerian Muslims, also interned in Vichy-era camps are not recognized by any 2004 German reparations because post-World War II German indemnifications did not perceive Muslims, unlike Jews as the former colonizers who became prisoners interned on racial grounds. Algerian Muslims as colonized natives had long been subjected to prison and forced labor beginning with France's conquest of Algeria in 1830. When such colonial atrocities overlapped chronologically to mesh with Vichy fascist practices, the savage treatment of the natives was not deemed specific to World War II. Dispossession and brutality were always their lot.

These different instances of German and French indemnifications, directed solely at Algerian Jewry, position Algerian Jews as a recipient group unavoidably within the context of colonial and settler-colonial projects. For France, after Algerian independence and the so-called return of Algerian Jews in 1962 to France, a country that was never their place of origin, the mass exodus from their native country was bureaucratically named "repatriation" to France, thereby providing access to indemnities once the French state lumped Algeria's Jews together again with the European settler colonists. To compensate the class of *colons* (settler colonists) for the end of French colonialism in Algeria after independence in 1962, France allocated reparations to European settler colonizers (in which category they included Algerian Jews). Once the Algerian colony was taken away, in the context of a transaction between metropole and settler colonists, a debt was established. France acknowledged the collective claims of moral debt in the sense of the nation's indebtedness to settler colonialists. Property and livelihoods were lost, and, as with damage and tort laws, French reparations were premised on the hypothetical, counterfactual belief in eternal colonial domination. Therefore, indemnification was calculated in terms of what colonists would have been worth had French colonialism in Algeria endured, a form of self-interest conjoined to the economic notion of interest, defined by David Graeber as "insatiable desires under the guise of impersonal math, since what is 'interest' but the demand that money *never cease* to grow?"[16] Of the three moral principles that establish economic relations—communism, mutuality, and hierarchy, according to Graeber—hierarchy, in many ways the opposite of reciprocity, characterizes French cash awards to their former settler colonists repatriated to France:

Whenever the lines of superiority and inferiority are clearly drawn and accepted as the framework of a relationship, and relations are sufficiently ongoing that we are no longer simply dealing with arbitrary force, then relations will be seen as being regulated by a web of habit or custom. Sometimes the situation is assumed to have originated in some founding conquest.[17]

Graeber's assumption is that money obligations (the debt between France and its settler colonists) historically precede the exchange of goods (so-called primitive societies and their barter economies) and, therefore, allows me to explain France and Germany's past-oriented reparations to settler colonists for the loss of colonialism. Specifically, the French version reinforces colonialist ideology by accepting the end of France's domination over North Africa as a national expression of indebtedness, meaning a moral debt convertible to a monetary one, buttressed by a system of credit to indemnify not the Algerian natives for dispossession but their former European rulers for the loss of the colony.

For Germany, Algerian Jews were granted German *Wiedergutmachung* payments in 2004 because Vichy authorities over Algeria during World War II, in abrogating the Crémieux Decree, no longer considered Jews as French settler-colonists with French citizenship but relegated them to the status of natives discriminated against for racial reasons. Germany pays for Vichy France and, similar to France, compensates colonists for the loss of status as colonists and the loss of colonialism. Moreover, Germany is consistent in refusing responsibility in Southwest Africa for crimes of colonialism. That country's colonial ventures have so far merited apologies but nothing like the post-World War II *Wiedergutmachung*, "making-good-again" reparations for European Jewry. For example, Germany's dispossession and near extermination of the Herero and Namaqua tribes took place in their colonial possession of Southwest Africa (present-day Namibia) during the wars of 1904–1907. Walther Rathenau, dispatched to the region as a contemporary observer shortly after the end of the Herero Wars, characterized the aftermath even at the time as "the greatest atrocity that has ever been brought about by German military policy."[18] In 1995, during the visit of Germany's chancellor Helmut Kohl to the region, Herero leader Kuaimi Isaac Riruako demanded reparations for large-scale German confiscations of lands and cattle, and especially for the deaths of two-thirds of his people eighty years before through slave labor, torture, and medical experimentation:

After delivering the petition, Riruako stated, "We think we have a legitimate claim for reparations as a result of the war and genocide committed against the Hereros by the German army." The Herero Traditional Authority, he continued, was prepared to take its case to the United Nations if Bonn rejected the claim. And, in a surprising move, Chief Riruako, through the Chief Hosea Kutako Foundation, recently [in 2001] filed a lawsuit against three German companies in the Superior Court of the District of Columbia, asking for $2 billion (U.S.) in reparations, asserting the companies were in a "brutal alliance" with imperial Germany in the Herero War.[19]

Germany's refusal of financial compensation for the Herero genocide brings back arguments on behalf of a dark teleology. Hannah Arendt in *Origins of Totalitarianism* espoused teleological linkages between colonialism in South Africa and the rise of National Socialism in Germany, as does Herero Chief Riruako: "What Hitler did to the Jewish people was something that originated in German colonization of Namibia. The Holocaust started with us here."[20] The pre-World War I genocide of the indigenous peoples of colonized German Africa is not admitted into the extensive and ever-expanding ambit of German reparations, although Germany assigns favorable trade agreements and development aid for Namibia as attenuated forms of rewards. In sum, if some Europeans somewhere and for some reason are treated in ways that correspond to colonized non-Europeans, Germany must rectify and repair only this breach. As late as 2012, Germany's sole reparative action was to restore Herero skulls to Namibia, thereby removing evidence of what was done to the actual physical bodies of the colonized through their repatriation to the former colony. Some twenty Herero individuals, who died between 1905 and 1907 from starvation and forced labor in the Shark Island prison camp, had been dissected by German military and colonial doctors. Their heads were preserved, then shipped to the metropole's research centers for further examination of the colonized's physiognomy, then displayed in museums.[21]

The Herero case affords one explanation as to why German reparations distinguish between Arab and Jewish inmates of North African camps. Germany, according to this rationale, is not responsible for the crimes of colonialism; instead, it holds itself accountable solely for importing the crimes of colonialism into the European metropolitan space and against noncolonized European peoples and groups. Neither German reparations nor French indemnifications constitute a critique of colonialism, merely a profound regret at its demise. If colonialism and settler colonialism are based on over-lapping processes of domination and displacement of the native, the Germans regret the end of displacement and the end of the fundamental distinction between Europe and non-Europe, while the French regret the end of their colonial domination. Both states interpret only the end of displacement and domination as crimes, and only these crimes establish a debt each colonizer country must repay.

Reparations and Comparing Settler Colonialisms

German reparations for the Holocaust are past-oriented and utterly unlike the future-oriented repair of crimes of colonialism. Pertinent questions for my advocacy of reparations within the framework of colonialism and settler colonialism are not merely "How much is a life worth" but also "Who counts as human and compensable?" What are the ways that crimes of colonialism merit reparations? How do reparations compel a powerful colonizer to earn legitimacy by persuading the colonized that, in fact, settler colonialism is justified or even inevitable? Given the money and power of colonialism to determine vastly unequal transactions between colonized and colonizer, what possible freedom of choice to accept or reject reparations exists for colonized natives anywhere when they are faced with extensive land expropriation, cultural eradication, and ethnic cleansing? Do these kinds of reparations from a colonizer willing to pay the colonized for the continuation of settler colonialism share features with the vast programs of reparations between a perpetrator German state and its Jewish victims? Is this comparison between reparations for settler colonialism and reparations for the Holocaust a distortion in the realms of victimhood too sacred to be traded? Even if there are constraints on comparison, specifically to the 1948 forcible depopulation of Palestinians from their homeland that became the State of Israel in 1948, nonetheless, in terms of aftermaths and afterlives, is the Palestinian *Nakba* (catastrophe) of 1948 an event subject to a discussion of what is calculable and compensable to Palestinians Arabs by Jewish Israelis?

A range of responses to the question of comparison draws on the disciplines of psychology, history, and economics. A psychological perspective, although historian Ilan Pappé notes that he himself avoids such analogies, maintains counterintuitively that there is power in promoting likenesses to elicit Jewish Israeli empathy: "one has to understand that everything in Israel is measured vis-à-vis the holocaust. Only in fact when the association is made—rightly or wrongly—the moral space of Israelis begins to include the Palestinian victims of their government's policies."[22] Historically, Israeli government proposals for financially compensating the expelled Palestinian population were directed toward resettlement and integration outside their homeland and always in opposition to the right of refugee return, despite UN General Assembly Resolution 194:

> The refugees wishing to return to their homes and live at peace with their neighbors should be permitted to do so at the earliest practicable date, and that the compensation should be paid for the property of those choosing not to return and for loss of or damage to property which, under principles of international law or in equity, should be made good by the governments responsible. (UNGA Res. 194, December 11, 1948, Article 11)

Around a year after Israel became an independent state in October 1949, by which time the majority of the indigenous Palestinian population had been expelled, the Israeli government established a series of advisory bodies to consider the issue of compensating Palestinian refugees, such as the 1949 Compensation Committee, the 1950 Lif Committee, and the 1953 Horowitz Committee. One after the other, each investigating panel reflected identical, inflexible state policies in rejecting both repatriation (avoidance of a Palestinian influx) and restitution of properties (already expropriated and redistributed to new Jewish ownership).[23] There was some attention paid, if only during the early years of statehood, to the prospect of financial compensation to Palestinian refugees in the form of a lump sum collective payment to a designated, internationally overseen fund.[24] In contrast to the Palestinian Arabs, the Israeli government did eventually accord compensation to the German Templers, or Tempelgesellschaft, a breakaway Lutheran group who settled in Palestine in the 1860s. Their complex World War II and postwar histories, as recounted by Suzanne D. Rutland, included service in the German Army for the men, internment as German enemies, confiscation of their property by Israel's German Property Law, and collective immigration for most of the community to Australia.[25] Partly due to political pressure exerted on their behalf by the Australian government, the Templers successfully negotiated for Israeli compensation by 1962:

the Templers in Australia compiled a document opposing the German Property Bill and stating their case for compensation from Israel, while also supporting the Jewish claim for material compensation from Germany. The Templer leaders, Fritz Lippmann and Walter Hoffmann, stressed that there was a need to differentiate between property in Israel owned by the German government and that owned by religious communities and individuals. They criticized the impending German Property Law as making an assumption that "two blacks make a white" and they noted that the fact that "Hitler wronged the Jews does not entitle Israel to wrong a religious community, its members or friends."[26]

Among Suzanne Rutland's conclusions are Australia's effective political savvy as a recipient of Israeli compensation for resettling what were deemed to be German Nazi refugees, while scholars compare and contrast this historical anomaly with Israel's ongoing refusal to address Palestinian human rights and the claim for restitution and compensation.[27]

Jewish claims to restitution and reparations during those very same early years of statehood resulted in the transfer of German *Wiedergutmachung* funds into Israel's economy beginning in the 1950s. For historian Ronald Zweig, it is necessary to draw explicitly on the principles of postwar German indemnification to Jews as the model for future Palestinian restitution and reparations from Israel:

> There were lessons to be learned from the Jewish-German reparations process that were relevant to the Palestinian Arab refugee problem. . . . Beyond the specific historical experiences of these two cases, restitution of material assets could be an important tool in dealing with refugee crises in general. Enforcing material restitution prevents states from enriching themselves by expelling ethnic or other minorities. Restitution will be paid when there are significant sanctions for not doing so. . . . If restitution of material assets is considered part of the armoury of the international community's efforts to resolve refugee problems, it should be possible to enforce by making aid, trade and participation in the international financial community conditional on the resolution of refuge claims. Payment of commercial debts is enforced in this manner.[28]

From an economic perspective, Karl Marx, Georg Simmel, and Max Weber would support the analogy between actual German *Wiedergutmachung* to Jews and potential Jewish Israeli reparations to Palestinian Arabs, if only because "capitalist moneys render everything quantifiable according to one scale of value and permit previously unthinkable comparisons among objects, persons, and activities."[29] Money from reparations diminishes, levels, and flattens to measure and scale disparate events according to widely shared international protocols of indemnification, even if reparations are morally marked or "repugnant." If money from reparations is a gift, as viewed by Marcel Mauss in so-called primitive societies, then gifts can be measured, quantified, and calculated. If they are commodities, they still possess a moral dimension.[30] Simmel makes the point that reparations are never anonymous because perpetrator and victim identities are crucial to the exchange of cash. In multiple ways, money does not depersonalize social exchanges; instead, in the form of reparations of every variety, money invites and seeks to create new connections.[31]

Money exchanges involved in reparations are frequently subject to failure, partial resolutions, controlled remedial efforts, deflated outcomes, disregarded claims, and the absence of acknowledging perpetrator culpability. Some countries established remedy programs directed at their own citizens or foreign nationals that appear to resemble torts, restitution, or reparations, but payment protocols are labeled something else. Governments camouflage these transactions to obscure their reparative nature, but in reparations begin possibilities, whether the word is mentioned or not. Two examples are "blood money" payments by the United States government for military operations in parts of the Muslim-majority world and Israeli payments of *pitsuyyim* to Palestinians.

Paying Reparations by Calling Them Something Else (1): American "Blood Money" in Middle East Conflicts

American payments for civilian killings continue to be widespread and effective silencing mechanisms aimed at subverting local legal practices while simultaneously effacing covert U.S. operations.[32] Consider the events that unfolded in the city of Lahore, Pakistan, on January 27, 2011, when a thirty-six-year-old American CIA contractor named Raymond Davis was charged with double murder in the deaths of two Pakistani men, Faizan Haider and Fahim Shamshad. Newspaper accounts describe Davis as firing his gun at two men on motorcycles, whom he believed were armed and attempting to rob him as he stopped his vehicle at a traffic signal. At the same time, reports place another American employee driving a truck nearby, who, in his rush to rescue Davis, hit and killed a third passing motorcyclist. The driver of the truck somehow managed to leave the country, but Davis was unable to disappear from what escalated into a tense international and legal incident between Pakistan and the United States.

According to the *Washington Post*, "Davis has spent much of the past two years working as part of a group of covert CIA operatives, whose mission appears to have centered on conducting surveillance of militant groups in large cities, including Lahore."[33] Davis claimed self-defense as the victim of a botched attempted robbery. He also insisted on his right to diplomatic immunity. Pakistan's lower court rejected his immunity since no prior documentation attested to any protected diplomatic status. A Lahore trial court judge concluded that Davis's actions constituted intentional murder based on police investigations of ballistics and witness testimony. According to newspaper accounts, the matter was resolved when the families of Davis's two victims— nothing is reported about the truck driver's victim—agreed to receive compensation totaling close to $2.4 million, even though the source of the money remains in dispute. Secretary of State Hillary Clinton declared in interviews that the U.S. government did not pay anything. On March 16, 2011, Davis was released, and it seems that most of the victims' family members as well as Davis left Pakistan. The grieving wife of one of the slain Pakistanis, however, is said to have committed suicide, declaring, "Blood for blood."

To spring Davis, did the United States deploy the mechanism in Islamic law called *diyat*, a term that translates as "blood money"? If so, it was an interesting turn of events, given the attempts of some states and municipalities to promulgate anti-shari'a laws. In 2010, for example, Oklahoma voters passed State Question 755 (or "Save Our State") to block the remote possibility that shari'a would be applied in that state's courts. Oklahoma's version was eventually ruled unconstitutional, but, in the Davis case, it seems that the United States and the CIA looked to shari'a to free an American spy abroad. Money paid to Davis's victims was not determined by international protocols for reparation but instead allocated through *diyat*. Enshrined in Pakistan's penal code, *diyat* demonstrates the ways in which tenets of shari'a intersect with criminal justice and judicial process in Pakistani law: a victim is permitted to pardon a murderer through a determination of actual or symbolic "blood money" payments. It is important to note that, according to Pakistani law, pardon by the victims' families can only take place after a court decides on a murder conviction: Davis had stood trial in a Pakistani court and was convicted of murder before the victims' families could contemplate *diyat*.

The presence of aspects of shari'a in contemporary legal systems of Muslim-majority states varies from country to country. Civil codes, not Islamic ones, often regulate damages and indemnities by relying on tort law. In fact, shari'a provisions may or may not be present to deal with reparations and damages under the general rubric of *diyat*, in which involuntary manslaughter clearly calls for compensation, while voluntary manslaughter may include the perpetrator's flight or family vengeance. The intent of *diyat*, achieved primarily through financial reparations, is to avert private vengeance yet restore public order and social accord at the local level. It is not meant solely as an indemnity payment to victims while absolving the guilty. In Pakistan, certain crimes of violence between persons, for example, murder, can be transformed by recourse to *diyat* into crimes between individuals, during which proceedings the state withdraws from the role of representing the victim. In contrast, in the American legal system absent *diyat*, the state represents "the people" against the alleged perpetrator. *Diyat* bought the life of Davis, if that is his real name, but it was never envisioned as a mechanism to settle disputes between sovereign states.

Critics of CIA operations throughout the world view this deployment of *diyat* as the latest example of wealthy America killing Third World civilians with impunity. By refusing Davis diplomatic immunity and pursuing criminal justice, Pakistani law transformed his murderous actions into an incident of interpersonal violence eligible for *diyat*, as opposed to an instance in a pattern of American state perpetration of violence throughout the region. The move to fudge and obscure American state violence as the aberrant acts of individuals is characteristic of the U.S. overseas presence, whether in clandestine or official military operations. For example, data about annual U.S. payouts for so-called accidental shootings of civilians, especially in Iraq and Afghanistan, remain incomplete. Based on information forwarded from the Department of the Army under the Freedom of Information Act in 2007, the American Civil Liberties Union (ACLU) compiled a partial record of Pentagon payments that totaled $32 million for the years 2005–2006. Although often limited to $2,500, amounts were offered "as an expression of sympathy" but "without reference to fault."[34] Most descriptions of the civilian deaths in the ACLU sample end with the chilling phrase, "No statements from Iraqi witnesses were taken."[35] In other words, the wads of cash were neither reparations nor even blood money but a Pentagon-approved system of "condolence" payments to silence victims and hold no perpetrator accountable.

Compare these Iraqi civilian deaths to the outrage of families from the 1988 Lockerbie airplane bombing that killed 270 people. In response to the 2003 Libyan government offer of compensation, many of the victims' families cried "blood money." If the principle is that offenders who pay money to resolve murder cases are making a clear and public admission of guilt to the surrounding society, then Libya and the Pentagon are counterexamples. For Libya, the price for lifting international sanctions prompted payments of approximately $8 million to each family, while Libya denied guilt. Libya's former minister of justice Mustafa 'Abd al-Jalil claims that Muammar Qaddafi personally ordered the Lockerbie bombing. Setting explosives in the airplane was part of a cycle of violence in which a prior 1986 American airstrike that killed members of Qaddafi's family was itself a response to Libyan bombs in a Berlin nightclub that killed American soldiers. A spiral of retaliation and violence was cut short by the widow of Raymond Davis's victim and the depth of her grief: her suicide and refusal of U.S. blood money made clear her protest against any buy-off because reparative values are also attached to the source of money.

As U.S. drone-borne missile strikes pummel Pakistan and Afghanistan, causing collateral civilian damages and deaths, leaders in Muslim-majority countries seek recourse in international law by pointing to American actions as violations of humanitarian norms and laws. They do not demand blood money through the Islamic dimension of their societies embedded in meaningful cultural and legal traditions. So-called collateral damage to civilians ranges from the violent responses of Raymond Davis against the local population in which he was embedded as a CIA operative to the U.S. military in Afghanistan, Pakistan, and Iraq. Drone attacks are evidence of large-scale U.S. government actions and must be compared with other types of violence, even those adjudicated by *diyat*, precisely because they draw on the mechanism of cash payments. In all these cases, the United States is the perpetrator state, even though, in the Davis case, *diyat* appears to push both the Pakistani and the American states outside a relationship of violence in favor of monetized solutions between individuals. In this way, the United States has responded and adapted to the asymmetric nature of the declared wars on terror by invoking local legal practices such as *diyat*, which coincidentally overlap and already share the financial features of U.S. military practice to dispense derisory cash payouts to Afghan and Iraqi civilian victims.

Legal scholar George Bisharat describes the ability of states to reconfigure and integrate new forms of violence into the law as "legal entrepreneurialism."[36] The adage "might makes right," Bisharat concludes, encourages government ambitions to incorporate violence into the law. An egregious example was the 2002 "torture memos" by then Deputy Assistant Attorney General John Yoo and collaborators in which torture was determined to be legally permissible under new and expanded interpretations of presidential authority in the era of the "war on terror." Arguably, by widening the possibility of buy-outs for killing civilians while eliminating Pakistan's *diyat* provisions of a trial and conviction, the ad hoc character of U.S. payments is driven more by political than legal imperatives.

Perhaps if nothing else worthwhile emerges from the Davis case, future victims and their families should consider blood money as one possible economic and legal sanction and elevate it internationally in the form of economic reparations between states exacted for examples of destruction and death by U.S. drones. As many more Raymond Davises roam the region, recent WikiLeaks—notably the 2007 "JTF-GTMO Matrix of Threat Indicators for Enemy Combatants" files on detainees held in the U.S. military prison at Guantanamo Bay—reveal that those in charge at the prison included Pakistan's Inter-Services Intelligence (ISI) directorate on their list of some sixty-five "terrorist and terrorist support entities." Yet, regardless of various laws and competing legal systems—the 1961 Vienna convention on diplomatic impunity, criminal law, reparation protocols, international human rights law, or shari'a—the partnership between two likeminded organizations, the CIA and the ISI, remains unbroken. The Davis case, the killing of Osama bin Laden, and ongoing U.S. drone strikes may momentarily halt coordinated efforts, but money flows channeled to the ISI by the CIA since September 11, 2001 continue unabated. My questions are whether these American funds are hush money, compensation, "condolence" payments, or *diyat*? And in what ways do they compare with Israeli payments to Palestinians since the 1948 establishment of the State of Israel?

Paying Reparations by Calling Them Something Else (2): *Pitsuyyim* Not *Shilumim* to Palestinians

Pakistanis, Iraqis, and Afghans are quietly paid off by American administrators with deep secretive pockets. This process signals a game about names (for example, the "condolence" payments), but, in the American case, there is evidence that cash payouts diminish relations between the United States and the citizenry of affected countries. American interests abroad view the death of foreign nationals as inevitable products of collateral damage. Like their American counterparts, Israeli administrations have long invoked versions of a tort system to deal with Palestinian casualties and other so-called collateral damages they inflict. The Hebrew word in certain cases is *pitsuyyim*, which translates as "damages, compensation, workmen's compensation," and cash awards to Palestinians. In contrast, the Hebrew word *shilum* in the singular is "reward, requital, payment; bribery," while the plural *shilumim* is "reparations (especially from Germany), reward, remuneration, retribution, restitution."[37] The plural form became the term used by Israelis specifically for Germany's Holocaust reparations:

> The term (*shilumim*) was borrowed from the book of Isaiah [34:8] and indicated that these payments did not imply an expiation of guilt, nor did their acceptance connote a sign of forgiveness. The term embraces an element of vengeance, which at the same time can be a presupposition for bringing about peace (*shalom*). *Shilumim* is fundamentally different from the German word *Wiedergutmachung*, which etymologically means returning to former conditions and, in a broader sense, to a former state of co-existence. . . . The problem of choosing a suitable expression was due to the fact that Jewish claims were in a sense revolutionary and as unique as the Holocaust. Finally, the term *Shilumim* was agreed upon. It was Professor [Yeshayahu A.] Jelinek who reintroduced this term into the scholarly language, and it seems to be the most adequate word we have.[38]

An early example from the first decade of Israeli statehood in which *pitsuyyim* were disbursed to Palestinians followed the events of Thursday, October 29, 1956. Shortly after 5 p.m., Palestinian citizens of Israel, returning home at the end of the agricultural workday, were unaware that a curfew had been declared during their absence in the fields. Men, women, and children of the village of Kafr Qasim were shot by units of the Israeli army charged with guarding Israel's eastern border with Jordan. Until 1967, the village of Kafr Qasim was situated one kilometer from Israel's border with Jordan at the easternmost point of what was once thought of as Israel's *beten rakhah* (soft underbelly), the densely populated narrow coastal strip of Israel extending a mere fifteen kilometers from the Mediterranean Sea to neighboring Jordan. Palestinian border villages shared specific legal and socio-cultural features until the 1967 war brought former Jordanian-ruled West Bank under Israeli occupation, thereby shifting a border farther east to the Jordan River.[39] On the Israeli side of the pre-1967 border, inhabitants lived in the "Little Triangle" and were neither refugees nor "present absentees," the latter defined as Palestinians who are internal refugees displaced from their original homes and lands but still residing within the borders of 1948–1967 Israel. Instead, they became dispossessed farmers, transformed into low-wage laborers for the Israeli economy.[40] On the Jordanian side, the United Nations Relief and Works Agency (UNRWA) did not classify border villagers as refugees.[41] Nonetheless, Palestinians on both sides of the 1949 Israel-Jordan armistice boundaries lost considerable agricultural lands to Israel depending on which side of the border they found themselves: Palestinians living on the Jordanian side lost land because of the Israel-Jordan partition lines, while Palestinian Israeli's land was expropriated by the State of Israel under succeeding emergency regulations that promoted Jewish settlements as strategic defense units along Israel's borders with Jordan.[42]

Kafr Qasim's geographical proximity to a contested militarized border contributed to the ensuing tragedy. Historian Benny Morris notes that, between 1949 and 1956, Israel's "free-fire policy" prevailed along the border and resulted in a series of "atrocities,"[43] including the massacre. Of the forty-nine Kafr Qasim dead, the majority were killed at the western entrance to the village of Kafr Qasim, a few in the center, and some to the north of the center; this last group, known as "the women's group" consisted of fourteen women, a boy, and four men. Two years after the shootings in Kafr Qasim and after a year-and-a-half long, highly publicized military trial (January 15, 1957–October 16, 1958), eleven Border Police (Mishmar ha-Gevul), including the battalion commander, Major Shmuel Malinki, were sentenced to lengthy prison terms. During the trial, testimony was presented by sixteen-year-old Hana Sulayman Amir, a survivor of the massacre, who describes the killings of seventeen people in the third group of women. Hana repeated the words of two Israeli officers as they confronted, then shot, the pregnant Fatimah Salih Sarsur: Officer Shmuel Malinky said to Sergeant Shalom Ofer, *kadur ehad maspik* (a single bullet is sufficient).[44]

In a second swift military trial, the responsible brigade commander, Issachar Shadmi, was convicted of a minor administrative offence and sentenced to pay a fine equivalent to a penny.[45] All convicted Border Police were freed after three years, having received presidential pardons or administrative reductions of sentences, which they served in a Jerusalem sanitorium and not in prison. Lieutenant Gabriel Dahan, found guilty of killing forty-three citizens, was sentenced to seventeen years. He too was freed after three years and rehabilitated, so to speak, with an appointment in 1960 as officer for Arab affairs in the nearby municipality of Ramleh. When Dahan retired, Kafr Qasim villagers reported his latest assignment as a security guard in the Rosh Ha-Ayin mall, a nearby Jewish settlement built on expropriated Kafr Qasim agricultural lands.

A year after the Kafr Qasim massacre, on November 10, 1957, and in the midst of the military trial of the Israeli soldiers, the Public Committee was hastily formed to consider compensation awards for the wounded, the slain, and the heirs. Each victim was valued at 5,000 Israeli *lira* (pound) with the exception of the one pregnant victim, Fatimah Salih Sarsur, whose family was allotted an additional 1,000 pounds "in consideration of the fact that she was in the last days of her pregnancy at her death."[46] One consequence of Fatimah's death is that the number of Palestinians killed by the Israeli Border Police continues to be a figure in dispute: Israelis acknowledge thirteen injured and forty-nine dead, whereas Palestinians count fifty dead because they include as a fiftieth victim the unborn child carried by the pregnant Fatimah. A monument and fountain constructed in 1973 inside the Kafr Qasim municipality complex memorialize the fifty dead, with forty-nine white headstones inscribed with the names of the dead; the fiftieth remains starkly blank.[47]

The aftermath of the Kafr Qasim massacre demonstrated selective cross-cultural features of reparative justice, such as reconciliation and apology, rarely in evidence during subsequent Palestinian demands for justice, restitution, and reparation against the State of Israel. In 1957, the Public Committee's report ended with a recommendation to both sides to set up a *sulhah* ceremony at government expense in Kafr Qasim "in accord with customary Arab tradition" (*be-hetem la-masoret ha-'aravit ha-mekubelet*).[48] The reconciliation ceremony and the financial compensation report were intimately related in time and content. On November 20, 1957, more than a year after the massacre, a mere seventeen days after the Public Committee's recommendation and in the midst of the first trial, a ceremony in Kafr Qasim was staged in the village that was designated by Israeli authorities with the Arabic word *sulhah*. The *sulhah* is a much-studied sociocultural event in Western and Israeli anthropology about the Arab world. Israeli anthropologist

Abner Cohen undertook fieldwork in 1958 in this area not long after the massacre in Kafr Qasim.[49] Cohen illustrates the differences between Jewish Israeli justice and "Arab justice," the latter being a term applied by Cohen to complex Palestinian and Arab juridical institutions such as *sulh* (reconciliation) and *sulhah* (reconciliation ceremony), as they were conducted among Kafr Qasim's *hamulah*s (village clans). Cohen concludes that "Perhaps the most serious divergence between Arab concepts of justice and those implicit in Israeli legislation is the abolition, in Israel, of the death penalty. This abolition runs counter to the Arab notion of justice based on retribution, although allowance is made in Arab justice for the payment of blood money."[50]

Eliminating the death penalty, however, is no guarantee that the state will not find other means to execute its citizens: witness the killings at Kafr Qasim. Cohen's fieldwork conclusions were that "disputes are not regarded by villagers as settled until indigenous procedures of arbitration and reconciliation took place. Often the police themselves helped in setting these procedures in operation. In some of the cases the police were requested by the villagers not to take the disputants to courts, when the matter was settled according to 'Arab Justice'."[51]

Given that Cohen's fieldwork took place a year after the Kafr Qasim massacre, his ahistorical research findings are strikingly oblivious to the reasons Palestinian villagers in Israel, under military rule from 1948 to 1966, preferred local legal controls to Jewish Israeli courts. Nonetheless, how to account for the spectacle of an Israeli government appropriating and financing traditions of "Arab justice"? Ibrahim Sarsur, town mayor during my 1998 visit, said that he and other villagers had come to see the *sulhah* as a response to wrongful murder, powered by the need to cover up through denial and betrayal. Sarsur's description of the *sulhah* is a powerful testimony of the event:

The food was prepared; the food was not eaten. Village inhabitants and a small part of the victims' families were brought to a tent erected in the only village school. During the forced sulhah, notables participated from neighboring Arab villages that were an integral part of the regime's rule in the State of Israel. The media reported that the sulhah was conducted according to the best of Arab tradition. The massacre, according to this definition, was kind of a quarrel of village clans that ended in a sulhah, food, drinks, peace. Ben-Gurion needed a sulhah before the end of the trial of the murderers, a sulhah that supposedly enabled him to make a deal with Malinki and the rest of the soldiers: after the inhabitants of Kafr Qasim forgive, there is no reason for the murderers to remain in jail. "It is a moral obligation to free them," Ben-Gurion claimed. The second reason for Ben-Gurion wanting a sulhah is that it would "release" the Israeli government from any further responsibilities towards the victims. . . . From many conversations I have had with victims' families it emerges that pressure was applied to them and strong threats including threats of deportation and being fired in order that they should participate in the sulhah process. Until today, in Kafr Qasim, there is no one who agrees with the manner of treatment of the government of Israel concerning the massacre and its consequences.[52]

The *sulhah*, when a genuine Arab reconciliation ceremony, mediates publicly disputes among and between individuals, families, and clans; it is not intended to resolve conflicts between persons and governments. Yet the conundrum remains: since Arab justice in Israel is devalued by Israeli Jewish views of the Arab population, for whom did the Israeli government organize the Kafr Qasim *sulhah* and why? Not for the mourning families, Sarsur insists, who were forced to attend and participate in their degradation.[53] A contemporary newspaper account ends with the words of Hamdelelullah Sarsur, a son of a victim: "Not one member of the bereaved families would come to the proposed sulhah with the man standing trial for killing 43 [sic] villagers. He charged that the villagers were 'forced' to sign in favour of the Rashish Committee finding."[54] Israel's leaders reproduced early anthropological "culturalist" views of the Arab world in which Israel's own culturally constructed stereotypes keep non-Western groups as frozen representatives in unvarying societies that are resistant to historical time and contexts theorized as a static, internally coherent social system unaffected by the external impact of colonialism.[55] A potent mix of Orientalism, the settler colonialist's impulse to imitate indigenous ways, the weight of Israeli military rule and administrative control over Arabs in Israel, and crude pressure on the Kafr Qasim families to participate underlies the discourse of *sulhah* as a process toward healing and reconciliation. Similarly, current American military payoff protocols that suborn Pakistani legal mechanisms of *diyat* echo Israel's early practice to appropriate and corrupt indigenous juridical mechanisms traditionally intended to avoid violence and reestablish internally validated moral orders.

Indemnification may be paired with an official spoken apology, and a rare Israeli version was pronounced in 1997. On the forty-first anniversary of the massacre, minister of tourism Moshe Katsav was present to voice an apology as a government representative. Kafr Qasim's mayor Ibrahim Sarsur countered by calling on the government to return 6,000 *dunams* (1,500 acres) of confiscated village lands, a request never implemented. Then Justice Minister Yossi Beilin reiterated the government position "that Israel could not take responsibility for the massacre, saying that the government at the time did not order the shootings."[56] The initial Israeli responses to the massacre in 1956 relied on criminal law administered through military courts, followed by amnesties for all convicted perpetrators. In spite of the outcome, the Kafr Qasim trials established clear legal precedent in Israeli civil and military law that following orders or transmitting the order to shoot is sufficient grounds for determining guilt if murder is the consequence, even if the transmitter of those orders to shoot did not have murderous intentions. Following such legal terminology of the doctrine of a "manifestly unlawful order" in which a "black flag" had been raised and, thus, a "partnership in crime" invoked, the "black flag" criterion of Kafr Qasim was evoked five years later in 1961 during a more internationally famous trial, when Israeli judges condemned Adolf Eichmann to death for his role in exterminating European Jewry. Nonetheless, the Kafr Qasim military trials of soldiers and the "black flag" have never served as deterrents to future hostilities between the Israeli army and Palestinian civilians, despite a famous verdict by Israeli judges (who were borrowed for the army trial from the civil court system) condemning "manslaughter by army personnel" (in Hebrew *harigah 'al yidey ish tsava*) and asserting that soldiers must refuse "a patently illegal order that carries a black flag of criminality."[57]

Paying Reparations by Calling Them Something Else (3): A Limited Financial Compromise for Palestinians in the Occupied Territories

Israeli settler colonialism within the 1948–1967 borders successfully expropriated Palestinian lands while permitting remnants of the native Arab population to remain as landless citizens of the State of Israel, politically neutralized and never fully absorbed into Israel's post-1948 society. Subsequent categorizations and proliferating categories of Palestinians are entirely the creation of

the State of Israel: Palestinian citizens of Israel, Palestinians designated as
"permanent residents" of East Jerusalem, Occupied West Bank Palestinians
with West Bank identity cards, Occupied Gazan Palestinians with Gaza
identity cards, and, finally, exiled, diasporic Palestinians bearing a variety
of passports and citizenships. It would seem that citizenship, and lack
thereof, can be correlated with cash awards. Despite the system of *pitsuyyim*
for loss of life in the village of Kafr Qasim in the form of lump sum cash
awards funneled through a government social welfare system, this mechanism underscores the hollow promise of Israeli citizenship for the Arab
minority as merely the right to be bought off. In the Occupied Palestinian
Territories (OPT) of the West Bank and Gaza, where Palestinians do not
possess minimal rights as citizens, Israeli policies remain consistently minimalist responses in the face of Palestinian demands for reparations as a
means of redress. This means that Israel rejects restitution of Palestinian
land and houses seized since the illegal 1967 occupation, although occasionally it has permitted limited applications of financial compensation as long
as they are understood as the State of Israel's economic, humanitarian op-
tion in cases of wrongful death, material losses, and displacement. Prior to
the watershed year of reversal in 2002 against any form of financial redress
to Palestinians by Jewish Israelis, on occasion Palestinians in the OPT achieved
success in suing the state for compensation in cases of bodily injury or property damage. In 2002 and again in 2005, Israeli state liability laws regarding
torts held that "the state is not civilly liable for an act done in the course of a
war operation" and in a "declared war zone," a designation that may be ret-
roactively assigned by the State of Israel's own Ministry of Defense. Payments may be made in exceptional circumstances at the discretion of a
"Compensation Committee" and "without admitting liability."[58]

"Operation Cast Lead," the name devised by Israel for the invasion and
bombardment of Gaza from December 27, 2008, to January 18, 2009, opened
up a new chapter in the history of Palestinian demands for reparations from
Israel. "Cast Lead" resulted in the deaths of thirteen Israelis (four from
friendly fire) and approximately 1,400 Palestinians, which in turn produced
1,046 criminal complaints to the Israeli Military Advocate General and an
equivalent number of civil complaints to the Compensation Committee of
the Israeli Ministry of Defense. As of 2012, two cases of Israeli court-ordered
payments to Palestinians were negotiated, but only as a settlement minus the
word "compensation." These successes were owed to the Gaza-based Palestinian Centre for Human Rights (PCHR), despite difficulties in bringing

Palestinian witnesses to Israeli courts through the Israel-instigated forced closure of the Gaza Strip border. Cash awards of $108,000 were allocated to the Shurrab family, whose two sons, both civilian noncombatants, were killed by Israeli troops, one shot to death as he lay wounded. A second amount of $120,000 was awarded to the Abu Hajjaj family on behalf of sixty-seven-year-old Raya Abu Hajjaj and her thirty-seven-year-old daughter Majeda, a mother and daughter shot in cold blood in an area of Gaza controlled by the Israeli army. When the civilian population, mainly women and children, were ordered to move out, Raya and Majeda Abu Hajjaj were targeted leaving their house as they tried to comply with army orders and while holding up white flags of surrender. After dropping charges from "involuntary manslaughter" to "misuse of a weapon," the Israeli military court sentenced the soldier in the Abu Hajjaj murders to forty-five days of imprisonment. The PCHR lawyer concluded, "It is clear that the Israeli military court's decision against the soldier confirms the absence of individual criminal responsibility and provides further judicial protection for Israeli soldiers, especially as the penalty for involuntary killing may amount to 20 years of imprisonment."[59]

The military-operated "Compensation Committee" refused the very word "compensation" in their own bureaucratic title in favor of a mediated "compromise," one in which a cash settlement foreclosed further claims.[60] The bureaucracy of cash payoffs with no liability eases the way to disclaimers of responsibility for any criminal policies that may have been carried out. Especially in these cases of compensation that cannot be named "compensation," such solutions by the Israeli civil and military court systems reinscribes and reinforces the complete separation between the Israeli colonizing settler and the native colonized Palestinian populations, effectively building—in Geshon Shafir's typology—a Zionist variant of a pure settlement colony separated in every way from the Palestinian native.[61]

During numerous wars of disproportionate Israeli weaponry unleashed on the Palestinian population, the status of the Arab native as "victim" and potential "claimant" endures unacknowledged, both existentially and bureaucratically. The abysmal nature of Israel's minimalist approach to compensation for the loss of Palestinian lives at the hands of Israeli soldiers is in evidence in the following account redacted from an anonymous Israeli army veteran who served during the Second Intifada (2000–2005) in Balata Camp, a densely populated township that is the largest Palestinian refugee camp in the West Bank, OPT:

[Israeli soldier]: . . . When there are riots, you get permission to shoot at the legs of the kids who throw bricks, and if I happen to shoot and I'm just a rifleman (not a sharpshooter) and I aim at the knee.

[Interviewer]: Can any soldier shoot?

[Israeli soldier]: Yes from his personal weapon. If the commander during the procedure is a deputy company commander, he can authorize this. And if by mistake I hit him in the back or kill him, and we had this 2–3 times just in the last service team.

[Interviewer]: Soldiers killed kids.

[Israeli soldier]: Killed kids by mistake. Aimed at the legs, shot them in the back and killed them.

[Interviewer]: How do you know afterwards if soldiers killed them?

[Israeli soldier]: Reports arrived from the DCL (District Coordination Liaison), the Palestinians report, there is coordination in that sense. So kids get killed. It's nothing to a soldier. And for this an officer can get (fined) 100, 200 shekels.

[Interviewer]: 100, 200 shekels for a kid?

[Israeli soldier]: Yes.

[Interviewer]: Prison?

[Israeli soldier]: No, no.

Interviewer]: A trial? Any serious inquiry about things?

[Israeli soldier]: No. I'm sure it doesn't go above the battalion commander. I don't know of people undergoing an inquiry. I can't say for sure.[62]

The post-World War II pedigree of reparations (restitution, compensation, reparative justice), circumscribed by Israel as financial compensation to Palestinian citizens of Israel, is downgraded to limited, negotiated settlements without liability to Palestinians in the OPT and shrinks to a grotesque semblance in the internal system of military fines paid by Israeli soldier to Israeli soldier with minimal reference to the numbers of Palestinian killed. These three forms of Israeli payments—money as compensation (*pitsuyyim*) for Palestinian citizens of Israel, money as negotiated cash "compromise" for Gazan victims of "Operation Cast Lead," and derisory military fines levied on Israeli soldiers—are embedded in structures of settler colonialism to control Palestinians, whether they reside in the OPT or within the borders of Israel. This is because each type of Jewish Israeli payment to Palestinians is a function of inevitable financial outcomes to ensure the social formations of colonialism and settler colonialism.[63] Jewish Israeli settler colonialism in the OPT seeks to eliminate the natives by simultaneously displacing them and also enriching their own Israeli institutions, hence the circularity of fines that the Israeli army pays itself for indigenous eradication. Israel's colonialism with regard to its own Palestinian citizens of Israel is based on systemic controls over the native rather than killing their citizens. Therefore, Israeli *pitsuyyim* allocated in the Kafr Qasim aftermath reaches the limits of what the state in violent confrontation with its non-Jewish citizens achieved in terminology, cash, and liability. In all instances, Israeli soldiers and the Israeli military are held to minimal accountability through minimal prison time, or no accountability at all through derisory cash payments and fines. The State of Israel mediates for the military to perpetuate a protective cover of refusals—no right of return for either Palestinian refugees or internally displaced Palestinian citizens of Israel, no restitution, and no reparations.

Reparations and the *Nakba*

Since 1948, there have been numerous maximalist and minimalist proposals to resolve the fates of Palestinian refugees by those outside the homeland and those internally displaced within Israel. For the Israeli state and many Jewish Israelis, the ideal encompasses a hoped-for absorption (that is, disappearance) of Palestinians into host countries elsewhere. For Palestinians, the rights of return and reparations (restitution and compensation for lost properties and human suffering) are nonnegotiable. Questions are endless, solutions seemingly insoluble, and my brief review represents an inadequate summary of the discussion, as each aspect is in dispute. For example, discussions continue concerning the ways to calculate current equivalent values for Palestinian losses or even determine recipients to whom compensation is owed. Israel contests the baseline definitions of "refugee" established by UNRWA, the international assistance organization for humanitarian aid to Palestinians.[64] Even as part of my thought experiment of a miraculous reversal in which Israel recognizes the Palestinian right of return, further roadblocks are raised to question whether this refers to repatriation within the 1948–1967 borders of Israel or only within the framework of a two-state solution into the OPT constituted from the West Bank and Gaza: Would Palestinians accept the principle of acknowledgment of the right of return but not its full practical application? Are financial compensation and restitutions collective or individual? Did Palestinian Authority President Mahmoud Abbas, who relinquished his right to the Palestinian right of return for refugees, speak for the Palestinian collectivity or merely for himself during his November 2012 television appearance?

> In the interview [with Israel's Channel 2], Abbas said that although he is a refugee from Safed, he does not intend to return to the city as a resident—if anything, he would visit as a tourist. "Palestine for me is the 1967 borders with East Jerusalem as the capital, this is Palestine, I am a refugee, I live in Ramallah, the West Bank and Gaza is Palestine, everything else is Israel."[65]

None of these issues are insoluble and many remarkable proposals have been circulated. Numerous visionary overtures and practical recommendations concerning reparations, restitution, return, and compensation have been set forth by a plethora of actors and are available in books, articles, lectures, and Internet groups.[66] In all cases, it seems that reparations by definition are indifferent to the political entity that dispenses compensation, which may be a one-state Palestine/Israel, the two separate states of Israel and Palestine in negotiation with each other, or any semblance of a federal or confederated framework. This holds true for philosopher Sari Nusseibeh's modest proposal for an interim single state with second-class citizenship for OPT Palestinians (no rights to vote or hold electoral office), while Jewish Israelis control the military and state bureaucracy. His viewpoint assumes that Palestine/Israel is a settler colonial formation, a land under occupation with every Jewish Israeli city, town, and village a colonial settlement, and Jewish settlement of the Occupied Territories of the West Bank and Gaza irreversible. His conclusion is a call for

> a transitional stage [that] would maintain *Jewish ownership of the state* while guaranteeing Palestinians their human rights and all services a state normally provides for its citizens, including their collective cultural rights. . . . From the Palestinian perspective, this scenario would be a far more bitter pill to swallow. It would require them to

give up the dream of a Palestinian state, and those now living under occupation, as well as those in the diaspora who decided to participate in this experiment, would have to make do, psychologically, with being subjects rather than citizens in their own country.[67]

Palestinians under Nusseibeh's proposal would retain the rights of return and material compensation for lost properties. In theory, compensation to internally displaced and diasporic Palestinian Arab refugees may be endorsed and underwritten by any number of potential parties and agencies— the State of Israel, the American government redirecting $3 billion of its annual weapons budget to Israel for reparation and repatriation, and overseas Jewish organizations and donors, including those in which my mother was active (for example, if B'nai Brith and Hadassah-WIZO would enlarge their humanitarian aid to encompass projects of communal reparations to Palestinians).

Finally, what does it means to advocate for compensation and repatriation when these processes are embedded in settler colonial and colonial frameworks of Jewish Israeli colonizer and indigenous Palestinian Arab colonized? As with the United States, Canada, Australia, and New Zealand, settler colonial societies triumphed because they held on to the majority of land, and they did not depart; they succeeded because they laid claim to indigeneity and native-ness for themselves.[68] In fact, do reparations signal the moment of the natives' utter dispossession as noted by Awni al-Mashni?

> Even the millions of dollars in compensation cannot erase the reality of Palestinian displacement, which is no longer a mere objective fact, but has rather come to shape and has taken over the Palestinian conscience, much like what the crematories and the concentration camps have done to the Jews. Have German reparations, in spite of their exorbitant amounts, drawn attention away from the crematory?[69]

Acknowledging the triumph of Jewish Israeli settler colonialism in Palestine goes hand in hand with a one-state solution in which Palestinians are ideally equal citizens but just as likely, and one hopes temporarily, transformed into Nusseibeh's second-class citizens. Provisionally, there is the small consolation proposed by historian Gabriel Piterberg in which settler societies, even when attempting to erase the native, can never eliminate the interpenetrating histories and interactions between settler and native:

> Whether or not the presence of indigenous people is consequential to how settler societies were shaped, is possibly the most elusive, and the one that exposes the exclusionary, or segregationist, nature of white liberalism, and perhaps multiculturalism as well. The more liberal versions of hegemonic settler narratives may admit that along the path to creating a nation bad things were done to the indigenous people; they may even condemn these "bad things" and deem them unacceptable. At the same time these narratives deny the possibility that the removal and dispossession of indigenous peoples and the enslavement of others is an intrinsic part of what settler nations are—indeed the most pivotal constituent of what they are—rather than an extrinsic aberration or corruption of something essentially good. My point is not whether settler nations are good or bad, but the extent to which the act of exclusion in reality is congruous with the hegemonic rendering of that reality. The exclusionary fundamental that inheres in these white hegemonic narratives lies not in sovereign settlers' denial of the wrong they have done to those whom they have disinherited or enslaved (though such denials are protested all too often), but in their denial of the interaction with the dispossessed is the history of who the settlers collectively are. In short, what is denied is the extent to which the non-white world has been an intrinsic part of what is construed as European or Western history.[70]

I can imagine the Jewish Israeli settler and the Palestinian native inhabiting a hypothetical single state. Perhaps there could be some lingering histories and memories of pre-1948 coexistences when both groups were under British Mandatory rule. Or, despite Nusseibeh's predictions of second-class citizenship, Palestinians would attain parity in terms of population, since repatriation (however limited and partial) tips demography in favor of a Palestinian majority. As a Jewish Israeli settler nation with a potential Palestinian majority, would reparations from the minority settlers to the majority native reinforce or diminish the power of settler colonialism? Indemnifications targeted to settler colonists are most in evidence in variously defined indigenous reconciliation processes throughout settler societies. However, when compensation went to the colonized native, as in the example of the indigenous Maori of New Zealand, the aim was to make up for the manifest legacies of colonialism but also to maintain the continuation of the white settler colonial regime. Although reparation to the colonized temporarily restructures the hierarchy of social inferiors hitherto forced to make material tribute to higher-status colonizers, it must never be forgotten that reconciliation between native and settler is about rationalizing ongoing settler colonialism through the colonizer's compensations that reinforce the lowly place of the colonized in the social hierarchy.[71] Thus, compensation remains mired in the messy realities of festering disputes between colonizer and colonized or settler colonist and native, even when opposing sides such as the Maori native and the white New Zealander are in agreement that reparative processes must advance.[72]

Another point of dissimilarity is that the vast majority of Jewish beneficiaries of German Holocaust reparations do not reside in Germany. Many survivors created new lives in countries distant from Europe (with the State of Israel possessing the largest number of survivors). My Czechoslovakian Jewish survivor family was free to choose or reject reparations in Canada, as were Holocaust survivors elsewhere who could avoid interactions with Germans and Germany, and many did so. Not so Jewish Israelis and Palestinians in their small, densely populated shared territory. Consequently, the prospect of reparations does not answer these questions posed by Salman Natour, a Palestinian citizen of Israel living "inside" the 1948–67 borders of the state:

> The relationship with the Jewish Israeli other—who is he? This is a relationship of knowledge: it compels the Palestinians to know about the other given that he is a part of our daily lives and landscapes. So he is a subject of knowledge for us. This situation consequently raises our curiosity and evokes questions about the other's identity, history, ideology, and actions, not for surveillance purposes ("know your enemy"), but out of scientific, academic, and philosophical inquisitiveness. Can I live with him? This relationship raises a serious ethical question: how can the victim live with the oppressor (and executioner)? This question has historically taken and still takes the center of Palestinian culture in the Inside since the Nakba, as exhibited by most Palestinian literary texts. What is our future and what is his future? . . . In dialogue and engagement with the other, our culture is

the only one (not the European) which can offer a humanitarian solution to this question, so that we—identified by Jews as the other—
would not repeat the sins of the European. Remember that the
Europeans committed unforgivable crimes stemming from extreme
nationalist positions and inclinations, of which we remain the latest
of their victims.[73]

By way of an inconclusive ending, although Immanuel Kant reminds us
that as human beings and "by virtue of this [inner] worth we are not for sale
at any price," paradoxically setting a price on ourselves serves to emphasize
our place as humans within economic exchanges driven by our humanity:
"The satisfaction of all human needs—not just those that can be met through
private market transactions, but also the need for public goods, such as education, security and a healthy environment, and for intangible qualities such
as dignity that cannot be reduced to dollars spent per capita."[74] Money cannot buy everything, but it does open up connections to indemnifications
that individuals and collectivities imbue with meaning. Following anthropologist Keith Hart, money becomes the concrete, material embodiment of
our links to each other and to society:

> money enables individuals to stabilise their personal identity by
> holding something durable that embodies the desires and wealth
> of all members of society. I would go further. Communities exist by
> virtue of their members' ability to exchange meanings that are sub-
> stantially shared between them. People form communities to the
> extent that they understand each other for practical purposes. And
> that is why communities operate through culture (meanings held in
> common). Money is, with language, the most important vehicle for
> this collective sharing.[75]

From prior discussions and family experiences of German *Wiedergutmachung*, I can assert that reparations are financially useful, symbolically
powerful, politically fraught, and resonate as an indisputable remedy with
which to acknowledge the value of human life. Reparations become not
merely a matter of law and economic protocols but a social movement and
an extension of a political project. My ruminations about the future of Palestinians and Israelis are based on notions of maintaining the movement of
money, sustained by empathetic possibilities that take me away from the

realms of memory, remembrance, and memorialization toward innovative political projects. Intellectually and emotionally shaped by familial story-telling and filial engagement and despite frameworks of settler colonialism, I advocate for Jewish Israeli reparations to Palestinian Arabs, underpinned by the Palestinian right of return, in order that my Holocaust postmemories may be put in the service of imagining a world, a region, and myself in new ways.[76]

My Grandmother's First
Reparations Claim (1956)

Eidliche Erklarung

Zur Verwendung in dem Entschadigungsverfahren .. ..

der: .. Gizella **HOLLAENDER** , geb. Elefant verw. Hellaender
(Vor-und Zuname, bei Frauen auch Madchenname)

anhangig bei: . . . . **Mainz 13388** . . . .
(Entschadigungsbehorde oder - gericht, Aktenzeichen)

Zeuge: . **Antragsteller** : . . . **siehe oben** . . . .

Geburstag und -ort: . . . . 6. 7. 1905 in Buchtima (C.S.R.)

Familienstand: . . . . **verheiratet**

jetzige Anschrift: . . . **Montreal** , **Queb.** (**Canada**) **286 Villeneuve St.** W.

ausgewiesen durch (Lichtbildausweis erforderlich). . . . .
.C.S.R. Pass. 4430 . . . . ausgestellt am: . . .14.3. 1948 . . .
durch . . . . P R A G . . . .
. . . . Staatsangehorigkeit - nicht feststellbar.

Nur fur Zeugen: Mit dem Antragsteller nicht verwandt und nicht
verschwagert - der Antragsteller ist (Verwandtschaftsgrad angeben
. . . . **entfaellt**. . . . .
Mein sigenes Entschadigungsverfahren ist - war - anhangig bei:
. . . . **entfaellt**. . . . .
(Entschadigungsbehorde oder - gericht, Aktenzeichen)
Ich habe Entschadigung nicht beantragt.
Zu wahrheit ermahnt und in Konntnis der Bedeutung des Eides,
insbesondere der Strafbarkeiteiner vorsatzlich oder fahrlassig
falschen eidlichen Aussage, sowie daruber belehrt, dass der Entschadi-
gungsanspruch bei wissentlich oder grobfahrlassig unrichtigen oder
irrefuhrenden Angaben uber Grund und Hohe des Schadens zu versagen ist,
erklare ich foldendes: ')

Als der Krieg ausbrach lebte ich in Buchtima

C.S.R. und als die Deutschen im April 1944 einmarschierten,musste ich den

Judenstern tragen und Zwangsarbeit verrichten.------------------

----------------------- **Transport Seite 2** ----------------------
') Die Unterschrift ist nach Verlesung und Genehmigung der Erklarung
erst nach Ableistung des Eides zu vellziehen.

Die Übereinstimmung der Fotokopie
mit dem vorliegenden Original wird
beglaubigt **19. Jan. 2006**
Saarburg, den . . . .

5a

------------------------------ Seite 2 ------------------------------

Im April 1944 kam ich ins Ghetto Matisalka und hier blieb ich bis
Mai 1944.Dann kam ich ueber K.Z. Auschwitz nach K.Z.Plaszow und hier blieb
ich bis September 1944.
Ende Juli

Hier arbeitete ich im Steinbruch.
Ende Juli
Im September 1944 kam ich wieder ueber K.Z.Auschwitz nach K.Z.Mark-
leben b/Leipzig und hier blieb ich bis Mai 1945.Ich arbeitete in der Munitionsfabrik der Junkers Werke.Der Leiter hiess Ingenieur WITT.

Einige Tage vor der Befreiung ,nachdem die deutsche Wache gefluechtet
war,verliess ich das Lager und wurde einige Tage spaeter durch die Amerikaner
befreit.

Nach der Befreiung ging ich nach Prag,habe 1948 geheiratet und wander-
te mit meinem Mann im Mai 1948 nach Cuba aus.Im Oktober 1949 wanderten wir
in Canada ein.

Ich erklaere ausdruecklich,dass ich mich am 1.1.1947 in Prag aufge-
halten habe und dort polizeilich gemeldet war.

I certify that I have seen
the number 19459 on the left arm
of Mrs. Gizella Hollaender.
Laut Eintragung der canadischen Immigrationsbehoerde auf meinem Ausweis
bin ich im Oktober 1949 in Canada eingewandert und habe seitdem meinen
staendigen Wohnsitz in Montreal Canada).

Gizella Hollaender .

SWORN TO BEFORE ME
THIS 13th DAY OF May 1956
AT MONTREAL, QUE.

eidliche
~~Eidesstattliche~~ Erklärung

Heute, den *13. Mai 1956* erschien

vor mir *Charles J. Cahn*
(Urkundsperson oder Notar)

d ie G i z e l l a H O L L A E N D E R geb.Elefant verw.
Hollaender
Montreal,Que.(Canada)
von Beruf: wohnhaft in: 286 Villeneuve St.W.

Die Persönlichkeit der erschienenen Person wurde zur Gewißheit der Urkundsperson durch Vorlage der Identitätskarte Nr. 64774 , die mit Lichtbild und eigenhändiger Unterschrift versehen war, ausgewiesen.

Die erschienene Person erklärte:

Ich will eine eidliche Erklärung abgeben, die den Zweck hat, auf Grund des Bundesergänzungsgesetzes zur Entschädigung für Opfer der nationalsozialistischen Verfolgung vom 18. September 1953 (BEG) gemäß §§ 71—75 eine Entschädigungsleistung zu erlangen.

Ich weiß, daß eine falsche ~~Versicherung an Eides Statt~~ strafbar ist und daß nach § 2 des genannten Gesetzes ihretwegen der Anspruch auf Entschädigung versagt werden kann. Außerdem bin ich auf die Strafbestimmungen über die Abgabe einer falschen eidstattlichen Versicherung des in meinem derzeitigen Aufenthaltslande geltenden Strafgesetzbuches hingewiesen worden.

In diesem Bewußtsein ~~versichere~~ ich zur Glaubhaftmachung des mir nach § 71 BEG bei Erfüllung der sonstigen Voraussetzungen zustehenden Anspruches insbesondere folgendes:

I. Zur Person:

Ich heiße G i z e l l a H O L L A E N D E R geb. ~~17.5.1931~~ 6.7.1905

in Buchtina (CSR) , vor der nationalsozialistischen

Verfolgung wohnhaft in Buchtina CSR.

II. Zur Sache:

1) Die Gründe, aus meinem Heimatland zu flüchten bzw. die Nichtrückkehr in mein Heimatland nach der nationalsozialistischen Verfolgung waren folgende:

Wegen meiner anti-kommunistischen Einstellung

bin ich nicht gewillt in meine fruehere Heimat zurueckzukehren.-

Die Übereinstimmung der Fotokopie mit dem vorliegenden Original wird beglaubigt
Saarburg, den 19. Jan. 2006

(Turbing)
Reg. Hauptsekretär

Formblatt I

2) Ich habe mich nicht, nachdem ich als Flüchtling im Sinne der Genfer Konvention vom 28. Juli 1951 am ..25.10.1949.... in ....Canada................ eingewandert. bin, freiwillig erneut dem Schutz meines Heimatlandes unterstellt.

3) Im Hinblick auf den in Artikel 1 F der Genfer Konvention vom 28. Juli 1951 vorgesehenen Ausschluß als politischer Flüchtling versichere ich,

   a) daß ich ein Verbrechen gegen den Frieden, ein Kriegsverbrechen oder ein Verbrechen gegen die Menschlichkeit im Sinne der internationalen Vertragswerke nicht begangen habe, die ausgearbeitet worden sind, um Bestimmungen bezüglich dieser Verbrechen zu treffen;

   b) daß ich ein schweres nichtpolitisches Verbrechen außerhalb des Aufnahmelandes nicht begangen habe, bevor ich dort als Flüchtling aufgenommen wurde;

   c) daß ich mir keine Handlungen zuschulden kommen ließ, die den Zielen und Grundsätzen der Vereinten Nationen zuwiderlaufen.

4) Ich besitze die Staatsangehörigkeit von .... C A N A D A ....
   seit ....1.9.5.6........... *)

   Vor Erwerb dieser Staatsangehörigkeit besaß ich die Staatsangehörigkeit von.................;
   ....Rumänien................... *)
   Ich habe die Staatsangehörigkeit von-------------............................... noch nicht verliehen erhalten, bin jedoch im Besitze ordnungsgemäßer Einwanderungspapiere. *)

5) Ich bin wegen des infolge der nationalsozialistischen Verfolgung erlittenen Schadens von keinem Staat oder keiner zwischenstaatlichen Organisation durch Kapitalabfindung betreut worden — und — werde auch nicht durch Zuwendungen laufend betreut.
   Ich bin Juedin und stamme von juedischen Eltern ab.-

Ich bestätige durch Eid die Wahrheit vorstehender Erklärung und unterzeichne dieselbe in Gegenwart des Urkundsbeamten / des Notars in freier Willensäußerung.

_____, den _13. Mai 1956_

_____
(Vor- und Zuname)

Ich, der unterzeichnete Urkundsbeamte / Notar bestätige, daß der Antragsteller durch Eid die Erklärung vor mir abgegeben und unterschriftlich vollzogen hat.

_____, den _13. Mai 1956_

(Siegel) _____
(Unterschrift)

My Grandmother's Subsequent Reparations Claims (1965–68)

EIGENE EIDESSTATTLICHE VERSICHERUNG.

Vor mir, dem unterfertigten Notar, erscheint heute Frau GISELLA HOLLAENDER, wohnhaft 414 Elmwood Ave., Brooklyn 30,N.Y., und gibt in ihrer eigenen Entschaedigungssache zur Vorlage beim Wiedergutmachungsamt folgende eigene eidesstattliche Versicherung ab, nachdem sie auf die strafrechtlichen Folgen einer falschen eidesstattlichen Versicherung hingewiesen wurde.

Ich lebte bis zum Beginn der Verfolgung in Buchtina/CSR und war bis zu diesem Zeitpunkt vollkommen gesund. Im Zuge der Verfolgungsmassnahmen der Nazis wurde ich im April 1944 in das Ghetto Matisalka eingeliefert und von dort ueber das KZ Auschwitz in das KZ Plaszow verbracht.

An allen diesen Plaetzen war ich unter den bekannten unhygienische und unmenschlichen Bedingungen untergebracht, litt Hunger, war jeder Witterung ohne den notwendigsten Schutz ausgesetzt und musste schwerste koerperliche Zwangsarbeiten leisten. Ich habe in Steinbruechen gearbeitet und Lasten heben muessen, die weit ueber das Maass meiner Kraefte gingen, sodass ich glaubte zusammenzubrechen. Ich wurde bei diesen Arbeiten, die mir aeusserst schwer fielen, von den Aufsichtsorganen angetrieben und tagtaeglich schwerstens misshandelt. Auch anschliessend im KZ Markleberg wurde ich zu schwersten Zwangsarbeiten herangezogen, und zwar in einer Munitionsfabrik der Junkerswerke, und auch dort wurde ich zu widerholten Malen schwerstens misshandelt. Ich wurde einmal in Auschwitz und ein zweites Mal in Markleberg ueber Kopf und Ruecken geschlagen, bis ich bewusstlos zusammenbrach.

Waehrend dieser Verfolgungszeit habe ich auf Grund der schrecklichen Umstaende und der Angst vor den sich immer wiederholenden Misshandlungen, sowie der Befuerchtung einer endgueltigen Liquidierung gesundheitlich sehr gelitten. Ich wurde besonders nach den Misshandlungen ueber Kopf und Ruecken von staendigen heftigen Kopfschmerzen und Kopfschwindel geplagt, litt an Schmerzen in meinem Ruecken und durch die Witterungseinfluesse auch an Schmerzen in meinen Gelenken, besonders in beiden Knien und Haenden. Ich wurde sehr oft von Weinanfaellen heimgesucht und konnte keinen Schlaf mehr finden. Die uns verabreichte Nahrung war nicht nur unzureichend, sondern bestand auch meistens aus Ersatzmitteln und verursachte mir Magenbeschwerden und kolikartige Anfaelle, sowie Durchfall abwechselnd mit Verstopfung. Zu meinen Kopfschmerzen und Kopfschwindel hatte ich auch Geraeusche in meinen Ohren.

Bei der Befreiung war ich psychisch und physisch nur noch ein menschliches Wrack. Mein erster Ehemann ist durch die Moerderhaende der Nazis in der Verfolgung umgekommen.

30

Obwohl ich seit der Befreiung bis heute wegen der mir in der
Verfolgung zugezogenen Leiden in staendiger aerztlicher Behandlung
bin, habe ich meinen Gesundheitszustand nicht wieder herstellen
koennen. Die noch immer bestehenden Symptome dieser Krankheiten
machen mir ein normales Leben unmoeglich. Zusaetzlich werde
ich von Angsttraeumen heimgesucht, in denen ich die Schrecken,
Misshandlungen und Erniedrigungen, denen ich in der Nazizeit
ausgesetzt war, wiedererlebe, und nach denen ich dann in tiefe
Depression verfalle. Waehrend solcher Zeit verliere ich jegliches
Interesse an meiner Umgebung, kann keinerlei Taetigkeit ausueben
und trage mich mit Selbstmordgedanken.

Gisella Hellanosker

Subscribed and sworn to before me
this.3...day of.........1965

MELVIN C. ELLENBOGEN
NOTARY PUBLIC, State of New York
No. 30-6172500
Qualified in Nassau County
Commission Expires March 30, 1966

Vor mir, dem unterzeichneten Notar, erscheint heute Frau

Gisella Hollander, wohnhaft zu 414 Elmwood Avenue, Brooklyn 30,

New York, und gibt zur Vorlage in ihrer Entschaedigungssache bei der

Entschaedigungsbehoerde folgende eidesstattliche Versicherung ab,

nachdem sie auf die strafrechtlichen Folgen einer falschen eides-

stattlichen Versicherung hingewiesen worden ist:

Mein Mann SAMUEL HOLLANDER, der 1902 in der CSR geboren ist, war

ein gebildeter Mann. Er hat eine Handelsschule absolviert. Wir haben

im Jahre 1926 geheiratet und mein Mann hat im Jahre 1928 ein Textil-

und Kurzwarengeschaeft gegruendet mit Hilfe der Eltern, welche uns cie.

diese als Mitgift gegeben haben. Das Geschaeft hat sich sehr gut

entwickelt und uns viel Einkommen gebracht. Mein Mann hatte auch die

Vertretung von B. Altmann Brun von Kopf und Halstuechern bekommen

fuer ganz Podkarpatsky Rus. Wir hatten vier Angestellte. Wir hatten

einen Umsatz von ueber 300.000.-- Kronen und ein jaehrliches Netto-

einkommen von 70.000.-- bis 80.000.-- Kronen. Wir haben in einem

eigenen schoenen 8-Zimmer Haus gewohnt. Das Geschaeftslokal und

Magasin befanden sich im selben Haus. Das Haus war auf Namen von

Samuel Hollander.

Infolge der Judenverfolgungen wurde uns das Gewerbeschein in 1941

weggenommen. Aus dem Erloes der Geschaeftsliquidierung habe ich

ein grosses Appartmenthaus in Munkaceva auf meinem Namen Gisella

Hollander gekauft, von welchem Einkommen wir gut leben konnten.

Ausserdem haben wir viele Grundstuecke besessen.

Im Jahre 1944 wurde die ganze Familie in das Ghetto Mstesalka ver-

bracht und von dort in das Konzentrationslager Auschwitz. Mein Mann

ist im Jahr 1944 (22.11.)infolge Hunger gestorben, was mir von Zeugen

berichtet wurde. *Unsere Wöhnung und Geschaeft var in Bustino*

ČSR

SWORN TO BEFORE ME

this 26th day of March 1968

Gisella Hollander

Unterschrift

NOTES

Prologue: Reparations and My Family

1. See Stéphane Courtois et al., *The Black Book of Communism: Crimes, Terror, Repression* (Cambridge, Mass.: Harvard University Press, 1999), and for Czechoslovakia, 394–456.

2. My father became eligible for an additional set of indemnities after the fall of communism that targeted all those who returned to the Czech Republic as he had decided to do. See the Czechoslovakian compensation law available in English as "Law on the Mitigation of the Consequences of Certain Wrongs Affecting Property, Passed by the Czechoslovak Federal Assembly on October 2, 1990," *Czechoslovak Economic Digest* 1 (1991): 29–32; see also Jiřina Šiklová, "Lustration, or the Czech Way of Screening," *East European Constitutional Review* 6, 1 (1996): 57–62.

3. Joseph B. Schechtman, *Post-War Population Transfers in Europe: 1945–1955* (Liverpool: Charles Birchall, 1962), 44.

4. The literature on the expulsion of the German-speaking population from Czechoslovakia's Sudetenland is vast. Relevant English-language works consulted are Wilhelm K. Turnwald, *Documents on the Expulsion of the Sudeten Germans* (Munich: University Press, 1953) and *Renascence or Decline of Central Europe: The Sudeten German-Czech Problem* (Munich: University Press C. Wolf, 1954); *The Expulsion of the German Population from Czechoslovakia: A Selection and Translation* (Bonn: Federal Ministry for Expellees, Refugees and War Victims, 1960); Luza Radomir, *The Transfer of the Sudeten Germans: A Study of Czech-German Relations, 1933–1962* (New York: New York University Press, 1964); Alfred De Zayas, *A Terrible Revenge: The Ethnic Cleansing of the East European Germans, 1944–1950* (New York: Saint Martin's, 1994); and Norman M. Naimark, *Fires of Hatred: Ethnic Cleansing in Twentieth-century Europe* (Cambridge, Mass.: Harvard University Press, 2001). Former Czech Republic president Václav Havel was the rare politician who advocated for some form of compensation owed to the expelled Sudeten Germans of Czechoslovakia: "Havel had always considered this expulsion both morally wrong and politically disastrous, because it was an inhuman act carried out on dubious legal and moral grounds, and because it established a precedent that he felt had prepared the way for the Communist putsch in 1948. And though he later claimed that he had not, as president, offered any formal

apologies to the Germans, he certainly believed that some sort of compensation was in order for those expelled, perhaps in the form of Czech citizenship. His position caused an uproar at home that has still not entirely died down, but he stuck to his guns." Paul Wilson, "Václav Havel (1936–2011)," *New York Review of Books*, February 9, 2012, 8.

5. Nicholas Balabkins, *West German Reparations to Israel* (New Brunswick, N.J.: Rutgers University Press, 1971), 89.

6. Joseph B. Schectman, "Case Against Negotiations with Germany," *Jewish Herald* 15, 19 (1951): 7, quoted in Tomer Kleinman, "Did the Holocaust Play a Role in the Establishment of the State of Israel?" Pro-Seminar Paper, UCSB Oral History Project, accessed November 5, 2012, http://www.history.ucsb.edu/projects/holocaust /Research/Proseminar/tomerkleinman.htm#_ftn3. For debates on accepting reparations, see Elazar Barkan, *The Guilt of Nations: Restitution and Negotiating Injustices* (New York: Norton, 2000), and Tom Segev, *The Seventh Million: The Israelis and the Holocaust* (New York: Hill and Wang, 1993).

7. See section on "Junkers à Markkleeberg," in Mémorial du Maréchal de Hauteclocque et de la Libération de Paris, at Musée Jean Moulin, *Les femmes oubliées de Buchenwald: 22 avril–30 octobre 2005* (Paris: Musées, 2005), 39–41.

8. Otto Graf Lambsdorff, "The Long Road Towards the Foundation 'Remembrance, Responsibility and the Future'," in *Sharing the Burden of the Past*, ed. Andrew Horvat (Tokyo: Asia Foundation, 2003), 152–60, 152.

9. Conference on Jewish Material Claims Against Germany, *Twenty Years Later: Activities of the Conference on Jewish Material Claims Against Germany, 1952–1972* (New York: Conference on Jewish Material Claims Against Germany, 1972), 127.

10. Theodore Lavi, ed., "Mateszalka," *Pinkas ha-Kehillot Hungarya* (Encyclopedia of Jewish Communities in Hungary) (Jerusalem: Yad Vashem, 1975), 348–49 (English translation available at http://www.jewishgen.org/yizkor/pinkas_hungary /hun348.html).

11. The tale of Jews judging God in the camps and ghettoes is found in other sources. The Public Broadcasting Service aired a 2008 *Masterpiece Contemporary* production of "God on Trial" set in a men's barrack at Auschwitz, synopsis at http://www .pbs.org/wgbh/masterpiece/godontrial/index.html. Elie Wiesel claims to have witnessed such a trial while in Auschwitz; see Jennie Frazer, "Wiesel: Yes, We Really Did Put God on Trial," *Jewish Chronicle Online*, September 19, 2008.

12. On Holocaust dormant accounts in Swiss banks, see Stuart E. Eizenstat, "All That Glitters," in his *Imperfect Justice: Looted Assets, Slave Labor, and the Unfinished Business of World War* (New York: Public Affairs, 2003), 90–114.

13. From the website of the Claims Conference, the consortium of Jewish organizations that administers the "Article 2 fund": Article 2 of the Implementation Agreement to the German Unification Treaty of October 3, 1990, which reads: "The Federal Government is prepared, in continuation of the policy of the German Federal Republic, to enter into agreements with the Claims Conference for additional Fund arrange-

ments in order to provide hardship payments to persecutees who thus far received no or only minimal compensation according to the legislative provisions of the German Federal Republic." The resulting agreement, known as the Article 2 Fund, was the outcome of 16 more months of difficult negotiations. Compensation is in the form of monthly payments of €270 (approximately $320), increased after negotiations in 2003. The Claims Conference administers the fund according to German government regulations, see www.claimscon.org/index.asp?url=article2/overview

14. Letter from Bettina Seifert to Vera Slyomovics, August 2, 2004. For the English-language text of the law establishing the Foundation, see http://www.stiftung-evz.de /eng/the-foundation/law.html.

15. On legal peace from future legal suits, see Articles 16(2) and 17(2) of Foundation Law above; see also commentary by Michael J. Bazyler, *Holocaust Justice: The Battle for Restitution in America's Courts* (New York: New York University Press, 2003), 83.

16. Names of German companies still in operation that used slave labor are found in two major registers: *Mittestaendische Unternehmen 1999*, vols. 1–3 (Darmstadt: Hoppenstedt, 1999), and *Handbuch der Grossunternehmen 1999*, vols. 1–2 (Darmstadt: Hoppenstedt, 1999). See also Michael Thad Allen, *The Business of Genocide: The SS, Slave Labor, and the Concentration Camps* (Chapel Hill: University of North Carolina Press, 2002); Paul Jaskot, *The Architecture of Oppression: The SS, Forced Labor and the Nazi Monumental Building Economy* (London: Routledge, 2000); Eizenstat, *Imperfect Justice*; and Bazyler, *Holocaust Justice*.

17. Miroslav Kárný et al., eds., *Terezínská pamětní kniha: Theresienstaedter Gedenkbuch*, 2 vols. (Prague: Melantrich, 1995). See vol. 2, "Transports to Terezin from the Protectorate Bohemia and Moravia (2.7.1942–26.1.1945)," 802. Descriptions of the camp are found in Zdenek Lederer, "Terezin," in Avigdor Dagan, *The Jews of Czechoslovakia: Historical Studies and Surveys*, vol. 3 (Philadelphia: Jewish Publication Society of America and Society for the History of Czechoslovak Jews, 1984), 104–64; and Hans Gunther Adler, *Theresienstadt 1941–1945: Das Antlitz einer Zwangsgemeinschaft. Geschichte, Soziologie, Psychologie* (Tübingen: Mohr, 1955).

18. In the literature about the Plaszow Camp, I have found only these infamous woman camp guards: Gertrud Heise, Luise Danz, Alice Orlowski, and Anna Gerwing.

19. "Female Jews had a lower chance of survival in comparison to men, since most of the working facilities were meant for male prisoners," Dieter Pohl, "Krakau-Plazow Main Camp," in *The United States Holocaust Memorial Museum Encyclopedia of Camps and Ghettos, 1933–45*, ed. Geoffrey Megargee, vol. 1, Part B (Bloomington: Indiana University Press, 2009), 863–64. See also Malvina Graf, *The Kraków Ghetto and the Płaszów Camp Remembered* (Tallahassee: Florida State University Press, 1989).

20. Randolf L. Braham, "Hungary and the Holocaust: The Nationalist Drive to Whitewash the Past," *Radio Free Europe/Radio Liberty Reports* 3, 18 (October 17, 2001).

21. Jeffrey K. Olick, "Genre Memories and Memory Genres: A Dialogical Analysis of May 8, 1945 Commemorations in the Federal Republic of Germany," *American Sociological Review* 64, 3 (1999): 381–402.

22. *Kapo* is said to derive from the Italian for "boss." Other dictionary definitions are from the French *caporal* (corporal) or possibly an abbreviation of *Kameradschaftspolizei*. During summer 2008, thanks to a fellowship at the International Tracing Service in Bad Arolsen, Germany, I met historian of the Holocaust Konrad Kwiet, who teaches in Australia. He informed me that the legendary Auschwitz tattooer was Lou Sokolov; see Konrad Kwiet, "Designing Survival: A Graphic Artist in Birkenau," in *Approaching an Auschwitz Survivor: Holocaust Testimony and Its Transformations*, ed. Jürgen Matthäus (Oxford: Oxford University Press, 2009), 7–26.

23. Raul Hilberg, *The Politics of Memory: The Journey of a Holocaust Historian* (Chicago: Ivan Dee, 1996), 74.

Chapter 1. Financial Pain

Epigraph: Karl Jaspers, *The Question of German Guilt* (New York: Fordham University Press, 2001), 16 (originally published in 1947 as *Die Schuldfrage*).

1. A survey of the moral and economic justification for reparations as a remedy is in Dinah Shelton, *Remedies in International Human Rights Law* (Oxford: Oxford University Press, 1999).

2. United Nations, *Basic Principles and Guidelines on the Right to a Remedy and Reparation for Victims of Violations of International Human Rights and Humanitarian Law*, E/CN.4/2005/L.48.

3. Nehemiah Robinson, *Restitution Legislation in Germany* (New York: Institute of Jewish Affairs, World Jewish Congress, 1949); and Ariel Colonomos and Andrea Armstrong, "German Reparations to Jews After World War II: A Turning Point in the History of Reparations," in *The Handbook of Reparations*, ed. Pablo de Greif (New York: Oxford University Press, 2006), 391–419. On the early German resistance to the restitution program, see Jurgen Lillteicher, "Die Rückerstattung in Westdeutschland," in *Nach der Verfolgung: Wiedergutmaching nationalsozialistischen Unrechts in Deutschland?* ed. Hans Gunter Hockerts and Christian Kuller (Gottingen: Wallstein, 2003), 61–77.

4. Ronald W. Zweig, *German Reparations and the Jewish World: A History of the Claims Conference* (London: Frank Cass, 2001), 17.

5. Chancellor Adenauer's speech was widely disseminated, and an English translation appears on the website of the American partner organization to German reparations, namely, "The Conference on Jewish Material Claims Against Germany," http://www.claimscon.org/?url=history, accessed January 10, 2010.

6. U.S. Department of Justice, Foreign Claims Settlement Commission, "German Compensation for National Socialist Crimes," March 6, 1996, reprinted in Roy

L. Brooks, *When Sorry Isn't Enough: The Controversy over Apologies and Reparations for Human Injustice* (New York: New York University Press, 1999), 61–67; and Nana Sagi, *German Reparations: A History of the Negotiations* (Jerusalem: Magnes Press, 1980).

7. On apology, see Brooks, "The Age of Apology," *When Sorry Isn't Enough*, 3–11; Richard L. Abel, *Speaking Respect, Respecting Speech* (Chicago: University of Chicago Press, 1998); Nicholas Tavuchis, *Mea Culpa: A Sociology of Apology and Reconciliation* (Stanford, Calif.: Stanford University Press, 1991); and Michael R. Marrus, "Official Apologies and the Quest for Historical Justice," Occasional Paper 111, University of Toronto Munk Centre, 2006.

8. Georg Simmel, *The Philosophy of Money* (London: Routledge & Kegan Paul, 1978), 211.

9. Ibid., 355 (emphasis original).

10. See René Girard, *Violence and the Sacred* (Baltimore: Johns Hopkins Press, 1977), and Susan Slyomovics, "Reparations in Morocco: The Symbolic Dirham," in *Waging War, Making Peace: Reparations and Human Rights*, ed. Barbara Rose Johnston and Susan Slyomovics (Walnut Creek, Calif.: Left Coast Press, 2008), 94–114.

11. Viviana A. Zelizer, *The Social Meaning of Money* (Princeton, N.J.: Princeton University Press, 1997), 18. I borrow the notion of special-purpose money from anthropologist Paul Bohannon, "The Impact of Money on an African Subsistence Economy," *Journal of Economic History* 19 (1959): 491–503.

12. Daniel Levy and Natan Sznaider, "Forgive and Not Forget: Reconciliation Between Forgiveness and Resentment," in *Taking Wrongs Seriously: Apologies and Reconciliation*, ed. Elazar Barkan and Alexander Karn (Stanford, Calif.: Stanford University Press, 2006), 83–100.

13. John Torpey, *Making Whole What Has Been Smashed: On Reparation Politics* (Cambridge, Mass.: Harvard University Press, 2006), 47.

14. Zelizer, *The Social Meaning of Money*, 5.

15. See Richard Cherry, *Lectures on the Growth of Criminal Law in Ancient Communities* (New York: Macmillan, 1890); and surveys by Keith F. Otterbein and Charlotte Swanson Otterbein, "An Eye for an Eye, a Tooth for a Tooth: A Cross-Cultural Study of Feuding," *American Anthropologist* 67, 6 (1965): 1470–82.

16. For a tale to contradict these anthropological findings, compare the outcomes between Jared Diamond's father-in-law, a Polish Jew who did not exact revenge for his family's murderers, to the satisfaction of a New Guinea Highlander who achieved revenge through killings. Jared Diamond, "Vengeance Is Ours: What Can Tribal Societies Tell Us About Our Need to Get Even?" *New Yorker*, April 21, 2008, 74–87.

17. Quote from Mrs. Feuer in *Massive Psychic Trauma*, ed. Henry Krystal (New York: International Universities Press, 1968), 96.

18. Marguerite Feitlowitz, *A Lexicon of Terror: Argentina and the Legacies of Torture* (New York: Oxford University Press, 1998), 257–28n2.

19. See Susan Slyomovics, "Morocco and Algeria: Financial Reparations, Blood Money, and Human Rights Witness Testimony," in *Humanitarianism and Suffering: The Mobilization of Empathy*, ed. Richard Ashby Wilson and Richard D. Brown (Cambridge: Cambridge University Press, 2009), 277.

20. Kenneth R. Feinberg, *What Is Life Worth?* (New York: Public Affairs, 2005), 26. On distaste for tort lawyers, see also William Haltom and Michael McCann, *Distorting the Law: Politics, Media, and the Litigation Crisis* (Chicago: University of Chicago Press, 2004). Feinberg's approach toward the families of victims of September 11, 2001, led to his subsequent role as overseer for many similar funds, such as the 2007 Virginia Tech shooting, the 2010 BP oil spill, and the 2012 Denver Aurora Theater massacre. For the 2012 massacre, money donated from around the world was not sufficient to cover emotional and psychological issues, while Feinberg, as is now his custom, generously waived his fee for this case; see Jenny Deam, "Massacre Funds to be Distributed," *Los Angeles Times*, October 17, 2012, A14.

21. Burt Neuborne, "Preliminary Reflections on Aspects of Holocaust-Era Litigation in American Courts," *Washington University Law Quarterly* 80 (2002): 828n119.

22. Feinberg, *What Is Life Worth?* 54–55.

23. See Henry Greenspan, "Listening to Holocaust Survivors: Interpreting a Repeated Story," *Shofar: An Interdisciplinary Journal of Jewish Studies* 17, 4 (1999): 83–88.

24. Feinberg, *What Is Life Worth?* 162. On the refusal to monetize civic relationships with the state, see Sandel's discussion about Swiss villagers who refused to be "bribed" about locating a nuclear waste repository in their environs, yet were more readily willing to consider the same issue absent any government compensation. Michael J. Sandel, *What Money Can't Buy: The Moral Limits of the Market* (New York: Farrar, Straus and Giroux, 2012), 114–22.

25. For descriptions of Germany's compensation as it operated in Germany, see John Borneman, "Money and Memory: Transvaluating the Redress of Loss," in *Restitution and Memory: Material Restoration in Europe*, ed. Dan Diner and Gotthart Wunberg (New York: Bergahn, 2007), 27–50.

26. Christian Pross, *Paying for the Past: The Struggle over Reparations for Surviving Victims of Nazi Terror* (Baltimore: Johns Hopkins University Press, 1998), 175–76. See also Pross, "Breaking Through the Postwar Coverup of Nazi Doctors in Germany," *Journal of Medical Ethics Supplement* 4 (1991): 13–16.

27. Pross, *Paying for the Past*, 17–19.

28. Michael J. Bazyler, "Suing Hitler's Willing Business Partners: American Justice and Holocaust Morality," *Jewish Political Studies Review* 16 (2004): 3–4. For another critique, see Norman G. Finkelstein, *The Holocaust Industry: Reflection on the Exploitation of Jewish Suffering* (New York: VERSO, 2000).

29. John Maynard Keynes, *Essays in Persuasion* (New York: Norton, 1963), 358–73.

30. "German Government Ghetto Work Payment Program" (Bundesamt für zentrale Dienste und offene Vermögensfragen, BADV) stands for the government department handling claims to the Ghetto Fund. Claim forms and information about the fund are available at http://www.badv.bund.de/002_menue_oben/007_english/005_ghettowork/index.html.

31. Tom Baker, "Blood Money, New Money and the Moral Economy of Tort Law in Action," *Law and Society Review* 35, 2 (2001): 276.

32. Tom Baker, "The Blood Money Myth," *Legal Affairs* (September/October 2002).

33. Simmel, *Philosophy of Money*, 364.

34. Accounts of strong mother-daughter dyads among camp inmates (besides psychiatrist Anna Ornstein's memoir), are analyzed in Johanna Bodenstab, "Under Siege: A Mother-Daughter Relationship Survives the Holocaust," *Psychoanalytic Inquiry* 24 (2004): 731–51.

35. I wrote down my recollection of my mother's talk, and she approved this version during our interview years later (Vera Slyomovics, interview by author, Vancouver, Canada, June 3, 2007).

36. It took Ornstein until 2004 to publish her memoirs: Anna Ornstein and Stewart Goldman, *My Mother's Eyes: Holocaust Memories of a Young Girl* (Cincinnati: Emmis Books, 2004).

37. Anna Ornstein, "Survival and Recovery," *Psychoanalytic Inquiry* 5 (1985): 99–130.

38. Lawrence Weinbaum, "Defrosting History: The Theft of Jewish Property in Eastern Europe," in *The Plunder of Jewish Property During the Holocaust*, ed. Avi Beker (New York: Palgrave, 2001), 94–100.

39. Randolph L. Braham, *Genocide and Retribution: The Holocaust in Hungarian-Ruled Northern Transylvania* (Boston: Kluwer-Nijhoff, 1983).

40. S. Y. Gross and Y. Yosef Cohen, eds., *Sefer Marmarosh: Mea ve-shishim kehilot kedoshot be-yishuvan u-ve-hurbanan* [The Marmaros Book: In Memory of a Hundred and Sixty Thousand Jewish Communities] (Tel Aviv: Beit Marmaros, 1983). Quote appears in chap.7, "The Holocaust of Jewish Marmaros," 93–112, English trans. Moshe A. Davis, accessed January 10, 2010, http://www.jewishgen.org/yizkor/Maramures/mar093.html.

41. Eugene Hollander, *From the Hell of the Holocaust: A Survivor's Story* (New York: Ktav, 2000), 3.

42. Timothy Snyder, *Bloodlands: Europe Between Hitler and Stalin* (New York: Basic Books, 2010). On the Kamenetz-Podolsk deportations, see Ágnes Ságvári, *The Holocaust in Carpatho-Ruthenia* (Budapest: Á. Ságvári, 1998).

43. Office of U.S. Chief Counsel for Prosecution of Axis Criminality, *Nazi Conspiracy and Aggression* (Washington, D.C.: Government Printing Office, 1946), 8 vols. See "The First Indictment," vol. 1, chap. 3, 38: "In Kamenetz-Podolsk Region 31,000

Jews were shot and exterminated, including 13,000 persons brought there from Hungary." See also Ray Brandon and Wendy Lower, eds., *The Shoah in Ukraine: History, Testimony, Memorialization* (Bloomington: Indiana University Press, 2008).

44. Example quoted in Viviana Zelizer, *Morals and Markets: The Development of Life Insurance in the United States* (New York: Columbia University Press, 1979), 46.

45. Elazar Barkan, *The Guilt of Nations: Restitution and Negotiating Historical Injustices* (New York: Norton, 2000), 3.

46. Michael J. Bazyler, *Holocaust Justice: The Battle for Restitution in America's Court* (New York: New York University Press, 2003), 286.

47. Bazyler, "Suing Hitler's Willing Business Partners."

48. On local moral discourses about money, see Maurice Bloch and Jonathan Parry, "Introduction: Money and the Morality of Exchange," in *Money and the Morality of Exchange*, ed. Maurice Bloch and Jonathan Parry (Cambridge: Cambridge University Press, 1989), 1–32.

49. Richard Abel, "General Damages Are Incoherent, Incalculable, Incommensurable, and Inegalitarian (But Otherwise a Great Idea)," *DePaul Law Review* 55, 2 (2006): 255.

50. Feinberg, *What Is Life Worth?* 89.

51. Ibid., 94.

52. Kathleen Hennessey, "Overseer of Gulf Victim Fund a Force of Nature," *Los Angeles Times*, June 18, 2010, A18.

53. Feinberg, *What Is Life Worth?* 184.

54. Pierre Bourdieu, *Distinction: A Social Critique of the Judgment of Taste* (Cambridge, Mass.: Harvard University Press, 1984), and *Practical Reason: On the Theory of Action* (Stanford, Calif.: Stanford University Press, 1998).

55. Henry Rousso, *The Vichy Syndrome: History and Memory in France Since 1944*, trans. Arthur Goldhammer (Cambridge, Mass.: Harvard University Press, 1991), 24. See testimony by French resistance fighter Jacqueline Marie Fleury who was interned in Markkleeberg, in Association des Amis de la Fondation de la Résistance, "Nous les oublions pas: Fleury née Marie Jacqueline," *Mémoire et Espoirs de la résistance*, http://www.memoresist.org/spip.php?page=oublionspas_detail&id=1761, accessed November 1, 2012.

56. Established by law under Vichy France in February 1943 as an alternative to French military service; see Robert Gildea, *Marianne in Chains: Everyday Life in the French Heartland Under the German Occupation* (New York: Metropolitan Books, 2003), 277.

57. On the various camp hierarchies, with the Jew on the bottom, see the concentration camp memoirs of a French survivor of Buchenwald, David Rousset, *L'Univers concentrationnaire* published in English as *The Other Kingdom*, trans. and intro. Ramon Guthrie (New York: Reynal & Hitchcock, 1947). Daniel Blatman, *The Death Marches: The Final Phase of Nazi Genocide* (Cambridge, Mass.: Belknap Press of Harvard University Press, 2011) devotes several chapters to April 1945 and provides con-

texts for responses by French non-Jewish workers to the arrival of escaped Jewish slave laborers.

58. Philippe Bourgois, "Bringing the Past into the Present: Family Narratives of Holocaust, Exile and Diaspora: Missing the Holocaust: My Father's Account of Auschwitz from August 1943 to June 1944," *Anthropological Quarterly* 78, 1 (2005): 89–123.

59. Benjamin B. Ferencz, *Less Than Slaves: Jewish Forced Labor and the Quest for Compensation* (Bloomington: Indiana University Press, 2002), xxv.

60. Ulrich Herbert, *A History of Foreign Labor in Germany, 1880–1980: Seasonal Workers, Forced Laborers, Guest Workers* (Ann Arbor: University of Michigan Press, 1990), 162–63.

61. On the German law, see *Gesetz zur Errichtung einer Stiftung "Erinnerung, Verantwortung, Zukunft"*, accessed December 12, 2009, http://www.stiftung-evz.de/eng /the_foundation_remembrance_responsibility_and_future/.

62. On legislation, legal and diplomatic history leading to the establishment of the foundation, see *Zwangsarbeit im Dritten Reich. Erinnerung und Verantwortung. Juristische und zeithistorische Betrachtungen = NS-Forced Labor.* Peer Zumbansen, ed., *Remembrance and Responsibility. Legal and Historical Observations* (Baden-Baden: Nomos, 2002). For commentary on the foundation, and in particular some doubts concerning whether the settlement was helpful to broader concerns, such as addressing historical memory and acknowledgment of responsibility for atrocities by German industry, see Libby Adler and Peer Zumbansen, "The Forgetfulness of the Noblesse: A Critique of the German Foundation Law Compensating Slave and Forced Laborers of the Third Reich," *Harvard Journal of Legislation* 39, 1 (2002): 1–61.

63. Numbers are found on the Foundation website, http://www.stiftung-evz.de /eng/.

64. Lawrence Wechsler, "The Son's Tale: Art Spiegelman," republished in his collected essays *Vermeer in Bosnia: Selected Writings* (New York: Vintage, 2004), 194–95.

65. Douglas Hollan, "Dreaming in a Global World," in *A Companion to Psychological Anthropology: Modernity and Psychocultural Change*, ed. Conerly Casey and Robert B. Edgerton (Oxford: Blackwell, 2005), 91.

66. "Senate Approves Permanent Tax Exemption for Holocaust Victims," *Accounting Web*, November 25, 2002. A full description can be found at the Claims Conference website, "Tax Exemptions on Holocaust Compensation and Restitution Payments," http://www.claimscon.org/. Most U.S. states allow tax exemptions for Holocaust payments.

67. Marcel Mauss, *The Gift: The Form and Reason for Exchange in Archaic Societies*, trans. W. D. Halls (New York: Norton, 1990).

68. Ibid., 82.

69. F. H. Damon, "The Kula and Generalised Exchange: Considering Some Unconsidered Aspects of the Elementary Structures of Kinship," *Man* n.s. 15 (1980): 282;

and Bronislaw Malinowski, "Kula: The Circulating Exchange of Valuables in the Archipelagoes of Eastern New Guinea," *Man* 20 (1920): 97–105.

Chapter 2. The Limits of Therapy: Narratives of Reparation and Psychopathology

1. Robert A. LeVine, *Culture, Behavior and Personality* (Chicago: Aldine, 1982); Douglas Hollan, "The Relevance of Person-Centered Ethnography to Cross-Cultural Psychiatry," *Transcultural Psychiatry* 34, 2 (1997): 219–234; and Robert I. Levy and Douglas Hollan, "Person-Centered Interviewing and Observation in Anthropology," in *Handbook of Methods in Cultural Anthropology*, ed. H. R. Bernard (Walnut Creek, Calif.: Altamira, 1998), 333–64.

2. Douglas Hollan, "Setting a New Standard: The Person-Centered Interviewing and Observation of Robert I. Levy," *Ethos* 33, 4 (2005): 462. An exemplary extended study of a single survivor by various authors is Jürgen Matthaus, ed., *Approaching an Auschwitz Survivor: Holocaust Testimony and Its Transformations* (New York: Oxford University Press, 2009).

3. Alisse Waterston and Barbara Rylko-Bauer, "Out of the Shadows of History and Memory: Personal Narratives in Ethnographies of Rediscovery," *American Ethnologist* 33, 3 (2006): 397.

4. On the narrated self, see Elinor Ochs and Linda Capps, "Narrating the Self," *Annual Review of Anthropology* 25 (1996): 19–43. Linda Garro's process-oriented perspective on narrative and relevant cultural resources that endow the past with meaning sheds light on my mother's religious interpretations of her camp experience; see her "Narrating Troubling Experiences," *Transcultural Psychiatry* 40, 1 (2003): 5–43.

5. Annette Wieviorka, *L'ère du témoin* (Paris: Plon, 1998), and Ana Douglass and Thomas A. Vogler, "Introduction," in *Witness and Memory: The Discourse of Trauma*, ed. Ana Douglass and Thomas A. Vogler (New York: Routledge, 2003), 1–53.

6. Although few Israelis attended the trial or could view TV broadcasts, approximately 60 percent of the population (over age fourteen) are believed to have followed opening day radio broadcasts, according to Hanna Yablonka, *The State of Israel vs. Adolf Eichmann* (New York: Schocken, 2004), 60–61.

7. Hannah Arendt, *Eichmann in Jerusalem: A Report on the Banality of Evil* (New York: Viking, 1963), 232–33. Gideon Hausner's own account of the trial is in his *Justice in Jerusalem* (New York: Harper & Row, 1966). On Hausner's self-described role as storyteller for the six million dead, see his *Six Million Accusers; Israel's Case Against Eichmann: The Opening Speech and Legal Argument of Mr. Gideon Hausner, Attorney-General* (Jerusalem: Jerusalem Post, 1961).

8. Bernhard Schlink, *Guilt About the Past* (Toronto: Anansi, 2010), 119.

9. Researchers have emphasized periodizing Holocaust narratives over the life of the survivor, for example, narratives emerging from "pre-Holocaust, Early and Late

Holocaust, post-Holocaust"; see Peter Suedfeld, Robert Krell, Robyn E. Wiebe, and Gary Daniel Steel, "Coping Strategies in the Narratives of Holocaust Survivors," *Anxiety, Stress & Coping: An International Journal* 10 (1997):153–79.

10. Hannah Arendt, "Auschwitz on Trial," in *Responsibility and Judgment*, ed. Jerome Kohn (New York: Schocken, 2003), 254–55.

11. Karl Leonhard, *The Classification of Endogenous Psychoses* (New York: Irvington Publishers, 1979), 62

12. Elie Wiesel, "A Plea for Survivors," in *A Jew Today* (New York: Random House, 1978), 200.

13. Henry Krystal, interview, University of Michigan-Dearborn "Voice/Vision Holocaust Survivor Oral History Archive," accessed November 28, 2012, http://holocaust .umd.umich.edu/interview.php?D=krystal&section=25.

14. For a discussion on "freezing," see Henry Krystal, "Psychoanalytic Approaches to Trauma: A Forty-Year Perspective," in *Mapping Trauma and Its Wake: Autobiographic Essays by Pioneer Trauma Scholars*, ed. Charles Figley (New York: Routledge, 2006), 115–16.

15. Although there is an extensive literature on gender and the Holocaust and despite the restricted sample of my immediate family, nonetheless, my approach is gender-inflected in focus both by subjects interviewed and topics; see Joan Ringelheim, "Women and the Holocaust: A Reconsideration of Research," *Signs* 10, 4 (1985): 741–61. Carol Gilligan's research on coping mechanisms of women (nurturing, bonding, talking) have been applied to gender-specific approaches to women survivors.

16. Krystal, interview, September 19, 1996. University of Michigan-Dearborn "Voice/ Vision Holocaust Survivor Oral History Archive," accessed November 28, 2012. http:// holocaust.umd.umich.edu/interview.php?D=krystal&section=27.

17. Schlink, *Guilt About the Past*, 119–20.

18. Bernhard Schlink, *The Reader*, trans. Carol Brown Janeway (New York: Vintage, 2008), 212.

19. Ibid., 214.

20. Axel Honneth, *Reification: A New Look at an Old Idea*, ed. Martin Jay (Oxford: Oxford University Press, 2008), 35–86.

21. Christian Pross, *Paying for the Past: The Struggle over Reparations for Surviving Victims of the Nazi Terror* (Baltimore: Johns Hopkins University, 1998), xii.

22. Tobias Winstel, "'Healed Biographies'? Jewish Remigration and Indemnification for Nationalist Socialist Injustice," *Leo Baeck Institute Year Book* 4, 1 (2004): 152.

23. Max Weber, *Economy and Society: An Outline of Interpretative Sociology*, ed. Claus Wittich and Guenther Roth (Berkeley: University of California Press, 1978).

24. Michael Herzfeld, *The Social Production of Indifference: Exploring the Symbolic Roots of Western Bureaucracy* (Chicago: University of Chicago Press, 1993), 2.

25. For a critique of Matussek's work, see Pross, *Paying for the Past*, 101–4. The English translation of Matussek, *Die Konzentrationslagerhaft und ihre Folgen* (Berlin:

Springer, 1971) appeared as Paul Matussek, *Internment in Concentration Camps and Its Consequences*, trans. Derek and Inge Jordan (New York: Springer, 1975).

26. Zahava Szász Stessel, *Snow Flowers: Hungarian Jewish Women in an Airplane Factory, Markkleeberg, Germany* (Madison, N.J.: Fairleigh Dickinson University Press, 2009), 316–17.

27. Nazi anthropology's close relation to medicine is embodied in the life and work of Josef Mengele, educated in both disciplines with a medical degree from Frankfurt and a doctorate in anthropology from Munich. Medicine and anthropology combined with psychiatry developed theoretical and practical approaches to race and the identification of inferior non-Germans to be eliminated. Two important works are Gretchen E. Schafft, *From Racism to Genocide: Anthropology in the Third Reich* (Urbana: University of Illinois Press, 2004), and Benno Muller-Hill, *Murderous Science: Elimination by Scientific Selection of Jews, Gypsies, and Others, Germany 1933–45* (New York: Oxford University Press, 1988). See the well-known images, often reproduced and titled "Selection on the Juden-rampe" depicting the arrival of Jews from Carpathian Ruthenia in May or June 1944, part of some 160 photographs known as the "Auschwitz Album" taken by SS-Hauptscharführer Bernhard Walter and SS-Unterscharführer Ernst Hofmann, http://www.youtube.com /watch?v=yQXlMNMcPqo, accessed November 10, 2010

28. J. S. Kestenberg, "Discriminatory Aspects of the German Indemnification Policy: A Continuation of Persecution," in *Generations of the Holocaust*, ed. Martin A. Bergmann and Milton E. Jucovy (New York: Basic Books, 1982), 67–79. Kestenberg mentions the complex application and filing procedures including a provision to deny claimants making inaccurate statements.

29. Helen Epstein, *Children of the Holocaust: Conversations with Sons and Daughters of Survivors* (New York: Putnam, 1979), 85–86.

30. Werner E. Platz and Franklin Oberlaender, "On the Problems of Expert Opinion on Holocaust Survivors Submitted to the Compensation Authorities in Germany," *International Journal of Law and Psychiatry* 18, 3 (1995): 307–8. For an earlier important critique of the reparation system, there is Kurt Eissler's "Die Ermordung von wievielen seiner Kinder muß ein Mensch symptomfrei ertragen können, um eine normale Konstitution zu haben?" ["The murder of how many of one's children must one be able to bear without symptoms to have a normal constitution?"] *Psyche: Zeitschrift fur Psychoanalyse und ihre Anwendunger* 17 (1963): 241–91.

31. See the conference publication with Hillel Klein's contribution, "Wiedergut-machung: Ein Act des Retraumatisierung," in *Die Bundesrepublik Deutschland und die Opfer des Nationalsozialismus*, Tagung vom 25–27 November 1983 in Bad Boll (Bad Boll: Evangelische Akademie, 1984). Relevant comparative cases were witnesses in the South African Truth Commission, on whose behalf it was claimed that reliving pain and sharing feelings could facilitate recovery or result in its horrific opposite, to retraumatize in the form of flashbacks, hysteria, and depression; see Brandon Hamber, "The Burdens of Truth: An Evaluation of the Psychological Services and Initiatives Undertaken by the South African Truth and Reconciliation Commission," *American*

Imago 55, 1 (1998): 9–28. On relived trauma, see also Cathy Carruth, *Unclaimed Experience: Trauma, Narrative and History* (Baltimore: Johns Hopkins University Press, 1996). As I have noted about rape victims elsewhere (Morocco, Palestine), most never testified about rape; see Susan Slyomovics, "The Argument from Silence: Morocco's Truth Commission and Women Political Prisoners," *Journal of Middle East Women's Studies* 1, 3 (2005): 73–95; and "The Rape of Qula, a Destroyed Palestinian Village," in *Nakba: Palestine, 1948, and the Claims of Memory*, ed. Ahmad Sa'di and Lila Abu-Lughod (New York: Columbia University Press, 2007), 44–45.

32. Hillel Klein, "Problems in the Psychotherapeutic Treatment of Israeli Survivors of the Holocaust," in *Massive Psychic Trauma*, ed. Henry Krystal (New York: International Universities Press, 1968), 234.

33. In 1985, Krell and Eitinger edited a comprehensive bibliography on medical and psychological affects of the concentration camps, updated in 1997. See Robert Krell and Marc I. Sherman, *Medical and Psychological Effects of Concentration Camps on Holocaust Survivors* (New Brunswick, N.J.: Transaction, 1997).

34. Anna Ornstein and Steward Goldman, *My Mother's Eyes: Holocaust Memories of a Young Girl* (Cincinnati: Emmis Books 2004), 16.

35. Emanuel Tanay, "On Being a Survivor," in *Bearing Witness to the Holocaust, 1939–1989*, ed. Alan L. Berger (Lewiston, N.Y.: Edwin Mellen, 1989), 16–31; then followed by his memoir, *Passport to Life: Autobiographical Reflections on the Holocaust* (Ann Arbor, Mich.: Forensic Press, 2004).

36. Tanay, "On Being a Survivor," 26.

37. Ibid., 28.

38. Bruno Bettelheim, *The Informed Heart; Autonomy in a Mass Age* (Glencoe, Ill.: Free Press, 1960). Bettelheim and fellow inmate Curt Bondy, a German psychologist, were both imprisoned in Dachau and Buchenwald and both published their analyses in the same 1943 issue of the *Journal of Abnormal Psychology*, with radically different conclusions: compare Bettelheim's article "Individual and Mass Behavior in Extreme Situations," 38, 4 (1943): 417–52, preceded by Bondy's, "Problems of Internment Camps," 38, 4 (1943): 453–75.

39. Emanuel Tanay, "Initiation of Psychotherapy with Survivors of Nazi Persecution," in *Massive Psychic Trauma*, 219–33, 222. See Henry Krystal and William G. Niederland, "Clinical Observations on the Survivor Syndrome," in *Massive Psychic Trauma*, 326–39, followed by their later coauthored book, *Psychic Traumatization: Aftereffects in Individuals and Communities* (Boston: Little, Brown, 1971).

40. Karl Marx, *Economic and Philosophic Manuscripts of 1844* (Moscow: Foreign Languages Publishing House, 1961).

41. Robert J. Lifton, "Observations on Hiroshima Survivors," in *Massive Psychic Trauma*, 174. This theme also appears in his other writings on Japanese survivors of the atomic bomb; see also his "Psychological Effects of the Atomic Bomb in Hiroshima: The Theme of Death," *Daedalus* 92 (1963): 462–97; and *Death in Life: Survivors of Hiroshima* (New York: Random House, 1968).

42. Emanuel Tanay, in "Case Presentations," in *Massive Psychic Trauma*, 37–38.

43. Emanuel Tanay, Interview, March 16, 1987, University of Michigan-Dearborn "Voice/Vision Holocaust Survivor Oral History Archive," http://holocaust.umd.umich .edu/tanay/section014.html, accessed November 28, 2012.

44. Albert B. Kerenyi, Comment, in *Massive Psychic Trauma*, 200.

45. Important counterexamples are a series of studies of former Auschwitz prisoners that have appeared in Polish since the early 1990s under the auspices of Stanislaw Klodzinski, a psychiatrist and Auschwitz survivor at the University of Krakow. Researchers reported an enthusiastic and special rapport in therapy with former camp inmates; see Antoni Kepinski, "KZ-Syndrome," *Archives of Psychiatry and Psychotherapy* 4 (2008): 77–84. At the risk of reinscribing questionable hierarchies of victimhood, it seems that none of the patients were displaced Jews, but rather Poles who were welcomed home after liberation.

46. H. Grauer, "Psychodynamics of the Survivor Syndrome," *Canadian Psychiatric Association Journal* 14, 6 (1969): 619.

47. *Mental Disorders: Diagnostic and Statistical Manual* (Washington, D.C.: American Psychiatric Association, 1952), and Mick Carpenter, "It's a small world": Mental Health Policy Under Welfare Capitalism Since 1945," *Sociology of Health and Illness* 22, 5 (2000): 602–19

48. "Belsen Concentration Camp: The Medical Services Take Over," *The Lancet*, 12 (May 1945): 604–5. (First report in a medical journal reporting on period from April 12 to 17, 1945.)

49. William Robert Fitz-Gerald Collis, "Belsen Camp: A Preliminary Report," *British Medical Journal* (June 9, 1945): 814. See Johannes-Dieter Steinert, "British Relief Teams in Belsen Concentration Camp: Emergency Relief and the Perception of Survivors," in *Belsen 1945: New Historical Perspectives*, ed. Suzanne Bardgett and David Cesarani (London: Vallentine Mitchell, 2006), 62–78.

50. See Joanne Reilly, *Belsen: The Liberation of a Concentration Camp* (London: Routledge, 1998).

51. Collis, "Belsen Camp," 815.

52. Eugene Hollander, my mother's second cousin, liberated by the American Army from Mauthausen camp in Austria, also described the miraculous arrival of the Czech buses in his memoir *From the Hell of the Holocaust: A Survivor's Story* (New York: Ktav, 2000), 132–33: "But then luck was with us. Pondering our fate we noticed a huge truck pull into camp. Someone stood up on top of the driver's cabin and hoisted up the Czech flag. One of the men announced that they were here to pick up any Czechoslovakian citizens who wished to return home. My friend and I stepped forward and told them we were Czechoslovakian citizens and we wished to be repatriated to our native land, but lacked any documentation or identification except the number tattooed on our forearms. The driver assured us that we didn't need have to bother to obtain documentation and would receive such documentation in Czechoslovakia."

53. Paul Friedman, "The Road Back for the DP'S: Healing the Psychological Scars of Nazism," *Commentary* 6 (1948): 502–10.

54. Ibid., 507.

55. Eugène Minkowski, "L'anésthesie affective," *Annales Médico-Psychologiques* 104 (1946): 80–88.

56. René Targowla, "Sur une forme du syndrome asthénique des déportés et prisonniers de la guerre 1939–45 [On a form of asthenia syndrome of deportees and prisoners of war] *Presse Médicale* 58 (1950): 728–30.

57. The original article is Knud Hermann and Paul Thygesen, "KZ-syndromet," *Ugeskrift for Laeger* (1954): 825–36, with a simultaneous 1954 French publication that I consulted: Knud Hermann and Paul Thygesen, "Le syndrome des camps de concentration 8 ans après la liberation," [The concentration camp syndrome eight years after liberation], in *La Déportation dans les camps de concentration Allemands et ses séquelles* [Deportation in the German Concentration Camps and its consequences], ed. Paul Thygesen (Copenhagen: Danish Red Cross, 1954), 56–69. English citations are Paul Thygesen, "The Concentration Camp Syndrome," *Danish Medical Bulletin* 27 (1980): 224–28, and Leo Eitinger, "Psychosomatic Problems in Concentration Camp Survivors," *Journal of Psychosomatic Research* 13 (1969): 185.

58. William G. Niederland, "The Problems of the Survivor-Part I," *Journal of the Hillside Hospital* 10 (1961): 233–47.

59. Niederland's 165 reports on indemnification claims are housed in the Leo Baeck Institute, Center for Jewish History Archives, New York City, AR 7165, Series V: Psychiatric Cases, subseries 1, with limited access.

60. Early works in English by Leo Eitinger are "The Symptomatology of Mental Disease Among Refugees in Norway," *Journal of Mental Science* 106 (1960): 947–66; "Pathology of the Concentration Camp Syndrome," *Archives of General Psychiatry* (1961) 5: 371–79; and "Refugees and Concentration Camp Survivors in Norway," *Israel Journal of Medical Sciences* 21 (1962): 21–27.

61. The psychological literature highlights survivors' difficulties with trust; see, for example, the writings of Shamai Davidson, especially "The Clinical Effects of Massive Psychic Traumatization in Families of Holocaust Survivors," *Journal of Marital and Family Therapy* 6, 1 (1980): 11–21. Survivors were reported to experience social isolation and hostile and paranoid reactions to the world; see, for example, the influential research from the 1960s by Hillel Klein, Julius Zellermayer, and Joel Shannan, "Former Concentration Camp Inmates on a Psychiatric Ward," *Archives of General Psychiatry* 8 (1963): 334–42; and Eddy DeWind, "The Confrontation with Death," *Psychoanalytic Quarterly* 37, 2 (1968): 322–24.

62. J. Tas, "Psychical Disorders Among Inmates of Concentration Camps and Repatriates," *Psychiatric Quarterly* 25 (1946): 690.

63. William G. Niederland, "The Psychiatric Evaluation of Emotional Disorders in Survivors of Nazi Persecution," in *Masssive Psychic Trauma*, 10.

64. F. Kennedy, "The Mind of the Injured Worker: Its Effect on Disability Periods," *Compensation Medicine* 1 (1946): 19–24.

65. Johannes Rigler, *Über die Folgen der Verletzungen auf Eisenbahn* (Berlin: G. Reimer, 1879) discussed in Danuta Mendelson, "The History of Damages for Psychiatric Injury," *Psychiatry, Psychology and Law* 4, 2 (1997): 169–75; and Andreas Killen, *Berlin Electropolis: Shock, Nerves, and German Modernity* (Berkeley: University of California Press, 2006), 81–127.

66. Paul Lerner, *Hysterical Men: War Psychiatry and the Politics of Trauma in Germany 1890–1930* (Ithaca, N.Y.: Cornell University Press, 2003).

67. Killen, *Berlin Electropolis*, 214.

68. Herzfeld, *Social Production of Indifference*, 143. Walter von Baeyer, H. Hafner, and K. P. Kisker, *Psychiatrie der Verfolgten* [Psychiatry of the Persecuted] (Berlin: Springer-Verlag, 1964).

69. American Psychiatric Association, *Diagnostic and Statistical Manual of Mental Disorders*, 3rd ed. (Washington, D.C.: American Psychiatric Association, 1980), 485 (DSM-III).

70. Robert Jay Lifton, *Home From the War* (New York: Simon and Schuster, 1973), 318, and Cathy Caruth, "An Interview with Robert Jay Lifton," in *Trauma: Explorations in Memory*, ed. Cathy Caruth (Baltimore: Johns Hopkins University Press, 1995), 128–47.

71. See histories of the addition of PTSD to the 1980 DSM-III involving these psychiatrists in Ben Shephard, *A War of Nerves: Soldiers and Psychiatrists in the Twentieth Century* (Cambridge, Mass.: Harvard University Press, 2001); Candace M. Monson, Matthew J. Friedman, and Heidi A. J. La Bash, "A Psychological History of PTSD," in *Handbook of PTSD: Science and Practice*, ed. Matthew J. Friedman, Terence M. Keane, Patricia A. Resick (New York: Guilford Press, 2007), 30; and Ruth Leys, *From Guilt to Shame: Auschwitz and After* (Princeton, N.J.: Princeton University Press, 2007), 54.

72. Chaim Shatan, "The Grief of Soldiers: Vietnam Combat Veterans' Self-Help Movement," *American Journal of Orthopsychiatry* 43, 4 (1973): 640–53. In this influential article, Shatan twice compares Vietnam veterans and Holocaust survivors in terms of postwar problems. His opening paragraph begins: "Atrocities perpetrated upon the Vietnamese while saving them from Communism are now almost as well known as those of Hitler's extermination camps. Less obvious, however, is the Vietnam veterans are themselves victims of atrocity, as well as being former executioners," 640. In terms of delayed onset of symptoms, Shatan refers to Niederland's research: "William Niederland, who has devoted 25 years to work with concentration camp survivors, has noted that the same delay precedes their 'survivor syndrome.' He suggests that in both groups, 'the initial exultation over surviving prevents immediate symptoms; only as the advanced psychic numbing wears off do symptoms become prominent'," 645.

73. Allan Young, *The Harmony of Illusions: Inventing Post-Traumatic Stress Disorder* (Princeton, N.J.: Princeton University Press, 1995), 108–11; and Wilbur Scott, "PTSD in DSM-III: A Case in the Politics of Diagnosis and Disease," *Social Problems* 37, 3 (1990): 294–310.

74. Bruce J. Ennis and Thomas R. Litwack, "Psychiatry and the Presumption of Expertise: Flipping Coins in the Courtroom, "*California Law Review* 62, 3 (1974): 693–752.

75. Judith L. Herman, *Trauma and Recovery: The Aftermath of Violence from Domestic Abuse to Political Terror* (New York: Basic Books, 2004), 369.

76. Thomas Szasz, *The Myth of Mental Illness: Foundations of a Theory of Personal Conduct* (New York: Harper & Row, 1961).

77. Thomas Szasz, *The Second Sin* (New York: Doubleday, 1973).

78. See Ilana Rosen, *Sisters in Sorrow: Life Histories of Female Holocaust Survivors from Hungary* (Detroit: Wayne State University Press, 2008). Rosen researched her mother and other Holocaust family histories, in many cases after their deaths, to produce a memoir, a work of scholarship, and a set of interviews that compared Jewish women survivors who chose to remain in Hungary with those who left for Israel.

79. Ernest E. Becker, *The Birth and Death of Meaning: A Perspective in Psychiatry and Anthropology* (New York: Free Press of Glencoe, 1962), 172–73.

80. C. Jason Throop, "Latitudes of Loss: On the Vicissitudes of Empathy," *American Ethnologist* 37, 4 (2010): 771–82; and Douglas W. Hollan and C. Jason Throop, "The Anthropology of Empathy: An Introduction," in *The Anthropology of Empathy: Experiencing the Lives of Others in Pacific Societies*, ed. Douglas W. Hollan and C. Jason Throop (New York: Berghahn, 2011), 1–21.

81. Henrik Hoffmeyer, "Principes thérapeutiques," in *La Déportation dans les camps de concentration Allemands*, ed. Thygesen, 77.

Chapter 3. The Will to Record and the Claim to Suffering: Reparations, Archives, and the International Tracing Service

Epigraph: Laura Stoler, *Against the Archival Grain: Epistemic Anxieties and Colonial Common Sense* (Princeton: N.J.: Princeton University Press, 2009), 24.

1. See special issue "Archives, Records and Power: The Making of Modern Memory," *Archival Science* 2 (2002).

2. Ernst Posner, "Public Records Under Military Occupation," *American Historical Review* 49, 2 (1944): 222.

3. Ilana Feldman, "Working in the In-Between: Archives, Ethnography, and Research in Gaza," in *Anthrohistory: Unsettling Knowledge, Questioning Discipline*, ed. Edward Murphy et al. (Ann Arbor: University of Michigan Press, 2011), 97–109.

4. Jacques Derrida, *Archive Fever: A Freudian Impression*, trans. Eric Prenowitz (Chicago: University of Chicago Press, 1995), 16–17.

5. Ibid., 91.

6. Hannah Arendt, "The History of the Great Crime: A Review of *Bréviaire de la haine: Le IIIe Reich et les juifs*," in *The Jewish Writings*, ed. Jerome Kohn and Ron H. Feldman (New York: Schocken, 2007), 460.

7. For a comparison with the billion and a half name entries in the archive created by the Mormon Church in Salt Lake City, see Alex Shoumatoff, *The Mountain of Names: A History of the Human Family* (New York: Simon & Schuster, 1985).

8. See the four-volume International Committee of the Red Cross, *Report of the International Committee of the Red Cross on Its Activities During the Second World War* (Geneva: ICRC, 1948), which was based on *Documents sur l'activité du CICR en faveur des civils détenus dans les camps de concentration en Allemagne 1939–1945* (Geneva, 1946), and *Inter Arma Caritas: The Work of the ICRC During the Second World War* (Geneva, 1947): "Not only the washing places, but installations for baths, showers and laundry were inspected by the delegates. They had often to take action to have fixtures made less primitive, and to get them repaired or enlarged" (3: 594).

9. I thank Bernd Joachim Zimmer, local historian and schoolteacher, who gave me a tour of the SS-barracks with the wartime history of Arolsen during my June 2008 research trip to Arosen. There were some 180 prisoners by the end of the war attached to the *Auskommando*; see Bernd Joachim Zimmer, *Deckname Arthur: Das KZ-Aussenkommando in der SS-Führerschule Arolsen* (Kassel: Gesamthochschul-Bibliothek, 1994).

10. For a critical history of the formation of the ITS, see Jean-Marc Dreyfus, "À Bad Arolsen, dans la forêt des archives nazies," *La Vie de idées.fr.*, September 11, 2008. See also Robert Wolfe, ed., *Captured German and Related Records: A National Archives Conference* (Athens: Ohio University Press, 1974).

11. See Charles-Claude Biedermann, *Sixty Years of History and Benefit of the Personal Documentary Material About the Former Civilian Persecutees of the Nationalist Socialist Regime Preserved in Bad Arolsen* (Bad Arolsen: International Tracing Service, 2003), 10 and ITS homepage under "History," based on the 1960 Amendments.

12. Interview with Jacques Derrida by Michal Ben-Naftali, trans. Moshe Ron. Shoah Resource Center, Jerusalem, January 8, 1998, accessed January 12, 2010, http://www.yadvashem.org/odot_pdf/Microsoft%20Word%20-%203851.pdf. My writing about my use of my mother's and grandmother's files conforms to the imaginative ethnographic writings by Matthew Hull; see especially "Ruled by Records: The Appropriation of Land and the Misappropriation of Lists in Islamabad," *American Ethnologist* 34, 4 (2008): 508–18, on the importance of each individual document and its bureaucratic contexts. In this case, files constitute the missing Jewish body.

13. Biedermann, *Sixty Years of History*, 26.

14. Ernst Posner, *Memorandum Concerning the Protection and Salvage of Cultural Objects and Records in War Areas* (Washington, D.C.: American Council of Learned Societies, 1944). Posner's "Public Records Under Military Occupation," first published in 1944, is included in Ernst Posner, *Archives and the Public Interest: Selected Essays*, ed. Ken Munden (Washington, D.C.: Public Affairs Press, 1967), 186. I thank my UCLA colleague Anne Gilliland for these details on his career trajectory in the United States: "Ernst Posner already had quite a distinguished career in the Prussian State Archives and as an author and lecturer before being pushed out after the Nuremberg Laws be-

cause of his mixed Lutheran and Jewish ancestry. His wife was able to petition for his release from Sachsenhausen after Kristallnacht because he was a WWI veteran decorated at the battle of Tannenberg. When he finally reached the United States, via Sweden, however, he was blackballed in what became known as the McKellar Affair by Senator McKellar, chair of the Senate Appropriations Committee, because he was German. He was expressly forbidden to hold any position with the National Archives in case he might be a spy—to the point where McKellar was prepared to withhold appropriations not only from the new National Archives but also from the entire department of the Army in the middle of the war, if either worked with Posner. Posner had terrible trouble finding any work in D.C. and eventually got a lectureship and then a faculty position at American University. He went on to become dean and also president of the Society of American Archivists and to write highly regarded monographs and articles. He was also instrumental in the identification and protection of records during the Allied invasion of Europe, although that was kept secret until recently." Email correspondence from Anne Gilliland to author, February 11, 2011. On the role of Ernst Posner, see Oliver W. Holmes, "The National Archives and the Protection of Records," *American Archivist* 9, 1 (1946): 110–17.

15. Michael J. Kurtz, *America and the Return of Nazi Contraband: The Recovery of Europe's Cultural Treasures* (Cambridge: Cambridge University Press, 2006), 52.

16. Mark Lendler, "Archive to Expand Access to Files on the Holocaust," *New York Times*, August 5, 2007, 6.

17. Kate Doyle, "The Atrocity Files: Deciphering the Archives of Guatemala's Dirty War," *Harper's*, December 2007, 59. See also Trudy Huskamp Peterson, *Final Acts: A Guide to Preserving the Records of Truth Commissions* (Baltimore: Johns Hopkins University Press, 2005).

18. For a review of the arguments to preserve individual privacy and, hence, restrict access to the archive, see Collin McDonald, "Reconciling Holocaust Scholarship and Personal Data Protection: Facilitating Access to the International Tracing Service Archive," *Fordham International Law Journal* 30, 4 (2007): 1360–91. Germany's postwar management of its own archives is discussed in Astrid M. Eckert, "Managing Their Past: German Archivists Between National Socialism and Democracy," *Archival Science* 7, 3 (2007): 223–44. According to Eckert, in 1939, fully 80 percent of German archivists were members of the Nazi party, and almost all of them survived the postwar denazification inquests.

19. Max Weber, "Bureaucracy," in *From Max Weber: Essays in Sociology*, ed. H. H. Gerth and C. Wright Mills (New York: Oxford University Press, 1946), 196–240. Matthew Hull's work on bureaucracy as ritual captures a positive aspect of my feelings in producing more paperwork to bind the dead to the living; see Matthew Hull, *Government of Paper: The Materiality of Bureaucracy in Urban Pakistan* (Berkeley: University of California Press, 2012).

20. Biedermann, *Sixty Years of History*, 17, 20.

21. On pressures to open the ITS archives, see Paul Belkin, "Opening of the International Tracing Service's Holocaust-Era Archives, in Bad Arolsen, Germany," *Congressional Research Service Report for Congress*, April 27, 2007 (RS22638); and Astrid M. Eckert, "The Fight for the Files: Captured German Records After World War II," *German Historical Institute Bulletin* 32 (2003): 144–48.

22. Hannah Arendt, *Eichmann in Jerusalem: A Report on the Banality of Evil* (New York: Viking, 1963), 85–86.

23. Joan Marshall, "LC Labeling: An Indictment," in *Revolting Librarians*, ed. Celeste West, Elizabeth Katz, et al. (San Francisco: Booklegger Press, 1972), 45–49. Marshall defined her 1971 "majority reader" as "white, Christian (often specifically Protestant), male, and straight (heterosexual)," 46. As a cataloguer-librarian in 1974–1976 during the precomputerized catalog era, I confess that my reluctance on behalf of updated subject headings owes much to the fact that I was the one who painstakingly altered by hand many of the now-outdated three-by-five catalog cards by using whiteout and retyping. See also Sanford Berman, *Prejudices and Antipathies: A Tract on the LC Subject Heads Concerning People* (Metuchen, N.J.: Scarecrow Press, 1971).

24. Daniel Schorn, "Revisiting the Horrors of the Holocaust," *60 Minutes*, December 17, 2006, updated June 21, 2007. CBSNews.com.

25. Giorgio Agamben, *Homo Sacer: Sovereign Power and Bare Life*, trans. Daniel Heller-Roazen (Stanford, Calif.: Stanford University Press, 1998), 114.

26. Kenneth Waltzer, "Opening the Red Cross International Tracing Service Archives," *John Marshall Journal of Computer and Information Law* 21, 6 (2009), 176.

27. Robert S. Marcus, "Report on Leipzig," Headquarters, In Tactical Command, Office of the Chaplain, May 12, 1945, one page report found in ITS Archives.

28. On Marcus, see Alex Grobman, *Rekindling the Flame: American Jewish Chaplains and the Survivors of European Jewry, 1944–1948* (Detroit: Wayne State University Press, 1993), 22, 40, 48–52, and 131. I learned that Marcus was assigned to the 36th Infantry Division formed from the Texas National Guard, which corroborated my mother's tales of six-foot Texans loading her up with food (Prologue). This division has also been recognized by the U.S. Holocaust Memorial Museum for their role in liberating several Nazi *auskommandos*.

29. Zahava Szász Stessel, *Snow Flowers: Hungarian Jewish Women in an Airplane Factory, Markkleeberg, Germany* (Madison, N.J.: Fairleigh Dickinson University Press, 2009), 11, 20–21.

30. Miriam Porat, *Li-lo shihrur: zikhronotai mi-tekufat ha-Sho'ah* (Tel-Aviv: Eked kelali, 1982), 69–71. My translation from Hebrew with help from Osnat Slyomovics.

31. Stessel, *Snow Flowers*, 177–78.

32. Verne Harris, "The Archival Sliver: Power, Memory and Archives in South Africa," *Archival Science* 2 (2002): 64–65.

33. See ITS website, http://www.its-arolsen.org/en/homepage/index.html.

34. Anton Gill, *The Journey Back from Hell* (New York: William Morrow, 1988), 375. Elie Cohen's interview, pp. 366–85. His 1952 Ph.D. thesis in psychiatry from Utrecht State University, "The German Concentration Camp: A Medical-Psychological Study," an early scientific work by a survivor and psychiatrist, was translated into English as Elie A. Cohen, *Human Behaviour in the Concentration Camp* (New York: Norton, 1953).

35. Their multilingual website is available at http://www.afw-saarburg.de/.

36. Biedermann, *Sixty Years of History*, 37–38.

37. Yael Danieli, "Families of Survivors of the Nazi Holocaust: Some Short- and Long-Term Effects," in *Stress and Anxiety*, ed. Charles D. Spielberger, Irwin G. Sarason, and Norman Milgram (Washington, D.C.: Hemisphere, 1982), 8: 406.

38. Joseph Kage, *With Faith and Thanksgiving* (Montreal: Eagle, 1962), 260; and Franklin Bialystock, *Delayed Impact: The Holocaust and the Canadian Community* (Montreal: McGill-Queen's University Press, 2000), 44.

39. Yisrael Gutman and Michael Berenbaum, eds, *Anatomy of the Auschwitz Death Camp* (Bloomington: U.S. Holocaust Memorial Museum and Indiana University Press, 1994), 389.

40. See essays in Richard Ashby Wilson and Richard D. Brown, eds., *Humanitarianism and Suffering: The Mobilization of Empathy* (Cambridge: Cambridge University Press, 2009), especially the work of Ron Dudai, "'Can You Describe This?' Human Rights Reports and What They Tell Us About the Human Rights Movement," 245–64.

41. Didier Fassin and Richard Rechtman, *The Empire of Trauma: An Inquiry into the Condition of Victimhood* (Princeton, N.J.: Princeton University Press, 2009), 275–76.

Chapter 4. Canada

1. Hans Günther Adler, *Panorama: A Novel*, trans. Peter Filkins (New York: Random House, 2011), 379.

2. Jean-Claude Moscovici, *Voyage à Pitchipoï* (Paris: École des Loisirs, 1995).

3. A later edition, which I own, was retitled as Rudolf Vrba, *I Escaped from Auschwitz* (Fort Lee, N.J.: Barricade Books, 2002), 26, 132, but see also 126–44.

4. For this approach, see John Braithwaite, *Restorative Justice and Responsive Regulation* (New York: Oxford University Press, 2002), 46.

5. Paul Chodoff, "Late Effects of the Concentration Camp Syndrome," *Archives of General Psychiatry* 8 (1963): 323–33, and "Depression and Guilt in Concentration Camp Survivors," *Psychotherapy and Psychosomatics* 15, 1 (1967): 11–12.

6. For a stellar analysis of reframing known phrases, see Barbara Kirshenblatt-Gimblett, "A Parable in Context: A Social Interactional Analysis of Storytelling

Performance," in *Folklore: Performance and Communication*, ed. Dan Ben-Amos and Kenneth S. Goldstein (The Hague: Mouton, 1975), 105–30.

7. Esther Herzog, "The Suspicious Anthropologist: Documenting My Mother's Holocaust," in *Serendipity in Anthropological Research*, ed. Haim Hazan and Esther Hertzog (Farnham: Ashgate, 2012), 242.

8. Ben Shephard, *After Daybreak: The Liberation of Belsen, 1945* (London: Jonathan Cape, 2005).

9. Alfred Garwood, "The Holocaust and the Power of Powerlessness: Survivor Guilt, an Unhealed Wound," *British Journal of Psychotherapy* 13, 2 (1996): 243–58.

10. Victor E. Frankl, *Man's Search for Meaning*, part 1 trans. Ilse Lasch (Boston: Beacon Press, 2006), 65–66.

11. The ITS paperwork in Bad Arolsen gives the date and port of my parents' departure (based on copies of the IRO). On the history of the SS *Scynthia*, Cunard Lines, see www.cunard.com.

12. There is a loving memoir of my parents during their first years in Canada by writer Renee Rodin, *Subject to Change* (Vancouver: Talonbooks, 2010), 21–31.

13. For Winnipeg, see Joseph Gordon, "The Litvak as a Leader," *Canadian Jewish Chronicle*, June 4, 1965, 5–6; and for Toronto, see Stephen Speisman, *The Jews of Toronto: A History to 1937* (Toronto: McClelland and Stewart, 1979), 178, 283. An excellent study of the formation of religious Jewish Toronto is in Etan Diamond, *And I Will Dwell in Their Midst: Orthodox Jews in Suburbia* (Chapel Hill: University of North Carolina Press, 2000).

14. The phrase "home to the third largest proportion of Holocaust survivors in the world" appears on the website of The Montreal Holocaust Memorial Centre, a museum and educational center established in 1979, accessed November 26, 2012, http://www.mhmc.ca/en/events/view/38. See David G. Roskies, *Against the Apocalypse: Responses to Catastrophe in Modern Jewish Culture* (Cambridge, Mass.: Harvard University Press, 1984), 3.

15. For Montreal as the Yiddish-speaking "Jerusalem of the North," see Sherry Simon, *Translating Montreal: Episodes in the Life of a Divided City* (Montreal: McGill-Queen's University Press, 2006), 90.

16. On the Montreal survivor community and their children, see also Franklin Bialystock, *Delayed Impact: The Holocaust and the Canadian Jewish Community* (Montreal: McGill-Queen's University Press, 2000), 194.

17. Julian Brauer, "Jewish Communities, Jewish Education and Quebec Nationalism," *Social Compass* 31, 4 (1984): 400.

18. Aron Horowitz, *Hebrew Camps Massad: Their Impact on Canadian Life and Culture* (Toronto: Aron Horowitz, 1990), 11–12.

19. One example of her outreach is captured in the Canadian Jewish Heritage Network photograph titled "Dedication of new Chapel Room in Hillel House, McGill University, Montreal, dated May 31, 1964 and with this description: Student officers of

McGill and Sir George Hillel societies participated in inscription ceremony. Sefer Torah donated to B'nai B'rith Hillel Foundation at McGill University by the B'nai B'rith
Women's Chapters in Montreal. The scroll served to dedicate a new Chapel Room in
Hillel House (similarly presented by the women of B'nai B'rith). People in photograph
identified on verso—incl, . . . Mrs. Vera Slymovics [sic]," accessed December 10, 2012,
http://www.cjhn.ca/en/explore.aspx?q=vera+slyomovics.

20. Susan McDonald and Andrea Hogue, "An Exploration of the Needs of Victims
of Hate Crimes," Report for the Department of Justice, Canada, November 15, 2007,
http://www.justice.gc.ca/eng/pi/rs/rep-rap/2007/rr07_vic1/p2.html.

21. Canadian Legal Information Institute, *R. v. Keegstra*, [1990] 3 SCR 697.

22. See Canadian Information Institute, *R. v. Keegstra*, 1984, CanLII 1313 (Ab QB),
http://www.canlii.org/en/ab/abqb/doc/1984/1984canlii1313/1984canlii1313.html. Ex-
cerpts of Doug Christie's summation to the jury were published in booklet form by
Doug Christie, *Thought Crimes: The Keegstra Case* (Toronto: Citizens for Foreign Aid
Reform, 1986). See also David J. Bercuson and Douglas Wertheimer, *A Trust Betrayed:
The Keegstra Affair* (New York: Doubleday, 1986).

23. *R. v. Keegstra*, 1996 ABCA 308 (CanLII), accessed October 2, 2012, http://
canlii.ca/t/2ddgh.

24. For arguments supporting hate-speech prohibitions, see Jeremy Waldron, *The
Harm in Hate Speech* (Cambridge, Mass.: Harvard University Press, 2012).

25. Alan Davies, "The Keegstar Affair," in *Antisemitism in Canada: History and
Interpretation*, edited by Alan Davies (Waterloo: Wilfrid Laurier University Press,
1992), 245n8.

26. Ben Kayfetz, "Students Get Lesson on the Holocaust," *Jewish Telegraphic Agency*,
September 22, 1983.

27. The organization's materials and history are available through the Canadian
Jewish Heritage Network, accessed September 29, 2012, http://www.cjhn.ca/permalink
/92.

28. Leon Kahn, *No Time to Mourn: A True Story of a Jewish Partisan Fighter* (Vancouver: Laurelton Press, 1978), 207.

29. Jean Gerber, "Immigration and Integration in Post-War Canada: A Case Study
of Holocaust Survivors in Vancouver 1947–70," MA Thesis, University of British Columbia, 1989, 87; and Faith Jones, "Between Suspicion and Censure: Attitudes Towards
the Jewish Left in Postwar Vancouver," *Canadian Jewish Studies* 6 (1998): 1–25.

30. From the *Jewish Western Bulletin*, quoted in Barbara Schober, "Holocaust
Commemoration in Vancouver, BC, 1943–70," MA Thesis, Simon Fraser University,
1998, 29.

31. Hasia R. Diner, *We Remember with Reverence and Love: American Jews and the
Myth of Silence After the Holocaust, 1945–1962* (New York: New York University Press,
2009), 200; Myra Giberovitch, "The Contributions of Montreal Holocaust Survivor
Organizations to Jewish Communal Life," MSW thesis, McGill University, 1988);

Gerber, "Immigration and Integration in Post-War Canada; and Schober, "Holocaust Commemoration in Vancouver, BC, 1943–70."

32. Jean Gerber, "Opening the Door: Immigration and Integration of Holocaust Survivors in Vancouver," *Canadian Jewish Studies* 4–5 (1996–97): 63–86.

33. Canadian Broadcast Company, Digital Archives, "Auschwitz: The Young Must Learn."

34. See, for example, the discussion in Henry Greenspan, "The Awakening of Memory: Survivor Testimony in the First Years After Liberation, and Today," Mona and Otto Weinmann Annual Lecture, U.S. Holocaust Memorial Museum, 2001. See especially comparative, cross-cultural work of Carol A. Kidron, "Toward an Ethnography of Silence: The Lived Presence of the Past in the Everyday Life of Holocaust Trauma Survivors and Their Descendants in Israel," *Current Anthropology* 50, 1 (2009): 5–27.

35. Leo Lowy interview by Franklin Bialystok, in *Delayed Impact*, 178–79. Lowy's son Richard was instrumental in bringing about a film of his father's life: *Leo's Journey: The Story of the Mengele Twins* (2001), dir. Shel Piercy.

36. Graham Forst, "Kristallnacht Keynote Speaker Rob Krell," *Zachor/Remember Vancouver Holocaust Education Centre Newsletter*, October 4, 2008, 3.

37. Vrba, *I Escaped from Auschwitz*, and Kahn, *No Time to Mourn*.

38. Robert Krell, "The Audiovisual Documentation of Survivors of the Holocaust: Obtaining Eyewitness Accounts for History and Education," Photocopy typed memorandum, dated February 1974, courtesy of the Vancouver Holocaust Education Centre. Although Krell presciently outlined his proposed project in 1974, videotaping survivors began only in 1978.

39. Robert Krell, "Children Who Survived the Holocaust: Reflections of a Child Survivor/Psychiatrist," *Echoes of the Holocaust* 4 (1995).

40. Robert Krell, "Confronting Despair: The Holocaust Survivor's Struggle with Ordinary Life and Ordinary Death," *Canadian Medical Association* 157 (1997): 741–44.

41. Robert Krell, "Holocaust Families: The Survivors and Their Children," *Comprehensive Psychiatry* 20, 6 (1979): 567.

42. Arnold J. Toynbee, *A Study of History*, abridgement of Volumes 1–6 by David Churchill Somervell (Oxford: Oxford University Press, 1946), 1:135: "There remains the case where the victims of religious discrimination represent an extinct society which only survives as a fossil. . . . but by far the most notable is one of the fossil remnants of the Syriac Society, the Jews."

43. Dori Laub, "Testimonies in the Treatment of Genocidal Trauma," *Journal of Applied Psychoanalytic Studies* 4 (2002): 73. See also Amit Pinchevski, "The Audiovisual Unconscious: Media and Trauma in the Video Archive for Holocaust Testimonies," *Critical Inquiry* 39, 1 (2012): 142–66: "videotestimony might be seen as a hybrid mutation. Speech and writing give way to screen and camera—a taping cure in lieu of a talking cure," 152.

44. See Joanne Weiner Rudoff, "A Yale University and New Haven Community Project: From Local to Global," on the Fortunoff Video Archive website, accessed October 23, 2012, http://www.library.yale.edu/testimonies/publications/Local_to_Global .pdf. Canadian testimonies are discussed in Janice Rosen, "Holocaust Testimonies and Related Resources in Canadian Archival Repositories," *Canadian Jewish Studies* 4–5 (1996–1997): 163–75. One of the earliest Holocaust testimony projects available to me in English and undertaken in Europe immediately after the war was by David Boder, recently the subject of a book by Alan Rosen, *The Wonder of Their Voices: The 1946 Holocaust Interviews by David Boder* (New York: Oxford University Press, 2010).

45. Robert Krell, "History of Holocaust Education in Vancouver, BC, 1975–2000," quoted in Olga Livshin and Basye Laye, "Holocaust Centre Milestone," *Jewish Independent*, November 16, 2012, 1.

46. Geoffrey Hartman, "Tele Suffering and Testimony in the Dot Com Era," in *Visual Culture and the Holocaust*, edited by Barbie Zelizer (New Brunswick, N.J.: Rutgers University Press, 2000), 116.

47. Lawrence Langer, *Holocaust Testimonies: The Ruins of Memory* (New Haven, Conn.: Yale University Press, 1991), 67. For problems surrounding video testimonies including the bond between interviewer and survivor, see Owen Baruch Stier, "Framing the Witness: The Memorial Role of Holocaust Videotestimonies," in *Remembering for the Future: The Holocaust in an Age of Genocide*, vol. 3, ed. John K. Roth and Elisabeth Maxwell (New York: Palgrave, 2001), 189–204.

48. *Voices of Survival*, Alan Handel dir., Canadian Jewish Congress, 1988/89. The documentation and film project is described in Bialystok, *Delayed Impact*, 180–84. Bialystock and Sharon Weintraub wrote the accompanying teaching guide to the video.

49. Kathy Faludi, "Interview Methodology and Format," Annex II to Canadian Jewish Congress, typed and photocopied memorandum, dated May 8, 1981, courtesy VHEC.

50. Dori Laub and Shoshana Felman, *Testimony: Crises of Witnessing in Literature, Psychoanalysis, and History* (New York: Routledge: 1992), 70. For overarching studies on Holocaust video testimonies, see Robert N Kraft, *Memory Perceived: Recalling the Holocaust* (Westport, Conn.: Praeger, 2002).

51. Anna Sheftel and Stacey Zembrzycki, "'We Started over Again, We Were Young': Postwar Social Worlds of Child Holocaust Survivors in Montreal," *Urban History Review/Revue d'histoire urbaine* 39, 1 (2010): 21. See Montreal Life Stories project at http://www.lifestoriesmontreal.ca/. See also Peter Suedfeld, Robert Krell, John Blando, and Patricia Southward, "The Holocaust as a Context for Telling Life Stories," *International Journal of Aging and Development* 60, 3 (2005): 213–28.

52. Giberovitch, "The Contributions of Montreal Holocaust Survivor Organizations to Jewish Communal Life," 71–72, plus Appendix F.

53. The North African Jewish spiritual phenomena have been much studied by anthropologists; see Yoram Bilu, *The Saints' Impresarios: Dreamers, Healers, and Holy Men*

in Israel's Urban Periphery (Brighton, Mass.: Academic Studies Press, 2010), and Alex Weingrod, *The Saint of Beersheba* (Albany: State University of New York Press, 1990).

54. In my readings of the works of Christopher Browning on slave labor, he indicates that Jewish attempts to survive through slave labor were not misplaced strategies since some like my mother and grandmother survived, see Christopher R. Browning, *Remembering Survival: Inside a Nazi Slave-Labor Camp* (New York: Norton, 2010).

55. See Talmud, Tractate *Moed Katan* 18b; *Sotah* 2. In folklore scholarship, this is the Jewish version of tale types 930A: "The Predestined Wife."

56. Marc Dvorjetsky, "Adjustment of Detainees to Camp and Ghetto Life and Their Subsequent Re-Adjustment to Normal Society," *Yad Vashem Studies* 5 (1963): 204n7. See also Nachman Blumenthal, "Magical Thinking Among the Jews During the Nazi Occupation," *Yad Vashem Studies on the European Jewish Catastrophe and Resistance* 5 (1963): 221–36.

57. James E. Young, *The Texture of Memory: Holocaust Memorials and Meaning* (New Haven, Conn.: Yale University Press, 1993), 4.

58. Peretz Lavie and Hanna Kaminer, "Dreams That Poison Sleep: Dreaming in Holocaust Survivors," *Dreaming: A Journal of the Association for the Study of Dreams* 1 (1991): 11–21.

59. Peretz Lavie and Hanna Kaminer, "Sleep and Dreaming Holocaust Survivors: Dramatic Decrease in Dream Recall in Well-Adjusted Survivors," *Journal of Nervous and Mental Disease* 179, 11 (1991): 664–69.

60. Heinz Kohut, *The Restoration of Self* (New York: International Universities Press, 1977), and Douglas Hollan, "Dreaming in a Global World," in *A Companion to Psychological Anthropology: Modernity and Psychocultural Change*, ed. Conerly Casey and Robert B. Edgerton (Oxford: Blackwell, 2005), 90–102.

61. Zhava Szász Stessel, *Snow Flowers: Hungarian Jewish Women in an Airplane Factory, Markkleeberg, Germany* (Madison, N.J.: Fairleigh Dickinson University Press, 2009), 161–64.

Chapter 5. Children of Survivors: The "Second Generation"
in Storytelling, Tourism, and Photography

1. See "The Holocaust: Our Generation Looks Back," *Response: A Contemporary Jewish Review* 9, 1 (1975): 3–100. The success of this issue led to its publication as a book, a copy of which is still on my bookshelf: Lucy Y. Steinitz and David M. Szonyi, eds., *Living After the Holocaust* (New York: Bloch, 1976).

2. Helen Epstein, "Heirs of the Holocaust: The Lingering Legacy for Children of Survivors," *New York Times Magazine*, June 19, 1977, 14; and *Children of the Holocaust: Conversations with Sons and Daughters of Survivors* (New York: Putnam, 1979).

3. "Five Children of Survivors: A Conversation," in *Living After the Holocaust*, 52–53.

4. Harvey Peskin, "Observations on the First International Conference on Children of Holocaust Survivors," *Family Process* 20, 4 (1981): 391–94. Publications continue to emerge, including a second generation of Germans: Alan L. Berger and Naomi Berger, eds., *Second Generation Voices: Reflections by Children of Holocaust Survivors and Perpetrators* (Syracuse, N.Y.: Syracuse University Press, 2001). From this literature, I single out certain studies useful to me, for example, Aaron Hass, *In the Shadow of the Holocaust* (London: Tauris, 1990); Hass, *The Aftermath* (Cambridge: Cambridge University Press, 1995); and especially, Marianne Hirsch's writings.

5. See, for example, from the 1980s, the work of John J. Sigal, Vincenzo DiNicola, and Michael F. Buonvino. "Grandchildren of Survivors: Can Negative Effects of Prolonged Exposure to Excessive Stress Be Observed Two Generations Later?" *Canadian Journal of Psychiatry* 33 (1988): 207–12; and Yael Danieli, "Families of Survivors of the Nazi Holocaust: Some Short- and Long-Term Effects," in *Stress and Anxiety*, vol. 8, ed. Charles D. Spielberger, Irwin G. Sarason, and Norman Milgram (Washington D.C.: Hemisphere, 1982), 405–21.

6. Vivian G. Rakoff, "Long-Term Effects of the Concentration Camp Experience," *Viewpoints: Labor Zionist Movement of Canada* 1 (1966): 18. A 1973 study of Montreal survivors, whom the authors label SNP (survivors of the Nazi Persecution), concludes with the survivors themselves, as parents report on greater personality problems and lack of coping behaviors in their own children; see John J. Sigal, D. Silver, Vivian G. Rakoff, and B. Ellin, "Some Second-Generation Effects of Survival of Nazi Persecution," *American Journal of Orthopsychiatry* 43, 3 (1973): 320–27.

7. John J. Sigal and Morton Weinfeld, *Trauma and Rebirth: Intergenerational Effects of the Holocaust* (New York: Praeger, 1989), 6.

8. John J. Sigal, "The Nature of Evidence for Intergenerational Effects of the Holocaust," *Simon Wiesenthal Center Annual* 3 (1986): 363–76; for additional research on the Montreal Jewish population, see Vivian G. Rakoff, John J. Sigal, and Nathan V. Epstein, "Children and Families of Concentration Camp Survivors," *Canada's Mental Health* 14 (1966): 24–25.

9. Bernard Trossman, "Adolescent Children of Concentration Camp Survivors," *Canadian Psychiatric Association Journal* 13, 2 (1968): 122.

10. Ibid.

11. John J. Sigal and Morton Weinfeld, "Control of Aggression in Adult Children of Survivors of the Nazi Persecution," *Journal of Abnormal Psychology* 94, 4 (1985): 562.

12. Saul Hayes, Foreword to Ben Lappin, *The Redeemed Children: The Story of the Rescue of War Orphans by the Jewish Community of Canada* (Toronto: University of Toronto Press, 1963), vi–vii; and Fraidie Martz, *Open Your Hearts* (Montreal: Vehicule Press, 1996). See also the video *Children of the Storm*, Kuper Productions, Toronto and Vision TV, Jack Kuper dir, 2000; and the website "Open Hearts—Closed Doors: The War Orphans Project," www.virtualmuseum.ca/Exhibitions/orphans/english.

13. Eva Hoffman, *After Such Knowledge: Memory, History, and the Legacy of the Holocaust* (New York: Public Affairs, 2004), 198. See also Rebecca Phillips, "The

Second Generation's Task," interview with Eva Hoffman, 2004, accessed December 27, 2012, http://www.beliefnet.com/Faiths/Judaism/2004/04/The-Second-Generations -Task.aspx.

14. My St. George's high school classmate, anthropologist Caroline Bretell, wrote a biography of her mother Zoe Bieler, a noted journalist in Montreal; see her *Writing Against the Wind: A Mother's Life History* (Wilmington, Del.: SR Books, 1999). Bretell's introduction (xi–xxiv) discusses Mary Catherine Bateson's biography of her mother Margaret Mead, other important professional women writing about their mothers, and a useful bibliographic review of life histories of women.

15. John Felstiner, *Paul Celan: Poet, Survivor, Jew* (New Haven, Conn.: Yale University Press, 1995), 113. See also Paul Celan, "Das, was Geschah?" in *Atemwende* (Frankfurt am Main: Suhrkamp, 1982 [1967]); also *Poems of Paul Celan*, trans. and intro. Michael Hamburger (London: Anvil Press Poetry, 1995), 108, 204; and Bernhard Böschenstein and Heino Schmull, eds., *The Meridian: Final Version—Drafts—Materials*, trans. and preface by Pierre Jorris (Stanford, Calif.: Stanford University Press, 2011).

16. Richard Schechner, *Between Theater and Anthropology* (Philadelphia: University of Pennsylvania Press, 1985), 35, 37.

17. See my discussion of Palestinian naming practices for children that include calling daughters for lost and destroyed Palestinian villages in Israel: Susan Slyomovics, *The Object of Memory: Arab and Jew Narrate the Palestinian Village* (Philadelphia: University of Pennsylvania Press, 1998), 201–3.

18. Emil Fackenheim, *The Jewish Return into History: Reflections in the Age of Auschwitz and a New Jerusalem* (New York: Schocken, 1978), 23–24: "we are, first, commanded to survive as Jews, lest the Jewish people perish. We are commanded, second, to remember in our very guts and bones the martyrs of the Holocaust, lest their memory perish. We are forbidden, thirdly, to deny or despair of God, however much we may have to contend with him or with belief in him, lest Judaism perish. We are forbidden, finally, to despair of the world as the place which is to become the kingdom of God, lest we help make it a meaningless place in which God is dead or irrelevant and everything is permitted. To abandon any of these imperatives, in response to Hitler's victory at Auschwitz, would be to hand him yet other, posthumous victories"; see also Reeve R. Brenner, *The Faith and Doubt of Holocaust Survivors* (New York: Free Press, 1980), and Paul Marcus and Alan Rosenberg, "The Holocaust Survivor's Faith and Religious Behavior and Some Implications for Treatment," *Holocaust and Genocide Studies* 3, 4 (1988): 413–30. Although my mother never used the term "memorial candles," the configuration of her attitudes toward her children are aptly described in Dina Wardi, *Memorial Candles: Children of the Holocaust* (New York: Tavistock, 1992).

19. Rudolf Kasztner is either a loved hero or hated collaborator of the Holocaust. For the former viewpoint, besides my grandmother, see Anna Porter, *Kasztner's Train: The True Story of Rezső Kasztner, Unknown Hero of the Holocaust* (Vancouver: Douglas & McIntyre, 2007). Kasztner bargained with Adolf Eichmann for the lives of 1,700 Hungarian Jews, including my step-grandfather's, exchanging cash and jewels

for a special train that traveled to Bergen-Belsen concentration camp, then safely on to Switzerland.

20. See Jewish Museum of Prague website, www.jewishmuseum.cz/en/a-ex-pinkas .htm.

21. Marianne Hirsch, *Family Frames: Photography, Narrative and Postmemory* (Cambridge, Mass.: Harvard University Press, 1997), 22.

22. Roland Barthes, *Camera Lucida: Reflections on Photography* (New York: Hill and Wang, 1981), 76, italics original.

23. Susan Sontag, *On Photography* (New York: Anchor Doubleday, 1973), 10.

24. Ibid., 19–20.

25. See Herman Dicker, *Piety and Perseverance: Jews from the Carpathian Mountains* (New York: Sepher-Hermon Press), 1981; Livia Rothkirchen, "Deep-Rooted Yet Alien: Some Aspects of the History of the Jews of Subcarpathian Ruthenia," *Yad Vashem Studies* 12 (1977): 147–97; Hugo Stransky, "The Religious Life in Slovakia and Subcarpathian Ruthenia," in *The Jews of Czechoslovakia* (Philadelphia: Jewish Publication Society 1968–84), 2: 347–92; Aryeh Sole, "Subcarpathian Ruthenia, 1918–38," in *The Jews of Czechoslovakia* (Philadelphia: Jewish Publication Society 1968–84), 1:125–54; Paul Robert Magocsi, *The Shaping of a National Identity: Subcarpathian Rus, 1848–1948* (Cambridge, Mass.: Harvard University Press, 1978), and his *Historical Atlas of East Central Europe* (Toronto: University of Toronto Press, 1993).

26. Although everyone I interviewed from the region would begin with this joke, folklorists have documented similar tellings in other contested regions characterized by turmoil and shifting geopolitical boundaries. On this topic, see Dov Noy, "The Jewish Versions of the 'Animal Languages' Folktale (AT 670): A Typological Structural Study," *Scripta Hierosolymitana* 22 (1971): 171–208; and Eli Yassif, "New Perspectives on the Oicotypification of Modern Jewish Folktales," *Jerusalem Studies in Jewish Folklore* 13–14 (Dov Noy Festschrift) (1992): 275–302.

27. See the chapter devoted to the one-day existence of Carpatho-Ukraine in Norman Davies, *Vanished Kingdoms: The History of Half-Forgotten Europe* (New York: Penguin Books, 2011). An earlier version of this chapter includes sections previously published with additional photographs documenting my voyage to my parent's region; see Susan Slyomovics, "Rebbele Mordkhele's Pilgrimage in New York City, Tel Aviv and Carpathian Ruthenia." In *Going Home*, ed. Jack Kugelmass (Evanston, Ill.: Northwestern University Press and Yivo Institute for Jewish Research, 1993), 369–94.

28. Edward S. Casey, *Remembering: A Phenomenological Study* (Bloomington: Indiana University Press, 1987), 184.

29. James E. Young, "Interpreting Literary Testimony: A Preface to Rereading Holocaust Diaries and Memoirs," *New Literary History* 18 (1986–87): 403–23.

30. While Holocaust memorials and burial society activities appeared to be the major functions of the two *landsmanshaftn*, in their early years, they created and participated in a wide range of cultural activities; see, for example, the special issue on *landsmanshaftn*, "Jewish Landsmanshaftn in America," *American Jewish History* 76

(September 1986). See also Dov Dinur, *Shoat Yehudei Rusia ha-Karpatit-Uzhorod* [The Holocaust of the Jews of Subcarpathian-Rus] (Jerusalem: Hebrew University Press, 1983).

31. S. Y. Gross and Y. Yosef Cohen, eds., *Sefer Marmaros: mea ve-shishim kehilot kedoshot be-yishuvan u-ve-hurbanan* [The Marmaros Book: In Memory of a Hundred and Sixty Thousand Jewish Communities] (Tel Aviv: Beit Marmaros, 1983), 54.

32. Ibid., 55.

33. Jack Kugelmass and Jonathan Boyarin, *From a Ruined Garden: The Memorial Books of Polish Jewry* (New York: Schocken, 1983), 1–19.

34. Alexander Kraus, *Our Village (as Remembered by Heimus fun Bishtine)* (London: Irgun Yotzei Bustina, 1996). I am a grateful to Alex Kraus for providing me with a copy of his privately published manuscript.

35. Roland Barthes, "Rhétorique de l'image," *Communications* 4 (1964): 40–51.

36. There are many transliterated versions of Yiddish, which causes confusion, especially since I use several in this book. "Yortsayt," the commemoration of the dead, is also spelled "jahrzeit," "yahrzeit," while "landslayt" may appear elsewhere as "landsleit." "Rebbele" according to the YIVO transliteration system should be "rebele," family name Melech is "Melekh" in the Library of Congress transliteration system, and so on. At least in the case of personal names, I follow written forms established by their bearers or families regardless of transliteration protocols, so "Melech" and not "Melekh." I ask the reader's indulgence for the added confusion of place names that may appear in their Yiddish, Rusyn or Hungarian forms in a variety of orthographies.

37. See Kraus, *Our Village*, 26; and Gross and Cohen, eds., *Sefer Marmaros*, 288.

38. Aharon Appelfeld, "Buried Homeland," *New Yorker*, November 23, 1998, 55. A similar tale of Jewish spirits that must be placated is recounted in Poland, when a Polish businessman, who survives a serious car accident, dreams of a Jewish girl who asks him to return her ring, one he was given by his grandmother who found it near Belzec Concentration Camp. He returns the ring with a letter, where it is on display in the State Museum of Majdanek; see Jan Tomasz Gross and Irena G. Gross, *Golden Harvest: Events at the Periphery of the Holocaust* (New York: Oxford University Press, 2012), 123–24. Throughout my travels in North Africa, I have come across tombs of Jewish rabbis as sites of veneration and pilgrimage, prayer and candle lighting by the surrounding Muslim population even as Maghribi Jews have largely departed.

39. Michael Alpert reported to me that at the Khist (Khust) synagogue on November 3, 1990, he encountered six Nadvorner Hasidim from the Bnei Brak community in Israel on their way to Rebbele Mordkhele's grave.

40. Ari Goldman, "Rosh ha-Shanah Journey to Hasidic Master's Tomb," *New York Times*, September 27, 1989, B2.

41. Parenthetically and for now, I believe my reading of ethnographically informed academic analyses, for example, by Feldman, Kugelmass, Stier, and other fine works help substitute for my actually visiting Auschwitz. See Jackie Feldman, *Above the Death-Pits, Beneath the Flag: Youth Voyages to Poland and the Performance of Is-*

raeli National Identity (New York: Berghahn, 2008); Jack Kugelmass, "Bloody Memories: Encountering the Past in Contemporary Poland," *Cultural Anthropology* 10, 3 (1995): 279–301; and Oren Baruch Stier, *Committed to Memory: Cultural Mediations of the Holocaust* (Amherst: University of Massachusetts Press, 2003).

42. For a description of the Markkleeberg commemoration service of 1998, see Zahava Szász Stessel, *Snow Flowers: Hungarian Jewish Women in an Airplane Factory, Markkleeberg, Germany* (Madison, N.J.: Fairleigh Dickinson University Press, 2009), 320–31.

43. Walter Benjamin, "On the Concept of History," originally in *Gesammelten Schriften* 1, 2 (Frankfurt am Main: Suhrkamp, 1974), trans. Dennis Redmond, http://members.efn.org/~dredmond/ThesesonHistory.html.

Chapter 6. Algerian Jews Make the Case for Reparations

1. On legislation and legal and diplomatic history leading to the establishment of the foundation, see Peer Zumbansen, ed., *Remembrance and Responsibility: Legal and Historical Observations* (Baden-Baden: Nomos, 2002). A history of the foundation is by J. D. Bindenagel, "Justice, Apology, Reconciliation, and the German Foundation: 'Rememberance, Responsibility and the Future'," in *Taking Wrongs Seriously: Apologies and Reconciliation*, ed. Elazar Barkan and Alexander Karn (Stanford, Calif.: Stanford University Press, 2006), 286–310. For commentary on the foundation, in particular some doubts concerning whether the settlement was helpful to broader concerns, such as addressing historical memory, see Libby Adler and Peer Zumbansen, "The Forgetfulness of the Noblesse: A Critique of the German Foundation Law Compensating Slave and Forced Laborers of the Third Reich," *Harvard Journal of Legislation* 39, 1 (2001): 1–61.

2. Susan Slyomovics and Sarah Abrevaya Stein, "Jews and French Colonialism in Algeria: An Introduction," *Journal of North African Studies* 17, 5 (2012): 751. See also my "French Restitution, German Compensation: Algerian Jews and Vichy's Financial Legacy," *Journal of North African Studies* 17, 5 (2012): 881–901; and "Geographies of Jewish Tlemcen," *Journal of North African History* 5, 2 (2001): 81–96.

3. Yitzchak Kerem, "Sephardic and Oriental Oral Testimonies: Their Importance for Holocaust Commemoration and Memory," in *Remembering for the Future: The Holocaust in the Age of Genocide*, ed. John K. Roth and Elisabeth Maxwell (New York: Palgrave, 2001), 3: 142–49; and Solomon Gaon and M. Mitchell Serels, eds., *Del Fuego: Sephardim and the Holocaust* (New York: Safra Institute, Yeshiva University, 1987).

4. See Robert Satloff, *Among the Righteous: Lost Stories from the Holocaust's Long Reach into Arab Lands* (New York: Public Affairs, 2006); and Gilbert Achcar, *The Arabs and the Holocaust: the Arab-Israeli War of Narratives* (St. Paul: Saqi Books, 2010).

5. Yehouda Shenhav, "What Do Palestinians and Arab-Jews Have in Common? Nationalism and Ethnicity Examined Through the Compensation Question," Palestinian Refugee Research Net, accessed December 28, 2012, http://prrn.mcgill.ca/research/papers/shenhav2.htm.

6. Bruce Golding, "Fraud Clerk Guilty: Holocaust Scam," *New York Post*, June 6, 2012.

7. United Nations, *Basic Principles and Guidelines on the Right to a Remedy and Reparation for Victims of Violations of International Human Rights and Humanitarian Law*, E/CN.4/2005/L.48.

8. There is a large legal literature on reparations; for one overview, see Dinah Shelton, *Remedies in International Human Rights Law* (Oxford: Oxford University Press, 1999).

9. Nehemiah Robinson, *Indemnification and Reparations: Jewish Aspects* (New York: Institute of Jewish Affairs, 1944), 133.

10. Ibid., 160.

11. Nahum Goldmann, "Nehemiah Robinson: Dedicated and Faithful Servant of the Jewish People," in *Ten Years of German Indemnification: Memorial Edition*, ed. Nehemiah Robinson (New York: Conference on Jewish Material Claims Against Germany, 1964), 8.

12. Jacques Derrida, *Of Hospitality: Anne Dufourmantelle Invites Jacques Derrida to Respond* (Stanford, Calif.: Stanford University Press, 2000), 141–42.

13. Frantz Fanon, *The Wretched of the Earth*, trans. Constance Farrington (New York: Grove Press, 1963), 102.

14. Michael Rothberg calls for a "countertradition in which remembrance of the Holocaust intersects with the legacies of colonialism and slavery and ongoing processes of decolonization" in *Multidirectional Memory: Remembering the Holocaust in the Age of Decolonization* (Stanford, Calif.: Stanford University Press, 2009), xiii.

15. For a history of early discussions involving Morris J. Cohen, Nahum Goldmann, and George Landauer, see Nicholas Balabkins, *West German Reparations to Israel* (New Brunswick, N.J.: Rutgers University Press, 1971), 81–82.

16. Inge Deutschkron, *Bonn and Jerusalem: The Strange Coalition* (Philadelphia: Chilton, 1970), 43: "The Stuttgart lawyer and restitution expert Dr. Otto Kuster explained that this term caught on in Germany after 1945 because it 'made sense' to the people, and it was also taken up by the legislature." See also her Deutschkron interview with Otto Kuster, September, 1967, at 42n5.

17. Robinson, *Indemnification and Reparations*, 198–209.

18. Michael Rothberg, "Between Auschwitz and Algeria: Multidirectional Memory and the Counterpublic Witness," *Critical Inquiry* 33, 1 (2006): 158–84.

19. Michael R. Marrus and Robert O. Paxton, *Vichy France and the Jews* (New York: Basic Books, 1981), viii; and Richard H. Weisberg, *Vichy Law and the Holocaust in France* (New York: New York University Press, 1996.) See also Paxton's groundbreaking study, *Vichy France: Old Guard and New Order, 1940–44* (New York, Knopf, 1972).

20. All citations for Vichy laws are drawn from the compilation in Dominique Rémy, *Les lois de Vichy: Actes dits "lois" de l'autorité de fait se prétendant "gouvernement de l'État français"* (Paris: Romillat, 1992). Citations for the original laws are

Loi du 3 octobre 1940 portant statut des Juifs; Loi du 4 octobre sur les ressortissants étrangers de race juive; and Loi du 7 octobre portant abrogation du décret Crémieux, in *Journal Officiel*, October 8, 1940, 5323, 5324, 5324, as cited in Rémy, *Les lois de Vichy*, 85–88, 91.

21. Warren Green, "The Fate of Oriental Jews in France," *Wiener Library Bulletin* 32, 49–50 (1979): 49–50. See also Michel Abitbol, *Les Juifs d'Afrique du Nord sous Vichy* (Paris: Maisonneuve et Larose, 1983); Henri Msellati, *Les Juifs d'Algérie sous le régime de Vichy* (Paris: L'Harmattan, 1999); Michel Ansky, *Les Juifs d'Algérie du décret Crémieux à la libération* (Paris: Éditions du Centre, 1950); Jacques Cantier, *L'Algérie sous le régime de Vichy* (Paris: O. Jacob, 2002); and Christine Levisse-Touzé, *L'Afrique du Nord dans la guerre 1939-1945* (Paris: A Michel, 1998).

22. Benedict Anderson, "Préface à l'édition francaise," in *L'imaginaire national: réflexions sur l'origine et l'essor de nationalism* (Paris: La Découverte, 2002), 9–14. Anderson's point is about Algerian Jews willfully forgetting their autochthonous origins,while Benjamin Stora's thesis in *La gangrène et l'oubli: la mémoire de la guerre d'Algérie* (Paris: La Découverte, 1991) is about French official nonrecognition and forgetting of the Algerian war.

23. Michel Abitbol, *The Jews of North Africa During the Second World War* (Detroit: Wayne State University Press, 1989), 60.

24. Estimates are from Jean Laloum, "La déportation des Juifs natifs d'Algérie," in *Les Juifs d'Algérie: Images et texts*, ed. Jean Laloum et al. (Paris: Éditions du Scribe, 1987), 36–41. See also "Algeria Sephardim Deported from France or Executed in, France During WW II," website based on Serge Klarsfeld, *La mémorial de la déportation des Juifs de France, 1942–45* (Paris: Klarsfeld, 1978), http://www.sephardicstudies.org/pdf /algeria-shoah.pdf. A study of a wartime Moroccan Jewish community south of Lyon reports that more than one hundred Jews, holders of Moroccan passports, were denounced by the local French and deported to camps; only half returned. See Elkbir Atouf, "Un communauté prolétaire: les Juifs marocains de Saint-Fons," *Archives Juives* 36, 2 (2003): 121–30.

25. Quote is taken from the title of the collections of laws, Rémy, *Les lois de Vichy*.

26. Marrus and Paxton, *Vichy France and the Jews*, 191–97. Vichy's role in saving or persecuting French Jews remains a matter for debates: Léon Poliakov, *Bréviaire de la haine* (Paris: Calmann-Lévy, 1951) credits Vichy with saving Jewish lives especially in 1943, while Raymond Aron in his *Mémoires* points to Vichy's participation in deportations as a "dishonor." The question whether Vichy was a buffer that protected French Jews from Nazi Germany continues; see Robert Paxton, "Letters to the Editor," *Times Literary Supplement*, January 21, 2001, 6, where he draws on Raul Hilberg's revised 2003 edition of *The Destruction of the European Jews* to emphasize that Vichy's more extreme initiatives against the Jews were not brought about by German coercion. Similarly, Paxton citing Léon Poliakov's work on Vichy in the Italian occupied zone notes that Vichy made matters worse for the Jews, According to Aron, while nothing the Pétain regime did could offset the power of Germany to do whatever it

wanted with French Jews, Vichy France should not have participated in the deportations; see Raymond Aron, *Memoires* (Paris: Julliard, 1983), 706.

27. Kristine McKenna, "The Three Ages of Jacques Derrida," *LA Weekly News*, November 6, 2002.

28. [Michel Rosenfeld], "Interview with Jacques Derrida," *Cardozo Life*, October 1998, http://www.cardozo.yu.edu/life/fall1998/derrida/.

29. Jacques Derrida, "Circumfession: Fifty-Nine Periods and Periphrases," in *Jacques Derrida*, ed. Geoffrey Bennington and Jacques Derrida (Chicago: University of Chicago Press, 1993), 58.

30. Robert Brunschvig, "Les measures antijuives dans l'enseignement en Algérie sous le régime de Vichy," *Revue d'Alger* 1, 2 (1944): 65.

31. For example, during academic year 1941–42, the year of Derrida's expulsion from school, Eisenbeth calculated that the 14 percent Jewish quota imposed on primary, secondary, or technical school level retained 11,962 Jewish students and expelled 13,168, while a harsher 7 percent quota for 1942–43 reduced the number to 6,582 with 18,544 expelled. At the university level, the 3 percent quota resulted in 110 Jewish students from a total of 452 retained in 1942–43. Maurice Eisenbeth, *Pages vécues, 1940–43* (Algiers: Charras, 1945), 41.

32. Ibid., 30.

33. See Laurent Joly, *Xavier Vallat: Du nationalisme chrétien à l'antisémitisme d'état, 1891–1972* (Paris: Grasset, 2001).

34. Catherine Malabou and Jacques Derrida, *Counterpath: Traveling with Jacques Derrida* (Stanford, Calif.: Stanford University Press, 2004), 82.

35. Norbert Bel Ange, *Quand Vichy internait ses soldats juifs d'Algérie: Bedeau, sud oranais, 1941–1943* (Paris: L'Harmattan, 2006).

36. No exact numbers are currently available; see the chapter devoted to the camps in Michel Ansky, *Les juifs d'Algérie du décret Crémieux à la libération*, 261–81; Abitbol, *The Jews of North Africa During the Second World War*, 102–4; Bel Ange, *Quand Vichy internait ses soldats juifs d'Algérie*; Jacob Oliel, *Les Camps de Vichy: Maghreb-Sahara 1939–44* (Montréal: Édition du Lys, 2005); Louis Cohn, "Une page non écrite des années 1940: Les camps d'internement en Algérie française," *Nouveaux Cahiers* 116 (1996): 27–29; Christine Levisse-Touzé, "Les camps d'internement en Afrique du Nord pendant le second guerre mondiale," in *Mélanges*, ed. Charles-Robert Ageron (Zaghouan: FTERSI, 1996), 601–5; Yves Claude Aouate, "Les juifs d'Algérie pendant la seconde guerre mondiale (1939–1945)," Ph.D. dissertation, University of Nice, 1984, 1: 47–58; Zosa Szajkowski, *Jews and the French Foreign Legion* (New York: Ktav, 1975); Michel Abitbol, *Mi-Kremyeh le-Peten: antishemiyut be-Alg'iryah ha-kolonyalit, 1870–1940* (Jerusalem: Merkaz Zalman Shazar le-Toldot Yisrael, 1993). The German Foundation determined that 3,000 Jews were interned from October 1940 to November 1942, with 300 hundred still alive and eligible for compensation in 2004.

37. See Bel Ange, *Quand Vichy internait ses soldats juifs d'Algérie*; Roger Bensadoun, *Les Juifs de la République en Algérie et au Maroc* (Paris: Publisud, 2003); Oliel,

Les Camps de Vichy; André Moine, *La déportation et la résistance en Afrique du Nord (1939–1944)* (Paris: Éditions sociales, 1972); Maurice Vanino-Wanikoff, "Le régime des camps en Afrique du Nord," in *Le combattant volontaire juif, 1939–45* (Paris: Ab-express, 1971), 80–82; and Satloff, *Among the Righteous*.

38. Roger Azoulay, interview with the author and Ariella Azoulay, Netanya, Israel, January 28, 2006. According to German historians Klaus-Michael Mallmann and Martin Cüppers, there was ample archival evidence for German plans to extend the Holocaust to the Jews of Arab lands through measures against the civilian population similar to those the SS Einsatzgruppen (Special Mobile Killing Units) were carrying out in the Soviet Union; see their "'Beseitigung der jüdisch-nationalen Heimstätte in Palästina.' Das Einsatzkommando der Panzerarmee Afrika 1942," in *Deutsche, Juden, Völkermord: Der Holocaust als Geschichte und Gegenwart*, ed. Jürgen Matthäus and Klaus-Michael Mallmann (Darmstadt: Wissenschaftliche Buchgesellschaft, 2006), 153–76.

39. Christian Eggers, "L'internement sous toutes ses forms: approche d'une vue d'ensemble du système d'internement dans la zone de Vichy," *Le Monde Juif* 153 (1995): 7–75.

40. An example of the circular found in Bel Ange, *Quand Vichy internait ses soldats juifs d'Algérie*, 90, states: "Les militaires juifs algériens récemment déchus de la nationalité francaises seront regroupés en une unité des travaileurs jusqua'à la liberation de la classe à laquelle ils sont attachés."

41. Yehouda Léon Askénazi, "L'histoire de ma vie" in *Ki MiTsion: notes sur la paracha.* (Jerusalem: Fondation Manitou, 1997).

42. Michel Abitbol, "North Africa (Tunisia, Algeria, Morocco)," in *Zionism in Transition*, ed. Moshe Davis (New York: Herzl Press, 1980), 197–210.

43. Keren Rouche, "Projecting Algerian Judaism, Formulating a Political Identity: Zionism in Algeria during the War of Independence," *Journal of North African Studies* 12, 2 (2007): 185–201.

44. Ariella Azoulay, "Sfat em, sfat av," in *Ḥazot mizraḥit* [Eastern appearance], ed. Yigal Nizri (Tel-Aviv: Bavel, 2004), 165.

45. René Cassin, "Vichy or Free France," *Foreign Affairs* 20, 1 (1941): 108n3.

46. Renée Poznanski, "French Apprehensions, Jewish Expectations: From a Social Imaginary to a Political Practice," 34, and Patrick Weil, "The Return of Jews in the Nationality or in the Territory of France (1943–73)," 58–72, both in *The Jews Are Coming Back: The Return of the Jews to their Countries of Origin After WWII*, ed. David Bankier (New York: Bergahn, 2005).

47. Hannah Arendt, "Why the Crémieux Decree Was Abrogated," originally published in *Contemporary Jewish Record* 6, 3 (April 1943); reprinted in *The Jewish Writings* (New York Schocken, 2007), 252–53.

48. See *Journal Officiel de la République Francaise* (JORF), October 28, 1943.

49. Claire Andrieu, "Two Approaches to Compensation in France," in *Robbery and Restitution: The Conflict over Jewish Property in Europe*, ed. Martin Dean,

Constantin Goschler, and Philipp Ther (New York: Berghahn in association with U.S. Holocaust Memorial Museum, 2007), 134–35. See also her *La persécution des Juifs de France (1940–1944) et le rétablissement de la légalité républicaine; Recueil des textes officiels 1940–1999* (avec la participation de Serge Klarsfeld et Annette Wieviorka, et la collaboration d'Olivier Cariguel et Cécilia Kapitz) (Paris: Mission d'Étude sur la Spoliation des Juifs de France, La Documentation Française, 2000).

50. Robinson, *Indemnification and Reparations*, 200n5.

51. Commission pour l'indemnisation des victimes des spoliations, report summary in French, http://www.civs.gouv.fr/

52. By 2001, the Drai Commission had received over seven thousand individual claims for compensation and accepted 1,276 for compensation, totaling €26.43 million. On the "triptych" of apology, trials, and reparations, see Julie Fette, "The Apology Moment: Vichy Memories in 1990s France," in *Taking Wrongs Seriously: Apologies and Reconciliation*, ed. Elazar Barkan and Alexander Karn (Stanford, Calif.: Stanford University Press, 2006), 259–385.

53. Bernadetta Nitschke, *Vertreibung und Aussiedlung der deutschen Bevölkerung aus Polen 1945 bis 1949* (Munich: Oldenbourg Wissenschaftsverlag, 2003).

54. Eftihia Voutira, "Post Soviet Diaspora Politics: The Case of the Soviet Greeks," *Journal of Modern Greek Studies* 24, 2 (2006): 379–414.

55. Todd Shepard describes this process in his *The Invention of Decolonization: The Algerian War and the Remaking of France* (Ithaca, N.Y.: Cornell University Press, 2006), 169–82.

56. Eric Savarèse, "After the Algerian War: Reconstructing Identity Among the Pieds-noirs," *International Social Science Journal* 58 (2006): 457–66; and *L'invention des pieds-noirs* (Paris: Séguier, 2002).

57. See Conference on Jewish Material Claims Against Germany website, accessed February 14, 2012, www.claimscon.org/?url=news/homecare_05.

58. "Facts and Files," accessed February 14, 2012, http://www.factsandfiles.com/.

59. Marc Masurovky, email correspondence with the author, October 24, 2005.

60. Christopher R. Browning, *Collected Memories: Holocaust History and Postwar Testimony* (Madison: University of Wisconsin Press, 2003), on collected survivor testimony to reconstruct the twenty-one-month existence of the Starachowice factory slave labor camp in Poland.

61. See the French government website on obtaining the "political internee" card: http://vosdroits.service-public.fr/F1493.xhtml.

62. Guy Teissier, written question number 1527 published in the *Journal Officiel*, July 31, 2007, 5005. The response by the ministry in charge of veterans was published in the *Journal Officiel*, September 18, 2007, 5666.

63. Achcar, *The Arabs and the Holocaust*, 146.

64. In addition, Achcar notes that some 6,300 Arabs from various countries served with the German military, while, according to historian Gerhard Höpp in *Blind für die*

Geschichte arabische Begegnungen mit dem Nationalsozialismus (Berlin: Klaus Schwarz 2004), 215–40, Arabs were interned in Nazi concentration camps.

65. Fanon, *The Wretched of the Earth*, 103.

66. Ibid.

67. Lorenzo Veracini, email correspondence, January 1, 2013. See also Lorenzo Veracini, *Settler Colonialism: A Theoretical Overview* (New York: Palgrave Macmillan, 2010).

68. Vincent Crapanzano, *The Harkis* (Chicago: University of Chicago Press, 2011), 159–60; and Sung Choi, "The Muslim Veteran in Postcolonial France: The Politics of the Integration of Harkis after 1962," *French Politics, Culture, and Society* 29, 1 (2011): 24–45.

69. Albert Memmi, *The Colonizer and the Colonized* (New York: Orion Press, 1967), xvi.

Chapter 7. Compensation for Settler Colonialism: Aftermaths and "Dark Teleology"

I draw on the term "dark teleology" from Heidegger on Aristotle, in Martin Heidegger, *Basic Concepts of Aristotelian Philosophy*, trans. Robert D. Metcalf and Mark B. Tanzer (Bloomington: Indiana University Press, 2009), 151.

Epigraph: Fady Joudah, "Revenge," in *Textu* (Port Townsend, Wash.: Copper Canyon Press, 2013), Kindle edition.

1. Imre Kertész, *The Holocaust as Culture* (London: Seagull Books, 2011), 77.

2. Barbara Rose Johnston, "Waging War, Making Peace: The Anthropology of Reparations," in *Waging War, Making Peace: Reparation and Human Rights*, ed. Barbara Rose Johnston and Susan Slyomovics (Walnut Creek, Calif.: Left Coast Press, 2008), 13.

3. Alvin E. Roth, "Repugnance as a Constraint on Markets," *Journal of Economic Perspectives* 21, 3 (2007): 40.

4. Information on this fund is available at the website for The Conference on Jewish Material Claims Against Germany, http://www.claimscon.org/?url=zrbg_apply. Pressure from Jewish organizations eliminated the German deadline of 2011. Many countries, including Canada, where my mother resides, do not consider this income taxable. Approximately half of some 56,000 reopened applications were approved.

5. Ibid., information on the website for The Conference on Jewish Material Claims Against Germany.

6. Georg Simmel, *The Philosophy of Money* (London: Routledge & Kegan Paul, 1978), 510–11.

7. See the works of C. Daniel Batson, especially *The Altruism Question: Toward a Social Psychological Answer* (Hillsdale, N.J.: Erlbaum, 1991). According to Elisabeth Young-Bruehl, "The usual, indeed, the clichéd way of describing empathy as 'putting

yourself in another's place' seems to me quite wrong. Empathizing involves, rather, putting another person in yourself, becoming another person's habitat. But this depends on your ability to tell the difference between the subject and yourself," see "The Biographer's Empathy with Her Subject," in *Subject to Biography: Psychoanalysis, Feminism, and Writing Women's Lives* (Cambridge, Mass.: Harvard University Press, 2000), 22.

8. David Graeber, "An Army of Altruists: On the Alienated Right to Do Good," *Harper's Magazine*, January 2007. On powerful narratives, see Linda C. Garro and Cheryl Mattingly, "Narrative as Construct and Construction," in *Narrative and the Cultural Construction of illness and Healing*, ed. Cheryl Mattingly and Linda C. Garro (Berkeley: University of California Press, 2000), 1–49.

9. Marcel Mauss, *The Gift: The Form and Reason for Exchange in Archaic Societies*, trans. W. D. Halls (New York: Norton, 1990), 3 (emphasis in original).

10. Johnston, "Waging War, Making Peace: The Anthropology of Reparations," 18.

11. John Torpey, " 'Making Whole What Has Been Smashed': Reflections on Reparations," *Journal of Modern History* 73, 2 (2001): 336.

12. A contrast is Germany's compensation to the few survivors from the 50,000 Ladino-speaking Greek Jewish community of Salonika deported to Auschwitz, who received individual German compensation. This was not the case for the German occupation of Greece during which, according to Greece's Ministry of Reconstruction, more than 1,200,000 Greeks became homeless, starvation was rampant, 5,000 schools were destroyed, and specific villages were targeted for mass destruction and death; see Ministry of Reconstruction, *The Sacrifices of Greece in the Second World War* (Athens: Ergostasiou Graphikai technai Aspiōtē-Elka, 1946). The majority of Greeks to this day insists on the inadequacy of German war reparations, an accusation revived at the onset of the 2011 Greek debt crisis.

13. Aimé Césaire, *Discourse on Colonialism*, trans. Joan Pinkham (New York: Monthly Review, 1972), 3. See also Mahmood Mamdani, "Making Sense of Political Violence in Postcolonial Africa," in *War and Peace in the Twentieth Century and Beyond: Proceedings of the Nobel Centennial Symposium*, ed. Geir Lundestad and Olav Njolstad (River Edge, N.J.: World Scientific, 2002), 71–100.

14. Césaire, *Discourse on Colonialism*, 13.

15. Frantz Fanon, *The Wretched of the Earth*, trans. Constance Farrington (New York: Grove Press, 1963), 101.

16. David Graeber, *Debt: The First 5,000 Years* (Brooklyn, N.Y.: Melville House, 2011), 332 (italics in original).

17. Ibid., 110.

18. Walther Rathenau, *Walther Rathenau: Industrialist, Banker, Intellectual, and Politician: Notes and Diaries, 1907–1922*, ed. Hartmut Pogge von Strandmann (Oxford: Clarendon, 1985), 81. Although Rathenau wrote against the system of deportation, concentration camps, and the status of the native reduced to slavery, he did not question Germany's right to rule over its colonial possessions.

19. Dominik J. Schaller, "'Every Herero Will Be Shot': Genocide, Concentration Camps, and Slave Labor in German South-West Africa," in *Forgotten Genocides: Oblivion, Denial, and Memory*, ed. René Lemarchand (Philadelphia: University of Pennsylvania Press, 2011), 51–70. On the legal case, see Sidney Harring, "German Reparations to the Herero Nation: An Assertion of Herero Nationhood in the Path of Namibian Development?" *West Virginia Law Review* 104, 2 (2002): 393–417. A 1985 UNReport, titled "The Whitaker Report" after its special rapporteur, Benjamin Whitaker, has been contested by researchers, especially the classification of the German assault on the Herero people as an extermination and one of the earliest attempts at genocide in the twentieth century. See the report, http://www.preventgenocide.org/prevent /UNdocs/whitaker/section5.htm. The Herero lawsuit against German companies was filed in 2001 in the Superior Court of the District of Columbia (U.S.A), Civil Division, "Case No 01-0004447," accessed November 12, 2012, http://www.baerfilm.de/PDF /prozess%20klageschrift.pdf.

20. See also Hannah Arendt, *The Origins of Totalitarianism* (New York: Harcourt, Brace, 1974) on European imperialism in Africa as the precursor to National Socialism. The notion of transfers of memory and comparison from the culture, time and space of the Holocaust to colonized Africa is part of Michael Rothberg's "multidirectional memory" (Chapter 6) and also Gabriele Schwab, *Haunting Legacies: Violent Histories and Transgenerational Trauma* (New York: Columbia University Press, 2010). Chief Riruako is quoted in David Bargueno, "Cash for Genocide? The Politics of Memory in the Herero Case for Reparations," *Holocaust and Genocide Studies* 26, 3 (2012): 402.

21. See the website of the German medical school, Charité Universitätsmedizin in Berlin:http://anatomie.charite.de/geschichte/human_remains_projekt/restitution_of _namibian_skulls/.

22. Ilan Pappé, *Out of the Frame: The Struggle for Academic Freedom in Israel* (London: Pluto Press, 2010), 140.

23. A small number of internally displaced Palestinians, termed "present absentees," who were legally living in post-1948 Israel qualified for a "settling of accounts"; see Yfaat Weiss, "Conflicting Memories, Unrestituted: Wadi Salib as an Israeli Political Metaphor," in *Restitution and Memory: Material Restoration in Europe*, ed. Dan Diner and Gotthart Wunberg (New York: Bergahn, 2007), 309–10.

24. Nur Masalha, "The Historical Roots of the Palestinian Refugee Question," in *Palestinian Refugees: The Right of Return*, ed. Naseer Aruri (London: Pluto, 2001): 36–67; and Shahira Samy, *Reparations to Palestinian Refugees: A Comparative Perspective* (Abingdon: Routledge, 2010). See also Michael R. Fischbach, *The Peace Process and Palestinian Refugee Claims: Addressing Claims for Property Compensation and Restitution* (Washington, D.C.: U.S. Institute of Peace Press, 2006), 67–84, who documents one victory, the restitution of some blocked refugee bank accounts from 1953–1956 to their rightful Palestinian owners but only if they resided outside Israel.

25. Suzanne D. Rutland, "'Buying out of the Matter': Australia's Role in Restitution of Templer Property in Israel," *Journal of Israeli History* 24, 1 (2005): 135–54.

26. Ibid., 144.

27. Rosemarie M. Esber, "When Israel Compensated Germans for Land in Israel," *Electronic Intifada*, June 5, 2013, accessed June 8, 2013.

28. Ronald W. Zweig, "Restitution of Property and Refugee Rehabilitation: Two Case Studies," *Journal of Refugee Studies* 6, 1 (1993): 63.

29. Bill Maurer, "The Anthropology of Money," *Annual Review of Anthropology* 35 (2006): 20.

30. In addition to Viviana Zelizer, discussed in Chapter 1, see Arjun Appadurai, "Introduction: Commodity and the Politics of Value," in *The Social Life of Things: Commodities in Cultural Perspective*, ed. Arjun Appadurai (Cambridge: Cambridge University Press, 1986), 3–63.

31. Simmel, 355–370.

32. An earlier version was published as Susan Slyomovics, "American 'Blood Money' and a Question of Reparations," *MERIP/Middle East Report* 41, 259 (2011).

33. See coverage in several articles including Karin Brulliard, "Pakistanis Say 'Blood Money' Might Win Release of Jailed CIA Contractor," *Washington Post*, March 4, 2011.

34. The information can be found at the website of the American Civil Liberties Union, "The Human Cost: Civilian Casualties in Iraq and Afghanistan," n.d., accessed January 10, 2012, http://www.aclu.org/human-cost-civilian-casualties-iraq-afghanistan.

35. See the list of payments at ACLU, "Documents Received from the Department of the Army in response to ACLU Freedom of Information Act Request, October 31, 2007, accessed January, 10, 2012, http://www.aclu.org/natsec/foia/log.html.

36. George Bisharat, "Violence's Law," lecture at the G.E. von Grunebaum Center for Near Eastern Studies, UCLA, April 20, 2011, accessed April 25, 2011, http://www.international.ucla.edu/cnes/podcasts/article.asp?parentid=120844.

37. Reuben Alcalay, *Hebrew-English Dictionary* (Tel Aviv: Masadah, 1959–1961), 2082.

38. Axel Frohn, "Introduction: The Origins of *Shilumim*," in *Holocaust and Shilumim: The Policy of Wiedergutmachung in the Early 1950s*, ed. Axel Frohn (Washington, D.C.: German Historical Institute, 1991), 2.

39. On border villages, see anthropologist Abner Cohen's ethnographic account of Kafr Qasim exemplifying the "border situation": "A distinct category . . . are villages, which (a) lie literally on the most strategically sensitive part of the [Israeli-Jordanian] border, (b) are cut off by that border from close associate villages, only a few miles away within Jordan, (c) are in intense interaction with the Jews in Israel with whom they have great economic interests, and (d) are seriously caught up in the strife between Israel and the Arab world"; Abner Cohen, *Arab Border-Villages in Israel: A Study of Continuity and Change* (Manchester: Manchester University Press, 1965), 17–18.

40. Henry Rosenfeld, "Processes of Structural Change Within the Arab Family," *American Anthropologist* 60, 6 (1958):1127–39, and "From Peasantry to Wage Labor

and Residual Peasantry: The Transformation of an Arab Village," in *Process and Pattern in Culture*, ed. Robert A. Manners (Chicago: Aldine, 1964), 211–34.

41. "A Palestinian refugee is a person whose normal residence was Palestine for a minimum of two years preceding the conflict in 1948 and who, as a result of the conflict, lost both his home and his means of livelihood and took refuge in one of the countries where UNRWA provides relief (Jordan, Lebanon, Syria, West Bank, Gaza)"; Shadia Matar, "Palestinian Refugees, a Material and Spiritual Homeland," n.d., accessed January 13, 2013, http://www.medmedia.it/review/numero3/en/art7.htm.

42. Menachem Hofnung, *Democracy, Law and National Security in Israel* (Aldershot: Ashgate, 1996) on Israeli government land confiscation from its Arab citizens.

43. Benny Morris, *Israel's Border Wars 1949–1956: Arab Infiltration, Israeli Retaliation, and the Countdown to the Suez War* (Oxford: Oxford University Press, 1993), 432–34.

44. Hana Sulayman Amir's testimony was recounted by Ibrahim Sarsur, interview with Waleed Kheif and Susan Slyomovics, Kafr Qasim, January 13, 1998.

45. Hebrew trial transcripts were published in Moshe Kordov, *Ahat esreh kumtot yerukot ba-din: parashat Kefar-Kasm* (Tel Aviv: A. Narkis, 1959).

46. The full report of the Public Committee (known as the Rashish Report after Pinchas Rashish, mayor of Petah Tikvah) appears in Rubik Rozental, ed., *Kefar Kasem: eru'im u-mitos* [Events and myth] (Kibbutz ha-Me'uchad, 2000), 237–39. See also "Four Hundred Attend Sulha at Kafr Qasim," *Jerusalem Post*, November 21, 1957, 1, 3.

47. Over time, a variety of ephemeral gestures and site-specific installations have appeared at each location where Kafr Qasim villagers were murdered; see Waleed Khleif and Susan Slyomovics, "Palestinian Remembrance Days and Plans: Kafr Qasim, Fact and Echo," in *Modernism and the Middle East: Architecture and Politics in the Twentieth Century*, ed. Kishvar Rizvi and Sandy Eisenstadt (Seattle: University of Washington Press, 2008), 186–217.

48. "Report of the Public Committee for Indemnities to the Dead and Wounded of Kafr Qasim, Petah Tikvah, November 10, 1957," republished in Rozental, *Kefar Kasem*, 239.

49. Cohen, *Arab Border-Villages*, and Abner Cohen, "Hamula," *Encyclopaedia of Islam* (Leiden: E.J. Brill, 1979(, 3: 149–50. Although Cohen renamed the pseudonymous Triangle village Bint el-Hudud (Arabic for "daughter of the borders"), he notes that "the whole village had been in mourning for the many villagers who had been killed in an incident two years earlier," 87. Cohen's ethnography is a transparent document, his disguise purportedly confected to protect his informants and their locales, and should be reread in terms of the legal fallout from a suppressed legacy of civilian dead. On the identity of Cohen's village of fieldwork, see Dan Rabinowitz, *Antropologyah veha-Palestinim* (Raananah: Institute for Israeli Arab Studies, 1998), 93–117.

50. Cohen, *Arab Border-Villages*, 135.

51. Ibid., 139–40n3.

52. Sarsur in Rozental, *Kefar Kasem*, 199. For a different description, see Lea Ben-Dor, "Marginal Column," *Jerusalem Post*, November 22, 1957, 1.

53. Interview with Ibrahim Sarsur by Khleif and Slyomovics, Kafr Qasim, January 13, 1998.

54. "Kafr Kasim Counsel Reject Terms of Payment," *Jerusalem Post*, November 18, 1957, 3.

55. See critiques and overviews of Western and Israeli anthropology on the *hamula* in Talal Asad, "Anthropological and Sociological Studies on the Arabs in Israel: A Critique," *Journal of Palestine Studies* 6 (1977): 41–70, and his "Anthropological Texts and Ideological Problems: An Analysis of Cohen on Arab Villages in Israel," *Economy and Society* 4 (1975): 274; Elia Zureik, *The Palestinians in Israel: A Study in Internal Colonialism* (London: Routledge Kegan Paul, 1979); and Aziz Haidar, *The Palestinians in Israel: Social Science Writings* (Kingston, Ont.: NECEF, 1987). Gil Eyal, in "Beyn mizrah le-ma'arav: ha-si'ah 'al ha-kfar ha-'aravi bi-yisra'el" [Between east and west: The Discourse on the Arab village in Israel], *Teoriya u-bikoret* 3 (1993): 39–55, contrasts the current discursive objectification of the Arab village (that produced harsh military rule policies) by Jewish Israelis with the pre-1948 state period that romanticized the Arab village as a locus for an authentic Jewish identity rooted in biblical ways. See my *The Object of Memory: Arab and Jew Narrate the Palestinian Village* (Philadelphia: University of Pennsylvania Press, 1998), chap. 3.

56. Joel Greenberg, "School Official Wants to Mark Israeli Atrocity" *New York Times*, October 7, 1999.

57. On the concept of "the black flag," see Rozental, *Kefar Kasem*, 117–77; Leora Bilsky, "Kufr Qassem: Between Ordinary Politics and Transformative Politics," *Adalah Review* 3 (2002): 69–80; and Danny Orbach, "Black Flag at a Crossroads: The Kafr Qasim Political Trial," *International Journal of Middle East Studies* 45 (2013): 491–511.

58. For critiques of the amended law, see Anne Massagee, "Rights Without Remedies: Israel's Compensation Laws, *Occasional Paper (Al-Haq)* 14 (October 2005), accessed January 21, 2013, http://www.ochaopt.org/documents/opt_prot_alhaq_compensation_law_oct_2005.pdf. For translations of the legal text, see B'Tselem: The Israeli Information Center for Human Rights in the Occupied Territories, "Denial of Compensation," January 1, 2011, updated July 22, 2012, accessed January 21, 2013, http://www.btselem.org/accountability/denial_of_compensation.

59. Palestinian Centre for Human Rights, "Israeli Military Court Continues to Provide Cover for IOF's Crimes," August 13, 2012, accessed January 21, 2013.

60. Rami Almeghari, "Family of Cast Lead Victims Wins 'Compromise, Not Compensation'," *Electronic Intifada*, September 26, 2012.

61. Gershon Shafir, "Zionism and Colonialism: A Comparative Approach," in *The Israel/Palestine Question: A Reader*, ed. Ilan Pappé (London: Routledge, 1999), 81–96.

62. Breaking the Silence, *Occupation of the Territories: Israeli Soldiers' Testimonies 2000–2010* (Jerusalem: Breaking the Silence, 2010), 111–12. Another interview con-

cerns a soldier asked how Balata becomes a "battle zone"; his reply is "Soldiers shoot so it becomes a battle zone," 114.

63. Lorenzo Veracini, *Israel and Settler Society* (Ann Arbor, Mich.: Pluto Press, 2006).

64. Yosef Mazur, *Zionism, Post-Zionism and the Arab Problem: A Compendium of Opinions About the Jewish State* (Bloomington, Ind.: WestBow Press, 2012); and Joseph Alpher and Khalil Shikaki, *The Palestinian Refugee Problem and the Right of Return* (Cambridge, Mass.: Weatherhead Center for International Affairs, Harvard University, 1998).

65. Barak Ravid, "PA President: As long as I am in power, there will be no third intifada," *Ha'aretz*, November 1, 2012.

66. For example, see the joint Israeli-Palestinian Zochrot-Badil program of refugee return and restitution emerging from their visit to the South African Truth and Reconciliation Commission: http://www.badil.org/component/k2/item/1806-2?lang=en. See also the concluding chapter, "Toward a New Regime," in Ariella Azoulay and Adi Ophir, *The One-State Condition: Occupation and Democracy in Israel/Palestine* (Stanford, Calif.: Stanford University Press, 2012), 249–71. For great imaginative élan, see Joshua Simon, ed., *Solution 196–213 United States of Palestine-Israel* (Berlin: Sternberg Press, 2011).

67. Sari Nusseibeh, *What Is a Palestinian State Worth?* (Cambridge, Mass.: Harvard University Press, 2011), 144–45.

68. Susan Slyomovics, "Who and What Is Native to Israel? On Marcel Janco's Settler Art and Jacqueline Shohet Kahanoff's 'Levantinism'," *Settler Colonial Studies* 4, 1 (2014): 27–47.

69. Awni Al-Mashni, "The Palestinian Refugees, Between the Impossible and the Possible," *Al Majdal* 16–17 (2003): 20.

70. Gabriel Piterberg, *The Returns of Zionism: Myths, Politics and Scholarship in Israel* (London: Verso, 2008), 56–57.

71. Paul G. McHugh, *Aboriginal Societies and the Common Law: A History of Sovereignty, Status, and Self-Determination* (Oxford: Oxford University Press, 2004).

72. Richard S. Hill and Brigitte Bönisch-Brednich, "Politicizing the Past: Indigenous Scholarship and Crown: Maori Reparations Processes in New Zealand," *Social and Legal Studies* 16, 2 (2007): 163–81.

73. Salman Natour, "The Culture of 'the Inside': The Post-Identity Question," *Jadal* 12 (February 2012).

74. Immanuel Kant, *Groundwork of the Metaphysic of Morals*, trans. H. J. Paten (New York: Harper, 1964), 101. See also John H. Zammito, *Kant, Herder, and the Birth of Anthropology* (Chicago: University of Chicago Press, 2002), and the authors' introduction in Chris Hann and Keith Hart, *Economic Anthropology: History, Ethnography, Critique* (Cambridge: Polity, 2011), 1–17.

75. Keith Hart, "Notes Towards an Anthropology of Money," *Kritikos* 2 (2005).

76. I am not alone in making this journey. Among other thinkers who explicitly see connections based on their legacy of Holocaust survivor families are Sara Roy, "Living with the Holocaust: The Journey of a Child of Holocaust Survivors," *Journal of Palestine Studies* 32, 1 (2002): 5–12. Also Roy writes, "In this way, among others, Gaza speaks to the unnaturalness of our own condition as Jews. For in Gaza, we seek remedy and consolation in the ruin of another people, 'Observing the windows of [their] houses through the sites of rifles, to borrow from the Israeli poet, Almog Behar. It is ironic then that our own salvation now lies in Gaza's. And no degree of distance or separation can ever change that"; Sara Roy, 2012 Edward Said Memorial Lecture, Palestine Center, Washington, D.C., October 10, 2012, ahttp://www.thejerusalemfund .org/ht/display/ContentDetails/i/36415/pid/897. See also Amira Hess, "Introduction: Notes on My Mother" and "Afterword: On My Parents" in Hanna Lévy-Hass, *Diary of Bergen-Belsen, 1944–45* (Chicago: Haymarket, 2009), 9–33, 123–49.

BIBLIOGRAPHY

Abel, Richard L. "General Damages Are Incoherent, Incalculable, Incommensurable, and Inegalitarian (But Otherwise a Great Idea)." *DePaul Law Review* 55, 2 (2006): 253–330.

———. *Speaking Respect, Respecting Speech*. Chicago: University of Chicago Press, 1998.

Abitbol, Michel. *The Jews of North Africa During the Second World War*. Detroit: Wayne State University Press, 1989.

———. *Les Juifs d'Afrique du Nord sous Vichy*. Paris: Maisonneuve et Larose, 1983.

———. *Mi-Kremyeh le-Peten: Antishemiyut be-Alg'iryah ha-kolonyalit, 1870–1940*. Jerusalem: Merkaz Zalman Shazar le-Toldot Yisrael, 1993.

———. "North Africa (Tunisia, Algeria, Morocco)." In *Zionism in Transition*, ed. Moshe Davis, 197–210. New York: Herzl Press, 1980.

Achcar, Gilbert. *The Arabs and the Holocaust: The Arab-Israeli War of Narratives*. Trans. G. M. Goshgarian. St. Paul: Saqi Books, 2010.

Adler, Hans Günther. *Panorama: A Novel*. New York: Random House, 2011.

———. *Theresienstadt 1941–1945: Das Antlitz einer Zwangsgemeinschaft; Geschichte, Soziologie, Psychologie*. Tübingen: Mohr, 1955.

Adler, Libby and Peer Zumbansen, "The Forgetfulness of the Noblesse: A Critique of the German Foundation Law Compensating Slave and Forced Laborers of the Third Reich." *Harvard Journal of Legislation* 39, 1 (2002): 1–61.

Agamben, Giorgio. *Homo Sacer: Sovereign Power and Bare Life*. Trans. Daniel Heller-Roazen. Stanford, Calif.: Stanford University Press, 1998.

Alcalay, Reuben. *Hebrew-English Dictionary*. Tel Aviv: Masadah, 1959–1961.

Allen, Michael Thad. *The Business of Genocide: The SS, Slave Labor, and the Concentration Camps*. Chapel Hill: University of North Carolina Press, 2002.

Al-Mashni, Awni. "The Palestinian Refugees, Between the Impossible and the Possible. *Al-Majdal* 16–17 (2003): 19–21.

Almeghari, Rami. "Family of Cast Lead Victims Wins 'Compromise, Not Compensation.'" *Electronic Intifada*, September 26, 2012.

Alpher, Joseph and Khalil Shikaki. *The Palestinian Refugee Problem and the Right of Return*. Cambridge, Mass.: Weatherhead Center for International Affairs, Harvard University, 1998.

American Civil Liberties Union. "Documents Received from the Department of the Army in Response to ACLU Freedom of Information Act Request." October 31, 2007, released March 2010. http://www.aclu.org/natsec/foia/log.html
———. "The Human Cost: Civilian Casualties in Iraq and Afghanistan." n.d. http://www .aclu.org/human-cost-civilian casualties-iraq-afghanistan.
American Psychiatric Association. *Diagnostic and Statistical Manual of Mental Disorders (Third Edition)*. Washington, D.C.: American Psychiatric Association, 1980.
Anderson, Benedict. "Préface à l'édition française." *L'imaginaire national: réflexions sur l'origine et l'essor de nationalism*, 9–14. Paris: La Découverte, 2002.
Andrieu, Claire, ed. *La persécution des Juifs de France (1940–1944) et le rétablissement de la légalité républicaine: Recueil des textes officiels 1940–1999*. Paris: Mission d'Étude sur la Spoliation des Juifs de France, La Documentation Française, 2000.
———. "Two Approaches to Compensation in France." In *Robbery and Restitution: The Conflict over Jewish Property in Europe*, ed. Martin Dean, Constantin Goschler, and Philipp Ther, 134–54. New York: Berghahn in association with U.S. Holocaust Memorial Museum, 2007.
Ansky, Michel. *Les Juifs d'Algérie du décret Crémieux à la liberation*. Paris: Éditions du Centre, 1950.
Aouate, Yves Claude. "Les juifs d'Algérie pendant la seconde guerre mondiale (1939–1945)." Ph.D. dissertation, University of Nice, 1984, 2 vols.
Appadurai, Arjun. "Introduction: Commodity and the Politics of Value." In *The Social Life of Things: Commodities in Cultural Perspective*, ed. Arjun Appadurai, 3–63. Cambridge: Cambridge University Press, 1986.
Appelfeld, Aharon. "Buried Homeland." *New Yorker*, November 23, 1998, 47–61.
Approaching an Auschwitz Survivor: Holocaust Testimony and Its Transformations, ed. Jürgen Matthaus. New York: Oxford University Press, 2009.
"Archives, Records and Power: The Making of Modern Memory." Special Issue, *Archival Science* 2 (2002).
Arendt, Hannah. "Auschwitz on Trial." In *Responsibility and Judgment*, ed. and intro. Jerome Kohn, 227–56. New York: Schocken, 2003.
———. *Eichmann in Jerusalem: A Report on the Banality of Evil*. New York: Viking, 1963.
———. "The History of the Great Crime: A Review of *Bréviaire de la haine: Le IIIe Reich et les juifs*." In *Hannah Arendt, the Jewish Writings*, ed. Jerome Kohn and Ron H. Feldman, 453–62. New York: Schocken, 2007.
———. *The Origins of Totalitarianism*. New York: Harcourt, Brace, 1974.
———. "Why the Crémieux Decree Was Abrogated." *Contemporary Jewish Record* 5, 3 (April 1943); reprint in *The Jewish Writings*, ed. Jerome Kohn and Ron H. Feldman, 244–53. New York: Schocken, 2007.

Aron, Raymond. *Mémoires*. Paris: Julliard, 1983.

Asad, Talal. "Anthropological and Sociological Studies on the Arabs in Israel: A Critique." *Journal of Palestine Studies* 6 (1977): 41–70.

———. "Anthropological Texts and Ideological Problems: An Analysis of Cohen on Arab Villages in Israel." *Economy and Society* 4 (1975): 251–82.

Askénazi, Yehouda Léon. "L'histoire de ma vie." In *Mi miTsion: notes sur la paracha*. Jerusalem: Fondation Manitou, 1997.

Association des Amis de la Fondation de la Résistance. "Nous les oublions pas: Fleury née Marie Jacqueline." *Mémoire et Espoirs de la Résistance*, n.d. Accessed November 1, 2012. http://www.memoresist.org/spip.php?page=oublionspas_detail&id=1761.

Atouf, Elkbir. "Un communauté prolétaire: les Juifs marocains de Saint-Fons." *Archives Juives* 36 (2003): 121–30.

Azoulay, Ariella. "Sfat em, sfat av." In *Ḥazot mizraḥit* [Eastern appearance], ed. Yigal Nizri, 159–68. Tel-Aviv: Bavel, 2004.

Azoulay, Ariella and Adi Ophir, *The One-State Condition: Occupation and Democracy in Israel/Palestine*. Stanford, Calif.: Stanford University Press, 2012.

Baeyer, Walter von, H. Hafner and K. P. Kisker, *Psychiatrie der Verfolgten*. Berlin: Springer-Verlag, 1964.

Baker, Tom. "Blood Money, New Money and the Moral Economy of Tort Law in Action." *Law and Society Review* 35, 2 (2002): 275–319.

———. "The Blood Money Myth." *Legal Affairs: The Magazine at the Intersection of Law and Life* (September/October 2002).

Balabkins, Nicholas. *West German Reparations to Israel*. New Brunswick, N.J.: Rutgers University Press, 1971.

Bargueno, David. "Cash for Genocide? The Politics of Memory in the Herero Case for Reparations." *Holocaust and Genocide Studies* 26, 3 (2012): 394–424.

Barkan, Elazar. *The Guilt of Nations: Restitution and Negotiating Injustices*. New York: Norton, 2000.

Barthes, Roland. *Camera Lucida: Reflections on Photography*. New York: Hill and Wang, 1981.

———. "Rhétorique de l'image." *Communications* 4 (1964): 40–51.

Batson, C. Daniel. *The Altruism Question: Toward a Social Psychological Answer*. Hillsdale, N.J.: Erlbaum, 1991.

Bazyler, Michael J. *Holocaust Justice: The Battle for Restitution in America's Courts*. New York: New York University Press, 2003.

———. "Suing Hitler's Willing Business Partners: American Justice and Holocaust Morality." *Jewish Political Studies Review* 16 (2004): 3–4.

Becker, Ernest E. *The Birth and Death of Meaning: A Perspective in Psychiatry and Anthropology*. New York: Free Press of Glencoe, 1962.

Bel Ange, Norbert. *Quand Vichy internait ses soldats juifs d'Algérie: Bedeau, sud oranais, 1941–1943*. Paris: L'Harmattan, 2006.

Belkin, Paul. "Opening of the International Tracing Service's Holocaust-Era Archives in Bad Arolsen, Germany." *Congressional Research Service Report for Congress*, April 27, 2007.

"Belsen Concentration Camp: The Medical Services Take Over." *The Lancet* 12 (1945): 604–5.

Ben-Dor, Lea. "Marginal Column." *Jerusalem Post*, November 22, 1957.

Benjamin, Walter. "On the Concept of History." In *Gesammelten Schriften*. Redmond. Frankfurt am Main: Suhrkamp, 1974. Trans. Dennis Redmond, http://members .efn.org/~dredmond/ThesesonHistory.html

Bensadoun, Roger. *Les Juifs de la république en Algérie et au Maroc*. Paris: Publisud, 2003.

Bercuson, David J. and Douglas Wertheimer. *A Trust Betrayed: The Keegstra Affair*. New York: Doubleday, 1986.

Berger, Alan L. and Naomi Berger, eds. *Second Generation Voices: Reflections by Children of Holocaust Survivors and Perpetrators*. Syracuse, N.Y.: Syracuse University Press, 2001.

Bergmann, Martin S. and Milton E. Jucovy, eds. *Generations of the Holocaust*. New York: Basic Books, 1982.

Berman, Sanford. *Prejudices and Antipathies: A Tract on the LC Subject Heads Concerning People*. Metuchen, N.J.: Scarecrow Press, 1971

Bettelheim, Bruno. "Individual and Mass Behavior in Extreme Situations." *Journal of Abnormal and Social Psychology* 38, 4 (1943): 417–52.

———. *The Informed Heart: Autonomy in a Mass Age*. Glencoe, Ill.: Free Press, 1960.

Bialystock, Franklin. *Delayed Impact: The Holocaust and the Canadian Community*. Montreal: McGill-Queen's University Press, 2000.

Biedermann, Charles-Claude. *Sixty Years of History and Benefit of the Personal Documentary Material About the Former Civilian Persecutees of the Nationalist Socialist Regime Preserved in Bad Arolsen*. Bad Arolsen, Germany: International Tracing Service, 2003.

Bilsky, Leora. "Kufr Qassem: Between Ordinary Politics and Transformative Politics." *Adalah Review* 3 (2002): 69–80.

Bilu, Yoram. *The Saints' Impresarios: Dreamers, Healers, and Holy Men in Israel's Urban Periphery*. Brighton, Mass.: Academic Studies Press, 2010.

Bindenagel, J. D. "Justice, Apology, Reconciliation, and the German Foundation: 'Rememberance, Responsibility and the Future.'" In *Taking Wrongs Seriously: Apologies and Reconciliation*, ed. Elazar Barkan and Alexander Karn, 268–310. Stanford, Calif.: Stanford University Press, 2006.

Bisharat, George. "Law's Violence." Lecture delivered at the G. E. von Grunebaum Center for Near Eastern Studies, UCLA, April 20, 2011, archived UCLA International Institute.

Blatman, Daniel. *The Death Marches: The Final Phase of Nazi Genocide*. Cambridge, Mass.: Belknap Press of Harvard University Press, 2011.

Bloch, Maurice and Jonathan Parry, "Introduction: Money and the Morality of Exchange." In *Money and the Morality of Exchange*, ed. Maurice Bloch and Jonathan Parry, 1–32. Cambridge: Cambridge University Press, 1989.

Blumenthal, Nachman. "Magical Thinking Among the Jews During the Nazi Occupation." *Yad Vashem Studies on the European Jewish Catastrophe and Resistance* 5 (1963): 221–36.

Bodenstab, Johanna. "Under Siege: A Mother-Daughter Relationship Survives the Holocaust." *Psychoanalytic Inquiry* 24 (2004): 731–751.

Bohannon, Paul. "The Impact of Money on an African Subsistence Economy." *Journal of Economic History* 19 (1959): 491–503.

Bondy, Curt. "Problems of Internment Camps." *Journal of Abnormal and Social Psychology* 38, 4 (1943): 453–75.

Böschenstein, Bernhard and Heino Schmull, eds. *The Meridian: Final Version—Drafts—Materials*. Trans. and preface Pierre Jorris. Stanford, Calif.: Stanford University Press, 2011.

Bourdieu, Pierre. *Distinction: A Social Critique of the Judgment of Taste*. Cambridge: Harvard University Press, 1984.

———. *Practical Reason: On the Theory of Action*. Stanford, Calif.: Stanford University Press, 1998.

Bourgois, Philippe. "Bringing the Past into the Present: Family Narratives of Holocaust, Exile and Diaspora: Missing the Holocaust: My Father's Account of Auschwitz from August 1943 to June 1944." *Anthropological Quarterly* 78, 1 (2005): 89–123.

Braham, Randolf L. *Genocide and Retribution: The Holocaust in Hungarian-Ruled Northern Transylvania*. Boston: Kluwer-Nijhoff, 1983.

———. "Hungary and the Holocaust: The Nationalist Drive to Whitewash the Past." *Radio Free Europe/Radio Liberty Reports* 3, 18 (October 17, 2001).

Braithwaite, John. *Restorative Justice and Responsive Regulation*. New York: Oxford University Press, 2002.

Brandon, Ray and Wendy Lower. *The Shoah in Ukraine: History, Testimony, Memorialization*. Bloomington: Indiana University Press, 2008.

Brauer, Julian. "Jewish Communities, Jewish Education and Quebec Nationalism." *Social Compass* 31, 4 (1984): 391–407.

Breaking the Silence. *Occupation of the Territories: Israeli Soldiers' Testimonies 2000–2010*. Jerusalem: Breaking the Silence, 2010.

Brenner, Reeve R. *The Faith and Doubt of Holocaust Survivors*. New York: Free Press, 1980.

Bretell, Caroline. *Writing Against the Wind: A Mother's Life History*. Wilmington, Del.: SR Books, 1999.

Brooks, Roy L., ed. *When Sorry Isn't Enough: The Controversy over Apologies and Reparations for Human Injustice*. New York: New York University Press, 1999.

Browning, Christopher R. *Collected Memories: Holocaust History and Postwar Testimony.* Madison: University of Wisconsin Press, 2003.

———. *Remembering Survival: Inside a Nazi Slave-Labor Camp.* New York: Norton, 2010.

Brulliard, Karin. "Pakistanis Say 'Blood Money' Might Win Release of Jailed CIA Contractor." *Washington Post,* March 4, 2011.

Brunschvig, Robert. "Les measures antijuives dans l'enseignement en Algérie sous le régime de Vichy." *Revue d'Alger* 2 (1944): 57–79.

Canadian Broadcast Company Digital Archives. "Auschwitz: The Young Must Learn." Video.

Canadian Legal Information Institute. *R. v. Keegstra,* 1984. Accessed October 2, 2012. http://www.canlii.org/en/ab/abqb/doc/1984/1984canlii1313/1984canlii1313.html.

———. *R. v. Keegstra,* [1990] 3 SCR 697. Accessed September 26, 2012. http://www.canlii.org/en/ca/scc/doc/1990/1990canlii24/1990canlii24.html.

Cantier, Jacques. *L'Algérie sous le régime de Vichy.* Paris: O. Jacob, 2002.

Carpenter, Mick. "'It's a Small World': Mental Health Policy Under Welfare Capitalism Since 1945." *Sociology of Health and Illness* 22, 5 (2000): 602–19.

Carruth, Cathy. "An Interview with Robert Jay Lifton." In *Trauma: Explorations in Memory,* ed. Cathy Carruth, 128–47. Baltimore: Johns Hopkins University Press, 1995

———. *Unclaimed Experience: Trauma, Narrative and History.* Baltimore: Johns Hopkins University Press, 1996.

Casey, Edward S. *Remembering: A Phenomenological Study.* Indiana: Indiana University Press, 1987.

Cassin, René. "Vichy or Free France." *Foreign Affairs* 20, 1 (1941): 102–12.

Celan, Paul. "Das, was Geschah?" In *Atemwende.* Frankfurt am Main: Suhrkamp, 1982 [1967].

———. *Poems of Paul Celan,* trans. and intro. Michael Hamburger. London: Anvil Press Poetry, 1995.

Césaire, Aimé. *Discourse on Colonialism.* New York: Monthly Review, 1972.

Cherry, Richard. *Lectures on the Growth of Criminal Law in Ancient Communities.* New York: Macmillan, 1980.

Chodoff, Paul. "Depression and Guilt in Concentration Camp Survivors." *Psychotherapy and Psychosomatics* 15, 1 (1967): 11–12.

———. "Late Effects of the Concentration Camp Syndrome." *Archives of General Psychiatry* 8 (1963): 323–33.

Choi, Sung. "The Muslim Veteran in Postcolonial France: The Politics of the Integration of Harkis After 1962." *French Politics, Culture, and Society* 29, 1 (2011): 24–45.

Christie, Doug. *Thought Crimes: The Keegstra Case.* Toronto: Citizens for Foreign Aid Reform, 1986.

Claims Conference. "Tax Exemptions on Holocaust Compensation and Restitution Payments." Accessed November 1 2012. http://www.claimscon.org/?url=tax_exemptions.

Cohen, Abner. *Arab Border-Villages in Israel: A Study of Continuity and Change.* Manchester: Manchester University Press, 1965.

———. "Hamula." *Encyclopaedia of Islam*, 3: 149–50. 1979.

Cohen, Elie A. *Human Behaviour in the Concentration Camp.* New York: Norton, 1953.

Cohn, Louis. "Une page non écrite des années 1940: Les camps d'internement en Algérie française." *Nouveaux Cahiers* 116 (1996): 27–29.

Collis, William Robert Fitz-Gerald. "Belsen Camp: A Preliminary Report." *British Medical Journal* (June 1945): 814–16.

Colonomos, Ariel and Andrea Armstrong. "German Reparations to Jews After World War II: A Turning Point in the History of Reparations." In *The Handbook of Reparations*, ed. Pablo de Greif, 391–419. New York: Oxford University Press, 2006.

Conference on Jewish Material Claims Against Germany. *Twenty Years Later: Activities of the Conference on Jewish Material Claims Against Germany, 1952–1972.* New York: Conference on Jewish Material Claims Against Germany, 1972.

Courtois, Stéphane et al. *The Black Book of Communism: Crimes, Terror, Repression.* Cambridge, Mass.: Harvard University Press, 1999.

Crapanzano, Vincent. *The Harkis.* Chicago: University of Chicago Press, 2011.

Dagan, Avigdor. *The Jews of Czechoslovakia: Historical Studies and Surveys.* Vol. 3. Philadelphia: Jewish Publication Society of America and Society for the History of Czechoslovak Jews, 1984.

Damon, F. H. "The Kula and Generalised Exchange: Considering Some Unconsidered Aspects of the Elementary Structures of Kinship." *Man* 15 (1980): 267–92.

Danieli, Yael. "Families of Survivors of the Nazi Holocaust: Some Short- and Long-term Effects." In *Stress and Anxiety*, vol. 8, ed. Charles D. Spielberger, Irwin G. Sarason, and Norman Milgram, 405–21. Washington, D.C.: Hemisphere, 1982.

Davidson, Shamai. "The Clinical Effects of Massive Psychic Traumatization in Families of Holocaust Survivors." *Journal of Marital and Family Therapy* 6, 1(1980): 11–21.

Davies, Alan. "The Keegstar Affair." In *Antisemitism in Canada: History and Interpretation*, ed. Alan Davies, 227–47. Waterloo: Wilfrid Laurier University Press, 1992.

Davies, Norman. *Vanished Kingdoms: The History of Half-Forgotten Europe.* New York: Penguin, 2011.

Deam, Jenny. "Massacre Funds to Be Distributed." *Los Angeles Times*, October 17, 2012, A14.

Derrida, Jacques. *Archive Fever: A Freudian Impression.* Trans. Eric Prenowitz. Chicago: University of Chicago Press, 1995.

———. "Circumfession: Fifty-Nine Periods and Periphrases." In *Jacques Derrida*, ed. Geoffrey Bennington and Jacques Derrida, 3–315. Chicago: University of Chicago Press, 1993.

———. *Of Hospitality: Anne Dufourmantelle Invites Jacques Derrida to Respond.* Stanford, Calif.: Stanford University Press, 2000.

Deutschkron, Inge. *Bonn and Jerusalem: The Strange Coalition.* Philadelphia: Chilton, 1970.

DeWind, Eddy. "The Confrontation with Death." *Psychoanalytic Quarterly* 37, 2 (1968): 322–24.

De Zayas, Alfred. *A Terrible Revenge: The Ethnic Cleansing of the East European Germans, 1944–1950.* New York: Saint Martin's, 1994.

Diamond, Etan. *And I Will Dwell in Their Midst: Orthodox Jews in Suburbia.* Chapel Hill: University of North Carolina Press, 2000.

Diamond, Jared. "Vengeance Is Ours: What Can Tribal Societies Tell Us About Our Need to Get Even?" *New Yorker,* April, 21, 2008: 74–87.

Dicker, Herman. *Piety and Perseverance: Jews from the Carpathian Mountains.* New York: Sepher-Hermon Press, 1981.

Diner, Hasia R. *We Remember with Reverence and Love: American Jews and the Myth of Silence After the Holocaust, 1945–1962.* New York: New York University Press, 2009.

Dinur, Dov. *Shoat Yehudei Rusia ha-Karpatit-Uzhorod* [The Holocaust of the Jews of Subcarpathian-Rus]. Jerusalem: Hebrew University Press, 1983.

Douglass, Ana and Thomas A. Vogler. Introduction to *Witness and Memory: The Discourse of Trauma*, ed. Ana Douglass and Thomas A. Vogler, 1–53. New York: Routledge, 2003.

Doyle, Kate. "The Atrocity Files: Deciphering the Archives of Guatemala's Dirty War." *Harper's*, December 2007, 52–64.

Dreyfus, Jean-Marc. "À Bad Arolsen, dans la forêt des archives nazies. *La vie des idées. fr.,* September 11, 2008.

Dudai, Ron. "'Can You Describe This?' Human Rights Reports and What They Tell Us About the Human Rights Movement." In *Humanitarianism and Suffering: the Mobilization of Empathy*, ed. Richard Ashby Wilson and Richard D. Brown, 245–64. Cambridge: Cambridge University Press, 2009.

Dvorjetsky, Marc. "Adjustment of Detainees to Camp and Ghetto Life and their Subsequent Re-Adjustment to Normal Society." *Yad Vashem Studies* 5 (1963): 193–220.

Eckert, Astrid M. "The Fight for the Files: Captured German Records After World War II." *German Historical Institute Bulletin* 32 (2003): 144–48.

———. "Managing Their Past: German Archivists Between National Socialism and Democracy." *Archival Science* 7, 3 (2007): 223–44.

Eggers, Christian. "L'internement sous toutes ses formes: approche d'une vue d'ensemble du système d'internement dans la zone de Vichy." *Le Monde juif* 153 (1995): 7–75.

Eisenbeth, Maurice. *Pages vécues, 1940–43.* Algiers: Charras, 1945.

Eissler, Kurt. "Die Ermordung von wievielen seiner Kinder muß ein Mensch symptomfrei ertragen können, um eine normale Konstitution zu haben?"*Psyche: Zeitschrift fur Psychoanalyse und ihre Anwendunger* 17 (1963): 241–91.

Eitinger, Leo. "Pathology of the Concentration Camp Syndrome." *Archives of General Psychiatry* 5 (1961): 371–79.

———. "Psychosomatic Problems in Concentration Camp Survivors." *Journal of Psychosomatic Research* 13 (1969): 183–89.

———. "Refugees and Concentration Camp Survivors in Norway." *Israel Journal of Medical Sciences* 21 (1962): 21–27.

———. "The Symptomatology of Mental Disease Among Refugees in Norway." *Journal of Mental Science* 106 (1960): 947–66.

Eizenstat, Stuart E. *Imperfect Justice: Looted Assets, Slave Labor, and the Unfinished Business of World War.* New York: Public Affairs, 2003.

Ennis, Bruce J. and Thomas R. Litwack, "Psychiatry and the Presumption of Expertise: Flipping Coins in the Courtroom." *California Law Review* 62, 3 (1974): 693–752.

Epstein, Helen. *Children of the Holocaust: Conversations with Sons and Daughters of Survivors.* New York: Putnam, 1979.

———. "Heirs of the Holocaust: The Lingering Legacy for Children of Survivors." *New York Times Magazine*, June 19, 1977, 12, 14.

Esber, Rosemarie. M. "When Israel Compensated Germans for Land in Israel." *Electronic Intifada*, June 5, 2013.

Eyal, Gil. "Beyn mizrah le-ma'arav: ha-si'ah 'al ha-kfar ha-'aravi bi-yisra'el." [Between east and west: Discourses on the Arab village in Israel], *Teoriya u-bikoret* [Theory and Criticism] 3 (1993): 39–55.

Fackenheim, Emil. *The Jewish Return into History: Reflections in the Age of Auschwitz and a New Jerusalem.* New York: Schocken, 1978.

Faludi, Kathy. "Interview Methodology and Format." Annex II to Canadian Jewish Congress, typed and photocopied memorandum, dated May 8, 1981, courtesy Vancouver Holocaust Education Centre.

Fanon, Frantz. *The Wretched of the Earth.* Trans. Constance Farrington. New York: Grove Press, 1963.

Fassin, Didier and Richard Rechtman, *The Empire of Trauma: An Inquiry into the Condition of Victimhood.* Princeton, N.J.: Princeton University Press, 2009.

Feinberg, Kenneth R. *What Is Life Worth?* New York: Public Affairs, 2005.

Feitlowitz, Marguerite. *A Lexicon of Terror: Argentina and the Legacies of Torture.* New York: Oxford University Press, 1998.

Feldman, Ilana. "Working in the In-Between: Archives, Ethnography, and Research in Gaza." In *Anthrohistory: Unsettling Knowledge, Questioning Discipline*, ed. Edward Murphy et al., 97–109. Ann Arbor: University of Michigan Press, 2011.

Feldman, Jackie. *Above the Death-Pits, Beneath the Flag: Youth Voyages to Poland and the Performance of Israeli National Identity.* New York: Berghahn, 2008.

Felstiner, John. *Paul Celan: Poet, Survivor, Jew.* New Haven, Conn.: Yale University Press, 1995.

Ferencz, Benjamin B. *Less Than Slaves: Jewish Forced Labor and the Quest for Compensation.* Bloomington: Indiana University Press, 2002.

Fette, Julie. "The Apology Moment: Vichy Memories in 1990s France." In *Taking Wrongs Seriously: Apologies and Reconciliation,* ed. Elazar Barkan and Alexander Karn, 259–285. Stanford, Calif.: Stanford University Press, 2006.

Finkelstein, Norman G. *The Holocaust Industry: Reflection on the Exploitation of Jewish Suffering.* New York: Verso, 2000.

Fischbach, Michael R. *The Peace Process and Palestinian Refugee Claims: Addressing Claims for Property Compensation and Restitution.* Washington, D.C.: U.S. Institute of Peace Press, 2006.

Forst, Graham. "Kristallnacht Keynote Speaker Rob Krell." *Zachor/Remember Vancouver Holocaust Education Centre Newsletter,* October 4, 2008, 3.

Frankl, Victor E. *Man's Search for Meaning.* Boston: Beacon Press, 2006.

Frazer, Jennie. "Wiesel: Yes, We Really Did Put God on Trial." *Jewish Chronicle Online,* September 19, 2008.

Friedman, Paul. "The Road Back for the DP'S: Healing the Psychological Scars of Nazism." *Commentary* 6 (1948): 502–10.

Frohn, Axel. "Introduction: The Origins of *Shilumim.*" In *Holocaust and Shilumim: The Policy of Wiedergutmachung in the Early 1950s,* ed. Axel Frohn, 1–6. Washington, D.C.: German Historical Institute, 1991.

Gaon, Solomon and M. Mitchell Serels, eds. *Del Fuego: Sephardim and the Holocaust.* New York: Safra Institute, Yeshiva University, 1987.

Garro, Linda C. "Narrating Troubling Experiences." *Transcultural Psychiatry* 40, 1 (2003): 5–43.

Garro, Linda C. and Cheryl Mattingly. "Narrative as Construct and Construction." In *Narrative and the Cultural Construction of Illness and Healing,* ed. Cheryl Mattingly and Linda C. Garro, 1–49. Berkeley: University of California Press, 2000.

Garwood, Alfred. "The Holocaust and the Power of Powerlessness: Survivor Guilt, an Unhealed Wound." *British Journal of Psychotherapy* 13, 2 (1996): 243–58.

Gerber, Jean. "Immigration and Integration in Post-War Canada: A Case Study of Holocaust Survivors in Vancouver 1947–70." Master's thesis, University of British Columbia, 1989.

———."Opening the Door: Immigration and Integration of Holocaust Survivors in Vancouver." *Canadian Jewish Studies* 4–5 (1996–97): 63–86.

Giberovitch, Myra. "The Contributions of Montreal Holocaust Survivor Organizations to Jewish Communal Life." MSW thesis, McGill University, 1988.

Gildea, Robert. *Marianne in Chains: Everyday Life in the French Heartland Under the German Occupation.* New York: Metropolitan Books, 2003.

Girard, René. *Violence and the Sacred.* Baltimore: Johns Hopkins University Press, 1977.

Golding, Bruce. "Fraud Clerk Guilty: Holocaust Scam." *New York Post*, June 6, 2012.

Goldman, Ari. "Rosh ha-Shanah Journey to Hasidic Master's Tomb." *New York Times*, September 27 1989, B2.

Goldmann, Nahum. "Nehemiah Robinson: Dedicated and Faithful Servant of the Jewish People." In *Ten Years of German Indemnification: Memorial Edition*, ed. Nehemiah Robinson, 7–12. New York: Conference on Jewish Material Claims Against Germany, 1964.

Gordon, Joseph. "The Litvak as a Leader." *Canadian Jewish Chronicle*. June 4, 1965, 5–6.

Graeber, David. "An Army of Altruists: On the Alienated Right to do Good." *Harper's Magazine*, January 2007, 31–38.

———. *Debt: The First 5,000 Years*. Brooklyn, N.Y.: Melville House, 2011.

Graf, Malvina. *The Kraków Ghetto and the Płaszów Camp Remembered*. Tallahassee: Florida State University Press, 1989.

Grauer, H. "Psychodynamics of the Survivor Syndrome." *Canadian Psychiatric Association Journal* 14, 6 (1969): 617–22.

Green, Warren. "The Fate of Oriental Jews in France." *Wiener Library Bulletin* 32, 49–50 (1979): 40–50.

Greenberg, Joel. "School Official Wants to Mark Israeli Atrocity." *New York Times*, October 7, 1999.

Greenspan, Henry. "The Awakening of Memory: Survivor Testimony in the First Years After Liberation, and Today." Annual Weinmann Lecture, U.S. Holocaust Memorial Museum, 2001.

———. "Listening to Holocaust Survivors: Interpreting a Repeated Story." *Shofar: An Interdisciplinary Journal of Jewish Studies* 17, 4 (1999): 83–88.

Grobman, Alex. *Rekindling the Flame: American Jewish Chaplains and the Survivors of European Jewry, 1944–1948*. Detroit: Wayne State University Press, 1993.

Gross, Jan Tomasz and Irena G. Gross. *Golden Harvest: Events at the Periphery of the Holocaust*. New York: Oxford University Press, 2012.

Gross, S.Y. and Y. Yosef Cohen, eds. *Sefer Marmaros: Mea ve-shishim kehilot kedoshot be- yishuvan u-ve-hurbanan* [The Marmaros Book: In Memory of a Hundred and Sixty Thousand Jewish Communities]. Tel Aviv: Beit Marmaros, 1983.

Gutman, Yisrael and Michael Berenbaum, eds. *Anatomy of the Auschwitz Death Camp*. Bloomington: U.S. Holocaust Memorial Museum and Indiana University Press, 1994.

Haidar, Aziz. *The Palestinians in Israel: Social Science Writings*. Kingston, Ont.: NECEF, 1987.

Haltom, William and Michael McCann. *Distorting the Law: Politics, Media, and the Litigation Crisis*. Chicago: University of Chicago Press, 2004.

Hamber, Brandon. "The Burdens of Truth: an Evaluation of the Psychological Services and Initiatives Undertaken by the South African Truth and Reconciliation Commission." *American Imago* 55, 1 (1998): 9–28.

Handbuch der Grossunternehmen 1999, Vols. 1–2. Darmstadt: Hoppenstedt, 1999.

Hann, Chris and Keith Hart. *Economic Anthropology: History, Ethnography, Critique.* Cambridge: Polity, 2011.

Harring, Sidney. "German Reparations to the Herero Nation: An Assertion of Herero Nationhood in the Path of Namibian Development?" *West Virginia Law Review* 104, 2 (2002): 393–417.

Harris, Verne. "The Archival Sliver: Power, Memory and Archives in South Africa." *Archival Science* 2 (2002): 63–86.

Hart, Keith. "Notes Towards an Anthropology of Money." *Kritikos* 2 (2005).

Hartman, Geoffrey. "Tele Suffering and Testimony in the Dot Com Era." In *Visual Culture and the Holocaust,* ed. Barbie Zelizer, 111–24. New Brunswick, N.J.: Rutgers University Press, 2000.

Hass, Aaron. *The Aftermath.* Cambridge: Cambridge University Press, 1995.

———. *In the Shadow of the Holocaust.* London: Tauris, 1990.

Hausner, Gideon. *Justice in Jerusalem.* New York: Harper & Row, 1966.

———. *Six Million Accusers; Israel's Case Against Eichmann: The Opening Speech and Legal Argument of Mr. Gideon Hausner, Attorney-General.* Jerusalem: Jerusalem Post, 1961.

Hayes, Saul. Foreword to Ben Lappin, *The Redeemed Children: The Story of the Rescue of War Orphans by the Jewish Community of Canada,* v–vii. Toronto: University of Toronto Press, 1963.

Heidegger, Martin. *Basic Concepts of Aristotelian Philosophy.* Trans. Robert D. Metcalf. Bloomington: Indiana University Press, 2009.

Hennessey, Kathleen. "Overseer of Gulf Victim Fund a Force of Nature." *Los Angeles Times,* June 18, 2010, A18.

Herbert, Ulrich. *A History of Foreign Labor in Germany, 1880–1980: Seasonal Workers, Forced Laborers, Guest Workers.* Ann Arbor: University of Michigan Press, 1990.

Herman, Judith L. *Trauma and Recovery: The Aftermath of Violence from Domestic Abuse to Political Terror.* New York: Basic Books, 2004.

Hermann, Knud and Paul Thygesen, "Le syndrome des camps de concentration 8 ans après la liberation." In *La déportation dans les camps de concentration allemands et ses séquelles,* ed. Paul Thygesen, 56–69. Copenhagen: Danish Red Cross, 1954.

Herzfeld, Michael. *The Social Production of Indifference: Exploring the Symbolic Roots of Western Bureaucracy.* Chicago: University of Chicago Press, 1993.

Herzog, Esther. "The Suspicious Anthropologist: Documenting My Mother's Holocaust." In *Serendipity in Anthropological Research,* ed. Haim Hazan and Esther Hertzog, 230–43. Farnham: Ashgate, 2012.

Hess, Amira. "Introduction: Notes on my Mother" and "Afterword: On My Parents" to Hanna Lévy-Hass, *Diary of Bergen-Belsen, 1944–45,* 9–33, 123–49. Chicago: Haymarket, 2009.

Hilberg, Raul. *The Politics of Memory: The Journey of a Holocaust Historian.* Chicago: Ivan Dee, 1996.

Hill, Richard S. and Brigitte Bönisch-Brednich. "Politicizing the Past: Indigenous Scholarship and Crown: Maori Reparations Processes in New Zealand." *Social and Legal Studies* 16, 2 (2007): 163–181.

Hirsch, Marianne. *Family Frames: Photography, Narrative and Postmemory.* Cambridge, Mass.: Harvard University Press, 1997.

Hoffman, Eva. *After Such Knowledge: Memory, History, and the Legacy of the Holocaust.* New York: Public Affairs, 2004.

Hoffmeyer, Henrik. "Principes thérapeutiques." In *La déportation dans les camps de concentration allemands et ses séquelles*, ed. Paul Thygesen, 73–77. Copenhagen: Danish Red Cross, 1954.

Hofnung, Menachem. *Democracy, Law and National Security in Israel.* Aldershot: Dartmouth, 1996.

Hollan, Douglas. "Dreaming in a Global World." In *A Companion to Psychological Anthropology: Modernity and Psychocultural Change*, ed. Conerly Casey and Robert B. Edgerton, 90–102. Oxford: Blackwell, 2005.

———. "The Relevance of Person-Centered Ethnography to Cross-Cultural Psychiatry." *Transcultural Psychiatry* 34, 2 (1997): 219–34.

———. "Setting a New Standard: The Person-Centered Interviewing and Observation of Robert I. Levy." *Ethos* 33, 4 (2005): 459–66.

Hollan, Douglas W. and C. Jason Throop, "The Anthropology of Empathy: An Introduction." In *The Anthropology of Empathy: Experiencing the Lives of Others in Pacific Societies*, ed. Douglas W. Hollan and C. Jason Throop, 1–21. New York: Berghahn, 2011.

Hollander, Eugene. *From the Hell of the Holocaust: A Survivor's Story.* New York: Ktav, 2000.

Holmes, Oliver W. "The National Archives and the Protection of Records." *American Archivist* 9, 1 (1946): 110–17.

"The Holocaust: Our Generation Looks Back." *Response: A Contemporary Jewish Review* 9, 1 (1975): 3–100.

Honneth, Alex. *Reification: A New Look at an Old Idea.* Ed. Martin Jay. Oxford: Oxford University Press, 2008.

Höpp, Gerhard, Peter Wien and René Wildangel. *Blind für die Geschichte? arabische Begegnungen mit dem Nationalsozialismus.* Berlin: Klaus Schwarz, 2004.

Horowitz, Aron. *Hebrew Camps Massad: Their Impact on Canadian Life and Culture.* Toronto: Aron Horowitz, 1990.

Hull, Matthew S. *Government of Paper: The Materiality of Bureaucracy in Urban Pakistan.* Berkeley: University of California Press, 2012.

———. "Ruled by Records: The Appropriation of Land and the Misappropriation of Lists in Islamabad." *American Ethnologist* 34, 4 (2008): 508–18.

International Committee of the Red Cross. *Report of the International Committee of the Red Cross on Its Activities During the Second World War.* Geneva: ICRC, 1948.

Jaskot, Paul. *The Architecture of Oppression: The SS, Forced Labor and the Nazi Monumental Building Economy*. London: Routledge, 2000.

Jaspers, Karl. *The Question of German Guilt*. New York: Fordham University Press, 2001.

Johnston, Barbara Rose. "Waging War, Making Peace: The Anthropology of Reparations." In *Waging War, Making Peace: Reparation and Human Rights*, ed. Barbara Rose Johnston and Susan Slyomovics, 11–28. Walnut Creek, Calif.: Left Coast Press, 2008.

Joly, Laurent. *Xavier Vallat: Du nationalisme chrétien à l'antisémitisme d'état, 1891–1972*. Paris: Grasset, 2001.

Joudah, Fady. "Revenge." In *Textu*. Port Townsend, Wash.: Copper Canyon Press, 2013. Kindle edition.

"Kafr Kasim Counsel Reject Terms of Payment." *Jerusalem Post*, November 18, 1957.

Kage, Joseph. *With Faith and Thanksgiving*. Montreal: Eagle, 1962.

Kahn, Leon. *No Time to Mourn: A True Story of a Jewish Partisan Fighter*. Vancouver: Laurelton Press, 1978.

Kant, Immanuel. *Groundwork of the Metaphysic of Morals*. Trans. H. J. Paten. New York: Harper, 1964.

Kárný, Miroslav et al, eds. *Terezínská pamětní kniha: Theresienstaedter Gedenkbuch*, 2 vols. Prague: Melantrich, 1995.

Kayfetz, Ben. "Students Get Lesson on the Holocaust." *Jewish Telegraphic Agency*, September 22, 1983.

Kennedy, F. "The Mind of the Injured Worker: Its Effect on Disability Periods." *Compensation Medicine* 1 (1946): 19–24.

Kepinski, Antoni. "KZ-Syndrome." *Archives of Psychiatry and Psychotherapy* 4 (2008): 77–84

Kerem, Yitzchak. "Sephardic and Oriental Oral Testimonies: Their Importance for Holocaust Commemoration and Memory." In *Remembering for the Future: The Holocaust in the Age of Genocide*, vol. 3, ed. John K. Roth and Elisabeth Maxwell, 142–49. New York: Palgrave, 2001.

Kertész, Imre. *The Holocaust as Culture*. London: Seagull Books, 2011.

Kestenberg, J. S. "Discriminatory Aspects of the German Indemnification Policy: A Continuation of Persecution." In *Generations of the Holocaust*, ed. Martin A. Bergmann and Milton E. Jucovy, 67–79. New York: Basic Books, 1982.

Keynes, John Maynard. *Essays in Persuasion*. New York: Norton, 1963.

Khleif, Waleed and Susan Slyomovics. "Palestinian Remembrance Days and Plans: Kafr Qasim, Fact and Echo." In *Modernism and the Middle East: Architecture and Politics in the Twentieth Century*, ed. Kishvar Rizvi and Sandy Eisenstadt, 186–217. Seattle: University of Washington Press, 2008.

Kidron, Carol A. "Toward an Ethnography of Silence: The Lived Presence of the Past in the Everyday Life of Holocaust Trauma Survivors and Their Descendants in Israel." *Current Anthropology* 50, 1 (2009): 5–27.

Killen, Andreas. *Berlin Electropolis: Shock, Nerves, and German Modernity*. Berkeley: University of California Press, 2006.

Kirshenblatt-Gimblett, Barbara. "A Parable in Context: A Social Interactional Analysis of Storytelling Performance." In *Folklore: Performance and Communication*, ed. Dan Ben-Amos and Kenneth S. Goldstein, 105–30. The Hague: Mouton, 1975.

Klarsfeld, Serge. *La mémorial de la déportation des Juifs de France, 1942–45*. Paris: Klarsfeld, 1978.

Klein, Hillel. "Problems in the Psychotherapeutic Treatment of Israeli Survivors of the Holocaust." In *Massive Psychic Trauma*, ed. Henry Krystal, 233–48. New York: International Universities Press, 1968.

———. "Wiedergutmachung: Ein Act des Retraumatisierung." In *Die Bundesrepublik Deutschland und die Opfer des Nationalsozialismus*, Tagung vom 25–27 November 1983 in Bad Boll. Bad Boll: Evangelische Akademie, 1984.

Klein, Hillel, Julius Zellermayer, and Joel Shannan. "Former Concentration Camp Inmates on a Psychiatric Ward." *Archives of General Psychiatry* 8 (1963): 334–42.

Kleinman, Tomer. "Did the Holocaust Play a Role in the Establishment of the State of Israel?" *UCSB Oral History Project Homepage*, June 2002.

Kohut, Heinz. *The Restoration of Self*. New York: International Universities Press, 1977.

Kordov, Moshe. *Ahat esreh kumtot yerukot ba-din: parashat Kefar-Kasm* [Eleven green berets under the law: The Kfar Kasim Affair]. Tel Aviv: Narkis, 1959.

Kraft, Robert N. *Memory Perceived: Recalling the Holocaust*. Westport, Conn.: Praeger, 2002.

Kraus, Alexander. *Our Village (as remembered by Heimus fun Bishtine)*. London: Irgun Yotzei Bustina, 1996.

Krell, Robert. "The Audiovisual Documentation of Survivors of the Holocaust: Obtaining Eyewitness Accounts for History and Education." Photocopy typed memorandum, dated February 1974, courtesy of VHEC.

———. "Children Who Survived the Holocaust: Reflections of a Child Survivor/Psychiatrist." *Echoes of the Holocaust* 4, 1995.

———. "Confronting Despair: The Holocaust Survivor's Struggle with Ordinary Life and Ordinary Death." *Canadian Medical Association* 157 (1997): 741–44.

———. "Holocaust Families: The Survivors and Their Children." *Comprehensive Psychiatry* 20, 6 (1979): 560–568.

Krell, Robert and Marc I. Sherman. *Medical and Psychological Effects of Concentration Camps on Holocaust Survivors*. New Brunswick, N.J.: Transaction, 1997.

Krystal, Henry. Interview, September 19, 1996. University of Michigan-Dearborn Voice/Vision Holocaust Survivor Oral History Archive.

———, ed. *Massive Psychic Trauma*. New York: International Universities Press, 1968.

———. "Psychoanalytic Approaches to Trauma: A Forty-Year Perspective." In *Mapping Trauma and Its Wake: Autobiographic Essays by Pioneer Trauma Scholars*, ed. Charles Figley, 111–19. New York: Routledge, 2006.

Krystal, Henry and William G. Niederland. "Clinical Observations on the Survivor Syndrome." In *Massive Psychic Trauma*, ed. Henry Krystal, 326–39. New York: International Universities Press, 1968.

———, eds. *Psychic Traumatization: Aftereffects in Individuals and Communities*. Boston: Little, Brown, 1971.

Kugelmass, Jack. "Bloody Memories: Encountering the Past in Contemporary Poland." *Cultural Anthropology* 10, 3 (1995): 279–301.

Kugelmass, Jack and Jonathan Boyarin. *From a Ruined Garden: The Memorial Books of Polish Jewry*. New York: Schocken, 1983.

Kurtz, Michael J. *America and the Return of Nazi Contraband: The Recovery of Europe's Cultural Treasures*. Cambridge: Cambridge University Press, 2006.

Kwiet, Konrad. "Designing Survival: A Graphic Artist in Birkenau." In *Approaching an Auschwitz Survivor: Holocaust Testimony and Its Transformations*, ed. Jürgen Matthäus, 7–26. Oxford: Oxford University Press, 2009.

Laloum, Jean. "La déportation des Juifs natifs d'Algérie." In *Les Juifs d'Algérie: Images et texts*, ed. Jean Laloum et al., 36–41. Paris: Éditions du Scribe, 1987.

Lambsdorff, Otto Graf. "The Long Road Towards the Foundation 'Remembrance, Responsibility and the Future.'" In *Sharing the Burden of the Past*, ed. Andrew Horvat, 152–60. Tokyo: Asia Foundation, 2003.

Langer, Lawrence. *Holocaust Testimonies: The Ruins of Memory*. New Haven, Conn.: Yale University Press, 1991.

Laub, Dori. "Testimonies in the Treatment of Genocidal Trauma." *Journal of Applied Psychoanalytic Studies* 4 (2002): 63–87.

Laub, Dori and Shoshana Felman, *Testimony: Crises of Witnessing in Literature, Psychoanalysis, and History*. New York: Routledge: 1992.

Lavi, Theodore, ed. "Mateszalka." *Pinkas ha-Kehillot Hungarya* [The Memorial Book of the Hungarian Communities]. Jerusalem: Yad Vashem, 1975.

Lavie, Peretz and Hanna Kaminer. "Dreams That Poison Sleep: Dreaming in Holocaust Survivors." *Dreaming: A Journal of the Association for the Study of Dreams* 1 (1991): 11–21.

———. "Sleep and Dreaming Holocaust Survivors: Dramatic Decrease in Dream Recall in Well-Adjusted Survivors." *Journal of Nervous and Mental Disease* 179, 11 (1991): 664–69.

"Law on the Mitigation of the Consequences of Certain Wrongs Affecting Property, Passed by the Czechoslovak Federal Assembly on October 2, 1990." *Czechoslovak Economic Digest* 1 (1991): 29–32.

Lendler, Mark. "Archive to Expand Access to Files on the Holocaust." *New York Times*, August 5, 2007, 6.

Lerner, Paul. *Hysterical Men: War Psychiatry, and the Politics of Trauma in Germany 1890–1930*. Ithaca, N.Y.: Cornell University Press, 2003.

Leonhard, Karl. *The Classification of Endogenous Psychoses*. New York: Irvington, 1979.

LeVine, Robert A. *Culture, Behavior and Personality*. Chicago: Aldine, 1982.

Levisse-Touzé, Christine. *L'Afrique du Nord dans la guerre 1939–1945*. Paris: A. Michel, 1998.

———. "Les camps d'internement en Afrique du Nord pendant le second guerre mondiale." In *Mélanges*, ed. Charles-Robert Ageron, 601–5. Zaghouan: FTERSI, 1996.

Levy, Daniel and Natan Sznaider, "Forgive and Not Forget: Reconciliation between Forgiveness and Resentment." In *Taking Wrongs Seriously: Apologies and Reconciliation*, ed. Elazar Barkan and Alexander Karn, 83–100. Stanford, Calif.: Stanford University Press, 2006.

Levy, Robert I. and Douglas Hollan. "Person-Centered Interviewing and Observation in Anthropology." In *Handbook of Methods in Cultural Anthropology*, ed. H. R. Bernard, 333–64. Walnut Creek, Calif.: Altamira Press, 1998.

Leys, Ruth. *From Guilt to Shame: Auschwitz and After*. Princeton, N.J.: Princeton University Press, 2007.

Lifton, Robert J. *Death in Life, Survivors of Hiroshima*. New York: Random House, 1968.

———. *Home from the War*. New York: Simon and Schuster, 1973.

———. "Observations on Hiroshima Survivors." In *Massive Psychic Trauma*, ed. Henry Krystal, 168–89. New York: International Universities Press, 1968.

———. "Psychological Effects of the Atomic Bomb in Hiroshima: The Theme of Death." *Daedalus* 92 (1963): 462–97.

Lillteicher, Jurgen. "Die Rückerstattung in Westdeutschland." In *Nach der Verfolgung: Wiedergutmaching nationalsozialistischen Unrechts in Deutschland?* ed. Hans Gunter Hockerts and Christian Kuller, 61–77. Gottingen: Wallstein, 2003.

Livshin, Olga and Basye Laye. "Holocaust Centre Milestone." *Jewish Independent*, November 16, 2012, 1.

Magocsi, Paul Robert. *Historical Atlas of East Central Europe*. Toronto: University of Toronto Press, 1993.

———. *The Shaping of a National Identity: Subcarpathian Rus, 1848–1948*. Cambridge, Mass.: Harvard University Press, 1978.

Malabou, Catherine and Jacques Derrida. *Counterpath: Traveling with Jacques Derrida*. Stanford, Calif.: Stanford University Press, 2004.

Malinowski, Bronislaw. "Kula; the Circulating Exchange of Valuables in the Archipelagoes of Eastern New Guinea." *Man* 20 (1920): 97–105.

Mallmann, Klaus-Michael and Martin Cüppers. "'Beseitigung der jüdisch-nationalen Heimstätte in Palästina.' Das Einsatzkommando der Panzerarmee Afrika 1942."

In *Deutsche, Juden, Völkermord: Der Holocaust als Geschichte und Gegenwart*, ed. Jürgen Matthäus and Klaus-Michael Mallmann, 153–76. Darmstadt: Wissenschaftliche Buchgesellschaft, 2006.

Mamdani, Mahmood. "Making Sense of Political Violence in Postcolonial Africa." In *War and Peace in the 20th Century and Beyond: Proceedings of the Nobel Centennial Symposium*, ed. Geir Lundestad and Olav Njolstad, 71–100. River Edge, N.J.: World Scientific, 2002.

Marcus, Paul and Alan Rosenberg. "The Holocaust Survivor's Faith and Religious Behavior and Some Implications for Treatment." *Holocaust and Genocide Studies* 3, 4 (1988): 413–30.

Marrus, Michael R. "Official Apologies and the Quest for Historical Justice." Occasional Paper 111, University of Toronto Munk Centre, 2006.

Marrus, Michael R. and Robert O. Paxton. *Vichy France and the Jews*. New York: Basic Books, 1981.

Marshall, Joan. "LC Labeling: An Indictment." In *Revolting Librarians*, ed. Celeste West, Elizabeth Katz, et al., 45–49. San Francisco: Booklegger Press, 1972.

Martz, Fraidie. *Open Your Hearts*. Montreal: Vehicule Press, 1996.

Marx, Karl. *Economic and Philosophic Manuscripts of 1844*. Moscow: Foreign Languages Publishing House, 1961.

Masalha, Nur. "The Historical Roots of the Palestinian Refugee Question." In *Palestinian Refugees: The Right of Return*, ed. Naseer Aruri, 36–67. London: Pluto, 2001.

Massagee, Anne. "Rights Without Remedies: Israel's Compensation Law." Occasional Paper 14. Al-Haq, Ramallah, 2006.

Mataar, Shadia. "Palestinian Refugees, a Material and Spiritual Homeland." Accessed January 21, 2013. MedMedia.org, 3.

Matussek, Paul. *Internment in Concentration Camps and Its Consequences*. New York: Springer, 1975.

Mauss, Marcel. *The Gift: The Form and Reason for Exchange in Archaic Societies*. Trans. Derek Jordan and Inge Jordan. New York: Norton, 1990.

Maurer, Bill. "The Anthropology of Money." *Annual Review of Anthropology* 35 (2006): 15–36.

Mazur, Yosef. *Zionism, Post-Zionism and the Arab Problem: A Compendium of Opinions about the Jewish State*. Bloomington, Ind.: WestBow Press, 2012.

McDonald, Collin. "Reconciling Holocaust Scholarship and Personal Data Protection: Facilitating Access to the International Tracing Service Archive." *Fordham International Law Journal* 30, 4 (2007): 1360–91.

McDonald, Susan and Andrea Hogue, "An Exploration of the Needs of Victims of Hate Crimes." Report for Department of Justice, Canada, November 15, 2007.

McHugh, Paul G. *Aboriginal Societies and the Common Law: A History of Sovereignty, Status, and Self-Determination*. Oxford: Oxford University Press, 2004.

McKenna, Kristine. "The Three Ages of Jacques Derrida." *LA Weekly News*, November 6, 2002.

Memmi, Albert. *The Colonizer and the Colonized*. New York: Orion Press, 1967.

Mendelson, Danuta. "The History of Damages for Psychiatric Injury." *Psychiatry, Psychology and Law* 4, 2 (1997): 169–175

Mental Disorders: Diagnostic and Statistical Manual. Washington, D.C.: American Psychiatric Association, 1952.

Ministry of Reconstruction. *The Sacrifices of Greece in the Second World War*. Athens: Ergostasiou Graphikai technai Aspiōtē-Elka, 1946.

Minkowski, Eugène. "L'anésthesie affective." *Annales Médico-Psychologiques* 104 (1946): 80–88.

Mittestaendische Unternehmen 1999. Vols. 1–3. Darmstadt: Hoppenstedt, 1999.

Moine, André. *La déportation et la résistance en Afrique du Nord (1939–1944)*. Paris: Éditions Sociales, 1972.

Monson, Candace M., Matthew J. Friedman, and Heidi A. J. La Bash. "A Psychological History of PTSD." In *Handbook of PTSD: Science and Practice*, ed. Matthew J. Friedman, Terence M. Keane, and Patricia A. Resick, 37–54. New York: Guilford Press, 2007.

Morris, Benny. *Israel's Border Wars 1949–1956: Arab Infiltration, Israeli Retaliation, and the Countdown to the Suez War*. Oxford: Oxford University Press, 1993.

Moscovici, Jean-Claude. *Voyage à Pitchipoï*. Paris: École des Loisirs, 1995.

Msellati, Henri. *Les juifs d'Algérie sous le régime de Vichy*. Paris: L'Harmattan, 1999.

Muller-Hill, Benno. *Murderous Science: Elimination by Scientific Selection of Jews, Gypsies, and Others, Germany 1933–45*. New York: Oxford University Press, 1988.

Musée Jean Moulin. *Les femmes oubliées de Buchenwald: 22 avril–30 octobre 2005*. Paris: Musées, 2005.

Naimark, Norman M. *Fires of Hatred: Ethnic Cleansing in Twentieth Century Europe*. Cambridge, Mass.: Harvard University Press, 2001.

Natour, Salman. "The Culture of 'the Inside': The Post-Identity Question." *Jadal* 12 (February 2012).

Neuborne, Burt. "Preliminary Reflections on Aspects of Holocaust-Era Litigation in American Courts." *Washington University Law Quarterly* 80 (2002): 795–832.

Niederland, William G. "The Problems of the Survivor—Part I." *Journal of the Hillside Hospital* 10 (1961): 233–47.

———. "The Psychiatric Evaluation of Emotional Disorders in Survivors of Nazi Persecution." In *Masssive Psychic Trauma*, ed. Henry Krystal, 8–22. New York: International Universities Press, 1968.

Nitschke, Bernadetta. *Vertreibung und Aussiedlung der deutschen Bevölkerung aus Polen 1945 bis 1949*. Munich: Oldenbourg Wissenschaftsverlag, 2003.

Noy, Dov. "The Jewish Versions of the 'Animal Languages' Folktale (AT 670): A Typological Structural Study." *Scripta Hierosolymitana* 22 (1971): 171–208.

Nusseibeh, Sari. *What is a Palestinian State Worth?* Cambridge, Mass.: Harvard University Press, 2011.

Ochs, Elinor and Linda Capps. "Narrating the Self." *Annual Review of Anthropology* 25 (1996): 19–43

Office of U.S. Chief Counsel for Prosecution of Axis Criminality. *Nazi Conspiracy and Aggression.* 8 vols. Washington, D.C.: Government Printing Office, 1946.

Orbach, Danny. "Black Flag at a Crossroads: The Kafr Qasim Political Trial." *International Journal of Middle East Studies* 45 (2013): 491–511.

Oliel, Jacob. *Les Camps de Vichy: Maghreb-Sahara 1939–44.* Montréal: Édition du Lys, 2005.

Ornstein, Anna. "Survival and Recovery." *Psychoanalytic Inquiry* 5 (1985): 99–130.

Ornstein, Anna and Stewart Goldman. *My Mother's Eyes: Holocaust Memories of a Young Girl.* Cincinnati: Emmis Books, 2004.

Olick, Jeffrey K. "Genre Memories and Memory Genres: A Dialogical Analysis of May 8, 1945 Commemorations in the Federal Republic of Germany." *American Sociological Review* 64, 3 (1999): 381–402.

Otterbein, Keith F. and Charlotte Swanson Otterbein. "An Eye for an Eye, a Tooth for a Tooth: A Cross-Cultural Study of Feuding." *American Anthropologist* 67, 6 (1965): 1470–82.

Palestinian Centre for Human Rights. "Israeli Military Court Continues to Provide Cover for IOF's Crimes." August 13, 2012.

Pappé, Ilan. *Out of the Frame: The Struggle for Academic Freedom in Israel.* London: Pluto Press, 2010.

Paxton, Robert O. "Letters to the Editor." *Times Literary Supplement*, January 21, 2001, 6.

———. *Vichy France: Old Guard and New Order, 1940–44.* New York: Knopf, 1972.

Peskin, Harvey. "Observations on the First International Conference on Children of Holocaust Survivors." *Family Process* 20, 4 (1981): 391–94.

Peterson, Trudy Huskamp. *Final Acts: A Guide to Preserving the Records of Truth Commissions.* Baltimore: Johns Hopkins University Press, 2005.

Phillips, Rebecca. "The Second Generation's Task." Interview with Eva Hoffman, 2004. Beliefnet.com.

Pinchevski, Amit. "The Audiovisual Unconscious: Media and Trauma in the Video Archive for Holocaust Testimonies." *Critical Inquiry* 39, 1 (2012): 142–66.

Piterberg, Gabriel. *The Returns of Zionism: Myths, Politics and Scholarship in Israel.* London: Verso, 2008.

Platz, Werner E and Franklin Oberlaender. "On the Problems of Expert Opinion on Holocaust Survivors Submitted to the Compensation Authorities in Germany." *International Journal of Law and Psychiatry* 18, 3 (1995): 305–21.

Pohl, Dieter. "Krakau-Plazow Main Camp." *The United States Holocaust Memorial Museum Encyclopedia of Camps and Ghettos, 1933–45*, vol. 1, Part B, ed. Geoffrey Megargee, 861–67. Bloomington: Indiana University Press, 2009.

Poliakov, Léon. *Bréviaire de la haine.* Paris: Calmann-Lévy, 1951.

Porat, Miriam. *Li-lo shihrur: zikhronotai mi-tekufat ha-Sho'ah* [Without Liberation: My Holocaust-era memories]. Tel-Aviv: Eked kelali, 1982.

Porter, Anna. *Kasztner's Train: The True Story of Rezső Kasztner, Unknown Hero of the Holocaust.* Vancouver: Douglas & McIntyre, 2007.

Posner, Ernst. *Archives and the Public Interest: Selected Essays.* Ed. Ken Munden Washington: Public Affairs Press, 1967.

———. *Memorandum Concerning the Protection and Salvage of Cultural Objects and Records in War Areas.* Washington: American Council of Learned Societies, 1944.

———. "Public Records Under Military Occupation." *American Historical Review* 49, 2 (1944): 213–27.

Pross, Christian. "Breaking Through the Postwar Coverup of Nazi Doctors in Germany." *Journal of Medical Ethics Supplement* 4 (1991): 13–16.

———. *Paying for the Past: The Struggle Over Reparations for Surviving Victims of Nazi Terror.* Baltimore: Johns Hopkins University Press, 1998.

Poznanski, Renée. "French Apprehensions, Jewish Expectations: From a Social Imaginary to a Political Practice." In *The Jews Are Coming Back: The Return of the Jews to Their Countries of Origin After WWII,* ed. David Bankier, 25–57. New York: Bergahn, 2005.

R. v. Keegstra. 1996 ABCA 308 (CanLII).

Rabinowitz, Dan. *Antropologyah veha-Palestinim.* Raananah: Institute for Israeli Arab Studies, 1998.

Radomir, Luza. *The Transfer of the Sudeten Germans: A Study of Czech-German Relations, 1933–1962.* New York: New York University Press, 1964.

Rakoff, Vivian G. "Long-term Effects of the Concentration Camp Experience." *Viewpoints: Labor Zionist Movement of Canada* 1 (1966): 17–22.

Rakoff, Vivian G., John J. Sigal, and Nathan V. Epstein. "Children and Families of Concentration Camp Survivors." *Canada's Mental Health* 14 (1966): 24–25.

Rathenau, Walter. *Walther Rathenau: Industrialist, Banker, Intellectual, and Politician: Notes and Diaries, 1907–1922.* Ed. Hartmut Pogge von Strandmann. Oxford: Clarendon, 1985.

Ravid, Barak. "PA President: As long as I am in power, there will be no third intifada." *Ha'aretz,* November 1, 2012.

Reilly, Joanne. *Belsen: The Liberation of a Concentration Camp.* London: Routledge, 1998.

Rémy, Dominique. *Les lois de Vichy: Actes dits "lois" de l'autorité de fait se prétendant "gouvernement de l'État français."* Paris: Romillat, 1992.

Rigler, Johannes. *Über die Folgen der Verletzungen auf Eisenbahn.* Berlin: G. Reimer, 1879

Ringelheim, Joan. "Women and the Holocaust: A Reconsideration of Research." *Signs* 10, 4 (1985): 741–61.

Robinson, Nehemiah. *Indemnification and Reparations: Jewish Aspects.* New York: Institute of Jewish Affairs, 1944.

———. *Restitution Legislation in Germany.* New York: Institute of Jewish Affairs, World Jewish Congress, 1949.

Rodin, Renee. *Subject to Change.* Vancouver: Talonbooks, 2010.

Rosen, Alan. *The Wonder of their Voices: The 1946 Holocaust Interviews by David Boder.* New York: Oxford University Press, 2010.

Rosen, Ilana. *Sisters in Sorrow: Life Histories of Female Holocaust Survivors from Hungary.* Detroit: Wayne State University Press, 2008.

Rosen, Janice. "Holocaust Testimonies and Related Resources in Canadian Archival Repositories." *Canadian Jewish Studies* 4–5 (1996–1997): 163–75.

Rosenfeld, Henry. "From Peasantry to Wage Labor and Residual Peasantry: The Transformation of an Arab village." In *Process and Pattern in Culture*, ed. Robert A. Manners, 211–34. Chicago: Aldine, 1964.

———. "Processes of Structural Change Within the Arab Family." *American Anthropologist* 60, 6 (1958): 1127–39.

Roskies, David G. *Against the Apocalypse: Responses to Catastrophe in Modern Jewish Culture.* Cambridge, Mass.: Harvard University Press, 1984.

Roth, Alvin E. "Repugnance as a Constraint on Markets." *Journal of Economic Perspectives* 21, 3 (2007): 37–58.

Rothberg, Michael. "Between Auschwitz and Algeria: Multidirectional Memory and the Counterpublic Witness." *Critical Inquiry* 33 (2006): 158–84.

———. *Multidirectional Memory: Remembering the Holocaust in the Age of Decolonization.* Stanford, Calif.: Stanford University Press, 2009.

Rothkirchen, Livia. "Deep-Rooted Yet Alien: Some Aspects of the History of the Jews of Subcarpathian Ruthenia." *Yad Vashem Studies* 12 (1977): 147–97.

Rouche, Keren. "Projecting Algerian Judaism, Formulating a Political Identity: Zionism in Algeria During the War of Independence." *Journal of North African Studies* 12, 2 (2007): 185–201.

Rousset, David. *The Other Kingdom.* Trans. and intro. Ramon Guthrie. New York: Reynal & Hitchcock, 1947.

Rousso, Henry. *The Vichy Syndrome: History and Memory in France Since 1944.* Cambridge: Harvard University Press, 1991.

Roy, Sara. "Living with the *Holocaust*: The Journey of a Child of Holocaust Survivors." *Journal of Palestine Studies* 32, 1 (2002): 5–12.

Rozental, Rubik, ed. *Kefar Kasem: eru'im u-mitos* [Events and myth]. Kibbutz ha-Me'uchad, 2000.

Rudoff, Joanne Weiner. "A Yale University and New Haven Community Project: From Local to Global." October 2007. Fortunoff Video Archive.

Rutland, Suzanne D. "'Buying Out of the Matter': Australia's Role in Restitution of Templer Property in Israel." *Journal of Israeli History* 24, 1 (2005): 135–54.

Sagi, Nana. *German Reparations: A History of the Negotiations.* Jerusalem: Magnes Press, 1980.

Ságvári, Ágnes. *The Holocaust in Carpatho-Ruthenia.* Accessed May 23, 2013. http://www.zsido.hu/tortenelem/holocaust.htm.

Samy, Shahira. *Reparations to Palestinian Refugees: A Comparative Perspective.* Abingdon: Routledge, 2010.

Sandel, Michael J. *What Money Can't Buy: The Moral Limits of the Market.* New York: Farrar, Straus and Giroux, 2012.

Satloff, Robert. *Among the Righteous: Lost Stories from the Holocaust's Long Reach into Arab Lands.* New York: Public Affairs, 2006.

Savarèse, Eric. "After the Algerian War: Reconstructing Identity Among the Pieds-noirs." *International Social Science Journal* 58 (2006): 457–66.

———. *L'invention des pieds-noirs.* Paris: Séguier, 2002.

Schafft, Gretchen E. *From Racism to Genocide: Anthropology in the Third Reich.* Urbana: University of Illinois Press, 2004.

Schaller, Dominik J. "'Every Herero Will Be Shot': Genocide, Concentration Camps, and Slave Labor in German South-West Africa." In *Forgotten Genocides: Oblivion, Denial, and Memory,* ed. René Lemarchand, 51–70. Philadelphia: University of Pennsylvania Press, 2011.

Schechtman, Joseph B. "Case Against Negotiations with Germany." *Jewish Herald* 15, 19 (1951): 7.

Schechtman, Joseph B. *Post-War Population Transfers in Europe: 1945–1955.* Liverpool: Charles Birchall, 1962.

Schechner, Richard. *Between Theater and Anthropology.* Philadelphia: University of Pennsylvania Press, 1985.

Schlink, Bernhard. *Guilt About the Past.* Toronto: Anansi, 2010.

———. *The Reader.* Trans. Carol Brown Janeway. New York: Vintage, 2008.

Schober, Barbara. "Holocaust Commemoration in Vancouver, BC, 1943–70." MA Thesis, Simon Fraser University, 1998.

Schorn, Daniel. "Revisiting the Horrors of the Holocaust." December 17, 2006, updated June 21, 2007. CBSNews.com.

Schwab, Gabriele. *Haunting Legacies: Violent Histories and Transgenerational Trauma.* New York: Columbia University Press, 2010.

Scott, Wilbur. "PTSD in DSM-III: A Case in the Politics of Diagnosis and Disease." *Social Problems* 37, 3 (1990): 294–310.

Segev, Tom. *The Seventh Million: Israelis and the Holocaust.* New York: Hill and Wang, 1993.

"Senate Approves Permanent Tax Exemption for Holocaust Victims." Accounting Web, November 25, 2002.

Shafir, Gershon. "Zionism and Colonialism: A Comparative Approach." In *The Israel/Palestine Question: A Reader,* ed. Ilan Pappé, 81–96. London: Routledge, 1999.

Shatan, Chaim. "The Grief of Soldiers: Vietnam Combat Veterans' Self-Help Movement." *American Journal of Orthopsychiatry* 43, 4 (1973): 640–53.

Sheftel, Anna and Stacey Zembrzycki. "'We Started Over Again, We Were Young': Postwar Social Worlds of Child Holocaust Survivors in Montreal." *Urban History Review/Revue d'Histoire Urbaine* 39, 1 (2010): 20–30.

Shelton, Dinah. *Remedies in International Human Rights Law.* Oxford: Oxford University Press, 1999.

Shenhav, Yehouda. "What Do Palestinians and Arab-Jews Have in Common? Nationalism and Ethnicity Examined Through the Compensation Question." Research Paper, Palestinian Refugee Research Net, 2003.

Shepard, Todd. *The Invention of Decolonization: The Algerian War and the Remaking of France.* Cornell University Press, 2006.

Shephard, Ben. *After Daybreak: The Liberation of Belsen, 1945.* London: Jonathan Cape, 2005.

———. *A War of Nerves: Soldiers and Psychiatrists in the Twentieth Century.* Cambridge, Mass.: Harvard University Press, 2001

Shoumatoff, Alex. *The Mountain of Names: A History of the Human Family.* New York: Simon & Schuster, 1985

Sigal, John J. "The Nature of Evidence for Intergenerational Effects of the Holocaust." *Simon Wiesenthal Center Annual* 3 (1986): 363–76.

Sigal, John J., Vincenzo DiNicola, and Michael F. Buonvino. "Grandchildren of Survivors: Can Negative Effects of Prolonged Exposure to Excessive Stress Be Observed Two Generations Later?" *Canadian Journal of Psychiatry* 33 (1988): 207–12.

Sigal, John J., D. Silver, Vivian Rakoff, and B. Ellin. "Some Second-Generation Effects of Survival of Nazi Persecution." *American Journal of Orthopsychiatry* 43, 3 (1973): 320–27.

Sigal, John J. and Morton Weinfeld. "Control of Aggression in Adult Children of Survivors of the Nazi Persecution." *Journal of Abnormal Psychology* 94, 4 (1985): 556–564.

———. *Trauma and Rebirth: Intergenerational Effects of the Holocaust.* New York: Praeger, 1989.

Šiklová, Jiřina. "Lustration, or the Czech Way of Screening." *East European Constitutional Review* 6, 1 (1996): 57–62.

Simmel, Georg. *The Philosophy of Money.* London: Routledge & Kegan Paul, 1978.

Simon, Joshua, ed. *Solution 196–213 United States of Palestine-Israel.* Berlin: Sternberg Press, 2011.

Simon, Sherry. *Translating Montreal: Episodes in the Life of a Divided City.* Montreal: McGill Queen's University Press, 2006.

Slyomovics, Susan. "American 'Blood Money' and a Question of Reparations." *MERIP/Middle East Report* 44, 259 (2011).

———. "The Argument from Silence: Morocco's Truth Commission and Women Political Prisoners." *Journal of Middle East Women's Studies* 1, 3 (2005): 73–95.

———. "French Restitution, German Compensation: Algerian Jews and Vichy's Financial Legacy." *Journal of North African Studies* 17, 5 (2012): 881–901.

———. "Geographies of Jewish Tlemcen." *Journal of North African History* 5, 2 (2001): 81–96.

———. "Morocco and Algeria: Financial Reparations, Blood Money, and Human Rights Witness Testimony." In *Humanitarianism and Suffering: The Mobilization of Empathy,* ed. Richard Ashby Wilson and Richard D. Brown, 265–84. Cambridge: Cambridge University Press, 2009.

——. *The Object of Memory: Arab and Jew Narrate the Palestinian Village.* Philadelphia: University of Pennsylvania Press, 1998.

——. "The Rape of Qula, a Destroyed Palestinian Village." In *Nakba: Palestine, 1948, and the Claims of Memory,* ed. Ahmad Sa'di and Lila Abu-Lughod, 44–45. New York: Columbia University Press, 2007.

——. "Rebbele Mordkhele's Pilgrimage in New York City, Tel Aviv and Carpathian Ruthenia." In *Going Home,* ed. Jack Kugelmass, 369–394. Evanston, Ill.: Northwestern University Press and Yivo Institute for Jewish Research, 1993.

——. "Reparations in Morocco: The Symbolic Dirham." In *Waging War & Making Peace: Reparations and Human Rights,* ed. Barbara Rose Johnston and Susan Slyomovics, 94–114. Walnut Creek: Left Coast Press, 2008.

——. "Who and What Is Native to Israel? On Marcel Janco's Settler Art and Jacqueline Shohet Kahanoff's 'Levantinism.'" *Settler Colonial Studies* 4, 1 (2014): 27–47.

Slyomovics, Susan and Sarah Abrevaya Stein, "Jews and French Colonialism in Algeria: An Introduction." *Journal of North African Studies* 17, 5 (2012): 749–55.

Snyder, Timothy. *Bloodlands: Europe Between Hitler and Stalin.* New York: Basic Books, 2010.

Sole, Aryeh. "Subcarpathian Ruthenia, 1918–38." In *The Jews of Czechoslovakia: Historical Studies and Surveys,* vol. 1, 125–54. Philadelphia: Jewish Publication Society, 1968–84.

Sontag, Susan. *On Photography.* New York: Anchor Doubleday, 1973.

Speisman, Stephen. *The Jews of Toronto: A History to 1937.* Toronto: McClelland and Stewart, 1979.

Steinert, Johannes-Dieter. "British Relief Teams in Belsen Concentration Camp: Emergency Relief and the Perception of Survivors." In *Belsen 1945: New Historical Perspectives,* ed. Suzanne Bardgett and David Cesarani, 62–78. London: Vallentine Mitchell, 2006.

Steinitz, Lucy Y. and David M. Szonyi, eds. *Living After the Holocaust.* New York: Bloch, 1976.

Stessel, Zahava Szász. *Snow Flowers: Hungarian Jewish Women in an Airplane Factory, Markkleeberg, Germany.* Madison, N.J.: Fairleigh Dickinson University Press, 2009.

Stier, Oren Baruch. *Committed to Memory: Cultural Mediations of the Holocaust.* Amherst: University of Massachusetts Press, 2003.

——. "Framing the Witness: The Memorial Role of Holocaust Videotestimonies." In *Remembering for the Future: The Holocaust in an Age of Genocide,* vol. 3, ed. John K. Roth and Elisabeth Maxwell, 189–204. New York: Palgrave, 2001.

Stoler, Ann Laura. *Against the Archival Grain: Epistemic Anxieties and Colonial Common Sense.* Princeton, N.J.: Princeton University Press, 2009.

Stora, Benjamin. *La gangrène et l'oubli: la mémoire de la guerre d'Algérie.* Paris: Découverte, 1991.

Stransky, Hugo. "The Religious Life in Slovakia and Subcarpathian Ruthenia." In *The Jews of Czechoslovakia*, vol 2, 347–92. Philadelphia: Jewish Publication Society, 1968–84.

Suedfeld, Peter, Robert Krell, Robyn E. Wiebe, and Gary Daniel Steel. "Coping Strategies in the Narratives of Holocaust Survivors." *Anxiety, Stress & Coping: An International Journal* 10 (1997): 153–79.

Suedfeld, Peter and Robert Krell, John Blando, and Patricia Southward. "The Holocaust as a Context for Telling Life Stories." *International Journal of Aging and Development* 60, 3 (2005): 213–28.

Szajkowski, Zosa. *Jews and the French Foreign Legion*. New York: Ktav, 1975.

Szasz, Thomas. *The Myth of Mental Illness: Foundations of a Theory of Personal Conduct*. New York: Harper & Row, 1961.

———. *The Second Sin*. New York: Doubleday, 1973.

Tanay, Emanuel. Interview, March 16 1987. University of Michigan-Dearborn Voice/ Vision Holocaust Survivor Oral History Archive.

———. "Initiation of Psychotherapy with Survivors of Nazi Persecution." In *Massive Psychic Trauma*, ed. Henry Krystal, 219–233. New York: International Universities Press, 1968.

———. "On Being a Survivor." In *Bearing Witness to the Holocaust, 1939–1989*, ed. Alan L. Berger, 16–31. Lewiston, N.Y.: Edwin Mellen, 1989.

———. "Case Presentations." In *Massive Psychic Trauma*, ed. Henry Krystal, 36–40. New York: International Universities Press, 1968.

———. *Passport to Life: Autobiographical Reflections on the Holocaust*. Ann Arbor: Forensic Press, 2004.

Targowla, René. "Sur une forme du syndrome asthénique des déportés et prisonniers de la guerre 1939–45." *Presse Médicale* 58 (1950): 728–30.

Tas, J. "Psychical Disorders Among Inmates of Concentration Camps and Repatriates." *Psychiatric Quarterly* 25 (1946): 679–90.

Tavuchis, Nicholas. *Mea Culpa: A Sociology of Apology and Reconciliation*. Stanford: Stanford University Press, 1991.

Throop, C. Jason. "Latitudes of Loss: On the Vicissitudes of Empathy." *American Ethnologist* 37, 4 (2010): 771–82.

Torpey, John. *Making Whole What Has Been Smashed: On Reparation Politics*. Cambridge, Mass.: Harvard University Press, 2006.

———. 'Making Whole What Has Been Smashed': Reflections on Reparations." *Journal of Modern History* 73, 2 (2001): 333–58.

Toynbee, Arnold J. *A Study of History*. Abridgement of Volumes 1–6 by David Churchill Somervell. Oxford: Oxford University Press, 1946.

Trossman, Bernard. "Adolescent Children of Concentration Camp Survivors." *Canadian Psychiatric Association Journal* 13, 2 (1968): 121–123.

Turnwald, Wilhelm K. *Documents on the Expulsion of the Sudeten Germans*. Munich: University Press, 1953.

———. *The Expulsion of the German Population from Czechoslovakia: A Selection and Translation*. Bonn: Federal Ministry for Expellees, Refugees and War Victims, 1960.

———. *Renascence or Decline of Central Europe: the Sudeten German-Czech Problem* Munich: University Press, 1954.

United Nations, *Basic Principles and Guidelines on the Right to a Remedy and Reparation for Victims of Violations of International Human Rights and Humanitarian Law*. E/CN.4/2005/L.48.

United States Department of Justice, Foreign Claims Settlement Commission. "German Compensation for National Socialist Crimes." In Roy L. Brooks, *When Sorry Isn't Enough: The Controversy over Apologies and Reparations for Human Injustice*. New York: New York University Press, 1999.

Vanino-Wanikoff, Maurice. "Le régime des camps en Afrique du Nord." In *Le combattant volontaire juif, 1939–45*, 80–82. Paris: Abexpress, 1971.

Veracini, Lorenzo. *Israel and Settler Society*. Ann Arbor, Mich.: Pluto Press, 2006.

———. *Settler Colonialism: A Theoretical Overview*. New York: Palgrave Macmillan, 2010.

Voices of Survival, directed by Alan Handel, Canadian Jewish Congress, 1988/89.

Voutira, Eftihia. "Post Soviet Diaspora Politics: The Case of the Soviet Greeks." *Journal of Modern Greek Studies* 24, 2 (2006): 379–414.

Vrba, Rudolf. *I Escaped from Auschwitz*. Fort Lee, N.J.: Barricade Books, 2002.

Waldron, Jeremy. *The Harm in Hate Speech*. Cambridge, Mass.: Harvard University Press, 2012.

Waltzer, Kenneth. "Bad Arolsen Journal." Accessed January 1, 2010. http://special .news.msu.edu/holocaust/journal.php?journal.

———. "Opening the Red Cross International Tracing Service Archives." *John Marshall Journal of Computer and Information Law* 21, 6 (2009): 161–81.

Wardi, Dina. *Memorial Candles: Children of the Holocaust*. New York: Tavistock, 1992.

Waterston, Alissa and Barbara Rylko-Bauer. "Out of the Shadows of History and Memory: Personal Narratives in Ethnographies of Rediscovery." *American Ethnologist* 33 (2006): 397–412.

Weber, Max. "Bureaucracy." In *From Max Weber: Essays in Sociology*, ed. H. H. Gerth and C. Wright Mills, 196–240. New York: Oxford University Press, 1946.

———. *Economy and Society: An Outline of Interpretative Sociology*. Berkeley: University of California Press, 1978.

Wechsler, Lawrence. "The Son's Tale: Art Spiegelman." In *Vermeer in Bosnia: Selected Writings*, 182–204. New York: Vintage, 2004.

Weil, Patrick. "The Return of Jews in the Nationality or in the Territory of France (1943–73)." In *The Jews Are Coming Back: The Return of the Jews to their Countries of Origin After WWII*, ed. David Bankier, 58–72. New York: Bergahn, 2005.

Weinbaum, Laurence. "Defrosting History: The Theft of Jewish Property in Eastern Europe." In *The Plunder of Jewish Property During the Holocaust*, ed. Avi Beker, 83–110. New York: Palgrave, 2001.

Weingrod, Alex. *The Saint of Beersheba*. Albany: State University of New York Press, 1990.

Weisberg, Richard H. *Vichy Law and the Holocaust in France*. New York: New York University Press, 1996.

Weiss, Yfaat. "Conflicting Memories, Unrestituted: Wadi Salib as an Israeli Political Metaphor." In *Restitution and Memory: Material Restoration in Europe*, ed. Dan Diner and Gotthart Wunberg, 301–19. New York: Bergahn, 2007.

Wilson, Paul. "Václav Havel (1936–2011)." *New York Review of Books*, February 9, 2012, 4–8.

Wilson, Richard Ashby and Richard D. Brown. *Humanitarianism and Suffering: The Mobilization of Empathy*. Cambridge: Cambridge University Press, 2009.

Winstel, Tobias. "Healed Biographies'?: Jewish Remigration and Indemnification for Nationalist Socialist Injustice." *Leo Baeck Institute Year Book* 49, 1 (2004): 139–52.

Wolfe, Robert, ed. *Captured German and Related Records: A National Archives Conference*. Athens: Ohio University Press, 1974.

Yablonka, Hanna. *The State of Israel vs. Adolf Eichmann*. New York: Schocken, 2004.

Yassif, Eli. "New Perspectives on the Oicotypification of Modern Jewish Folktales." *Jerusalem Studies in Jewish Folklore* 13–14 (The Dov Noy Festschrift) (1992): 275–302.

Young, Allan. *The Harmony of Illusions: Inventing Post-Traumatic Stress Disorder*. Princeton, N.J.: Princeton University Press, 1995.

Young, James E. "Interpreting Literary Testimony: A Preface to Rereading Holocaust Diaries and Memoirs." *New Literary History* 18 (1986–87): 403–23.

———. *The Texture of Memory: Holocaust Memorials and Meaning*. New Haven, Conn.: Yale University Press, 1993.

Young-Bruehl, Elisabeth. "The Biographer's Empathy with Her Subject." In *Subject to Biography: Psychoanalysis, Feminism, and Writing Women's Lives*, 17–25. Cambridge, Mass.: Harvard University Press, 2000.

Zammito, John H. *Kant. Herder and the Birth of Anthropology*. Chicago: University of Chicago Press, 2002.

Zelizer, Viviana A. *The Social Meaning of Money*. Princeton, N.J.: Princeton University Press, 1997.

Zimmer, Bernd Joachim. *Deckname Arthur: Das KZ-Aussenkommando in der SS-Führerschule Arolsen*. Kassel: Gesamthochschul-Bibliothek, 1994.

Zumbansen, Peer, ed. *Remembrance and Responsibility: Legal and Historical Observations*. Baden-Baden: Nomos Verlagsgesellschaft, 2002.

Zureik, Elia. *The Palestinians in Israel: A Study in Internal Colonialism*. London: Routledge Kegan Paul, 1979.

Zweig, Ronald W. *German Reparations and the Jewish World: A History of the Claims Conference*. London: Frank Cass, 2001.

———. "Restitution of Property and Refugee Rehabilitation: Two Case Studies." *Journal of Refugee Studies* 6, 1 (1993): 56–64.

INDEX

Note: Page numbers in boldface represent photographs.

children of survivors "continued"
trauma, 177–81, 307n6; Krell studies,
159–60, 177–78; linguistic differences
with parents, 147–48; Montreal Jewish
youth, 147–48, 177–79, 307n6; mother-
daughter memoirs, 181, 308n14; and
names, 182–85; the 1979 New York
conference on, 176–77; photographs and
"postmemory," 184–87; and postwar
"conspiracy of silence," 158; recovering
ancestral origins (East-Central Europe),
187–206; research, conferences, and
organizations, 159–60, 175–81, 307n6;
Schechner theories on "restoration of
behavior," 181–82; "second generation"
label, 175–76; and Vancouver Holocaust
Testimony Audiovisual Project, 159–60
Children of the Holocaust (Epstein), 176
Chirac, Jacques, 232
Chodoff, Paul, 136–37, 169
Christie, Doug, 151–52
Claims Conference (Conference on Jewish
Material Claims Against Germany), 4,
6–7, 227; "Article 2 Fund," 6, 282n13; JCC
in North America, 56, 122, 210, 227–28,
237; and North African Jews, 227–28
Clinton, Hillary, 250
Cohen, Abner, 257, 320n39, 321n49
Cohen, Elie, 119
Collis, William Robert Fitz-Gerald, 81–82
colonialism, crimes of, 212–13, 231–34;
Algerian Muslims, 230–32, 234, 243;
comparing reparations to Holocaust
reparations, 246–49; dark teleology and
the Holocaust, 240–46, 312n14; Derrida
on reparations for, 212–13; Fanon on "just
reparation" for, 212–13, 231–32; French
colonialism and Algerian Jewry, 207–8,
212–22, 230–34, 242–44; German
reparations for, 234, 242–46; Herero tribe
of Southwest Africa, 244–46, 319n19; and
pension payments, 233; Vichy France,
212–22, 232–33, 242–44. *See also*
colonialism, settler
colonialism, settler, 232–34, 235–69; and
American "blood money" for military
operations in the Middle East, 249–53;
comparing reparations to Holocaust
reparations, 246–49; dark teleology,
240–46, 312n14; French Algeria, 233–34;

and indigenous Maori of New Zealand,
267; Israeli payments of *pitsuyyim* to
Palestinians, 253–59, 262–63; Israeli
reparations and the *Nakba*, 246, 247,
263–69, 319n23; Israel's limited
financial compromise for Palestinians
in the OPT, 247–48, 259–63; and
ongoing interactions/relationships
between settler and native, 266–68;
paying reparations by calling them
something else, 249–63
Comité Français de la Libération Nationale
(French Committee for National
Liberation), 223
Commission pour l'Indemnisation des
Victimes des Spoliations (Mattéoli
Commission), 224–25
Communist Party of Canada, 155
"compensation neurosis" (CN), 89–90
"concentration camp syndrome" (*KZ-
syndromet*), 81–95; DSMs I-III, 81–82,
91–92; and PTSD, 91–92
Concordia University "Life Stories of
Montrealers Displaced by War, Genocide,
and Other Human Rights Violations,"
165
COS. *See* children of survivors
Crémieux Decree, 215, 217–18, 223, 233–34,
242–44
Cüppers, Martin, 315n38
Czech Republic: indemnities for returnees,
281n2; Josef Slyomovics return to, 1, 188;
Prague Pinkas Synagogue, 167, 183–85
Czechoslovakia: annexation by Hungary,
37–38, 188–89; Bishtine, 5, 83, 167, 187,
190, 196–206; expulsion of Sudeten
Germans, 2, 8, 281n4; Karlovy Vary/
Carlsbad, 1, 2, 7–8, 63, 79, 188; Marmarosh province, 37–38, 187–206; postwar
Communist, 1–2, 79, 97, 124–25; postwar
rescue and return of camp survivors,
82–84, 294n52; postwar survivor
community and marriages, 124;
Subcarpathian Ruthenia, 2, 5, 36–39, 83,
187–91, 194, 196–206. *See also* Marmarosh province

Dachau Concentration Camp: liberation by
American soldiers, 141; postwar ITS
archives, 101–2

names: and archives, 100–104; Bet
Marmarosh synagogue of Tel Aviv
(memorial room), 166, 194; commemorative rituals and names of Jewish dead,
166–67, 168, 182–85, 194; Derrida on the
Shoah as attempted erasure, 102; ITS
collection and the Central Name Index
(CNI), 100–104; Pinkas Synagogue in
Prague, 167, 183–85, **184**; Torah scrolls,
168; Vancouver Jewish cemeteries, 167
Namibia, Herero tribe of, 244–46, 319n19
National Archives (Washington, D.C.),
102–3, 299n14
Natour, Salman, 267–68
Nazi anthropology and medicine: medical
examinations, 70–71; medical record
keeping, 119; Mengele and, 70–71,
292n27; and psychiatric symptoms, 81
Nazi record keeping, 99–107, 108–10, 119;
death certificates, 121; ITS collection of
Nazi documents in Bad Arolsen, 100–118,
121–25; language/terminology, 108–10;
medical record keeping at Auschwitz, 119.
See also archives; International Tracing
Service (ITS) collection of Nazi documents in Bad Arolsen, Germany
Netherlands, Nazi-occupied, 97
Neuborne, Burt, 27–28
Neuengamme Camp, 85
New York City: Jewish Claims Conference
(JCC), 6, 56, 122, 210, 227–28, 237;
Marmarosh *landsmanshaft* (hometown)
society meetings, 167, 189, 192–93;
recreated Marmarosh cemeteries and
diaspora community burial societies,
191–93, 309n30
Nicholls, William, 158
Niederland, William G., 75, 87; and
children of survivors, 176–77; and PTSD,
91–92; and "survivor syndrome," 87,
296n72
9/11 Fund and moral implications of the
claims process, 27–29, 41–42, 44, 48, 172,
286n24
North Africa: Moroccan Jews, 167, 313n24;
tombs of Jewish rabbis as sites of
veneration and pilgrimage, 310n38. *See
also* Algerian Jewry
Nuremberg Military Tribunal, 21, 39, 47, 57
Nusseibeh, Sari, 264–66

Occupied Palestinian Territories (OPT), 97,
259–63, 264–69; destruction of archives
in Gaza Strip, 97; Gazan victims of
"Operation Cast Lead" (December 2008),
260–63; Israeli payments since 1948
(limited financial compromise), 247–48,
259–63; Jewish Israeli settler colonialism
in, 259–63, 264–69, 324n76; reparations
and the *Nakba* (right of return), 246, 247,
263–69, 319n23. *See also* Palestinians
Ofer, Shalom, 255
"On Being a Survivor" (Tanay), 74–75
Oppenheim, Hermann, 89–90
Origins of Totalitarianism (Arendt), 245
Ornstein, Anna, 35–36, 74
Ornstein, Paul, 74

Pakistan: American "blood money"
payments (*diyat*) and Davis case, 249–53;
Inter-Services Intelligence (ISI)
directorate, 253
Palestinian Centre for Human Rights
(PCHR), 260–61
Palestinians: Gazan victims of "Operation
Cast Lead" (December 2008), 260–63;
internally-displaced "present absentees,"
255, 319n23; Israeli payments of
pitsuyyim (not *shilumim*), 253–59,
262–63; Israeli payments since 1948
(limited financial compromise), 247–48,
259–63; Israeli settler colonialism,
259–63, 264–69, 324n76; Kafr Qasim
village massacre and aftermath, 254–59,
262–63, 320n39, 321n49; OPT of West
Bank and Gaza, 97, 247–48, 259–63,
264–69; refugee status, 321n41; reparations and the *Nakba* (right of return),
246, 247, 263–69, 319n23; Second
Intifada, 261–62
Pappé, Ilan, 246–47
Paris Commune (1871), 97
Paxton, Robert, 214, 313n26
"person-centered ethnography," 54–58
Peterson, Trudy Huskamp, 103
The Philosophy of Money (Simmel), 23–24
photographs: as artifacts and postmemory,
184–87; myth of photographic truth, 196–
97; pre-World War I Bishtine postcard
and drawing, 196–99, **198**
Picquendar, Odilon, 219

Pinchevski, Amit, 304n45
Pinkas Synagogue in Prague, 167, 183–85, **184**; ghetto cemetery, 167, 183–84; inscribed names, 167, 183–85, **184**
Piterberg, Gabriel, 265–66
pitsuyyim payments to Palestinians, 253–59, 262–63
Plaszow Concentration Camp, 9, 59, 130, 139–40; women guards, 9, 283n18
Poliakov, Léon, 313n26
Porat, Miriam, 116–18
Posner, Ernst, 102–3, 298–99n14
"postmemory," 185, 240; photographs and children of survivors, 184–87
post-traumatic stress disorder (PTSD), 78, 91–92; and "concentration camp syndrome," 91–92; and DSM-III, 91
Pross, Christian, 30–31, 67–68
psychiatric treatment of Holocaust survivors, 74–95; Becker critique of, 92–95; Chodoff on realignment of trauma to socially restorative behaviors, 136–37, 169; "concentration camp syndrome," 85–92, 95; creative memorialization and healing, 142–43; in DP camps, 84–85; empathetic interventions, 95; and listeners'/practioners' guilt, 77, 85; and PTSD, 78, 91–92; recognition of psychiatric symptoms, 85–92; survivors' distrust/reluctance to seek treatment, 74–81, 92–95, 294n45; Szasz critique of, 92–93, 95; and "therapeutic optimism," 95; transference and countertransference, 77, 79–81
Psychiatrie der Verfolgten (Psychiatry of the Persecuted) (1964), 90
psychopathology and psychiatric effects for Holocaust survivors, 53–95; "affective anesthesia," 85–87; children and trauma ("freezing the past"), 63–64; children of survivors (COS) and transmittal of intergenerational trauma, 177–81, 307n6; "compensation neurosis" (CN), 89–90; "concentration camp syndrome," 91–95; delayed-onset symptoms/long-term psychiatric effects, 88–90, 295n61, 296n72; and German bureaucracy of documentation and testimony, 30–31, 67–74, 77, 89–90, 132; "happiness psychosis," 61; *Massive Psychic Trauma* (1968) and new attention to, 75–76, 91; reparations committees and conditions for disbursing funds, 53, 75–76, 88–92, 132; reparations for psychiatric trauma, 53, 75–76, 87–90, 130–33; reparations process and retraumatization, 73–74, 88–90, 292n31; suicidal thoughts, 131–32; survivor guilt, 35–36, 77, 136–37, 136–38; "survivor syndrome," 87, 296n72; survivors' psychiatric literature and treatment, 74–79; and survivors' storytelling, 56–67; Vera Slyomovics and, 55–61, 79–81, 92–95. *See also* psychiatric treatment of Holocaust survivors

Qaddafi, Muammar, 252

Rakoff, Vivian G., 176–78
Rathenau, Walther, 244, 318n18
The Reader (Schlink), 66–67
Rechtman, Richard, 132
Red Cross. *See* International Committee of the Red Cross (ICRC)
religious faith in the concentration camps, 6, 119–20, 282n11
reparations: anthropological theories of evolution from blood money to, 26, 285n16; and gifts, 25, 49–52, 239–40, 249; and human rights declarations, 235–36; restitution, compensation, rehabilitation, satisfaction, and guarantees of non-repetition, 21–22, 210–11; Robinson conditions for successful implementation, 211–12, 213; as term, 21–23, 236; UN guidelines on remedy and reparation (April 2005), 21–22, 210–11. *See also* financial reparations; German war reparations
Republic of Carpatho-Ukraine, 188
"repugnant markets," 236–37
Response (journal), 175, 176
Rigler, Johannes, 89–90
Riruako, Kuaimi Isaac, 244–45
Robinson, Jacob, 211–12
Robinson, Nehemiah, 211–12, 213, 224
Roma-Sinti (Gypsies), postwar reparations to, 67–68
Rosen, Ilana, 297n78
Rosenberg, Louis, 125
Roskies, David, 144

Roth, Alvin, 236–37
Rothberg, Michael, 312n14
Rouch, Keren, 221
Rousso, Henry, 45, 46
Roy, Sara, 324n76
Russian Karaites, 214
Rutland, Suzanne D., 247–48
Rwandan genocide, 165
Rylko-Bauer, Barbara, 54–55

Sachsenhausen Concentration Camp, 102,
  298–99n14
San Francico earthquake and fire (1906), 97
sanctions/boycotts on German culture,
  products, and language, 43–44
Sandel, Michael J., 286n24
Sarsur, Fatimah Salih, 255, 256
Sarsur, Ibrahim, 257–59
Schechner, Richard, 181–82
Schindler, Oskar, 139–40
Schindler's List (film), 9, 10
Schley, Jens, 209
Schlink, Bernhard, 58, 66–67
Schober, Barbara, 155
Schwartz, Emerech (Imy), 138
second generation. *See* children of survivors
  (COS)
Second Intifada (2000–2005), 261–62
September 11 Victim Compensation Fund.
  See 9/11 Fund
settler colonialism. *See* colonialism,
  settler
Shadmi, Issachar, 255–56
Shafir, Geshon, 261
Shamshad, Fahim, 249–50
shari'a law, 250–53
Shatan, Chaim, 91–92, 296n72
Shaw, Eugene Clay, Jr., 50
Shreter, Hayim, 201–2
Sigal, John J., 178
Simmel, Georg, 23–25, 33–34, 238, 249
Simmons College School of Library Science,
  109
slave labor: attempts to survive through,
  306n56; German Foundation and
  Foundation Law, 4, 6–7, 46–48, 207, 209,
  226; reparations claims and hierarchies of
  victimhood, 47, 226; Vera Slyomovics's
  work pension claim, 3–4, 6–7, 12–13,
  42–44, 48, 51–52, 92, 136, 170, 236. *See*

also Markkleeberg Camp (all-women's
  slave labor camp)
Slyomovics, Bluma Holder (author's
  paternal grandmother), 7, 9, 64–65, 107
Slyomovics, Hayim David (author's paternal
  grandfather), 105–7; author's ITS inquiry
  about, 105–7; death of, 7, 9, 64–65; short
  form certification ("Excerpt from
  Documents"), **106**
Slyomovics, Ida (author's father's sister), 9,
  64–65
Slyomovics, Josef (author's father), 1–2, 7–9,
  63–65; Czechoslovakian Brigade service,
  1–2, 7, 9, 64, 72, 97; parents, 7, 9, 64–65, 107;
  in postwar Canada, 97–98, 125, 145–46;
  refusing reparations, 2, 71–72, 281n2;
  return to Czech Republic, 1, 7; wartime
  narratives/witness testimony, 63–65
Slyomovics, Vera Hollander (author's
  mother), **20, 86, 164**; on American
  troops' liberation of Markkleeberg,
  14–15, 114–15, 141–42; audiovisual
  interviews/testimonies, 11–12, 71, 131–32,
  137–38, 159–60, 162–65, **164**; at
  Auschwitz, 3, 9–11, 13, 34–35, 58–61,
  70–71, 111, 169, 187; belief in *beshert*,
  168–69; birth date records, 111; and
  Canadian Jewish organizations, 136–37,
  143, 148–50, 156–66, 302n21; Card of
  Personal Effects at Buchenwald, 111–12;
  charitable giving, 49–50; on D-Day
  arrival at Auschwitz, 10–11; distrust of
  psychiatrists, 79–81, 92–95; dreams, 49,
  58–61, 80, 170–74; fear of medical exams,
  69–72; fear of thirst, 56; on food and
  hunger in the camps, 14–15, 59, 93–94,
  101; forgiveness by, 140–41; on "freezing
  the past," 63–64; and her father, Samuel,
  7, 10–12, 26–27, 61, 119–21, 138–39; and
  her father's "burial" in Vancouver Jewish
  cemetery, 166–67, 170–71; on her
  mother's reparation claims for psychological trauma, 131–33; as Holocaust
  educational speaker, 148–50, 153–54,
  156–58; immigration to Canada, 97–98,
  125, 136; and Keegstra hate crimes case,
  153–54; on *Lagerälteste* at Auschwitz,
  34–35; leaving postwar Czechoslovakia,
  79, 97, 124; living in "revenge against
  Hitler," 182–83; at Markkleeberg labor

ACKNOWLEDGMENTS

In 2005 I began thinking about my family history when I joined the monthly writers workshop convened at MIT by Professor Steven Strang, but then set aside the dozen or so pages that would eventually become the basis for the Prologue. In 2006 after moving to UCLA, I attended the Anthropology Department seminar, "Mind, Medicine and Culture" (MMAC) each Monday afternoon, a weekly interest group and discussion section devoted to psycho-cultural studies and medical anthropology. Integrating person-centered ethnography meta-discursively even during our scholarly presentations, the format consists of a presenter who talks for twenty minutes surrounded by empathetic listeners. I was encouraged to present versions of the Prologue to Chapter 2 for MMAC discussion on two occasions: April 7, 2008, "Money and Suffering: German Reparations to Jewish Survivors of Nazi Concentration Camps," and October 25, 2010, "The Limits of Therapy: Narratives of Reparation and Psychopathology." I owe a special debt of gratitude to Carole Browner, Linda Garro, Douglas Hollan, and Jason Throop, MMAC faculty conveners along with participants Kristin Yarris and Rebekah Park for comments, questions, and notes that continue to inspire.

On October 28, 2008, I lectured on "Accepting German Reparations" at the University of California, Irvine, for the "Anthropology of Modernity Colloquium Series" cosponsored with the UCI School of Law "Bridges" Workshop. I thank my respondent Susan Bibler Coutin as well as Julia Elyachar, Bill Maurer, and George Marcus for further discussions that stimulated progress on the manuscript. I presented Chapter 3 to a graduate seminar on "Archives and Human Rights" taught by my colleague Anne Gilliland at the UCLA Graduate School of Education and Information Studies. I thank Anne and the students for their thoughtful responses. Chapter 5 includes a greatly revised, expanded version of my 1993 essay, "Rebbele Mordkhele's Pilgrimage in New York City, Tel Aviv and Carpathian Ruthenia," published in *Going Home*, ed. Jack Kugelmass (Evanston, Ill.: Northwestern University Press and Yivo Institute for Jewish Research), 369–94, and reprinted with the permission of YIVO Institute for Jewish Research. On October 23–24, 2011, I presented a version of Chapter 6 for the UCLA conference, "New Approaches to Algerian Jewish Studies," that I coorganized with Sarah Abrevaya Stein during my directorship of the G. E. von Grunebaum Center for Near Eastern Studies. Conference proceedings were published as our joint, guest-edited December 2012 special issue of the *Journal of North African Studies*, "Jews and French Colonialism in Algeria." I thank Sarah Stein and conference participants for their feedback as I rewrote this section. Chapter 7 advances my research from two previously published articles: "American 'Blood Money' and a Question of Reparations," *MERIP/Middle East Report* 259 (2011): 44–46, and co-authored with Waleed Khleif, "Palestinian Remembrance Days and Plans: Kafr Qasim, Fact and Echo," in *Modernism and the Middle East: Architecture and Politics in the Twentieth Century*, ed. Kishvar Rizvi and Sandy Eisenstadt (Seattle: University of Washington Press, 2008), 186–217.

In Vancouver, I am grateful to Jean Gerber, Robert Krell, Graham Forst, and the staff of the Vancouver Holocaust Education Centre. In Berlin, I thank Frank Drauschke of "Facts and Files"; the staff of the German Foundation "Remembrance, Responsibility and the Future" (*Stiftung "Erinnerung, Verantwortung, Zukunft"*), especially Ulrike Vasily-Coulibaly; and Sonja Hegasy and Bettina Donnerlein of the Zentrum Moderner Orient. My participation and stay in Bad Arolsen, Germany, during the 2008 Summer Research Workshop, "Exploring the Newly Opened ITS Archive," coorganized by the U.S. Holocaust Memorial Museum's Center for Advanced Holocaust Studies and the International Tracing Service, contributed significantly to the development of research presented in Chapter 3. I thank Udo Jost, Bernd Joachim Zimmer, and my colleagues during my stay in Bad Arolsen. Research at the library of the U.S. Holocaust Memorial Museum in Washington, D.C. was greatly facilitated with help from the librarian, Michlean Amir.

For comments and correspondence, I am indebted to Rick Abel, Jon Anderson, Roslyn Eldar, Barbara Rose Johnston, the late Waleed Khleif, Marc Masurovsky, Gabriel Piterberg, Barbara Rylko-Bauer, Jeffrey Shandler, Nettanel Slyomovics, Chris Toensing, Alisse Waterston and Richard A. Wilson. To Lorenzo Veracini and Michael Herzfeld, my profoundest gratitude for our conversations and their close readings of the manuscript. Peter Tokofsky ably translated the German reparations documents in Chapter 3, Teruko Mitsuhara transcribed my mother's interview tapes, Alma Heckman turned my notes into the bibliography, and Naomi Bishop was an excellent reader and editor.

The University of California, Los Angeles has been generous in supporting my work: UCLA's Council on Research (COR) faculty grant program for 2012–13 provided funding for a book subvention. Research funds from the UCLA Anthropology Department supported my travels, fieldwork, and conference presentations. Title VI grants from the Department of Education with additional funding from UCLA help support the G. E. von Grunebaum Center for Near Eastern Studies, which I directed from 2007 to 2012, that remains a locus for scholarly exchanges, conferences, and visiting researchers. I'm grateful to David Hirsch, UCLA's Jewish and Middle East bibliographer, for years of friendship and scholarly support.

I hope that my love and attachment to my family find expression in every page.

CPSIA information can be obtained at www.ICGtesting.com
Printed in the USA
BVOW08s1430150715

408216BV00003B/3/P